EVALUATING THE LEGACY OF
ROBERT W. FUNK

BIBLICAL SCHOLARSHIP IN NORTH AMERICA

Number 28

EVALUATING THE LEGACY OF ROBERT W. FUNK

Reforming the Scholarly Model

Edited by

Andrew D. Scrimgeour

SBL PRESS

 **PRESS**

Atlanta

Copyright © 2018 by Society of Biblical Literature

Library of Congress Cataloging-in-Publication Data

Names: Scrimgeour, Andrew D., 1945– editor.
Title: Evaluating the legacy of Robert W. Funk : reforming the scholarly model / edited by Andrew D. Scrimgeour.
Description: Atlanta : SBL Press, 2018. | Series: Biblical scholarship in North America ; Number 28 | Includes bibliographical references.
Identifiers: LCCN 2018040636 (print) | LCCN 2018043892 (ebook) | ISBN 9780884143468 (ebk.) | ISBN 9781628372328 (pbk. : alk. paper) | ISBN 9780884143451 (hbk. : alk. paper)
Subjects: Funk, Robert W. (Robert Walter), 1926–2005.
Classification: LCC BX4827.F86 (ebook) | LCC BX4827.F86 E93 2018 (print) | DDC 225.092—dc23
LC record available at https://lccn.loc.gov/2018040636

Printed on acid-free paper.

For

Schubert Miles Ogden
who first introduced me to the promise and perils
of the quest for the historical Jesus

and

David Sten Herrstrom
my life-long mentor in how to be prophet,
priest, and poet with the pen

Yeats said it best:

Think where [our] glory most begins and ends,
And say my glory was I had such friends.

If the unexamined life is not worth living, the unexamined past is not worth possessing; it bears fruit only be being held continuously up to the light, and is as changeable and as full of surprises, pleasant and unpleasant, as the future.

—Brendan Gill

Contents

Foreword

Kent Harold Richards

> Legacies reach backward and forward. They are a continuum of the fundamental values that we gain from our past and which must reach ahead into the future.
>
> —Modified words of Paul Tsongas, 1941–1997

The assessments of several colleagues in this volume, as well as some of Bob Funk's own words open the window to Bob's legacy as a scholar and public figure. Much is made of the fact that there are few twentieth or twenty-first century names from biblical scholarship who are even whispered in public circles and the ubiquitous, growing impact of digital media. I think that one of Bob's legacies is that he was regarded both to have impacted positively the little world of biblical scholarship and the bigger world of public conversation.

Sending "white smoke" up as though electing a pope at the Vatican, Bob metaphorically sent smoke up with regard to the authenticity of what words in the New Testament really came from Jesus and what were only latter attributed to Jesus. He was praised for this balloting before casting the votes and after serious debates of the pros and cons. He was also chided for having done it. Legacies have disciples and detractors.

Whichever camp the reader of this volume finds themselves encamped might do well to take a hint from a minor Shakespeare character, Mariana, in *All's Well That Ends Well* (act 3, scene 5) when she says, "no legacy is so rich as honesty." These words were probably meant as a pun when spoken in the play.

However, one element of Bob's legacy, and in whatever of his many endeavors as scholar or public figure you wish to name, he strove for honesty with respect to the issue. You could disagree with him and even be shouted at. He could tell you that you were dead wrong. He could be angry with you.

Nevertheless, I would urge the readers of this small collection of Bob's legacy to hear the value of honesty. We all will have learned and confirmed an enormous value that at this particular moment in American history, if not in all moments and whatever the subject, is a foundational value. Thanks, Bob!

Preface

Andrew D. Scrimgeour

Shortly before the Annual Meeting of the Society of Biblical Literature in 2005 (New Orleans), it was learned that Robert W. Funk had died. Several of his colleagues quickly put together a program to honor him there. Kent Harold Richards, then Executive Director of the Society of Biblical Literature, suggested that a second session should be planned for a future year, when scholars would have had time to reflect more fully on Funk's contributions to the Society of Biblical Literature and biblical studies. With that encouragement, a program for 2007 in San Diego was organized. Under the title "Evaluating the Legacy of Robert W. Funk," six scholars reflected on the major areas of Funk's scholarship and academic leadership:

Greek Grammar: Lane C. McGaughy
Hermeneutics: James M. Robinson
Parables: Bernard Brandon Scott
Historical Jesus: John Dominic Crossan
The Jesus Seminar: Harold W. Attridge
The Academy and Publications: James Wiggins

Those papers are the heart of this volume.

Accompanying each essay are two to four writings by Funk that are illustrative of his contributions to that topic. Reflecting the breadth of his corpus, they range from scholarly articles to administrative reports and even include a fable. While most of these writings are intended for a scholarly audience, some of them were written for the general public and illustrate his insistence that scholars write clearly and without jargon and thereby contribute to the religious literacy of their communities. Included are several pieces that are being published for the first time. A final section includes two interviews with Funk and a letter that he wrote to the graduate students in one of his seminars.

Readers will no doubt observe that all the voices evaluating Funk's legacy in the 2007 session were male and that, as a result, the conference papers reproduced here reflect the same gender imbalance. We regret this greatly and wish that the session and, consequently, this volume offered a greater diversity of presenters and viewpoints.

Apart from correcting typographical errors and conforming the varied pieces to a consistent style, we have left the Funk essays as they were originally written, including the use of now-discouraged terms such as *man/men* for *human/humanity* and *Oriental* to refer to someone from the Near East.

Funk once wrote, "I write principally to find out what I think, or aspire to think, and so am my own first reader.... I am not infrequently amazed and often amused at what I write."[1] I suspect Bob would be both amazed and amused by the words—his own and those of his colleagues—assembled in this volume.

---

1. Robert W. Funk, *Honest to Jesus: Jesus for a New Millennium* (San Francisco: Harper-SanFrancisco, 1996), 14.

Acknowledgments

This volume, as most worthy enterprises, was a collaborative effort. My debts to colleagues, friends, scholars, librarians, and archivists are many, and I gratefully acknowledge them:

Jim Kasper and Lucy Hansen for covering the costs of the media companies that taped the sessions honoring Robert Funk at the 2005 (New Orleans) and 2007 (San Diego) Annual Meetings of the Society of Biblical Literature as well as other project expenses.

Kent Harold Richards for ensuring that the proposed Robert Funk programs for the Annual Meetings of the Society of Biblical Literature in 2005 and 2007 became a reality.

Harold W. Attridge, John Dominic Crossan, Lane C. McGaughy, James M. Robinson, Bernard Brandon Scott, and James B. Wiggins for their thoughtful reviews of Funk's work. Both Robinson and Wiggins died in 2017; I regret that they will not see their astute reflections in this volume.

Many archivists and librarians for their generous assistance:

- Matthew Beland, University Archivist and Brian Shetler, Methodist Librarian and Head of Special Collections, Drew University.
- Teresa Gray, Public Services Archivist, Special Collections Library, Vanderbilt University.
- Carrie Beth Lowe, Library Director, Glass Memorial Library, Johnson University.
- Kate Skrebutenas, Director, Research and Public Services, Princeton Theological Seminary Library.
- Brandon C. Wason, Curator of Archives and Manuscripts, and Debra A. Madera, Special Collections Reference Assistant, Pitts Theology Library, Candler School of Theology, Emory University.
- Beth Sheppard, Director of the Divinity Library, Duke University, for giving the project priority with her staff.
- Rebecca Bowers, Archivist and technological guru, at the Divinity School Library, Duke University, for her meticulous work in

scanning and proofreading the articles reprinted in this volume, including the supervision of the graduate students assisting her.

Roy W. Hoover and Bernard Brandon Scott for invaluable editorial advice.

Char Matejovsky and Lane C. McGaughy for innumerable searches of files and memory. Lane also suggested the title for this volume.

Robaire Ream for tracking down historic DVDs and audio tapes.

John Kutsko for supporting this project and for solving a permissions issue at the eleventh hour.

Michael G. Maudlin, Senior Vice President and Executive Editor, HarperOne, for assisting in the permissions process.

Bob Buller for counsel and encouragement.

David Herrstrom, Dorothy Scrimgeour, and Meghan Scrimgeour, once again, for eagle-eye editing.

I would also like to thank the following publishers for their permission to reprint Funk's work.

Part 2: Greek Grammar
- "The Narrative Parables: The Birth of a Language Tradition." Pages 43–58 in *God's Christ and His People: Studies in Honor of Nils Alstrup Dahl*. Edited by Jacob Jervell and Wayne A. Meeks. Oslo: Universitetsforlaget, 1977. Used by permission of Universitetsforlaget.
- "Biblical Languages in the Professional School Curriculum." Vanderbilt Divinity School, 1968. Archives, Westar Institute, Drew University Library.

Part 3: Hermeneutics
- "The Hermeneutical Problem and Historical Criticism." Pages 164–97 in *The New Hermeneutic*. Edited by James M. Robinson and John B. Cobb Jr. New York: Harper & Row, 1964. Used by permission of HarperCollins Publishers.
- "Language, Hermeneutic, and the Vocation of the Word." Pages 1–18 in *Language, Hermeneutic, and Word of God: The Problem of Language in the New Testament and Contemporary Theology*. New York: Harper & Row, 1966. Used by permission of HarperCollins Publishers.

Part 4: Parables
+ "The Old Testament in Parable: A Study of Luke 10:25–37." *Encounter* 26 (1965): 251–67. Used by permission of Christian Theological Seminary.
+ "Beyond Criticism in Quest of Literacy: The Parable of the Leaven." *Int* 25 (1971): 149–70. Used by permission of Sage Publications.
+ "Theoretical Frame of Parables." Email to Westar scholars, 6 November 2004. Archives, Westar Institute, Drew University Library.

Part 5: Historical Jesus
+ "The Looking-Glass Tree Is for the Birds: Ezekiel 17:22–24; Mark 4:30–32." *Int* 27 (1973): 3–9. Used by permission of Sage Publications.
+ Introduction to *The Five Gospels: The Search for the Authentic Words of Jesus*. New York: Scribner, 1993. Pages 1–6. Used by permission of Scribner.

Part 6: The Jesus Seminar
+ "The Issue of Jesus." *Forum* 1.1 (1985): 7–12. Used by permission of Polebridge Press.
+ "On Distinguishing Historical from Fictive Narrative." *Forum* 9.3–4 (1993): 179–216. Used by permission of Polebridge Press.
+ "The Jesus Seminar and the Quest." Pages 130–39 in *Jesus Then and Now: Images of Jesus in History and Christology*. Edited by Marvin Meyer and Charles Hughes. Harrisburg, PA: Trinity Press International, 2001. Used by permission of Bloomsbury Publishing Plc.

Part 7: The Academy and Publications
+ "Society of Biblical Literature—Report of the Executive Secretary, 1968–1973." *Bulletin of the Council of the Study of Religion* 4.4 (1973): 8–28. Used by permission of Equinox Publishing Ltd.
+ "The Learned Society as Publisher and the University Press." *Bulletin of the Council of the Study of Religion* 4.3 (1973): 3–13. Used by permission of Equinox Publishing Ltd.
+ "Religious Studies as Witches Brew." 1981. Westar Institute Archives, Special Collections, Drew University Library.
+ "Legends of the School of Scribes or The Seventy Pens of Power." Centennial Banquet, Society of Biblical Literature, Dallas, Texas, November 8, 1980. Westar Institute Archives, Special Collections, Drew University Library.

Part 8: A Letter and Interviews

- Letter to Graduate Seminar students, Graduate Department of Religion, Vanderbilt University, Spring 1969. Westar Institute Archives, Special Collections, Drew University Library.
- "A Conversation with Robert Funk about the Society of Biblical Literature." Edited transcription of a taped interview. Ernest W. Saunders, March 25, 1979. Society of Biblical Literature Archives, Pitts Library, Candler School of Theology, Emory University.
- Treloar, Richard. "Transcript of a Conversation with Robert Funk during His Visit to Melbourne." 6 July 2000. *Colloq* 32.2 (2000): 151–67. Used by permission of *Colloquium: The Australian and New Zealand Theological Review*.

Backmatter

- "Chronology." *The Fourth R* 19.2 (2006): 2. Used by permission of Westar Institute.
- "Publications of Robert W. Funk." *The Fourth R* 19.2 (2006): 21–23. Used by permission of Westar Institute.

Abbreviations

AASOR	Annual of the American Schools of Oriental Research
Ant.	Josephus, *Jewish Antiquities*
ASNU	Acta Seminarii Neotestamentici Upsaliensis
BA	*Biblical Archaeologist*
BAG	Bauer, Walter, William F Arndt, and Felix Wilbur Gingrich. *A Greek-English Lexicon of the New Testament and Other Early Christian Literature.* Chicago: University of Chicago Press, 1957.
BASOR	*Bulletin of the American Schools of Oriental Research*
BDF	Blass, Friedrich, Albert Debrunner, and Robert W. Funk. *A Greek Grammar of the New Testament and Other Early Christian Literature.* Chicago: University of Chicago Press, 1961.
BDR	Blass, Friedrich, Albert Debrunner, and Friedrich Rehkopf. *Grammatik des neutestamentlichen Griechisch.* 16th ed. Gottingen: Vandenhoeck & Ruprecht, 1984.
Ber.	Berakhot
BZNW	Beihefte zur Zeitschrift für die Neutestamentliche Wissenschaft
ChrCent	*The Christian Century*
Colloq	*Colloquium: The Australian and New Zealand Theological Review*
ConBNT	Coniectanea Neotestamentics
DrewG	*The Drew Gateway*
EvK	*Evangelische Kommentare*
FFF	*Foundations and Facets Forum*
fr	frame of reference
FR	Field of Reference
IDB	Buttrick, George A. *The Interpreter's Dictionary of the Bible.* 4 vols. New York: Abingdon, 1962.
HTR	*Harvard Theological Review*

Int	*Interpretation*
JAAR	*Journal of the American Academy of Religion*
JBL	*Journal of Biblical Literature*
JBR	*Journal of Bible and Religion*
JThC	*Journal for Theology and the Church*
JR	*Journal of Religion*
JTS	*Journal of Theological Studies*
NEB	New English Bible
RGG	Betz, Hans Dieter, et al., eds. *Religion in Geschichte und Gegenwart*. 3rd ed. Tübingen: Mohr Siebeck, 1956–1957.
RSV	Revised Standard Version
SBLDS	Society of Biblical Literature Dissertation Series
SBLSBS	Society of Biblical Literature Sources for Biblical Study
SEÅ	*Svensk exegetisk arsbok*
SemeiaSt	Semeia Studies
Shabb.	Shabbat
SNTSMS	Society for New Testament Studies Monograph Series
SymBU	Symbolae Biblicae Upsalienses
TDNT	Kittel, Gerhard, and Gerhard Friedrich, eds. *Theological Dictionary of the New Testament*. Translated by Geoffrey W. Bromiley. 10 vols. Grand Rapids: Eerdmans, 1964–1976.
ThLZ	*Theologische Literaturzeitung*
TG	transformational-generative
ThTo	*Theology Today*
ZNW	*Zeitschrift für die neutestamentliche Wissenschaft*
ZTK	*Zeitschrift für Theologie und Kirche*

Part 1
Biography

Tracking a Whirlwind: A Biography of Robert W. Funk

Andrew D. Scrimgeour

If you could choose one word to encapsulate Robert Funk, what would it be? The most cited descriptions of Funk are those of Ernest Saunders in his centennial history of the Society of Biblical Literature, *Searching the Scriptures: A History of the Society of Biblical Literature, 1880–1980.*[1] That book would be a good place to look for a singular noun, especially in a passage like:

> The six-year period of Robert W. Funk's leadership as executive secretary (1968–1973) inaugurated a new era in the history of the Society in which he played a decisive role. Without his imagination and engineering skills it might not have been brought off. A top-flight scholar whose publications testify to his competence, he possessed the twin gifts of an inspired imagination that dreams dreams and sees visions and technical skills that can convert these ephemera into structures.

He continues:

> Few combine the two roles. But Funk is equally at home in the diverse worlds of poetics and practice, brain storms and balance sheets, the catholic world of scholarship and the particular discipline of Christian studies. As such he is a controversial figure, but no one would challenge his seminal influence in reshaping biblical studies in America in general or the guild of biblical scholars in particular.[2]

---

1. See Funk's obituary by Robert Kraft, which is a series of quotes from Saunders. Robert A. Kraft, "Robert W. Funk and the SBL," *SBL Forum* (September 2005): https://tinyurl.com/SBL1128c.

2. Ernest W. Saunders, *Searching the Scriptures: A History of the Society of Biblical Literature, 1880–1980*, BSNA 7 (Chico, CA: Scholars Press, 1982), 63–64.

Despite this otherwise striking tribute, a signature word to capture Funk does not emerge. But Saunders does not disappoint. A few years later, in a paper he read at the Annual Meeting of the Society of Biblical Literature, he surveyed the evolution of the Society of Biblical Literature's historical consciousness and its first attempts to establish a formal archive. Again he paid tribute to Funk. Those efforts, he wrote, were "largely under the impetus of that human whirlwind, Robert W. Funk."[3] *A whirlwind?* Spot on. A one-word metaphor capturing Funk's boundless energy, restless drive, artesian flow of ideas, even the unintended consequences of a "full speed ahead" approach to life and work. One of his colleagues remarked, "We used to say that Bob had more creative ideas before breakfast than the rest of us did in our careers."[4]

My brief biography constructs a narrative framework for this volume's six-part exploration of Funk's legacy. It identifies pertinent coordinates—geographic, temporal, institutional, and interpersonal—that track the life of Robert W. Funk, the human whirlwind who reformed the scholarly model of biblical studies.[5] A valuable companion to my profile is the chronology located later in the volume, which provides a roster of important dates in Funk's professional life.

+ + +

"I am still proud to call myself a Hoosier," Funk declared to the delight of the commencement crowd at Butler University in Indianapolis in spring 2005. "It is good to be back home again in Indiana." Rather than a rhetorical flourish designed to ingratiate himself to the audience and gain honorary citizenship for the weekend, his words were an honest shout-out to his roots. Throughout his career, whenever Funk reflected on the influences on his life, he would invariably point to the river port city of

---

3. Ernest W. Saunders, "The SBL History I Couldn't Write" (paper presented at the Annual Meeting of the Society of Biblical Literature, Chicago, IL, December 9, 1984).

4. Karen L. King, "Remembering Robert Funk," *The Fourth R* 19.2, (2006): 3, emphasis added.

5. In so doing, it is deeply rooted in the authoritative biographical explorations of Funk by Lane McGaughy, who worked closely with Funk during his seminary days and doctoral studies, followed by teaching with Funk at the University of Montana, serving with him as Associate Director of Society of Biblical Literature and Scholars Press, and finally working with him at the Jesus Seminar, Polebridge Press, and Westar Institute.

Evansville in southern Indiana and pay tribute to the people who were his boyhood mentors and life-long heroes.[6] Two stood out.

Ruth Stamps Adams, his junior high school social studies teacher, could well have been the Midwest's poster child for leadership in secondary education. She discerned Funk's latent talents and the deficits of his home life—his father had abandoned the family during the Great Depression when Funk was eight—and took a special interest in him. Above all, she encouraged her students to be independent thinkers whatever the subject. She made reading the local paper with critical eyes a weekly assignment. She insisted that Funk learn the skills of group leadership and try his hand in student government, a practical outlet for experimenting with the theories they were studying. As a result, he began high school as a serious, tenacious student—one increasingly eager to challenge the views expressed in textbooks or on the chalkboard—and a leader on the basketball court, with debate teams, and in thespian productions. His growing self-confidence and study habits served him well as the first person in his family to go to college. Later in life, Funk reflected that Ruth Adams "instilled in me a love of learning which I have never forgotten." So strong was her stamp on his life that he kept a photograph of her on his desk all his adult life.

The Barker Avenue Christian Church (Disciples of Christ) in Evansville was a second home to Funk. Its young pastor, Rice Kelso, took Funk under his wing. Struck by the infectious brio that Funk brought to church activities and his unrelenting questions about core beliefs and practices, Kelso began to mentor him in the history and ministries of the church, introduced him to the study of biblical texts and New Testament Greek, and gave the teenager opportunities to teach Sunday School and preach.[7] Funk modeled his life after his pastor and also set a course to become a minister.

Aware that World War II was intensifying and with it the conscription of young men as they turned eighteen, he set a goal to complete a year of

---

6. By contrast, his colleague John Dillenberger, a Midwesterner from neighboring Illinois, wrote a memoir titled *From Fallow Field to Hallowed Halls* (Santa Rosa, CA: Polebridge, 2004). In it he wrote, " 'How do I get out of here,' is the pervasive memory of my childhood and it persisted until I went to college.... I grew up in a situation of cultural deprivation" (3, 5, 27). Funk did not seem to display that native Midwestern trait that Patricia Hampl calls "the desire to be elsewhere."

7. This was not unusual in churches in the Stone-Campbell Movement. Leadership training of young people for roles in their local churches was central to the tradition. Many of the young men with whom Funk went to college were assigned churches to pastor on the weekends given their leadership in their home churches.

ministerial studies before the local draft board could summon him.[8] So
he accelerated his high school studies, graduated a year early, and immediately enrolled at Johnson Bible College, a conservative Disciples school,
near Knoxville, Tennessee, his pastor's alma mater. With that maneuver,
Funk was enhancing his chances of being assigned to the army chaplain
corps rather than to the infantry.[9] If he was to serve in the army, he wanted
those years to further his pastoral education not disrupt it. But his plan did
not go smoothly. Because he explored the Johnson Bible College library to
supplement the required readings and asked too many questions in class
unsettling the faculty, the president of Johnson Bible College asked him to
leave after the end of his sophomore year. Without rancor, Funk returned
home, enrolled in summer school at Evansville College, and then in the
fall transferred to Butler University in Indianapolis, a more liberal school
in the Disciples tradition. He was eighteen years old.

Funk was never drafted. He completed college as well as two postbac-
calaureate degrees without leaving his home state: college (AB, Classics,
Butler University, Indianapolis, 1947), seminary (BD, Christian Theological
School, Butler University, 1950), and graduate school (MA, Semitics, Butler
University, 1951). Each of the schools was a Disciples of Christ institution.
During these years of academic work, Funk devoted his weekends to serv-
ing churches. Following the customary Disciples pattern, upon completing
his seminary degree, Funk was ordained in his home church.

The Disciples regarded themselves as a "New Testament church" and
were committed to "restoring" early Christianity. Thus, the study of the
biblical texts in their original languages was the intellectual anchor for
their scholars and pastors. It became the passion of Funk, too, and the
motivation for taking his PhD in New Testament. As he later observed,
"Interest in New Testament and Christian origins has dictated the direction of my scholarly pursuits in one form or another my entire career."[10]

---

8. As Funk began his junior year, President Roosevelt signed landmark legislation
that launched the first peacetime draft in the history of the country and lowered the
age of conscription from twenty-one to eighteen.

9. As he wrote in a college essay, "If I was called up, I wanted my developing pastoral skills to be put to use" (Robert W. Funk, "Autobiography of Robert Funk" [college
essay, n.d., possibly fall 1943, Johnson Bible College, Westar Institute Archives, Special
Collections, Drew University Library]).

10. Robert W. Funk, "Bridge over Troubled Waters: From Seminary to the Jesus
Seminar" (unpublished memoir, 3–4).

When he moved to Nashville, Tennessee to pursue his PhD at Vanderbilt University, he was not venturing far from his denominational roots. The Disciples of Christ had established a Disciples Divinity House on the Vanderbilt campus for their students enrolled at the Divinity School. With this residential asset, the denomination sought to encourage its students to prepare for the ministry in a place where "the scientific and historical study of religion flourished in the context of a research university."[11]

+ + +

Like other leading scholars in biblical and theological studies, Vanderbilt faculty members were writing books and articles in response to European scholars who were setting the theological agenda.[12] The names of Rudolf Bultmann, Karl Barth, Gerhard Ebeling, Martin Heidegger, Martin Dibelius, and others dominated their footnotes and bibliographies. As Funk began his PhD work, he was plunged into the German tradition of biblical and theological studies. He could not have found a more ideal mentor for his studies than Kendrick Grobel. Grobel had been a student of Bultmann and, when Funk arrived, was translating Bultmann's *Theology of the New Testament* from German into English and preparing for Bultmann's visit to campus to deliver the distinguished Cole Lectures.[13] Funk learned form criticism and the hermeneutics of demythologizing from Grobel.

Because of Funk's language acumen, Grobel urged him to begin translating, editing, and revising the venerable *A Greek Grammar of the New*

---

11. The Disciples Divinity House at the University of Chicago Divinity School was the first of the chartered houses. Scott D. Seay, "Disciples Divinity House," *The Encyclopedia of the Stone-Campbell Movement*, ed. Douglas A. Foster (Grand Rapids: Eerdmans, 2004), 273–74. See also Thomas H. Olbricht, "Hermeneutics," in Foster, *Encyclopedia of the Stone-Campbell Movement*, 387–90.

12. Vanderbilt was part of the group that Claude Welch labeled "older and established programs of the first rank" and characterized them as "the oligopoly or grandfather institutions in religious studies." The group included Harvard, Yale, Princeton, Union (New York), Chicago, Columbia, and Duke. Claude Welch, *Graduate Education in Religion: A Critical Appraisal* (Missoula: University of Montana Press, 1971), 90.

13. Konrad Hammann, *Rudolf Bultmann: A Biography*, trans. Philip E. Devenish (Santa Rosa, CA: Polebridge, 2013), 6, 350. Funk, "Bridge over Troubled Waters," 22–23. The Cole Lectures were delivered in November 1951 and were published as *Jesus Christ and Mythology* (New York: Scribner's Sons, 1958). Grobel married Bultmann's niece (Marianne Pleus), and Bultmann married them on his fiftieth birthday (Hammann, *Rudolf Bultmann*, 350).

Testament by Friedrich Blass and Albert Debrunner from German and New Testament Greek into English.[14] With the assistance of Karlfried Froehlich, it was published ten years later as *A Greek Grammar of the New Testament and Other Early Christian Literature* by the University of Chicago Press and was hailed as superior to the original.[15] As Lane McGaughy has noted, it "is still regarded as the definitive reference grammar of New Testament Greek in English" and is known by the shorthand, "Blass-Debrunner-Funk" or "BDF."[16] Interestingly, in some printings, on the spine of the volume, just below the title, only a single name appears: Funk.

After completing his dissertation, "The Syntax of the Greek Article: Its Importance for Critical Pauline Problems," Funk held brief teaching and research posts at Texas Christian University (1953–1956, Fort Worth, Texas), Harvard Divinity School (1956–1957, Cambridge, Massachusetts), W. F. Albright Institute of Archaeological Research (1957–1958, Jerusalem), and Emory University (1958–1959, Atlanta, Georgia) before putting down roots at Drew University (1959–1966, Madison, New Jersey). In each of the appointments in the United States, he continued a threefold pattern: teaching, writing, and, on weekends, providing pastoral leadership for a local congregation.

Funk's immersion in Continental scholarship intensified at Drew. Unique to campus life was the opportunity to engage in face-to-face conversation with European theologians. For two years Ebeling, a leading German theologian and proponent of the New Hermeneutic, was a visiting professor on campus. Drew also hosted three consultations on hermeneutics that brought distinguished European as well as young North American theologians to campus for intensive three-day discussions.[17] So spirited were these European-American exchanges that they caught the attention of the national media, including *The New York Times*, which had also been covering Barth's first visit to the United States.

As an outgrowth of the consultations, Funk and James Robinson recognized the need of a steady stream of current Continental scholarship

---

14. Friedrich Blass and Albert Debrunner, *Grammatick des neutestamentlichen Griechisch*, 9th ed. (Göttingen: Vandenhoeck & Ruprecht, 1954; 10th ed., 1959).

15. Robert W. Funk, *A Greek Grammar of the New Testament and Other Early Christian Literature* (Chicago: University of Chicago Press, 1961).

16. Lane C. McGaughy, "Robert W. Funk and the Evolution of New Testament Greek Grammar," in this volume.

17. The first consultation was April 26–28, 1962; the second was April 9–11, 1964.

for North American faculty and clergy who did not read German. To provide this resource, they launched a new journal, *Journal for Theology and the Church*.[18] It provided English translations of cutting-edge articles by German and Swiss biblical scholars and theologians and was an early example of Funk's life-long passion for getting the right resources to the right people. Funk and Robinson with Helmut Koester and Eldon Epp were also founding members of the influential Hermeneia commentary series, which in its initial years translated major German commentaries into English.

It was at Drew that Funk discovered the parables or, more accurately, rediscovered the parables. His seminal book, *Language, Hermeneutic and Word of God*, was beginning to take shape in his mind. His attention was shifting from a strict historical interpretation of biblical texts to the literary dimensions of the Jesus tradition. In order to test and refine some of his new ideas, he offered a graduate seminar on the parables. An unexpected influential interlocutor in the seminar was Owen Barfield, eminent poet, literary theorist, and author of *Saving the Appearances*, who was on campus as a visiting professor from London. *Language, Hermeneutic and Word of God* was completed during a sabbatical year (1965–1966) in Germany as Funk continued conversations with Ebeling at the University of Tübingen as well as with other luminaries in Europe's theological pantheon: Ernst Käsemann, Pannenberg, Bultmann, and others.

He was intent on assessing through personal conversation whether German New Testament scholarship would continue to lead the field or whether the new approaches of American scholars would expand the hermeneutical options. When he returned to the United States in 1966, he had arrived at a major intellectual juncture: "My impression," he said, was that "German theology was still constricted by Lutheran orthodoxy and was incapable of fully addressing the contours of the modern world that had opened up after the Enlightenment."[19]

The Drew years were also important to Funk on a personal level. It was when he met two people who became his fast friends and would give him unflagging support for his projects over the decades: Ray Hart, a colleague

---

18. It was the American counterpart of the German *Zeitschrift für Theologie und Kirche*. Funk was the editor, 1964–1974.

19. Lane C. McGaughy, "Why the Jesus Seminar Matters: The American Quest for the Historical Jesus" (Showers Lectures, University of Indianapolis, April 17, 2018). See also Joseph A. Bessler, "Scholarly Provocation, the Jesus Seminar and Its Contexts (Showers Lectures, University of Indianapolis, April 17, 2018).

on the faculty who taught philosophical theology, and Lane McGaughy, a seminary student who would later do his doctorate with Funk at Vanderbilt and become a faculty colleague in Montana. Students looking for Funk in his office midday were often advised, "Check out the coffee shop in the student center. He's probably there with Professor Hart translating Bultmann and Heidegger." It was also during that period that Funk and Hart bought cabins in Montana. Funk and his family spent their summers there, and he "wrote [his] books and articles in the intense stillness of a mountain retreat" overlooking the trout-rippled North Fork River, his fly rod at the ready.[20]

+ + +

The day before Funk boarded the ship for his sabbatical passage to Germany, his professional plans took an unexpected turn. A letter from Vanderbilt arrived inviting him to join the faculty of the Department of Religion and take the chair formerly occupied by his recently deceased teacher, Grobel. Few honors in academic outrank such an offer. Few honors signal more powerfully how one is regarded in an area of specialty. When Funk and his family returned from Germany a year later, they moved to Nashville.

Although Vanderbilt was located many zip codes away from the centers of influence in the Northeast, it was central to the leadership of the Society of Biblical Literature. To some it seemed that the Society of Biblical Literature's gavel of authority was permanently ensconced there. Grobel had been the Executive Secretary for three years (1962–1965). When he died, two Vanderbilt colleagues took the post for one year each. Walter Harrelson, also of the faculty, then took the position intending to have a much longer tenure, but was unexpectedly appointed dean of the Vanderbilt Divinity School. He recommended Funk to succeed him. The Society of Biblical Literature Council agreed and elected him in 1968. The position then stabilized as Funk held the position for five years (1968–1973).

But stabilization did not mean business as usual. Emboldened perhaps by the example of Pope John XXIII who a few years earlier had called for a major council that would "throw open the windows of the church to let the fresh air of the spirit blow through," Funk threw open the windows of the

---

20. Funk, "Bridge over Troubled Waters." The stream was the North Fork of the Flathead River.

academy, and the winds of change swept through.[21] The Society of Biblical Literature was radically reorganized, the result of a massive overhaul of the constitution and by-laws led by Funk, Robert Kraft, and other "young Turks," as the young rebels were called, with support from key members of the old guard (1969).[22] Saunders called it the "turning point" in the life of the Society.[23] No longer was the Society of Biblical Literature a small, staid enclave of senior Ivy League scholars reading papers to each other the week after Christmas at Union Theological Seminary in New York while other scholars audited from the periphery. The new meeting venues featured first-rate hotels rather than seminary dormitories, and younger scholars, even from unsung campuses, took active roles in the expanded program. Funk had inherited from Grobel a concern that younger scholars be given voice both in the annual program and in the leadership of the Society.[24] Book exhibits were added for the first time, quickly becoming an essential hub for discourse and discovery at the annual meeting. Attendance swelled. Most importantly, the format of the program was enlarged to encourage seminars that would foster a wide array of collaborative research projects resulting in major publications. An ambitious publication program was also established followed by the invention of Scholars Press "again under the leadership of Funk, and in collaboration with the [American Academy of Religion] and other societies."[25] In the assessment of Gene Tucker, "The effects of those changes, and the others that came in their train, have been far-reaching, reshaping both the *form and substance* of biblical scholarship."[26]

---

21. Formally known as the Second Vatican Ecumenical Council, it began October 11, 1962, and concluded October 8, 1965.

22. Others included Norman E. Wagner, Brevard S. Childs, Walter Harrelson, Helmut Koester, and George W. MacRae. See Douglas A. Knight, "Studies in the Hebrew Bible / Old Testament in the Americas of the Twentieth Century," in *Hebrew Bible/Old Testament: The History of Its Interpretation*, vol. 3 of *From Modernism to Post-modernism (The Nineteenth and Twentieth Centuries)* (Göttingen: Vandenhoeck & Ruprecht, 2015), 231–32.

23. Saunders, *Searching the Scriptures*, 58. See also Ernest W. Saunders, "A Century of Service to American Biblical Scholarship," *CSR Bulletin* 11.3 (1980): 69–72.

24. Saunders, *Searching the Scriptures*, 59.

25. Saunders, *Searching the Scriptures*, 34.

26. Gene M. Tucker, "The Modern (and Postmodern?) Society of Biblical Literature: Institutions and Scholarship," in *Foster Biblical Scholarship: Essays in Honor of Kent Harold Richards*, ed. Frank Ritchel Ames and Charles William Miller (Atlanta: Society of Biblical Literature, 2010), 33, emphasis added.

+ + +

Over time Funk and Hart became disillusioned with the seminary culture in which they worked. In their view, too frequently theological faculty, despite the intended protections of tenure, found it difficult to be candid with denominational leaders and local churches about the results of biblical scholarship and its implications for faith. They functioned more as care-taking chaplains to their denominations than as scholars who could speak the truth with kindness, candor, and unflinching honesty.[27] When the opportunity came to establish a department of religion in a secular university where they would enjoy greater faculty freedom, they jumped at the chance and took on that challenge at the University of Montana in Missoula.[28] They brought with them their leading roles in the Society of Biblical Literature and the American Academy of Religion. Funk was in his second year as the Executive Secretary, and Hart was the editor of the *Journal of the American Academy of Religion*, the flagship publication of the American Academy of Religion. To the disbelief of the old guard, the leadership of religious studies, long perceived as the birthright of east coast institutions, was now homesteading in the mountains of Montana.[29]

Scholars Press was launched in Missoula five years later (1974) under the welcoming auspices of the printing department of the university and its entrepreneurial director, Al Madison. Funk stepped down as Executive Secretary in order to become the director of the new enterprise—a collaborative undertaking by the Society of Biblical Literature, the American Academy of Religion, and several other learned societies in the humanities.[30] Central to the mission of Scholars Press was the conviction that scholars should take charge of the publication of their own work and not

27. A model for Funk was the faculty at Drew University during his tenure there. "It was the willingness to look the old traditions straight in the eye and ask whether they could survive the climate of modernity that made Drew the place that it was," he wrote, in "Bridge over Troubled Waters." The Hermeneutical Conferences at Drew were another exhibit A of the theological leadership that he admired.

28. For an analysis of integrity and academic freedom in the university for scholars in religious studies, see Schubert M. Ogden, "Theology in the University: The Question of Integrity," in *Doing Theology Today* (Valley Forge, PA: Trinity Press International, 1996), 80–91.

29. Tucker, "Modern (and Postmodern?) Society of Biblical Literature," 34.

30. Other sponsors included the American Society of Papyrologists and the American Philological Association.

outsource it to for-profit publishers as had been the long-standing practice. Consequently, with the services provided on site by the university, scholars began to initiate, edit, publish, and distribute their own work for a price much lower than the established denominational and university presses. The number of published books soared. The runaway costs of publishing the journals were cut in half even as the page counts of the issues more than doubled. Significant to young scholars was a new Dissertation Series that published without major revision the best of recent doctoral dissertations. It efficiently integrated recent research into scholarly discourse without the usual delay of years of revision, launching many careers. A new journal was also created, *Semeia: An Experimental Journal in Biblical Interpretation.* "It became the primary organ in the Americas for introducing and exploring a wide range of new methods and issues in biblical studies."[31] The hegemony of commercial publishers over the products of scholarly research now had a bona fide challenger.[32]

After a six-year partnership with the university's printing department, Scholars Press lost its favored-contract status due to major cuts to the university budget and was forced to find a new institutional home. At the invitation of California State University, the press in 1980 moved 929 miles south to Chico, in northern California.[33] The timing was far from ideal, as Funk was recuperating from open-heart surgery.[34] Nevertheless, he took an unpaid leave from the university and helped pack, load, and transport

---

31. Knight, "Studies in the Hebrew Bible," 233.

32. Lane C. McGaughy, "Greetings to Our Esteemed Colleague and Mentor, Robert W. Funk," *Forum* 8.3–4 (1992): 174. Some of the management challenges for this experiment in scholarly publishing were explored by Jack Miles, a former assistant to Funk at Scholars Press: Jack A. Miles, "Knowing the Score at Scholars Press," *Scholarly Publishing* 7 (1976): 221–34.

33. Charles E. Winquist was a professor in the Religious Studies Department at Chico State and was instrumental in negotiating the Chico-Scholars Press arrangement. He was also the Executive Director of the American Academy of Religion at that time (1978–1982) and a member of the Board of Trustees of Scholars Press.

34. In his report to the Board of Directors, Funk wrote: "My convalescence may have contributed to the problem, but I suspect we would have had a tough year under the best of circumstances; we simply were not prepared for the moves we had to make owing to the situation in Missoula. The most difficult trials are now behind us" (Robert W. Funk, "Report of the Director," September 19–20, 1980 [unpublished typescript], 10).

five thousand boxes of books and journals south.[35] Then, as if the move required apocalyptic signs and wonders, Mount Saint Helens, 400 miles to the west, blew its top on May 18, spewing a pall of volcanic ash across the west, compromising visibility on the highways, delaying the move. When Funk was finally able to leave town with a fully loaded U-Haul, he left "under a cloud of volcanic dust."[36]

As the boxes were being unpacked in Chico, members of the Scholars Press Board of Trustees arrived for their fall meeting. In the months leading up to the meeting, communication between Funk and the board had been tempestuous. His own report to the board stated, "We have just passed through one of our most difficult periods and have arrived at what portends to be a most promising era." Despite these conciliatory words, the first session of the board turned acrimonious, as Funk and the board could not resolve their differences on a number of fiscal and management matters. In frustration, he offered his resignation to be effective three months later (December 31, 1980) and left the room. In his absence, the board accepted his resignation but altered its timeline—they made it effective immediately and informed him of the decision. Funk was blindsided by the news. It had never occurred to him that immediate termination would be their response to his offer.

Because the Scholars Press Board of Trustees never issued an official statement to its constituency about the reasons for the separation nor countered the swirl of conspiracy theories that ensued, a rumor took hold that Funk was guilty of malfeasance and therefore fired. That was not the case. Put simply, there was a fiscal crisis exacerbated by the costs and disruption of the move to Chico. Despite the arrival of grants from the National Endowment for the Humanities and the Exxon Corporation totaling $410,000, the board no longer had confidence that the entrepreneurial genius of the founder was now sufficient to speedily resolve a tangle of management issues.[37] Funk lived under that cloud for the rest of his life.

While he was never exonerated by the Scholars Press board, the president of the Society of Biblical Literature, James Robinson, a year later issued a report on behalf of the Society of Biblical Literature in the *CSR*

---

35. Robert W. Funk, "Calculated and Uncalculated Moves," in *Annual Meeting 1980, AAR/SBL, Scholars Press Scholia XII*, 110.

36. Funk, "Calculated and Uncalculated Moves."

37. A $360,000 Challenge Grant from the National Endowment for the Humanities and $50,000 from Exxon.

Bulletin (December 1981).[38] It included the text of a resolution from the Society of Biblical Literature Council, which was "here published to put to rest once and for all unfounded rumors of impropriety that have circulated and to reaffirm the integrity that has been apparent to those who worked closely with Funk during his years as Executive Secretary and President of the Society of Biblical Literature and then as founder and Director of Scholars Press."[39]

Two months later at the banquet celebrating the centennial of the Society of Biblical Literature at the Annual Meeting in Dallas, Funk was honored with the William Rainey Harper Award for Statecraft in Support of Biblical Scholarship.[40] That evening he was also honored as one of the three featured speakers.[41] To the relief of the leadership of the Society of Biblical Literature and the American Academy of Religion, Funk, rather than publicly exegete the Chico debacle or deliver a standard academic talk, read a fictional tale of his own creation, "Legends of the School of Scribes or The Seventy Pens of Power" (included in §7 of this volume). In the Tolkien-like fantasy, many biblical scholars, past and present, were lampooned. Funk himself was one of the prime targets in his literary hijinks. After that historic evening, Funk never again participated in the life of the Society of Biblical Literature.

+ + +

Funk returned to his faculty position at University of Montana. He was fifty-three years old. He could have coasted toward retirement—writing, teaching, and fly fishing as he chose, secure in his tenured position, his list of publications lengthy and distinguished. But such is not the nature of a whirlwind. His mind never in neutral, Funk began to search for the keys to an alternative, independent future in biblical research.

---

38. A publication of the Council of the Study on Religion, an umbrella group for academic associations in religious studies, including the Society of Biblical Literature and American Academy of Religion.

39. James M. Robinson, "Statement regarding Robert Funk," *CSR Bulletin* 12 (1980): 143.

40. At the same time, James Robinson was presented with a companion honor, the Ernest Cadman Colwell Award for Statecraft in Support of Biblical Scholarship.

41. The other two speakers were Ernest W. Saunders (Garrett-Evangelical Theological Seminary) and Harry Orlinsky (Hebrew Union College/Jewish Institute of Religion, New York).

Within a year, thanks to the financial backing of former students, colleagues, and friends and augmented by new technologies provided by David Packard Jr., he began his own press.[42] He named it Polebridge Press. Polebridge was the tiny, remote community where his summer cabin was located on the western border of Glacier National Park. Funk worked as a field editor for Fortress, and Matejovsky set type for Fortress and other university presses. Four years later, Funk took early retirement from the University of Montana and moved the press to Sonoma, California, the heart of wine country. Then he made his boldest move. He created the Jesus Seminar (1985) and asked Dominic Crossan to be co-chair. Later in 1986, that project was folded into the Westar Institute, an independent think tank that he founded in 1986. As Crossan has observed, with those three interlocking initiatives, Funk "was creating in microcosm what he had helped create in macrocosm with the SBL itself."[43]

The Jesus Seminar was launched March 21–24, 1985, in Berkeley, California. Funk's opening words to the founding group of thirty scholars have often been quoted:

> We are about to embark on a momentous enterprise. We are going to inquire simply, rigorously after the *voice* of Jesus, after what he really said.... Our basic plan is simple. We intend to examine every fragment of the traditions attached to the name of Jesus in order to determine what he really said—not his literal words, perhaps, but the substance and style of his utterances. We are in quest of his *voice*, insofar as it can be distinguished from many other voices also preserved in the tradition.[44]

The announcement of the project was viewed as bold and innovative by many, but others, despite the reputations and credentials of its participants, were wary of the seminar's maverick status. However, discerning eyes with institutional memory recognized that the seminar was not in fact without precedent. Rather, like a palimpsest, it bore the tracings of an earlier project. Indeed, in 1978, Funk and George MacRae had proposed

---

42. Packard "donated all the Hewlett-Packard hardware and the Ibycus software for setting Hebrew, Greek, and Coptic to the Press" (McGaughy, "Why the Jesus Seminar Matters").

43. Crossan, "Honest to Bob, In Memory of Professor Robert W. Funk," *Religious Studies News* (2006): 23. This insight is shared by McGaughy; see Lane C. McGaughy, "Robert W. Funk—A Profile," *The Fourth R* 19.2 (2006): 6.

44. Robert W. Funk, "The Issue of Jesus," *Forum* 1.1 (1985): 7.

a similar research project to the Society of Biblical Literature as part of the celebration of its centennial: evaluating the authenticity of the words attributed to Jesus in all the gospels of the early Christian movement.[45] It would be a seminar under the auspices of *Semeia* and supported by third-party funding. But it proved too controversial and was turned down.[46] Funk, however, did not scuttle the proposal. Seven years later, recast and enlarged, it became the Jesus Seminar and Funk's all-consuming work for the next twenty years.

The work plan of the seminar may be viewed in four phases.[47] The first (1985–1991) was to create a database of all the sayings attributed to Jesus in the first three centuries of the common era. The seminar collected more than 1,500 versions of some 500 items. The inventory covered all the surviving gospels and reports from the period, not just the canonical gospels, since "canonical boundaries are irrelevant in critical assessments of the various sources of information about Jesus."[48] The scholars met twice a year to debate scholarly papers written on groups of sayings and come to a consensus through voting as to the degree of certainty about their authenticity. The results of the first phase of the seminar were published in *The Five Gospels: The Search for the Authentic Words of Jesus* (1993). The working papers were published in the *Forum*, the academic journal of the seminar. The seminar found that 18 percent of the sayings attributed to Jesus can be verified, using historical-critical criteria, as authentic.

The second phase of the seminar (1991–1996) critically examined the deeds in the Gospels of Q, Mark, Matthew, Luke, John, and Peter. The results were published in *The Acts of Jesus: The Search for the Authentic*

---

45. The proposal was titled "National Seminar on the Primary Pronouncements of Jesus" (16 pages).

46. The first planning session was held in New York at the 1979 Annual Meeting.

47. My comments on the four phases borrow heavily from McGaughy, "Why the Jesus Seminar Matters." Additional valuable overviews include: Arthur J. Dewey, "The Jesus Seminar: An Overview," in *The Gospel of Jesus according to the Jesus Seminar*, by Robert W. Funk with Arthur J. Dewey and the Jesus Seminar, 2nd ed. (Santa Rosa, CA: Polebridge, 2015), ix–xiii; Mark Allan Powell, *Jesus as a Figure in History: How Modern Historians View the Man from Galilee*, 2nd ed. (Louisville: Westminster John Knox, 2013), esp. 100–105; and Bernard Brandon Scott, "How Did We Get Here? Looking Back at Twenty Years of the Jesus Seminar," *The Fourth R* 19.5 (2006): 3–10.

48. Robert W. Funk, with Roy W. Hoover and the Jesus Seminar, *The Five Gospels: The Search for the Authentic Words of Jesus* (Santa Rosa, CA: Polebridge, 1993), 35.

Deeds of Jesus (1998) and showed that 16 percent of the events can be verified as historical.

As Brandon Scott has observed: "The strength of *The Five Gospels* and *The Acts of Jesus* is their clarity of presentation. It makes available to the reader a vast range of information that has been sorted and debated by a diverse group of scholars. [Because of the four-color schema reflecting the voting options], the reader can see at a glance the range of positions" as well as the consensus. "As a force advancing literacy about the Bible, it has surely raised the level of debate."[49]

Once the seminar had a database of the historically authentic words and deeds of Jesus, "scholars who were only interested in reconstructing the past (the career of Jesus) moved on to other scholarly projects, though they retained their membership in the Jesus Seminar."[50] But Funk had a longer agenda. He encouraged the fellows to begin constructing their own profiles of Jesus based on those fragmentary aphorisms, parables, dialogues, and deeds (1996–2000). His expectations were modest: "We cannot, of course, fill in all the detail, but we can catch sight of the historical figure here and there, now and then, in these tiny windows that open onto his words and work."[51] Funk, Crossan, Marcus Borg, and others published their profiles as books.[52] Still others published briefer portraits in an anthology, *Profiles of Jesus* (2002), edited by Roy W. Hoover.[53] Funk also published a short version of the gospels, containing only the authentic

---

49. Scott, "How Did We Get Here?," 10.

50. McGaughy, "Why the Jesus Seminar Matters," 5.

51. Robert W. Funk, *A Credible Jesus: Fragments of a Vision* (Santa Rosa, CA: Polebridge, 2002), 2.

52. Robet W. Funk, *Honest to Jesus: Jesus for a New Millennium* (San Francisco: HarperSanFrancisco, 1996); Funk, *A Credible Jesus*; Marcus J. Borg, *Jesus: A New Vision; Spirit, Culture, and the Life of Discipleship* (San Francisco: Harper & Row, 1987); Borg, *Meeting Jesus Again for the First Time: The Historical Jesus and the Heart of Contemporary Faith* (San Francisco: HarperSanFrancisco, 1994); John Dominic Crossan, *The Historical Jesus: The Life of a Mediterranean Jewish Peasant* (San Francisco: HarperSanFrancisco, 1991); Crossan, *Jesus: A Revolutionary Biography* (San Francisco: HarperSanFrancisco, 1994); Stephen J. Patterson, *The God of Jesus: The Historical Jesus and the Search for Meaning* (Harrisburg, PA: Trinity Press International, 1998); and Bernard Brandon Scott, *Re-imagine the World: An Introduction to the Parables of Jesus* (Santa Rosa, CA: Polebridge, 2001).

53. Roy W. Hoover, *Profiles of Jesus* (Santa Rosa, CA: Polebridge, 2002). Contributors include: Robert W. Funk, James M. Robinson, Bernard Brandon Scott, Roy W. Hoover, Charles W. Hedrick, Arthur J. Dewey, Mahlon H. Smith, Lance C. McGaughy,

(red and pink) sayings and deeds, *The Gospel of Jesus according to the Jesus Seminar* (1999).

The final phase of the Jesus Seminar (2000–2005) turned to the "so what?" question Funk was always asking. As his years as a pastor had taught him, Funk was ever mindful that, for persons in the pew or those alienated from the churches, historical scholarship was insufficient in itself. What is the payoff for life and living? What does serious scholarship on the Bible mean for faith in the modern world? The essays from these discussions and debates appear in *The Once and Future Jesus* (2000), *The Once and Future Faith* (2001), *The Historical Jesus Goes to Church* (2004), and *When Faith Meets Reason* (2008).[54]

Over the years more than two hundred scholars participated in the seminar. More than seventy-five signed each of the two major reports. As Mark Allan Powell has noted, "The harmony of so many usually independent voices is precisely what demands that attention be given to this chorus of scholars."[55] Powell also pointed out that one aspect of the Jesus Seminar went unreported:

> Two hundred historians, relying solely on the investigative techniques of secular, critical scholarship, affirmed the authenticity of some 18 percent of the sayings attributed to Jesus in books that were written a generation after his death by people who made no pretense of being objective or unbiased in what they wrote. The media, however, missed this story, reporting instead the rather bland and predictable instances in which critical scholarship was unable to affirm convictions of religious piety.[56]

To the delight of the press, the sessions of the Jesus Seminar were open to the public so that anyone could see the scholars debating and famously

---

Marcus J. Borg, Kathleen E. Corley, John Dominic Crossan, Hal Taussig, Stephen J. Patterson, and Robert T. Fortna.

54. Robert W Funk et al., *The Once and Future Jesus* (Santa Rosa, CA: Polebridge, 2000); Karen Armstrong et al., *The Once and Future Faith* (Santa Rosa, CA: Polebridge, 2001); Roy W. Hoover, *The Historical Jesus Goes to Church* (Santa Rosa, CA: Polebridge, 2004); and Charles W. Hendrick, ed. *When Faith Meets Reason: Religion Scholars Reflect on Their Spiritual Journeys* (Santa Rosa, CA: Polebridge, 2008).

55. Powell, *Jesus as a Figure in History*, 116. Cited by Scott, "How Did We Get Here?," 4.

56. Powell, *Jesus as a Figure in History*, 104.

using colored beads to register their judgments. As Funk had said in the first session of the seminar in Berkeley:

> We are not embarking on this venture in a corner. We are going to carry out our work in full public view; we will not only honor the freedom of information, we will insist on the public disclosure of our work and, insofar as it lies within our power, we shall see to it that the public is informed of our judgments. We shall do so, not because our wisdom is superior, but because we are committed to public accountability.

Consequently, the collaborative decisions on the gospel texts regularly captured headlines in newspapers and magazines—local and national alike. As Funk released the votes to the press, he reaped bushels of both ire and admiration from scholars, clergy, parishioners, and the public.[57] His life was even threatened, and on one occasion a police escort was required to protect him from hostile demonstrators on a university campus.[58] All of these responses point to one unambiguous achievement: the Jesus Seminar had become part of the religious consciousness of the country.[59]

+ + +

While working on a book he was calling *The Incredible Christ* and assisting a team of Jesus Seminar scholars on a new translation of Paul's authentic letters, Funk learned he had an aggressive brain tumor.[60] He died four months later on September 3, 2005, just six weeks shy of the twentieth anniversary celebration of the founding of the Jesus Seminar. He was seventy-nine.

---

57. See especially Luke Timothy Johnson, *The Real Jesus: The Misguided Quest for the Historical Jesus and the Truth of the Traditional Gospels* (San Francisco: HarperSanFrancisco, 1996), Robert J. Miller, *The Jesus Seminar and Its Critics* (Santa Rosa, CA: Polebridge, 1999), and Robert J. Miller, ed., *The Life and Legacy of Robert W. Funk*, *The Fourth R* 19.2 (2006).

58. Reported by Powell, *Jesus as a Figure in History*, xi–xii.

59. John Shelby Spong, "Robert Walter Funk, Founder of the Jesus Seminar, 1926–2005, A Tribute," Bishop Spong Newsletter (September 15, 2005); republished at http://www.renewedpriesthood.org/ca/page.cfm?Web_ID=676

60. That project was completed five years later: Arthur J. Dewey et al., *The Authentic Letters of Paul: A New Reading of Paul's Rhetoric and Meaning* (Santa Rosa, CA: Polebridge, 2010).

That spring he had given a talk to the largest audience of his career: the commencement address at his alma mater, Butler University, and received the honorary degree, Doctor of Humane Letters. His plans for the fall included a trip to Drew University to give a lecture and accept an honorary doctorate. The title of the talk had been announced as "The Jesus Seminar as Community."

Funk's obituary in *The New York Times* inventoried his scholarly bona fides but focused on the Jesus Seminar that launched him into public prominence.[61] It even included caustic quotes from a detractor—ample evidence that Funk, even, in death, continued to roil the waters where Jesus was concerned. Though controversy seemed always to dog his way, more often than not it was evidence that he had brought an important issue out into the open. Religious literacy mattered. That is the legacy for which he will be long remembered: he escorted biblical scholarship, long sequestered in the ivory tower, to the public square.

Bibliography

Armstrong, Karen, et al. *The Once and Future Faith*. Santa Rosa, CA: Polebridge, 2001.

Bessler, Joseph A. "Scholarly Provocation, the Jesus Seminar and Its Contexts." Showers Lectures, University of Indianapolis, April 17, 2018.

Blass, Friedrich, and Albert Debrunner. *Grammatick des neutestamentlichen Griechisch*. 9th ed. Göttingen: Vandenhoeck & Ruprecht, 1954. 10th ed., 1959.

Borg, Marcus J. *Jesus: A New Vision; Spirit, Culture, and the Life of Discipleship*. San Francisco: Harper & Row, 1987.

———. *Meeting Jesus Again for the First Time: The Historical Jesus and the Heart of Contemporary Faith*. San Francisco: HarperSanFrancisco, 1994.

Bultmann, Rudolf. *Jesus Christ and Mythology*. New York: Scribner's Sons, 1958.

Crossan, John Dominic. *The Historical Jesus: The Life of a Mediterranean Jewish Peasant*. San Francisco: HarperSanFrancisco, 1991.

---

61. Laurie Goodstein, "R. W. Funk, 79, Creator of Jesus Seminar, Dies," *The New York Times*, September 10, 2005.

———. "Honest to Bob, In Memory of Professor Robert W. Funk." *Religious Studies News* (2006): 22–23.

———. *Jesus: A Revolutionary Biography*. San Francisco: HarperSanFrancisco, 1994.

Dewey, Arthur J. "The Jesus Seminar: An Overview." Pages ix–xiii in *The Gospel of Jesus according to the Jesus Seminar*. By Robert W. Funk, with Arthur J. Dewey and the Jesus Seminar. 2nd ed. Santa Rosa, CA: Polebridge, 2015.

Dewey, Arthur J., Roy W. Hoover, Lane C. McGaughy, and Daryl D. Schmidt, *The Authentic Letters of Paul: A New Reading of Paul's Rhetoric and Meaning*. Santa Rosa, CA: Polebridge, 2010.

Dillenberger, John. *From Fallow Field to Hallowed Halls*. Santa Rosa, CA: Polebridge, 2004.

Funk, Robert W. "Autobiography of Robert Funk." College essay, n.d. [possibly fall 1943], Johnson Bible College. Westar Institute Archives, Special Collections, Drew University Library.

———. "Bridge over Troubled Waters: From Seminary to the Jesus Seminar." Unpublished memoir, August 2, 2002.

———. "Calculated and Uncalculated Moves." Page 110 in *Annual Meeting 1980, AAR/SBL, Scholars Press Scholia XII*.

———. *A Credible Jesus: Fragments of a Vision*. Santa Rosa, CA: Polebridge, 2002.

———. *A Greek Grammar of the New Testament and Other Early Christian Literature*. Chicago: University of Chicago Press, 1961.

———. *Honest to Jesus: Jesus for a New Millennium*. San Francisco: HarperSanFrancisco, 1996.

———. "The Issue of Jesus." *Forum* 1.1 (1985): 7–12.

———. "Report of the Director." September 19–20, 1980. Unpublished typescript.

Funk, Robert W., with Roy W. Hoover and the Jesus Seminar. *The Five Gospels: The Search for the Authentic Words of Jesus*. Santa Rosa, CA: Polebridge, 1993.

Funk, Robert W., Thomas Sheehan, Marcus Borg, John Shelby Spong, Karen King, John Dominic Crossan, Lloyd Geering, Gerd Luedemann, and Walter Wink. *The Once and Future Jesus*. Santa Rosa, CA: Polebridge, 2000.

Goodstein, Laurie. "R. W. Funk, 79, Creator of Jesus Seminar, Dies." *The New York Times*, September 10, 2005.

Hammann, Konrad. *Rudolf Bultmann: A Biography.* Translated by Philip E. Devenish. Santa Rosa, CA: Polebridge, 2013.

Hendrick, Charles W., ed. *When Faith Meets Reason: Religion Scholars Reflect on Their Spiritual Journeys.* Santa Rosa, CA: Polebridge, 2008.

Hoover, Roy W. *The Historical Jesus Goes to Church.* Santa Rosa, CA: Polebridge, 2004.

———, ed. *Profiles of Jesus.* Santa Rosa, CA: Polebridge, 2002.

Johnson, Luke Timothy. *The Real Jesus: The Misguided Quest for the Historical Jesus and the Truth of the Traditional Gospels.* San Francisco: HarperSanFrancisco, 1996.

King, Karen L. "Remembering Robert Funk." *The Fourth R* 19.2 (2006): 3, 20.

Knight, Douglas A. "Studies in the Hebrew Bible / Old Testament in the Americas of the Twentieth Century." Pages 221–52 in *Hebrew Bible/ Old Testament: The History of Its Interpretation.* Vol. 3 of *From Modernism to Post-Modernism (The Nineteenth and Twentieth Centuries).* Göttingen: Vandenhoeck & Ruprecht, 2015.

Kraft, Robert. "Robert W. Funk and the SBL." *SBL Forum* (September 2005): https://tinyurl.com/SBL1128c.

McGaughy, Lane C. "Funk, Robert W, (1926–)." Pages 423–24 in vol. 1 of *Dictionary of Biblical Interpretation.* Edited by John H. Hayes. Nashville: Abingdon, 1999.

———. "Funk, Robert W. (1926–2005)." Pages 422–24 in *Dictionary of Major Biblical Interpreters, A–J.* Edited by Donald K. McKim. Downers Grove, IL: InterVarsity Press, 2007.

———. "Greetings to Our Esteemed Colleague and Mentor, Robert W. Funk." *Forum* 8.3–4 (1992): 169–75.

———. "Robert W. Funk—A Profile." *The Fourth R* 19.2 (2006): 4–6.

———. "Why the Jesus Seminar Matters: The American Quest for the Historical Jesus." Showers Lectures, University of Indianapolis, April 17, 2018.

Miles, John A. "Knowing the Score at Scholars Press." *Scholarly Publishing* 7 (1976): 221–34.

Miller, Robert J. ed. *The Life and Legacy of Robert W. Funk. The Fourth R* 19.2 (2006).

———. *The Jesus Seminar and Its Critics.* Santa Rosa, CA: Polebridge, 1999.

Ogden, Schubert M. "Theology in the University: The Question of Integrity." Pages 80–91 in *Doing Theology Today.* Valley Forge, PA: Trinity Press International, 1996.

Olbricht, Thomas H. "Hermeneutics." Pages 387–90 in *The Encyclopedia of the Stone-Campbell Movement*. Edited by Douglas A. Foster. Grand Rapids: Eerdmans, 2004.

Patterson, Stephen J. *The God of Jesus: The Historical Jesus and the Search for Meaning*. Harrisburg, PA: Trinity Press International, 1998.

Powell, Mark Allan. *Jesus as a Figure in History: How Modern Historians View the Man from Galilee*. 2nd ed. Louisville: Westminster John Knox, 2013.

Robinson, James M. "Statement regarding Robert Funk." *CSR Bulletin* 12 (1980): 143.

Saunders, Ernest W. "A Century of Service to American Biblical Scholarship." *CSR Bulletin*. 11.3 (1980): 69–72.

———. "The SBL History I Couldn't Write." Paper presented at the Annual Meeting of the Society of Biblical Literature, Chicago, December 9, 1984.

———. *Searching the Scriptures: A History of the Society of Biblical Literature, 1880–1980*. BSNA 7. Chico, CA: Scholars Press, 1982.

Scott, Bernard Brandon, "How Did We Get Here? Looking Back at Twenty Years of the Jesus Seminar." *The Fourth R* 19.5 (2006): 3–10.

———. *Re-imagine the World: An Introduction to the Parables of Jesus*. Santa Rosa, CA: Polebridge, 2001.

Seay, Scott D. "Disciples Divinity House." Pages 273–74 in *The Encyclopedia of the Stone-Campbell Movement*. Edited by Douglas A. Foster. Grand Rapids: Eerdmans, 2004.

Spong, John Shelby, "Robert Walter Funk, Founder of the Jesus Seminar, 1926–2005, A Tribute." Bishop Spong Newsletter (September 15, 2005). Republished at http://www.renewedpriesthood.org/ca/page.cfm?Web_ID=676.

Tucker, Gene M. "The Modern (and Postmodern?) Society of Biblical Literature: Institutions and Scholarship." Pages 31–52 in *Foster Biblical Scholarship: Essays in Honor of Kent Harold Richards*. Edited by Frank Ritchel Ames and Charles William Miller. Atlanta: Society of Biblical Literature, 2010.

Welch, Claude. *Graduate Education in Religion: A Critical Appraisal*. Missoula: University of Montana Press, 1971.

Part 2
Greek Grammar

Robert W. Funk and the Evolution
of New Testament Greek Grammar

Lane C. McGaughy

The work of Robert W. Funk in the field of New Testament Greek reflects the evolution of grammatical theory from classical philology to contemporary linguistics. His work on ancient Greek spans two turning points in grammatical theory: the transition from classical philology to descriptive linguistics at the beginning of the twentieth century and the equally radical shift from descriptive linguistics to transformational generative approaches at the end of the twentieth century.

Funk was well prepared to apply new approaches to grammatical and pedagogical theory in the field of New Testament Greek. As an undergraduate, he was trained in Classical Greek at Butler University by Professor Janet MacDonald. In his memoirs Funk notes: "She was a strict task master. Fifty lines of Greek drama or a chunk of Plato's dialogues a day was her prescription. She had been trained at Bryn Mawr and had studied in Athens. Years later I would send her copies of my work on Greek grammar and she would advise and reprimand."[1] Thus Funk's scholarly work on New Testament Greek was built on the foundation of Classical Greek, a point worth noting since most traditional New Testament Greek grammars assume the student already knows Classical Greek and simply highlight major changes that occurred between the two stages in the history of the Greek language.

Funk's preparation for grammatical analysis was also honed by his Vanderbilt dissertation, "The Syntax of the Greek Article: Its Importance for Critical Pauline Problems."[2] The topic was assigned by his disserta-

---

1. Robert W. Funk, "Bridge over Troubled Waters: From Seminary to the Jesus Seminar" (unpublished memoir, August 2, 2002), Section Two, 10.

2. Robert W. Funk, "The Syntax of the Greek Article: Its Importance for Critical Pauline Problems" (PhD diss., Vanderbilt University, 1953).

tion director, Professor Robert Hawkins, and Funk accepted it reluctantly, but it led to his recognition that grammatical analysis at the word level is inadequate.

A Greek Grammar of the New Testament and Other Early Christian Literature

Professor Kendrick Grobel was Funk's doctoral advisor at Vanderbilt and probably the most important influence on his scholarly formation. Grobel was married to the niece of Rudolf Bultmann and was translating Bultmann's German *Theology of the New Testament*[3] and the recently discovered Coptic Gospel of Truth into English while Funk was studying with him. In his memoirs Funk credits Grobel's influence for his first major publication: "We tend to imitate our teachers. Because Kendrick Grobel was a translator, I became a translator. I began the translation of Blass-Debrunner's Greek [g]rammar when I was a graduate student at Vanderbilt."[4] One must assume that Funk's decision to translate the ninth–tenth edition of Friedrich Blass and Albert Debrunner's *Grammatick des neutestamentlichen Griechisch* was not accidental: given his solid training in Classical and Koine Greek, Funk was well prepared to translate the standard German New Testament Greek grammar into English. Funk's year as the Annual Professor at the American School in Jerusalem in 1957–1958 was a particularly fruitful time for progress on the translation of Blass-Debrunner that was subsequently published under the title *A Greek Grammar of the New Testament and Other Early Christian Literature.*[5] Now six decades later Funk's English translation—referred to as BDF—is still regarded as the definitive reference grammar of New Testament Greek in English, and it continues to sell about two hundred copies a year. But BDF is not just a translation. Because of the revisions and additions Funk made to the ninth–tenth edition of Blass-Debrunner, one of the reviewers, Professor

---

3. Rudolf Bultmann, *Theology of the New Testament*, 2 vols. (New York: Scribner's Sons, 1951, 1955).

4. Funk, "Bridge over Troubled Waters," Section Two, 16.

5. Robert W. Funk, *A Greek Grammar of the New Testament and Other Early Christian Literature* (Chicago: University of Chicago Press, 1961). Translation of Friedrich Blass and Albert Debrunner, *Grammatick des neutestamentlichen Griechisch*, 9th ed. (Göttingen: Vandenhoeck & Ruprecht, 1954; 10th ed., 1959).

Nils Dahl of Yale, wrote that BDF "is one of those rare cases in which a translation is definitely better than the original."[6]

The legacy of nineteenth-century classical philology shaped the various editions and revisions leading up to BDF. In the introduction to the first edition of 1896, Blass states that his aim was to investigate those features of New Testament Greek that could not be documented in Classical Greek texts. Blass thus assumed both that fifth-century Attic is normative for later developments in Greek and that New Testament scholars possessed a working knowledge of Classical Greek grammar. Blass's goal was to catalogue and describe the changes that had occurred in the intervening five centuries. The implications of these assumptions are that New Testament Greek should be judged against classical norms and that a New Testament grammar was essentially an idiom book of special, that is, undocumented, usages in the New Testament.

In the preface to the fourth edition of 1913, Debrunner modestly notes that the German publisher Vandenhoeck & Ruprecht had selected him to update Blass's grammar because of his "linguistic" expertise, presumably referring to advances made in comparative philology and the history of the Greek language made in the late nineteenth century. Debrunner thus added, in six editions from 1913 until his death in 1958, citations from newly discovered Greek papyri and inscriptions, the Septuagint, other early Christian texts, and comparisons with medieval and modern Greek. Still, the core of the grammar throughout the successive editions retained Blass's emphasis on Classical Greek as the norm for evaluating New Testament usage and its practical function as a tool for exegetes needing help with difficult or unusual scriptural syntax or vocabulary. As a result, even with Funk's extensive bibliographical additions and his reorganization of section contents to include the notes with their topical treatments, BDF still honors the conception and parameters of Blass's original project and, as Funk notes in his preface, should be assessed in light of the aims and strengths of Blass and Debrunner's work.

A Beginning-Intermediate Grammar of Hellenistic Greek

But much had changed both in language study and in New Testament scholarship between 1896 and 1961, when BDF first appeared. Funk was

---

6. Nils Dahl, personal letter, October 10, 1973.

aware of these seismic changes, particularly with reference to the emergence of the field of descriptive linguistics in the twentieth century, when he published his English edition of Blass-Debrunner. Rather than radically changing the conception of Blass-Debrunner, however, Funk almost immediately turned to the production of his own three-volume grammar, *A Beginning-Intermediate Grammar of Hellenistic Greek*, based on the insights of structural linguistics and a fresh analysis of the primary data.[7] The major innovations of Funk's conception of a Greek grammar can be summarized as follows:

(1) Description, not prescription. Modern linguists reject the assumption that any one stage in the evolving history of a language is normative but simply describe a particular stage in the history of a language in its own right; each dialect thus has its own integrity. Funk's grammar thus describes all the basic elements of Hellenistic Greek—what he calls its "bread and butter" features—and not just its exceptions from a classical norm. The result is a stand-alone, lesson and reference grammar that can be used by students who do not have a working knowledge of Classical Greek. This opens up the possibility of moving beyond the comparative work of Debrunner to a full-scale description of Hellenistic Greek as a distinctive stage of Greek, not a corruption of the Attic dialect. This was a step that Debrunner anticipated but hesitated to take. Because of Funk's embrace of modern linguistic theory on this point, a pedagogic debate erupted in the Society of Biblical Literature in the 1970s over whether students should still be required to learn Classical Greek before enrolling in New Testament exegetical courses or whether beginning with a course in Hellenistic Greek is sufficient for New Testament exegesis.

(2) Syntactical comprehension, not vocabulary and paradigm memorization. Structural linguistics describes the finite number of sentence patterns that are modified on the basis of syntactical rules to permit the formulation of an infinite number of actual sentences in any language. Funk's grammar is one of the first to analyze Hellenistic Greek on the basis of modern linguistic theory, rather than from the conventional philological approach. Funk's approach was eclectic, borrowing from the work of pre-Chomskian linguists such as Paul Roberts, C. C. Fries, and,

---

7. Robert W. Funk, *A Beginning-Intermediate Grammar of Hellenistic Greek*, 3 vols., SBLSBS 2 (Missoula, MT: Scholars Press, 1973).

in particular, Henry A. Gleason, with whom Funk spent a sabbatical year at the University of Toronto in 1973–1974.

Working in the days before desktop computer search engines, Funk, aided by seminary and graduate school students at Drew University, wrote out two thousand actual Greek sentences from thirty-eight sample passages on 4 x 6-inch index cards and analyzed each one using a parsing code he devised to indicate both the morphological description of word clusters and their syntactical relation to other word clusters in each sentence. He then classified the sentence descriptions; generated fresh analyses of noun phrases, verb clusters, and embedded clauses; and identified six kernel sentence patterns in the sample and their accompanying passive transformations. Funk also classified all the nouns and verbs in Walter Bauer, William F. Arndt, and Felix Wilbur Gingrich's *A Greek-English Lexicon of the New Testament and Other Early Christian Literature* (BAG), according to declension and verb base, and provided a catalogue of BAG's lexical stock in volume 3.[8]

(3) Pedagogical focus, not grammatical jargon. In keeping with current pedagogical advances, Funk's stated aim is to enable students to become proficient in reading actual Greek texts, rather than training them to become professional grammarians. Memorization of vocabulary lists and paradigms is replaced by an emphasis on the syntactic signals of Greek and by strategies for applying a few models to unfamiliar words and constructions. Funk's grammar also contains narrative explanations of each topic, so that lessons can be assigned as advanced reading, thus allowing instructors to use limited class time to answer student questions and elaborate on difficult issues. Anyone wanting to learn Greek on their own could conceivably do so with copies of Funk's grammar and the Greek New Testament.

Assessment of Funk's Work on New Testament Greek Grammar

While serving as the Executive Secretary of the Society of Biblical Literature, Funk created a new program section entitled Hellenistic Greek: Linguistics in 1969. This attracted a number of younger scholars who were influenced by new developments in the field of linguistics and were encour-

---

8. Walter Bauer, William F. Arndt, and Felix Wilbur Gingrich, *A Greek-English Lexicon of the New Testament and Other Early Christian Literature* (Chicago: University of Chicago Press, 1957).

aged by Funk and Eugene Van Ness Goetchius to apply these insights to Koine Greek. One of these younger scholars was Daryl Dean Schmidt whose Graduate Theological Union dissertation, *Hellenistic Greek Grammar and Noam Chomsky* was published in the Society of Biblical Literature Dissertation Series.[9] Schmidt assesses Funk's *A Beginning-Intermediate Grammar of Hellenistic Greek* as follows:

> In the final analysis, Funk's effort is an excellent witness both to the shortcomings of structuralism: elaborate classification of items without an adequate description of syntax, and to its major contribution: morphological analysis of word forms and types.[10]

Schmidt argues that Noam Chomsky's transformational-generative theory had "addressed the inadequacy of structuralism" and launched a "new revolution in linguistics." The one example of "structural inadequacy" Schmidt offers is Funk's analysis of passive sentences: although Funk does describe the passive voice as a "transformation," "his failure to comprehend its significance is reflected in the fact that sentences are dispersed under the various appropriate categories of their sentence structure," rather than being related to linguistic universals at the deep structure of Greek via an account of the operations that generate all such transformations.[11] From Schmidt's perspective as a proponent of transformational-generative grammar, the status of Funk's grammar is parallel to Debrunner's revision of Blass a century earlier: "Once again a new Hellenistic Greek grammar was making its appearance just when its linguistic basis was losing currency."[12] In Funk's defense, since his aim was to enhance the ability of students to read Greek texts, and not to advance transformational-generative theory, he employed an eclectic approach in creating *A Beginning-Intermediate Grammar of Hellenistic Greek*. One might reverse Schmidt's critique and argue that, if one locates BDF and Funk's own grammar at the end of prior epochs, he has produced elegant syntheses of the work of those two epochs. On the other hand, the cracks in the previous conventions that Funk made in both volumes opened the way for the next stage in

---

9. Daryl Dean Schmidt, *Hellenistic Greek Grammar and Noam Chomsky*, SBLDS 62 (Chico, CA: Scholars Press, 1981).

10. Schmidt, *Hellenistic Greek Grammar and Noam Chomsky*, 13.

11. Schmidt, *Hellenistic Greek Grammar and Noam Chomsky*, 13.

12. Schmidt, *Hellenistic Greek Grammar and Noam Chomsky*, 13.

the evolution of New Testament Greek grammar, and thus they can also be viewed as groundbreaking works. But Schmidt's critique does bring us back to an assessment of BDF.

In 1986 the University of Chicago Press invited Funk to prepare a second English edition of BDF based on the sixteenth German edition of Blass-Debrunner prepared by Friedrich Rehkopf (BDR).[13] Funk responded that he was willing to revise BDF but expressed reservations about Rehkopf's elimination of variant manuscript readings and older secondary sources, and his revision of "a few sections to make them conform to the views of his teacher, Joachim Jeremias."[14] An exchange ensued over how much of Rehkopf would need to be included in order to maintain the connection to the German Blass-Debrunner tradition. Funk then invited a team of New Testament scholars who are familiar with the latest developments in the field of linguistics, led by Daryl Schmidt, to review Rehkopf's revision and advise him as to how much of BDR could be incorporated in a new English edition. The committee concluded that Rehkopf's edition represented a step backward from BDF because Funk's improvements in BDF are not included in subsequent German editions of Blass-Debrunner. The review committee also concluded that, after a review of Rehkopf's seventeenth edition, only a small fraction of his work could be included in a new English edition.[15] In 1994 the new BDF editorial committee submitted an extensive outline for a revision that would have retained very little of BDR. Negotiations with the University of Chicago Press stalled at that point, since it was judged the proposal deviated too far from the conception of BDR.

Funk's work on Greek grammar—both in preparing an improved edition of Blass-Debrunner for English readers and in producing his own comprehensive description of Hellenistic Greek based on modern linguistic theory—is the basis for his scholarly reputation and represents a major contribution to the reference libraries of New Testament students and scholars even today. His two seminal grammars span the evolution from philology to linguistics in the late nineteenth century to the revolution of transformational-generative grammar in the late twentieth century—the

---

13. Blass, Friedrich, Albert Debrunner, and Friedrich Rehkopf, *Grammatik des neutestamentlichen Griechisch*, 16th ed. (Gottingen: Vandenhoeck & Ruprecht, 1984).

14. Robert W. Funk, letter, October 22, 1986.

15. Blass, Friedrich, Albert Debrunner, and Friedrich Rehkopf, *Grammatik des neutestamentlichen Griechisch*, 17th ed. (Gottingen: Vandenhoeck & Ruprecht, 1990).

two watershed moments in the history of linguistics symbolized by Ferdinand de Saussure and Noam Chomsky—and thus serve as boundary markers in the ongoing evolution of New Testament Greek grammar.

Bibliography

Bauer, Walter, William F. Arndt, and Felix Wilbur Gingrich. *A Greek-English Lexicon of the New Testament and Other Early Christian Literature.* Chicago: University of Chicago Press, 1957.

Blass, Friedrich, Albert Debrunner, and Friedrich Rehkopf. *Grammatik des neutestamentlichen Griechisch.* 16th ed. Gottingen: Vandenhoeck & Ruprecht, 1984. 17th ed. 1990.

Bultmann, Rudolf. *Theology of the New Testament.* 2 vols. New York: Scribner's Sons, 1951, 1955.

Funk, Robert W. *A Beginning-Intermediate Grammar of Hellenistic Greek.* 3 vols. SBLSBS 2. Missoula, MT: Scholars Press, 1973.

———. *A Greek Grammar of the New Testament and Other Early Christian Literature.* Chicago: University of Chicago Press, 1961. Translation of Friedrich Blass and Albert Debrunner. *Grammatick des neutestamentlichen Griechisch.* 9th ed. Göttingen: Vandenhoeck & Ruprecht, 1954. 10th ed. 1959.

———. "The Syntax of the Greek Article: Its Importance for Critical Pauline Problems." PhD diss., Vanderbilt University, 1953.

Schmidt, Daryl Dean. *Hellenistic Greek Grammar and Noam Chomsky.* SBLDS 62. Chico, CA: Scholars Press, 1981.

The Narrative Parables:
The Birth of a Language Tradition

Robert W. Funk

1.1. The Christian movement embodied its extant traditions in the common tongue of the hellenistic world, Koine Greek. Yet the language of the incipient movement was not simply congruent with the Greek vernacular as attested elsewhere, however difficult it is to define the difference. The emerging tradition adapted Greek to its ends, and Greek, for its part, took the tradition to its bosom. The union gave birth to a language tradition.

In pursuing the question of the specific vernacular in which the Christian tradition took shape and to which it, in turn, gave shape, it is necessary to move as close as possible to the fountainhead of that language tradition. Chronologically speaking, it is probably in portions of the Synoptic tradition attributed to Jesus that we stand closest to tradition and language aborning in the new idiom. In the balance of this essay, the major narrative parables will be subjected to analysis for the purpose of ascertaining whether the language of these parables bears the stamp of a linguistic tradition in process of formation.

1.2. The analysis will focus on one group of major narrative parables consisting of the laborers in the vineyard, the talents, the ten maidens, the great supper, the good Samaritan, and the prodigal son. These parables each have three principal characters and comparable plot structures.

The analysis will move from the more general to the more detailed. The point will be scored wherever possible in English. In some instances it will be necessary to resort to Greek.

2.0. The major narrative parables give evidence of having been carefully composed and constructed.

2.1. There is first of all the matter of vocabulary. Words and expressions are used parsimoniously, as though drawn from a stock dangerously low. Vocabulary is the simplest; there are no freighted terms, only everyday words like *laborer, field, go, rejoice, five*. Abstract nouns are lacking. Some very common terms appear to be especially suited to the concrete realism of the parable, e.g., *vineyard, go away, servant*.[1] These few words come preciously to the tongue of the narrator, like water to parched lips in a city under siege. Or, to change the figure, words are polished like mirrors: an image is reflected in them unblurred.

2.2. Descriptors and adjectives are kept to a minimum; characters are defined by what they do. Feelings and emotions are mentioned only where essential. The background of persons and events is not made explicit but left to the imagination. There is a penurious economy of words in depicting actions. However, where details are given, they are concrete in the extreme. Such details often afford clues to the direction of the narrative. Direct speech is preferred to third person narration.

2.3. The parsimony of words is joined by an economy of characters and conciseness of plot. Only the necessary persons appear. The plot is simple. Only two sets of relationships are developed, even in the full narrative, e.g., younger son/father, older son/father. Very little appears in the narrative that is non-functional.

2.4. There is repetition by twos and threes, occasionally by more, with variation. Together with other forms of rhythm and assonance, this endows the prose of the parables with certain poetic qualities.

2.5. Some of these characteristics are common to folk literature of other types, but many appear to be specific features of the Synoptic parables. With respect to details, it is of course difficult to attain certainty because of the editing to which the earliest traditions were subject.

3.0. The narrative or story line of the six parables is divided into three parts: opening, development, and crisis-denouement. The parts are signaled by certain surface markers hitherto unnoted.

---

1. Lloyd Gaston, *Horae Synoptica Electronicae: Word Statistics of the Synoptic Gospels*, SBLSBS 3 (Missoula, MT: Society of Biblical Literature, 1973), 43.

3.1. The development and crisis-denouement are initiated, as a rule, by temporal sequence phrases. In the talents, the principal characters are introduced in two sentences (= opening), and then the text reads:

> Matt 25:15 *Immediately* the five talent man ...

The crisis-denouement begins with:

> Matt 25:19 *After a good while*, the master ...

In other words, temporal sequence phrases indicate where the two principal subdivisions of the parable begin.

The first temporal marker in the ten maidens comes after an elaborate opening:

> Matt 25:6 *In the middle of the night* came a cry ...

And the brief denouement begins with the notice:

> Matt 25:11 *Later* came the rest of the maidens ...

In the laborers in the vineyard the opening appears to be conflated with the development. The first temporal phrase appears in the first sentence:

> Matt 20:1 (a householder) ... went out early in the morning ...

The reason for this move is the long, repetitive development, in which the householder ventures forth to hire laborers five times. The opening is therefore incorporated into the development, which serves also to introduce the principals. The laborers in the vineyard is an exception in this respect, although openings elsewhere are sometimes minimal, e.g., in the prodigal son.

The development in the laborers in the vineyard ends with verse 7. The crisis-denouement opens with these words:

> Matt 20:8 *When evening came* the master ...

There can be no doubt about the division of this and other parables on the basis of temporal sequence markers alone.

3.2. The principal character functioning as the axis of the story, so to speak, is introduced in the opening by a common noun, e.g., *householder, a man, a certain man*. As a rule, reference in the development is by pronoun or by zero anaphora. At the opening of the crisis-denouement, however, this same figure is reintroduced by a new common noun, i.e., the participant is identified by nominal substitution.

The householder of the laborers in the vineyard becomes the master of the vineyard at the opening of the crisis-denouement. A man going on a journey of the first sentence of the talents becomes the master of those servants at the beginning of the third division. In the great supper, a certain man becomes a householder at the commencement of scene three. There are some exceptions to the rule, but in general a shift in identification indicates the beginning of a new division.

3.3. There is another type of marker that indicates, as a general rule, that the crisis or denouement has arrived. As the Samaritan comes down the road and sees the victim in the ditch, he has "compassion" on him (ἐσπλαγχνίσθη, Luke 10:33). When the host in the great supper learns that the invited have rejected his summons, the closing scene opens with, "Then the householder became angry ..." (ὀργισθείς, Luke 14:21). Affective terms expressing compassion or wrath thus appear to mark the crisis or denouement.

The parable of the unmerciful servant belongs to another group of parables with a slightly different dramatic structure. There are actually two crisis in the parable, one when the servant first encounters his master and the master has "compassion" on him (σπλαγχνισθείς, Matt 18:27), the second when the master calls the servant to account for failing to have "compassion" on a fellow servant. On the second occasion, the master becomes "angry" (ὀργισθείς, Matt 18:34) and calls him a "worthless servant" (δοῦλε πονηρέ, Matt 18:32). In the talents, the master also calls the one talent servant a "worthless servant" (πονηρὲ δοῦλε, Matt 25:26) and deals with him angrily, although the term ὀργισθείς does not appear.

The prodigal son can be read in two ways. The first episode may be taken as a parable in its own right. In that episode the father has "compassion" (ἐσπλαγχνίσθη, Luke 15:20) on his younger son when he returns home. The second episode may be read as the crisis-denouement going with the first episode as the development (the opening is very brief). In episode two, the older son becomes "angry" (ὠργίσθη, Luke 15:28) and will not join in the celebration underway.

The terms σπλαγχνίζω and ὀργίζω thus appear to be linked to the parable in a special way and are associated with the crisis or denouement. The terms are preserved in single tradition parables preserved in both Matthew and Luke.

4.1. According to Charles Taber, a carefully planned and executed narrative in Sango, an African language, involves precise doses of repetition mixed with novelty.[2] Repetition and novelty in exact measure appear to be characteristic of the narrative parables also. A brief illustration at the gross level must suffice.

In the laborers in the vineyard, act 1 (the first division), scene 1 consists of three sense lines or themes:

(a)   who went out early in the morning to hire laborers for his vineyard

(b)   Upon agreeing with the laborers for a denarius a day

(c)   he sent them into his vineyard

These three lines are repeated in scene 2 with significant variation and in different order:

(a')   Going out at the third hour he saw others squatting idle in the marketplace

(c')   He said to them, You also go into the vineyard

(b')   and whatever is right I will give you.

Scenes 3 and 4 are carried by a repetition of a fragment of the opening clause and what amounts to ditto marks:

(a")   Again going out at the sixth and ninth hours he did likewise.

In the final scene, (b) is omitted, (c) is repeated from scene 2, while (a) is considerably expanded:

(a''')   And going out at the eleventh hour he found others squatting (abbreviated from scene 2)

And he says to them, "Why have you stood here idle all day?" They reply, "Because no one hired us."

---

2. Charles Russel Taber, *The Structure of Sango Narrative*, 2 vols., Hartford Studies in Linguistics 17 (Hartford: Hartford Seminary Foundation, 1966), 1:87.

Note that the same thematic words and phrases appear, e.g., going out at x hour, squatting idle, hire, go, vineyard. (c) then rounds off act 1:

(c‴)   You also go into the vineyard.

It is difficult to get a clear impression of the repetition and variation in act 1 without reading aloud or setting the lines down on paper in a schematic arrangement and then examining closely. There is, first of all, the broad (a)/(b)/(c) pattern with variations indicated above. Further, some phrases run like a thread through the entire act: εἰς τὸν ἀμπελῶνα (αὐτοῦ) ("into the [his] vineyard"); twice repeated in scene 1, once in scenes 2 and 5 always at the end of clauses. In scene 1 the householder ἐξῆλθεν ἅμα πρωΐ ("goes out early in the morning"); this phrase is repeated in scene 2, 3–4 (καὶ ἐξελθὼν περὶ τρίτην ὥραν; πάλιν ἐξελθὼν περὶ ἕκτην καὶ ἐνάτην ὥραν), with the elements in the same order. In the final scene, the order of the two principal phrases is reversed: "At about the eleventh hour he went out" (περὶ δὲ τὴν ἐνδεκάτην ἐξελθών). The variation in phrase order after so much repetition invites renewed attention. And the expanded form of (a) with the omission of (b) in the final scene of act 1 confirms that a significant development in the story is taking place.

4.2. Repetition and variation can be pursued, on a slightly smaller scale, through the parable as a whole.

In act 2, at the close of the parable, the master of the vineyard singles out one of the grumblers and directs several remarks to him. In the first, "Friend, I do you no injustice," the verb ἀδικῶ picks up a note struck in act 1, scene 2: "Whatever is right (δίκαιον) I will give you." There is thus a play on δίκαιον/ἀδικῶ across a considerable expanse of narrative. The master's second remark, "Did you not agree with me for a denarius?" renews a theme expressed in act 1, scene 1: "Upon agreeing with the laborers for a denarius a day …" And these two initial closing remarks of the master,

Friend, I do you no injustice.

Did you not agree with me for a denarius?

are also related to each other since they both renew what was identified as theme (b) in act 1.

The Master next tells the protester to take his denarius and be gone (ὕπαγε). Ὕπαγε recalls item (C) of act 1, which was twice repeated: ὑπάγετε καὶ ὑμεῖς εἰς τὸν ἀμπελῶνα. The householder told them to go into the vineyard; now he tells them to get out. This represents still another verbal link between acts 2 and 1.

In what is probably the final remark of the householder, he says, "I choose to give to this last fellow exactly what I gave to you." The verb δοῦναι, picks up δώσω of (b′) in act 1, scene 2: "Whatever is right I will *give you*." Meanwhile, the master has instructed his steward to "pay" ἀποδίδωμι the wages at the beginning of act 2. The verb δίδωμι represents a theme running through the entire parable. Moreover, the designation "last" for one of the workers hired at the eleventh hour goes back to the dichotomy also introduced at the outset of act 2: " ... pay the wages, beginning with the *last*, up to the first." Subsequently those hired at the first hour are referred to as "the first" (οἱ πρῶτοι), and they, in turn, call their lazy colleagues "the last" (οἱ ἔσχατοι). Again, there is wordplay on first/last in the second half of the parable.

The play upon or renewal of δίκαιον/ἀδικέω, συμφωνέω δηναρίου ὑπάγω, δίδωμι, πρῶτοι/ἔσχατοι across a large expanse of the narrative gives the story a textural unity and subtlety that would not have been missed by the ear, as difficult as it may be to catch by the untrained eye.

4.3. Some of the forms of repetition and variation indicated above are explored by J. D. Denniston in his work, *Greek Prose Style*. In the final chapter of that work, he takes up various forms of assonance, which he defines as "the recurrence of a sound in such a manner as to catch the ear."[3] The primacy of the spoken word in ancient Greek, and in other languages, before the age of printing, had a significant effect on composition, according to W. B. Stanford.[4] Prose as well as poetry was composed by the ear rather than by the eye. Euphony therefore played a large role in Greek rhetoric and composition.

Matthew Black has endeavoured to make a similar case for Aramaic.[5] He finds many examples of alliteration, assonance, and paronomasia (wordplay, pun) by translating portions of the New Testament back into Aramaic. I take his work to confirm the importance of the ear for the common languages of Hellenistic-Roman Palestine.

---

3. J. D. Denniston, *Greek Prose Style* (Oxford: Clarendon, 1952), 124.

4. W. B. Stanford, *The Sound of Greek: Studies in the Greek Theory and Practice of Euphony* (Berkeley: University of California Press, 1967).

5. Matthew Black, *An Aramaic Approach to the Gospels and Acts*, 3rd ed. (Oxford: Clarendon, 1967), 160–85.

4.3.1. I have modified to fit numbering sequence. The relation of sound to content need not be argued here. At the threshold of language—in *poiesis* in the root sense: the naming of the gods and in creation—it is taken for granted. It is no less obvious in the lullaby and jingle, ancient and modern. In an age dominated by the eye, the precincts of the ear are mostly vacant. Yet for those laboring to say something unheard of in the common tongue, the ear must have been crucial. And one expects rhythm and assonance in folk literature, to which the parables are closely related.

4.3.2. Repetition and variation in themselves contain forms of rhythm and assonance: the parallelism of clauses with variation; the repetition of thematic phrases; the play upon theme words; and the like. It is not surprising to find such cadences and euphony in prose that borders on poetry. It is perhaps somewhat surprising that the parables exhibit other interesting forms of assonance involving the sounds of Greek. A few examples drawn from the laborers in the vineyard must suffice to demonstrate the linguistic texture of the parables at the phonological level.

Act 1 of the laborers in the vineyard concerns a householder who goes out to hire ἐργάτας (laborers), some of whom stand ἀργούς (idle) in the ἀγορᾷ (marketplace). The use of these three terms exemplifies anagrammatic assonance (sound play on the same consonants in varying order). The juxtaposition of ἐργάτας/ἀργούς/ἀγορᾷ calls attention to act 1, scene 2: εἶδεν ἄλλους ἑστῶτας ἐν τῇ ἀγορᾷ ἀργούς. In this line, in addition to ἀγορᾷ ἀργούς, there is alternating alliteration with iota and alpha sounds (ε, α, ε, ε, α, α), This alliteration is continued in the first part of the next line: καὶ ἐκεῖνος εἶπεν, ὑπάγετε καὶ ὑμεῖς εἰς τὸν ἀμπελῶνα this time with *e* and *u*; the last phrase in the line of course renews a phrase already twice used. These two lines from scene 2 thus exhibit at least three forms of assonance: anagrammatic assonance, alliteration of initial vowel sounds, repetition of theme phrase.

The next line of scene 2 runs: καὶ ὃ ἐὰν ᾖ δίκαιον δώσω ὡμῖν. The alliteration in δίκαιον δώσω is striking in the context, especially when one recalls that δίκαιον and δίδωμι are both theme words, to which allusion is made in the final line of the parable.

In act 2 of the same parable, the protest of those hired first is introduced with the verb ἐγόγγυζον, itself an onomatopoeic word. And this is what they murmur: οὗτοι οἱ ἔσχατοι/μία ὥραν, ἐποίησαν καὶ ἴσους αὐτούς/ ἡμῖν ἐποίησας τοῖς βαστάσασι τὸ βάρος τῆς ἡμέρας καὶ τὸν καύσωνα. The repetition, -οι -οι -οι/-αν -αν -αν/-ους -ους, called *homoeoteleuta*,[6] appears to reinforce the sound effect succession of the verb. In the latter part of the line there is a succession of sounds with terminal σ: -ας, -οις, -ος, -ης with a similar effect. And there is alliteration with β, in βαστάσασι, βάρος.

4.4. The kinds of assonance noted in §4.3 doubtless occur, to a certain degree, in all levels of language—not just in poetry—when spoken by competent native speakers. The textures of the narrative parables is such that one has the impression they were "heard" originally in Greek by a competent native speaker.

5.1. The structural and surface evidence adduced from the parables is of more than one type. Some features may belong to deep structures which are translatable without essential loss into any language, e.g., the law of the parsimony of characters in folk tales. Whether all deep structures are universally translatable is a question which cannot be broached here. Some surface features may be suited to either Aramaic (Hebrew) or Greek and readily translatable into the other language. Temporal sequence markers would presumably belong to this category. Many so-called Semitisms can also be explained either as translation Semitisms or as spoken Semitic-Greek (Bl-D §4). Other features are difficult to account for on the basis of a Semitic (Aramaic or Hebrew) original, of which the Greek text preserved for us is a reasonably close translation. On balance, it seems to me that the major narrative parables provide ample evidence of having been composed in Greek.

5.2. J. Barre Toelken has suggested that the more significant aspects of Navaho Coyote tales lies in their texture, i.e., in any *coloration* given a traditional narrative as it is unfolded.[7] He then cites Alan Dundes with approval: "the more important the textural features are in a given genre of folklore, the more difficult it is to translate an example of that genre into another language."[8] The texture of the narrative parables would make it difficult to achieve the same effect in another language.

---

6. Denniston, *Greek Prose Style*, 135; BDF §488.1a.

7. J. Barre Toelken, "The 'Pretty Language' of Yellowman: Genre, Mode, and Texture in Navaho Coyote Narratives," *Genre* 2.3 (1969): 222f.

8. Alan Dundes, "Texture, Text, and Context," *Southern Folklore Quarterly* 28 (1964): 254; Toelken, "'Pretty Language' of Yellowman," 223.

5.2.1. The Greek of the parables strikes me not so much as translation Greek, as it does Greek which has been thoroughly vacuumed for the occasion. The Greek of the parables is as clean of resonances as the German of Kafka or the French of Beckett, both of whom were writing, interestingly enough, in a second language. Aramaic may well have been the first language of the narrator of the parables. However that may be, the composer employs Greek as though it were derived from a beginner's manual with only the immediate ordinary sense attached, just as Ionesco used beginner's English as the basis for his first play, *The Bald Soprano*. The Greek of the parables has been shorn of its rich history. Nevertheless, the unadorned and unnuanced simplicity of the style and diction marks an uncommon solemnity. The bare, uninterpreted act, such as a man going down from Jerusalem to Jericho (bristles) with anticipation. The way in which the narrator manipulates this language is therefore not unlike the way in which Kafka polishes German or Beckett washes French.

5.2.2. These less tangible features are joined by more obvious traits, such as repetition with variation, and assonance in various forms. Taken together, they indicate that creativity has been inscribed into the parables both on the surface and at the depths. As Leo Spitzer claims, poetic genius touches the linguistic act at all levels.[9]

5.3. The thesis, then, is that the narrative parables were composed in Greek. A claim of this order has long been thwarted by the assumption that a Palestinian tradition could not have taken shape in Greek. Now we have reason to believe differently. Further, from the distance of greater options, it becomes incredible that the original language of the tradition should have disappeared with only odd traces. Given the tenacity with which cultures and institutions cling to originating languages—to cite only two examples, the Latin church and French Canada—it is almost implausible that the Christian tradition took shape in Aramaic and then disappeared in that form in a few years or decades. Freedom from the earlier assumption and conclusion may permit us to examine the Synoptic tradition with an eye to the ear.

---

9. Leo Spitzer, *Linguistics and Literary History: Essays in Stylistics* (Princeton: Princeton University Press, 1967), 18.

5.4. There has been a steady refusal in this essay to attribute the narrative parables in their Greek form to Jesus. Such an attribution is by no means ruled out. The present argument, however, extends just this far: the narrative parable tradition took shape in Greek, whether at the hands of Jesus or some other, at some point proximate to the threshold of the Christian tradition.

Bibliography

Black, Matthew. *An Aramaic Approach to the Gospels and Acts.* 3rd ed. Oxford: Clarendon, 1967.

Blass, Friedrich, and Albert Debrunner. *A Greek Grammar of the New Testament and Other Early Christian Literature.* Translated and revised by Robert W. Funk. Chicago: University of Chicago Press, 1961.

Denniston, J. D. *Greek Prose Style.* Oxford: Clarendon, 1952.

Dundes, Alan. "Texture, Text, and Context." *Southern Folklore Quarterly* 28.4 (1964): 251–65.

Gaston, Lloyd. *Horae Synoptica Electronicae: Word Statistics of the Synoptic Gospels.* SBLSBS 3. Missoula: Society of Biblical Literature, 1973.

Spitzer, Leo. *Linguistics and Literary History: Essays in Stylistics.* Princeton: Princeton University Press, 1967.

Stanford, W. B. *The Sound of Greek: Studies in the Greek Theory and Practice of Euphony.* Berkeley: University of California Press, 1967.

Taber, Charles Russel. *The Structure of Sango Narrative.* 2 vols. Hartford Studies in Linguistics 17. Hartford: Hartford Seminary Foundation, 1966.

Toelken, J. Barre. "The 'Pretty Language' of Yellowman: Genre, Mode, and Texture in Navaho Coyote Narratives." *Genre* 2.3 (1969): 211–35.

Biblical Languages in the Professional School Curriculum

Robert W. Funk

Editorial Note: During the 1960s the increasing demand for multicultural courses had a dramatic impact on seminary curricula. The requirement that seminarians study the biblical languages either was reduced or turned into an elective. In this context, Dean Walter Harrelson and Professor Robert Funk convened a consultation of twenty-four Hebrew and Greek instructors at the Vanderbilt Divinity School on October 20–21, 1967. This was followed by a Summer Program in Biblical Languages and Linguistics July 1–August 9, 1968. Funk subsequently assessed the changing role of the biblical languages in the following short piece written on November 1, 1968, as he was beginning his term as Executive Secretary of the Society of Biblical Literature and working on his *Beginning-Intermediate Grammar of Hellenistic Greek*. (Lane C. McGaughy)

Theses

1a. The development of professional theological education in the American tradition since 1870 indicates that "exegetical theology" has been increasingly forced to the periphery of the professional curriculum, in spite of the residual affirmation that the study of scripture ought to occupy a significant, if not central, place in professional ministerial training. If we may extrapolate from this trend, "exegetical theology," i.e., the historical study of the original classical literatures of Judaism and Christianity, will be compelled to redefine and relocate itself in order to maintain its scholarly vitality.

1b. The waning of "exegetical theology" in the professional curriculum is correlative with the demise of the authoritative or normative function of scripture in theology. For this reason, the continuing attempt to justify the study of the biblical languages in the professional curriculum on the basis of the authority of scripture, whether in a literal or nonliteral sense, whether in a direct or indirect form, is doomed to failure.

1c. The authoritative and normative role of scripture (and tradition) has been displaced, in the American Protestant tradition, by the appeal to "experience," on the one hand, and by the hard data generated by the empirical sciences and a form of rationalism, on the other. These elements are compounded in varying proportions in the cake of American pragmatism, activism, and voluntarism.

1d. The shift from one basis to another (theses 1b and 1c) has created a growing hiatus between the knowledge bank alleged (in memory of the tradition) to fund professional ministerial training and the actual skills required for the practice of current ministerial crafts. By the middle of the twentieth century the disjunction had become acute.

2a. The redefinition and relocation of biblical studies involves forging new links between the study of biblical and related texts and classical humanistic learning. In historical perspective, this means returning to the *status quo ante.*

2b. The survival of the study of biblical languages, in anything like earlier scholarly depth, depends, in my judgment, on finding a context in which the scholar can give himself relentlessly to the "subject matter," and that means, without application of the Bible to the ministerial crafts. The seminary will not much longer tolerate nonapplied biblical studies, for the simple reason that it will not be able to support what it does not regard as essential. On the other hand, biblical studies, once divorced from professional training, may be welcome in a secular, humanistic context, and the secular, state-supported university may be the only institution that can afford such luxury.

2c. Functionally speaking, one second-rate teacher of English Bible would be adequate for most professional curricula, given the current operative definition of the knowledge and skills required for the ministerial crafts.

2d. The link with classical humanistic learning would be more propitious if that learning were not itself in need of fundamental reform. Humanists must be induced to give sustained attention to the trajectory of the Western tradition in order to facilitate an orderly and sane entry into the post-modern world. The reentry of biblical studies, as the analysis of the roots of the Judeo-Christian tradition, into the humanistic arena, can materially assist in this reform, provided biblical studies is willing to slough off its preoccupation with trivia and enforced professionalism.

2e. The contest is shaping up, as it seems to me, not in the professional school and church, but in the faculty of arts and sciences and its extensions in computer centers, laboratories, research centers, and the like. Biblical scholars, among others in the professional faculty, may look upon it as an evangelical call to join the fray at a crucial juncture.

3a. The study of the biblical languages, in particular, can be shifted into a fresh and vital context, viz., the problem of language as such. Several relatively discrete lines have converged in identifying language as a special problem, although the definition of the problem has its special merit: it allows the problem to emerge of and out of itself. There is evidence that the problem of language is deepening into a root problem.

3b. Among the various lines converging on language is descriptive and structural linguistics. Linguistics, if it continues in its present course, will impinge more and more on analytic philosophy and phenomenology of language: the phonological, morphological and syntactical analysis of language requires to be completed by semantic and phenomenal analyses if language is to be seized as a concrete phenomenon.

3c. Analytic philosophy, if it does not turn back from Wittgenstein and company, will be driven ultimately to the ontological status of language: semantic analysis, whether of a synchronic or diachronic sort, requires to be completed by an analysis of the whence and whither of language.

3d. Meanwhile, phenomenology has seized the problem of language as the locus where the transaction between self and "world" transpires, and thus as the spiral, in a temporal horizon, of the rise and fall of "worlds" and their correlative linguistic matrices.

3e. The convergence on language as a problem was anticipated in the literary arts, especially poetry and drama (e.g., the theatre of the absurd), and, analogously, in the graphic and plastic arts. In creative literature the problem of language takes the form of the artist seeking to kill words, on the one hand, and the artist in mad search of the real, i.e., new language, on the other. The recent history of the arts witnesses to a radical collapse of the linguistic tradition which has dominated the West.

3f. The problem of language has tended to become root by virtue of the acute disjunction between the linguistic tradition and the call of the "real": the problem of language becomes root only at the demise of old and the threshold of new worlds.

3g. As an especially significant ingredient in the linguistic debris of the Western tradition, biblical language, in its various forms—original and derived—offers a critical focal point for raising the synchronic and dia- chronic (systematic and historical) problems associated with the fate of the Western tradition. The study of the biblical languages can therefore participate at all levels in addressing the problem of language.

Part 3
Hermeneutics

Robert W. Funk and Hermeneutics

James M. Robinson†

Bob Funk had the Midas touch—not in the sense that everything literally turned to gold, since he did not always make money or become rich, but in the sense that things he undertook were not only competently handled, but they were raised to a higher plane, became something they would never have become without his Midas touch.

An early instance of this Midas touch was his interest, as any New Testament scholar of necessity has, in New Testament Greek. But in this case it became a major project of translating into English the basic grammar in this field, which we all have used ever since.[1]

This Midas touch is particularly true of his involvement in the new hermeneutic. This grew out of a German tradition going back to the existentialistic philosophy of Martin Heidegger. Heidegger had produced categories for the human sciences comparable to the table of categories used in the natural sciences to make of them such a highly successful undertaking of Western civilization. Rudolf Bultmann was Heidegger's colleague at the University of Marburg—Heidegger had even sat in on Bultmann's course on the Gospel of John! So Bultmann, realizing that the kerygma of the New Testament is unintelligible in our post-Christian culture, translated it into existentialistic terminology. He showed its primary relevance for the basic human quest to get free from the bondage of the past to live in an open future (which I trust you will recognize as what the church talks about as the forgiveness of sin and eschatology). So Bultmann launched *Entmythologisierung*, demythologizing the true,

---

1. Friedrich Blass and Albert Debrunner, *A Greek Grammar of the New Testament and Other Early Christian Literature*, trans. and rev. Robert W. Funk (Chicago: University of Chicago Press, 1961); trans. *Grammatik des neutestamentlichen Griechisch*, 9th ed. (Göttingen: Vandenhoeck & Ruprecht, 1954; 10th ed., 1959).

existential meaning of the primitive Christian kerygma into an understanding of existence one could embrace for today.

But after World War II things began to change, both in Heidegger's philosophy and in the Bultmannian school of theology. Heidegger argued that accrediting him as the founder of existentialism was a big mistake, since his interest all along had not been the existentials constitutive of human existence, but rather the unveiling of being, which comes not *from* humans, but rather *to* humans, in the language they inherit, the world in which they hence live.

This was then picked up theologically by Gerhard Ebeling, a church historian, who found in Luther's emphasis on the preaching of the *word* the modern locale for the *kerygma*, or, more precisely, for the *word* of Jesus behind the *kerygma*. Oscar Cullmann had preferred to kerygma the pietistic expression *Heilsgeschichte*, "salvation history," which Bultmann had revised to *Heilsgeschehen*, "salvation occurrence." Then Ebeling revised this again by coining the term *Wortgeschehen*, "word occurrence."

In New Testament scholarship, the new quest of the historical Jesus had been launched by Ernst Kasemann, who argued that we cannot continue to ignore the historical Jesus in favor of the kerygma, as form criticism had taught us to do, without ending up in some modern kind of Docetism. Hence Ernst Fuchs for his part elevated Jesus's word to what he called the basic gift of God. To express this he modulated the pious German term *Heilsereignis*, "saving event," into *Sprachereignis*, "language event." Ebeling and Fuchs then joined forces in a new hermeneutic, to translate the point of the kerygma, or more exactly of Jesus's word, from the impossibly antiquarian Hellenistic world into the modem technological world in which we, for better or worse, have to find our way. This then was the turbulent German post-Bultmannian epoch in which postwar American New Testament scholarship had its beginning.

The Annual Meeting of the Society of Biblical Literature took place in 1960 between Christmas and New Years at Union Seminary in New York, as we did back then three out of every four years. But a few of us held an important meeting just before the Annual Meeting began: Howard Kee had invited a few young Turks to have lunch with his publisher, Prentice-Hall, in Englewood Cliffs, New Jersey, to discuss a proposed new commentary series, to be chaired by him and Bernard Anderson, his Drew University colleague and author alongside him of their very popular introductions to the Old and New Testaments. Prentice-Hall wanted to expand this success story into a commentary. Funk led the interrogation of the staff of Prentice-Hall about the seriousness of its scholarly intentions in a discussion that dragged on until the end of the afternoon.

Kee returned to his home in nearby Madison, New Jersey, while the rest of us, including Funk, whose home was also in Madison, returned to Manhattan to have a caucus all evening, led by Funk, resulting in the agreement to withdraw from the proposed commentary in a block. But we decided to stay together and organized on the spot what became the New Testament Colloquium, which met annually for a day or so just prior to the Annual Meeting of the Society of Biblical Literature. We enlisted both Hans Jonas, who had produced the basic methodological study of how to translate Hellenistic culture into existentialistic terms,[2] and Kendrick Grobel, who had also studied with Bultmann before the war, as our non-voting "senior" sponsors. We met each year in the Jonas home in nearby New Rochelle. The idea of a commentary was retained and ultimately moved to Fortress Press as publisher, with Helmut Koester as New Testament chairperson. This new commentary was so closely related to the new hermeneutic that my proposal to name the commentary series Hermeneia was adopted. I published a rationale for "Hermeneutical Theology" in *The Christian Century* in 1966.[3]

Drew University then invited Fuchs and Ebeling to a colloquium where papers were presented that became the bulk of the volume *The New Hermeneutic* published in 1964.[4] Funk's contribution was entitled "The Hermeneutical Problem and Historical Criticism."[5] He was launched on his hermeneutical way.

Funk Americanized this new hermeneutic: the "word occurrence" or "language event" became "performative language,"[6] for language not only conveys information; it can very well do something simply by being spoken. Two familiar illustrations make this clear. When a person is put

---

2. Hans Jonas, *Gnosis und spätantiker Geist* (Gottingen: Vandenhoeck & Ruprecht, 1934), in a series edited by Bultmann.

3. James M. Robinson, "Hermeneutical Theology," *The Christian Century* 83 (1966): 579–82.

4. James M. Robinson and John B. Cobb Jr., eds., *The New Hermeneutic*, New Frontiers in Theology, vol. 2 (New York: Harper & Row, 1964).

5. Robert W. Funk, "The Hermeneutical Problem and Historical Criticism," in Robinson and Cobb, *New Hermeneutic*, 164–97.

6. Robert W. Funk, *Language, Hermeneutic, and Word of God: The Problem of Language in the New Testament and Contemporary Theology* (New York: Harper & Row, 1966).

on trial for a crime, that person is legally a "suspect" until proven guilty, at which point that person becomes legally "guilty," which changes that person's life; one is led off to prison. Or, on a happier note, when the clergy person says to the engaged couple "you are now man and wife," they are no longer "engaged" but rather "married"; the groom can even kiss the bride and take her off on their honeymoon. In such cases, talk is not just empty talk: it does what it says. Something happens. It "performs" what it says; it is "performative language."

Funk found his focus in Jesus's parables. Already more than a century earlier Adolf Jülicher has made the basic distinction between allegories, and parables: Jesus spoke in parables, which the church then made into allegories recounting in a veiled way biblical history and the plan of salvation. Jesus, on the other hand, told simple parables, scoring an obvious and simple ethical point. But, of course, one could then walk away from the parable itself and tuck its point into Jesus's other ethical sayings that were not parabolic, but said straight out what Jesus meant: turn the other cheek, walk the second mile, give the shirt off your back, give expecting nothing in return, love your neighbor and even your enemy, to be like God.

Funk, on the other hand, recognized parables as performative language: they not only pointed beyond themselves, but they themselves did something to you. They transplanted you into a strange new world different from the common-sense world in which you were at home. One should not retreat from the parable itself into some edifying moral but should stick with that strange new world and let it work on you. A group of young scholars clustered around Funk and his focus on parables. I contributed one article to this movement, defining parables as "God happening."[7] But Funk and others, such as Dominic Crossan, Bernard Brandon Scott, and Charles Hedrick, continued this focus on parables.

As usual, Funk not only led on the intellectual issues as such—he was an organization man: another outgrowth of the "young Turks" that had met in 1960 was *The Journal for Theology and the Church* (*JThC*), a journal making use of articles published in the German journal where the new hermeneutic had its center, the *Zeitschrift für Theologie und Kirche* (*ZTK*) edited by Gerhard Ebeling. The editor of *JThC* was Funk "in association with Gerhard Ebeling," with an editorial board of Frank M. Cross,

---

7. James M. Robinson, "Jesus' Parables as God Happening," in *Jesus and the Historian: Written in Honor of Ernest Cadman Colwell*, ed. F. Thomas Trotter (Philadelphia: Westminster, 1968), 134–50.

John Dillenberger, Gerhard Ebeling, Helmut Koester, Heiko A. Oberman, Schubert M. Ogden, and myself. Indeed, Funk spent a sabbatical year in Tübingen in 1965–1966 developing that association. Volume 1, published by Harper Torchbooks in 1965, was entitled *The Bultmann School of Biblical Interpretation: New Directions?* Funk wrote the foreword and I the explanatory opening essay, "For Theology and the Church."[8] It published some seven issues (the last at Herder & Herder in 1970) but then was discontinued. For Ebeling retired as editor of the *ZTK*, and a board of younger and less distinguished Germans was created, but without including any representative of the board of the *JThC*.

The Old and New Testament editorial boards of Hermeneia met each spring in Lexington, Massachusetts, in the homes of Helmut Koester and Frank Cross, respectively, with a final session each Sunday morning in the Cross home. On one such occasion I was called to the phone to speak to the Nominating Committee of the Society of Biblical Literature, inquiring if I would want to be considered for the position of Secretary of the Society of Biblical Literature. I explained for some good reason, I trust, that I was not, but that in the next room there was a certain Bob Funk whom they might be able to enlist. I put him on the phone, and the rest is history.

Bibliography

Blass, Friedrich, and Albert Debrunner. *A Greek Grammar of the New Testament and Other Early Christian Literature.* Translated and revised by Robert W. Funk. Chicago: University of Chicago Press, 1961. Translation of *Grammatik des neutestamentlichen Griechisch.* 9th ed. Göttingen: Vandenhoeck & Ruprecht, 1954. 10th ed., 1959.

Funk, Robert W. Foreword to *The Bultmann School of Biblical Interpretation: New Directions.* JThC 1. New York: Harper & Row, 1965.

——. "The Hermeneutical Problem and Historical Criticism." Pages 164–97 in *The New Hermeneutic.* Edited by James M. Robinson and John B. Cobb Jr. New Frontiers in Theology. Vol. 2. New York: Harper & Row, 1964.

---

8. Robert W. Funk, foreword to *The Bultmann School of Biblical Interpretation: New Directions,* JThC 1 (New York: Harper & Row, 1965), ix–xi; James M. Robinson, "For Theology and the Church," in *Bultmann School of Biblical Interpretation,* 1–19.

————. *Language, Hermeneutic, and Word of God: The Problem of Language in the New Testament and Contemporary Theology.* New York: Harper & Row, 1966.

Jonas, Hans. *Gnosis und spätantiker Geist.* Gottingen: Vandenhoeck & Ruprecht, 1934.

Robinson, James M. "For Theology and the Church." Pages 1–19 in *The Bultmann School of Biblical Interpretation: New Directions.* JThC 1. New York: Harper & Row, 1965.

————. "Hermeneutical Theology." *The Christian Century* 83 (1966): 579–82.

————. "Jesus' Parables as God Happening." Pages 134–50 in *Jesus and the Historian: Written in Honor of Ernest Cadman Colwell.* Edited by F. Thomas Trotter. Philadelphia: Westminster, 1968.

Robinson, James M., and John B. Cobb Jr., eds. *The New Hermeneutic.* New Frontiers in Theology. Vol. 2. New York: Harper & Row, 1964.

The Hermeneutical Problem and Historical Criticism

Robert W. Funk

By intention this essay turns on the axis of the hermeneutical problem as it has been developed by Rudolf Bultmann, Ernst Fuchs, and Gerhard Ebeling. In this respect the writer wishes to include himself among those who have learned much from Bultmann. Fuchs and Ebeling, too, have made distinctive contributions to the discussion, but in which follows it is the concern of Ebeling, set out in his programmatic essay of 1950 and articulated elsewhere, which is to be developed.[1]

It is taken for granted in this circle that a theological hermeneutic must be appropriate both to faith *and* to the categories of understanding which belong to man as man.[2] If this be allowed, it is not immediately apparent how historical criticism[3] can be of service in aiding the occurrence

---

Editorial note: In order to provide bibliographic clarity, some citations have been corrected and a few omitted.

1. Gerhard Ebeling, "Die Bedeutung der historisch-kritischen Methode für die protestantische Theologie und Kirche," *ZTK* 47 (1950): 1–46, repr. in *Wort und Glaube* (Tübingen: Mohr Siebeck, 1960), 1–49; English translation "The Significance of the Critical Historical Method for Church and Theology in Protestantism," in *Word and Faith*, trans. James W. Leitch (Philadelphia: Fortress, 1963), 17–61 [Subsequent citations will be to the English article. —Ed.]; Ebeling, *Die Geschichtlichkeit der Kirche und ihrer Verkündigung als theologisches Problem* (Tübingen: Mohr Siebeck, 1954); Ebeling, "The Meaning of 'Biblical Theology,'" *JTS* 6 (1955): 210–25, also appearing in *On the Authority of the Bible: Some Recent Studies by L. Hodgson, C. F. Evans, J. Burnaby, C. Ebeling and D. E. Nineham* (London: SPCK, 1960), 49–67, and in German as "Was heisst 'Biblische Theologie,'" in *Wort und Glaube*, 69–89 (*Word and Faith*, 79–97) [Subsequent citations will be to the English article in *Word and Faith* —Ed.]; etc.

2. This involves opting for Bultmann over against Barth.

3. Historical criticism is used throughout in a comprehensive sense as it has been developed in relation to biblical studies; i.e., it embraces both "lower" and "higher" criticism as well as the broader fields normally designated as historical criticism.

of the word of God, i.e., the proclamation. For is not historical criticism fundamentally inimical to the concept of the word of God, as well as to the concept of the Holy Spirit, operating as it does with scientific criteria? On the other hand, is it not dangerous to isolate the word of God from the exegesis of the text, if the word bears any significant relation to the text? In short, how does historical criticism function with respect to the text of faith through which faith believes that its life and its norm are mediated?

This question has been polarized at the less-sophisticated level into two antithetical questions: Is historical criticism the arbitrator, from an autonomous and objective locus, in the theological interpretation of Scripture, deciding what is and what is not allowable? Or, is historical criticism in the service of, and subservient to, theological exegesis which ultimately decides what meaning can be assigned to a text? This polarization obscures the hermeneutical problem which lies at the base of both questions. We should ask rather, can historical criticism be taken up in to the theological task in such a way that it does not lose its independent critical powers but nevertheless functions positively in the service of theology? The hermeneutical problem, as it relates to this formulation, can be posed as the question of how the word that has come to expression can come to expression anew.

Bultmann, Fuchs, and Ebeling have clung steadfastly to their liberal heritage in insisting that historical criticism has an integral role to play in the movement from text to proclamation. Bultmann in particular has developed the notion of the hermeneutical circle that decisively involves historical criticism with respect to the text. While I affirm this position, I see two aspects of the problem as requiring further elucidation. What precisely is the function of historical criticism[4] in relation to an *interpretation* of the text? This aspect is opened up in section 2. Further, it is not the *interpreter* himself involved in a historical circle to which historical criticism is also relevant? The treatment of the second aspect in section 3 betrays unmistakable affinities with Ebeling's concerns.

The American situation in this respect presents marked contrast to the situation on the Continent. Although Ebeling has set out good reasons for concern about the critical nerve of historical criticism in German language theology,[5] biblical studies on this side of the Atlantic have never

---

4. Historical criticism here is used as the equivalent of Bultmann's historical circle as defined by Dinkler. See below, n. 83.

5. Ebeling, "Significance of the Critical Historical Method," 18ff.

been theologically shaken to the same extent and so are in danger of continuing on their independent way, critical but increasingly irrelevant. Biblical criticism on the Continent has sustained a closer relation to theology, particularly since Barth, than it has in this country, with the result that the problem may be said to be relevant to both situations for opposite reasons. In Europe historical criticism has tended to become subservient to theological interests, thereby losing its critical powers; on the American side historical criticism has retained its nontheological orientation. Since that orientation received its decisive bent in the theological wars of the preceding era, the nontheological bias of historical criticism tends to take on theological import in the face of a new situation. Neither in Europe nor in America has historical criticism been able to break through to the hermeneutical issue that underlies both situations, i.e., the problem of the conditions under which understanding is possible at all. This essay, however, is aimed primarily at the peculiarities of the American development.

The hermeneutic of Fuchs and Ebeling, depending as it does on a doctrine of the word, both requires historical criticism and yet relativizes it. Why this is so can best be seen by attending to the place that justification by faith occupies in their theological programs. In the present essay the correlation between a doctrine of the word and the function of historical criticism, which is the overarching concern, is implicit in the juxtaposition of exegetical and methodological sections. In the exegetical section (1) an attempt is made to reflect upon the hermeneutical problem in the face of the text, i.e., to ask how the word is heard, how it comes to understanding, and what is concomitant therewith, what the word is. In the methodological sections (2, 3) the function of historical criticism, with respect to both text and interpreter, is defined in relation to *that* understanding of the word. The substantive affinities of this approach with that of Fuchs and Ebeling are apparent.

The choice of 2 Corinthians as text requires some special justification. The Corinthian correspondence has recently been brought back into the discussion in connection with the heresy-orthodoxy problem,[6] and it is because this problem can be conceived hermeneutically that the Corinthian letters take on special importance. That is to say, Paul's effort to grapple with the Corinthian heresy can be interpreted as an example of

---

6. James M. Robinson, "Basic Shifts in German Theology," *Int* 16 (1962): 79ff., 86–87.

his hermeneutic at work.[7] The exposition of 2 Corinthians lays the basis, therefore, for the methodological discussion which follows.

1. 2 Corinthians as Hermeneutic

In 2 Cor 2:14–7:4 (omitting 6:14–7:1) and 10:1–13:13 Paul is giving expression to the word of reconciliation (5:19) as it determines his work as apostle.[8] This theme is renewed from a different perspective in 1:1–2:13; 7:5–16.[9] His sentences are set in the context of a serious challenge to his legitimacy as an apostle, which Paul rightly views as a challenge also to his status as a Christian.[10] His line of defense is evident from the development of the argument in both 2:14–7:4 and 10:1–13:13. If the Corinthians understood what it means to be reconciled to God in Christ, to be a

---

7. One could even say that the Corinthian correspondence provides the battleground for the current theological debate. It is worth noting that H. Schlier identifies the pneumatic theology of heretical Corinthians with modern existentialist theology (Robinson, "Basic Shifts in German Theology," 87). This leads to the observation that Paul may have been trapped by his predilection to criticize from within rather than from without, and further that the orthodox way out was to reject not only false implications but also the whole context and language of a theological position (86). The debate thus has potentially far-reaching implications for theology as a whole. Thus far, however, the discussion does not seem to have come to grips with the central issue, which is whether Paul could meet the Corinthians on their ground and still remain true to the kerygma, or, as I would prefer to put it, whether he could remain true to the kerygma and *not* meet them on their own ground.

8. In the following analysis I am especially indebted to Ernst Kasernann, "Die Legitimität des Apostels: Eine Untersuchung zu II Korinther 10–13," *ZNW* 41 (1942): 33–71 (now published as a *Sonderausgabe* [Darmstadt: Wissenschaftliche Buchgesellschaft, 1956]), and Rudolf Bultmann, *Exegetische Probleme des zweiten Korintherbriefes*, Symbolae Biblicae Upsalienses 9 (Darmstadt: Wissenschaftliche Buchgesellschaft, 1947). Also relevant are W. Schmithals, *Die Gnosis in Korinth: Eine Untersuchung zu den Korintherbriefen* (Göttingen: Vandenhoeck & Ruprecht, 1956); U. Wilckens, *Weisheit und Torheit: Eine exegetisch-religionsgeschichtliche Untersuchung zu I Kor. I und 2* (Tübingen: Mohr Siebeck, 1959); G. Bornkamm, *Die Vorgeschichte des sogenannten Zweiten Korintherbriefes* (Heidelberg: Winter, 1961).

9. For the divisions of the letter, see Bultmann, *Exegetische Probleme des zweiten Korintherbriefes*, 14 n. 16; Schmithals, *Die Gnosis in Korinth*, 18–22; and now Bornkamm, *Die Vorgeschichte des sogenannten Zweiten Korintherbriefes*, 16–23.

10. 10:7. Käsemann, "Die Legitimität des Apostels," 36; Bultmann, *Exegetische Probleme des zweiten Korintherbriefes*, 16; also cf. 3–4 on the fluidity of the "we" (apostolic-general Christian) in 3:12–5:11.

new creation in him (5:16ff.), they would also understand the form of the Apostles' ministry, for its form is controlled by the norm of Christ (5:14). Thus, while working out from his own status as apostle, Paul ends by calling the Corinthians back to faith, i.e., he renews the word as proclamation (e.g., 5:20ff.; cf. 12:19–20; 13:5ff.).

Paul's articulation of his defense is actually a fresh exposition of the gospel set in the context of the charges raised against him. In order to confront the Corinthians with *the* norm against which all Christian endeavor is to be measured, and not with a comparison of himself and his opponents based on their norms, he is led to the presenting of the revelatory event within the horizon of their mutual status before the Lord. Consequently, he is required to set out the basis of his apostleship in relation to the kerygma. In so doing, the Apostle exposes the claims of his opponents for what they really are: idle claims based on self-commendation (10:18 and often). Unlike his opponents, who have no real measure for their boasting, Paul must keep to the measure that God has allotted him (10:13).[11]

Paul's exposition of the gospel, therefore, is a re-presentation of the kerygma in language that speaks to the controversy in which he is engaged. While pre-Pauline kerygmatic formulae have not been identified in 2 Corinthians,[12] it is clear that Paul is "listening" to the kerygma, but in such a way that the terms of the kerygma are heard in relation to the concrete realities of his own life and work (e.g., 1:3–10; 4:7–12; 6:3–10).[13] Especially instructive is his characterization of the Christ event in 13:4a: "True, he died on the cross in weakness, but he lives by the power of God" (NEB), a characterization that is immediately applied to the apostolic office (13:4b). Outside of the Corinthian correspondence *asthenēs* and its cognates are nowhere used to characterize the humiliation side of the kerygma,[14] but they are employed here because *asthenēs* is a catchword of Paul's opponents (10:10; 11:21, 29ff.).[15] Moreover, the four terms of 4:8–9 (afflicted,

---

11. Following Bultmann, *Exegetische Probleme des zweiten Korintherbriefes*, 21.

12. One has to allow for the possibility that pre-Pauline formulae lie back of such passages as 1:3ff. and 2:14ff.

13. James M. Robinson, *Kerygma und historischer Jesus* (Zürich: Zwingli, 1960), 179ff.

14. But note Heb 4:14–5:10 (5:2); cf. G. Stählin, "ἀσθενής," *TDNT* 1:492–93, Eduard Schweizer, *Lordship and Discipleship* (London: SCM, 1960), 71ff. (trans. of *Erniedrigung und Erhöhung bei Jesus und seinen Nachfolgern* [Zürich: Zwingli, 1955], 67–68).

15. Käsemann, "Die Legitimität des Apostels," 34ff.; Bultmann, *Exegetische Probleme des zweiten Korintherbriefes*, 20; cf. Wilckens, *Weisheit und Torheit*, 37–38, 212.

perplexed, persecuted, struck down), which arise out of the Apostle's immediate experience,[16] are set in a kerygmatic context (4:10–11) and show that the power of God is operative only in and through weakness (4:7 and 12:9 provide the norm).[17] A similar observation can be made with reference to 1:3–11, where a comparison of 1:5–6 with 1:8–9 makes clear the intimate relationship between Paul's situation and the way in which the kerygma comes to expression.[18] Other passages, such as 2:14ff., 6:3ff., and 8:9 likewise support this view.

Thus while the Apostle's thinking is informed by the kerygma throughout, the kerygma is coming to expression here in a new context, which requires that the language of the kerygma be shaped to that context. How else can the word occur? If the observation that Paul is here presenting the kerygma within the horizon of his and the Corinthians' mutual status before the Lord is correct, it follows that the word of reconciliation is coming to expression *anew* because it is being *heard* anew.[19] That is to say, it is being encountered in a context in which the categories, say of Romans or even 1 Corinthians, do not immediately speak, without translation, to the new situation. In such a context the articulation of the kerygma may, therefore, have little or no verbal continuity with the tradition, or with the Apostle's own articulation of it elsewhere.[20] It may, therefore, be set out as

---

16. *Thlibomenoi*: cf. 2:4 (occasioned by the Corinthians themselves); 1:8 (experienced in Asia); 7:5 (experienced in Macedonia); 6:4; 8:2 (also the lot of the Macedonian churches); *aporoumenoi*: cf. 1:8; *diōkomenoi*: cf. 11:23ff.; 12:10; 1 Cor 4:12.; *kataballomenoi* (only here in Paul): whether this term means that the Apostle was struck down with a weapon (6:5; 11:23–25), thrown into prison (6:5; 11:23), or simply abused (6:4ff.; 11:26ff.), it is descriptive of his history. The verbal parallels are significant, of course, only as 4:8–9 is read with 1:8ff.; 6:2ff., and 11:23ff. in view. Sentences such as 12:10 provide the basis for the Apostle's repeated reference to his personal history and bear out the contention that the language is evoked by his situation. In 4:8ff. the first term of each pair expresses his "weakness," the second gives negative expression to his "power"; i.e., his weakness does not and cannot lead to total defeat.

17. Cf. Käsemann, "Die Legitimität des Apostels," 53.

18. James M. Robinson, "The Historicality of Biblical Language," in *The Old Testament and the Christian Faith*, ed. Bernhard W. Anderson (New York: Harper & Row, 1963), 145, 149.

19. The connection between the word coming to expression anew and being heard anew is evident in a passage like 2 Cor 3:4ff. Perhaps the methodological text for Paul is 1 Cor 4:6.

20. D. Ernst Fuchs, *Zum hermeneutischen Problem in der Theologie: Die existentiale Interpretation* (Tübingen: Mohr Siebeck, 1959), 291, has warned against attempt-

a guiding principle that the discontinuity in the language of the kerygma is directly proportional to the discontinuity in the language character of the situation into which it is received. It is necessary, however, to go on and inquire whether the kerygma only *allows* for such discontinuity, or whether in fact it *demands* it. The answer is self-evident: if the kerygma is the norm that probes Christian life before God in the world, then it follows that the kerygma must come to expression in language that is bound up with that life.

It has to be reaffirmed, nevertheless, that it is the kerygma as tradition which is informing Paul's thinking throughout. This implies, among other things, that the word that comes to expression is one—if it is the true word. On the assumption that Paul was converted via the kerygmatic Christ, i.e., the Christ known to him in the kerygma,[21] it must be said that the kerygma functions for Paul as text, for it is back upon the text (= tradition) that he must ultimately fall for the *norm* of his gospel, as seen particularly in 1 Cor 15:1ff. (note especially 15:11 and Gal 2:2[22]). The kerygma as he knew it from the tradition (learned probably before his conversion) serves him as text as he unfolds the gospel. What is the relation between this text and the proclamation that arises out of it? It has already been affirmed that the text cannot merely be repeated but must be heard anew, and this means that it comes to expression in language indigenous to the context of hearing, if it is to function as propping word. It thus appears that the

---

ing to refer Paul's choice of antitheses and theological concepts only to actual occasions. It is a warning that is well taken. Nevertheless, Bornkamm, *Die Vorgeschichte des sogenannten Zweiten Korintherbriefes*, 14, notes that since Paul's opponents in Corinthians are not the Judaizers of Galatians, the doctrine of justification by faith plays no role in 2 Corinthians. The point to be made here is that it is precisely the doctrine of justification by faith that is coming to expression in 2 Corinthians in different language.

21. Rudolf Bultmann, *Theology of the New Testament*, 3 vols. (New York: Scribner's Sons, 1951), 1:187–88.

22. Paul's apprehension, expressed in the phrase "lest somehow I should be running or had run in vain," is related to the presentation of his gospel to the leaders of the Jerusalem community. Similar uses of *kenos* and *eikē*, elsewhere give expression to the potential failure of his work as apostles (*kenos*: 1 Cor 15:10, 14, 58; 2 Cor 6:1; Phil 2:16; *eikē*: Gal 3:4, 4:11; 1 Cor 15:2). In spite of the protest in Gal 1:11ff.—which is often misunderstood—Paul is not denying his dependence on the apostolic kerygma, but is insisting that his appropriation of it was the result of revelation (note especially his use of the phrase, "the truth of the gospel," in Gal 2:5, 14).

tradition-Scripture problem is implicit already within the New Testament, and with it the hermeneutical problem.[23]

The constellation to which the dialectic of hearing/speaking belongs consists, therefore, of the kerygma understood as protocreedal affirmation (in this instance, pre-Pauline), the kerygma understood as God's word to man, i.e., the incarnation, and the articulation of the kerygma as proclamation, e.g., in 2 Corinthians.[24] Since discontinuity within the protocreedal kerygma itself, and between the protocreedal kerygma and its articulation, presents itself already behind and in the New Testament, the problem of continuity becomes acute. From the foregoing it is clear that this problem cannot be solved *verbatim ac litteratim*, yet it is equally clear that it is a problem of language. If the language of the kerygma in all its forms is wholly historical, i.e., contingent, then it follows that the continuity must lie in that to which one is ultimately attending, if by this is meant that which one is hearing in and through language.

But that to which one is ultimately attending, i.e., God's word to man, never draws near except as word event (Ebeling), so that there is no escape from the linguistic character of the kerygma. The incarnation is itself word event. *What* one is hearing in and through language and the *hearing* are inextricably bound up together.

Historically speaking, the question with respect to Paul may be delimited as the relation between protocreedal affirmation and kerygmatic articulation in a new language context, since Paul's access to Jesus as the Christ is primarily through the protocreedal kerygma. The problem may, of course, be pushed back one step and turned into the question of Paul and the protocreedal kerygma in relation to Jesus as the Christ, but the hermeneutical problem is not thereby avoided, as has already been indi-

---

23. Cf. Gerhard Ebeling, *Theologie und Verkündigung: Hermeneutische Untersuchungen zur Theologie*, vol. 1 (Tübingen: Mohr Siebeck, 1962), 42.

24. Ebeling's criticisms of the ambiguity of the term kerygma when used in this manifold way are not to be overlooked. See *Theologie und Verkündigung*, 26–51, esp. 32ff., 39, 41–42, 49–50. While I am in agreement with the thrust of his remarks, I take it that one has the option of dropping the term altogether or using it with greater care.

The ambiguity is aggravated by the fact, noted by K. Stendahl ("Kerygma und kerygmatisch," *ThLZ* 77 [1952]: 719), that the kerygma in its formal sense (= protocreedal affirmation) is not necessarily kerygmatic. There is therefore the non-kerygmatic kerygma and the kerygmatic non-kerygma, as well as the potentially kerygmatic kerygma and the non-kerygmatic non-kerygma. But this observation points to the problem, already articulated, of the dialectic between speaking / hearing.

cated. Inasmuch as Paul is here under scrutiny, the problem may be posed as it presents itself to him.

Thus for Paul the proclamation arises out of hearing, but it is true word only insofar as it evokes faith, i.e., is a word that cannot fail. It must therefore be *heard* as the word of grace and received by faith. In this sense Paul's hermeneutic requires that the saving event be understood as word and word only,[25] as the word spoken by God in Christ (cf. 5:19). This hermeneutical principle may be explicated in relation to Paul's word to the Corinthians.

The apostolic ministry is characterized as the ministry entrusted with the word of reconciliation (5:19 which is equal to the word of the cross 1 Cor 1:18). The apostolic ministry is that which spreads the fragrance of Christ. To those perishing it is the fragrance of death, but to those being saved the fragrance of life (2:14–16; this theme dominates the whole of 2:14–7:4 and 10:1–13:13). The sufficiency (*hikanos*, 2:16, is another catchword[26]) of the apostle for such a ministry does not rest on self-commendation (3:1–3, 5; 5:12; 6:4; 10:17–18; cf. 12:11), but on the sufficiency which is of God (2:16b; 3:5–6; 4:1, 5, 7; 5:21, etc.). Out of such God-based sufficiency there flows, according to 2:14–4:6, the *pepoithēsis* and/or *parrēsia* of the apostle (3:4, 12; 4:1, 13–14, 16; 5:6, 11ff. [the last without specific restatement of the theme]).

But the fragrance of Christ, the *zōē*, the *doxa*, which is the fruit of this ministry, appears to the world as a fragrance of death and as weakness (2:14ff.; 4:7–12; 11:30; 12:9–10). Since, however, this ministry is in reality vested with the power of God, its form in the world is rife with ambiguity (6:4–10; cf. 12:11–12; 13:3ff.). But this is all for the sake of the basis of the ministry, which can be only the power of God (1:9; 4:7ff.; 12:9; etc.), and hence for the sake of the power of its message.

For this reason the word of reconciliation itself is the unveiling of the glory of the Lord (3:18; with which cf. 4:2ff.), which produces a new basis for life in Christ (5:17). The divine power is made perfect in weakness so that faith may be faith. The Corinthians, at the instigation of Paul's opponents, were asking that the Apostle legitimize himself to them, i.e., provide some extrinsic signs of his apostleship. To this demand Paul can only reply: to provide such authenticating signs of status *apart from the*

---

25. Cf. Ebeling, "Significance of the Critical Historical Method," 36.
26. Käsemann, "Die Legitimität des Apostels," 35.

word that calls faith into being, would itself be faith's corruption. So the word, too, is characterized as death (2:16), as that which is veiled (4:3), and as weakness (10:10; cf. 1 Cor 1:18ff.; 2:1ff.; etc.). With the hearing of faith, however, all this is reversed. The word cannot, therefore, be understood as pointing to something else, something extrinsic, which can been joined as the basis of faith—whether it be Jesus of Nazareth,[27] or the resurrection, or the faith of the early church itself! The word of reconciliation points only to itself. It is valid only as occurring word, as the word that evokes faith and concurrently arises as confession, as the word which is itself the saving event.

It is necessary to observe, however, that the presenting of the kerygma, its exposition, takes place as the expositing of him who hears and is, therefore, self-and community-probing.[28] It should not be understood that it is thereby a negative process. The authority that Paul exercises as apostle is for building up and not tearing down (10:8; 13:10), so that when he speaks in Christ he does so for their upbuilding (12:19b; cf. 13:9; 7:8ff.; 1:24; etc.). The word which he speaks is first of all a healing, saving word, the word of grace.[29] But because it is that, it is also a testing, probing word (13:5-7).

---

27. This injunction is used in the customary Bultmannian sense, i.e., that one cannot go *behind* the kerygma (which does not here mean traditional formulations: Ebeling, *Theologie und Verkündigung*, 41) in order to validate it extrinsically. Cf., e.g., Rudolf Bultmann, *Glauben und Verstehen*, vol. 3 (Tübingen: Mohr Siebeck, 1960; 2nd ed., 1962), 22–23, translated by S. M. Ogden in *Existence and Faith: Shorter Writings of Rudolf Bultmann* (New York: Meridian Books, 1960), 79. Ebeling has proposed to understand Jesus as the basis of faith in another sense: "Certainly not a support which relieves us in part of the need for faith. Rather, the basis of faith is that which lets faith be faith, which keeps it being faith, on which faith, that is to say, ultimately relies" (*Das Wesen des Christlichen Glaubens* [Tübingen: Mohr Siebeck, 1959], 83–84; English translation by R. G. Smith, *The Nature of Faith* [London: Collins, 1961], 70–71). Cf. "Jesus and Faith," 201–46, and *Theologie und Verkündigung*, 19–82. The matter may be formulated thus: Jesus *as the word* is the basis of the proclamation and therefore of faith. With this the injunction above does not stand in opposition.

28. Ernst Fuchs, *Zur Frage nach dem historischen Jesus* (Tübingen: Mohr Siebeck, 1960), 389ff., 400; Gerhard Ebeling, "Discussion Theses for a Course of Introductory Lectures on the Study of Theology," 428; Wilckens, *Weisheit und Torheit*, 214–15. Cf. Ebeling, "Hauptprobleme der protestantischen Theologie in der Gegenwart," *ZTK* 58 (1961): 125–26.

29. Cf. 2:2ff.; 5:20; 7:8ff. Cf. Fuchs's understanding of the word as permission in *Hermeneutik* (Bad Cannstatt: Müllerschön Verlag, 1954; 2nd ed., 1958), 6; Fuchs, *Zum hermeneutischen Problem in der Theologie*, 282–83; Fuchs, *Zur Frage nach dem histo-*

What it destroys when heard in faith is "all that rears its proud head against the knowledge of God" (10:5, NEB). As the word of reconciliation, the proclamation requires the participation of him who hears in the reality which is communicated, and therefore in faith.

It follows that the exposition of the text, in this case the kerygma that Paul knew from the tradition, fulfills its vocation only as proclamation, and that means precisely as the probing word that brings life. Exposition that does not lead to proclamation is sterile, just as proclamation that is not exposition tends to be uncritical.

It remains to inquire what the exposition of the kerygma in 2 Corinthians exposes. We may begin with the Apostle himself. It is clear that the body of the letter exposes the basis of the apostolic ministry and thus exhibits the inner connection between the nature of the word that is proclaimed and the basis of the ministry that proclaims it. In the section 2:14–4:15 (from thanksgiving to thanksgiving), Paul sets out the form of his ministry which gives the appearance, on the one hand, of weakness, self-commendation, deceitfulness, and guile, but, on the other hand, manifests sufficiency, confidence, and open appeal to the truth. His sufficiency, which is of God (3:5; etc.), is accessible only as he embraces the "weakness" of Christ (4:7–12; cf. 12:9). But it is for this very reason that he is confident and bold (introduced in 3:4 and reiterated often). In 3:12–18 *kalymma* is developed as the contrasting term to *parrēsia*, i.e., uncovering the face is boldness. He is thereby reversing the charges made against him: he is said to have acted deviously, clandestinely, with cunning and guile, to have adulterated the word of God (4:2; cf. 2:17), all of which are practices characterized by *kalyptō!* The opposite, he affirms, is in fact the case: he speaks in the sight of God, i.e., submits himself to the judgment of the word (2:17), and so can commend himself only by the open statement of the truth (4:2; cf. 3:2, 18).

Nevertheless, his question "Are we beginning to commend ourselves again?" suggests that he is never free from the temptation to boast a little on his own behalf. One expects the Apostle to refute the charges leveled against him by invoking his own powers as a pneumatic, by reference to his own achievements. In fact, in 10:7ff., 11:1ff., and 12:1ff. he appears to

---

rischen Jesus, 427; Bultmann, *Glauben und Verstehen*, vol. 2 (Tübingen: Mohr Siebeck, 1952; 3rd ed., 1961), 10, English translation by C. G. Grieg, *Essays Philosophical and Theological* (New York: Macmillan Company, 1955), 11–12 [Subsequent citations will be to the German. —Ed.], had already expressed a similar notion.

launch into just this type of defense. But at every crucial point he subtly shifts the burden of his argument, and ends by turning it upside down. The passage 11:21–30 is characteristic: he begins by noting that he speaks as a fool, a madman (11:21b, 23), and ends by reversing the thrust of his list of "achievements" so that all he can legitimately offer to support his claims are the things that show his weakness (11:29–30).

It is not without significance that the Apostle makes his defense in the form of a renewal of the proclamation, but in such a way, of course, that it is directly related to the problem at hand. The polemical cast of 2:14–7:5, though much milder to be sure than that of 10:1–13:13, is evident throughout, reaching its peak in the concluding section 5:11–6:10. Following the initial polemic,[30] which Paul grounds once again in a kerygmatic formulation (5:14–15), he proceeds to the ultimate basis of his confidence and boldness as apostle, which has dominated the argument since 2:14. With Christ the old way of knowing has passed away and the new has taken its place (5:16), with the result that the Corinthians can no more know Paul *kata sarka* than they can the Christ. The appeal for reconciliation that Paul directs to them (5:20) is then renewed in 6:1 as the appeal not to accept the grace of God in vain (cf. Gal 3:1–5 following on 2:20–21), both of which are bound up with the final polemical note in 6:3. Correctly understood, 6:3–10 is a peroration that sums up the character of his ministry as determined by the norm in 5:14–15.[31] As such, it calls for the Corinthians to view him as they must view Christ, and thus to adjust their seeing (or knowing) to their hearing.[32]

---

30. The phrase "we persuade men" (5:11) is here as in Gal 1:10 a slogan of opponents (cf. Bultmann, *Exegetische Probleme des zweiten Korintherbriefes*, 13); "what we are is known to God" is probably directed against the charge of furtiveness and insincerity (cf. 4:2); 5:12 refers to the charge of self-commendation (cf. 3:1; 4:2) which Paul now turns around in order to give the Corinthians a "handle" to use if they wish, in their defense of him (cf. 12:11); 5:13 is concerned with his failure to a credit himself as an ecstatic (cf. Käsemann, "Die Legitimität des Apostels," 67–68; Bultmann, *Exegetische Probleme des zweiten Korintherbriefes*, 14).

31. Cf. Bultmann, *Exegetische Probleme des zweiten Korintherbriefes*, 18–20.

32. Bultmann sets "seeing" over against "hearing" in the sense of a doctrine of God and the world as opposed to hearing as obedience (*Hören als Gehorchen*), e.g., *Glauben und Verstehen*, vol. 1. (Tübingen: Mohr Siebeck, 1933; 2nd ed., 1954), 271, 272–73, 324. The former goes with Weltanschauungen, with "theory" (*theoria*), with a spectator's and hence a detached knowing. There is, however, a "seeing" of faith, e.g.,

This integral relationship between defense or apology and proclamation, both of which are referred to the text, is specified here and there
throughout the epistle. The new situation[33] at Corinth that appears to have
provoked 2 Corinthians, especially chapters 10–13, is the appearance of
itinerant "superlative" apostles (11:5; 12:11) who preach another Jesus than
Paul preached and who, consequently, cause the Corinthians to receive a
different spirit and submit to a different gospel (11:4). If Paul is forced
to defend his ministry, it is because he sees that the gospel itself is being
called into question. The intruders in Corinth have seduced the congregation into believing that Paul lacked all the marks of a legitimate apostle
(12:12; 13:3) and that his ministry was therefore to be characterized as
weakness.[34] He is accused of being *tapeinos kata prosōpon*, i.e., of being
pliant, subservient, abject (Bauer) when in the presence of opposition,
but of being arrogant when away (10:1, 10). This goes together with his
lack of facility in extempore speaking (10:10; 11:6), which was regarded as
the mark of a true pneumatic.[35] He had apparently made little of his own
visions and ecstasies (12:1–6; cf. 5:13), but this, too, was taken as a sign of
weakness. Signs and wonders, which were also understood to be the mark
of a true apostle, were apparently performed by Paul among the Corinthians, but they had not recognized them as such (12:12).[36] Since Paul had
not given sufficient evidence of spirit possession, his authority (*exousia*) is
to be questioned (10:8; 13:10), and therefore his power (*dynamis*) (10:2ff.,
21; 12:9; 13:2ff.). Lacking the requisite authority and power, he could not

---

in the Gospel of John (*Glauben und Verstehen*, 1:293). To put the matter succinctly,
"seeing" as theology has always to be probed and corrected by "hearing" of the word.

33. Bornkamm, *Die Vorgeschichte des sogenannten Zweiten Korintherbriefes*,
15–16.

34. According to Käsemann, "Die Legitimität des Apostels," 34, the leading theme
of the objections and response.

35. Käsemann, "Die Legitimität des Apostels," 35.

36. It is significant that Paul qualifies his claim to signs and wonders in 12:12 with
the phrase *en pasē hypomonē*. This means that he places such deeds within the horizon of sufferings patiently endured for Christ, e.g., 1:6; 6:4ff.; 11:23ff. Kasemann, "Die
Legitimität des Apostels," 62–63. These elements—*sēmeia, terata, dynameis*—singly or
in combination, are regarded as legitimizing (e.g., Gal 3:5; Rom 15:19; Acts 2:22; Heb
2:4), although they may be quite deceptive (e.g., 2 Thess 2:9). The question is, what
are the legitimate signs, wonders, and mighty deeds? Paul had already dealt with this
question in 1 Cor 12–14, and Gal 3:5 makes it equally clear that such wonders can
arise, i.e., be "seen," only out of faith.

make a claim on the Corinthians for support (11:7ff.), nor could he offer letters of certification such as the intruders were able to present (3:1).[37]

It has already been noted that Paul specifies as the norm of his ministry the weakness of Christ, through which alone he has access to genuine power (12:9 and 13:3–4). His weakness signalizes his participation in the sufferings of Christ through which he is able to minister salvation and comfort (1:5–6).[38] It is precisely that which the Corinthians—prompted by the intruders—now find objectionable in Paul that the Apostle must offer as his only legitimate claim, although he can, to be sure, play the game of comparison on their terms (10:7–8; 11:17, 21–22; 12:1ff., 11). Nevertheless, if he is to boast, he can boast only of his weakness (11:30; 12:9–10), only of that which shows that his sufficiency is of God (3:5–6; 4:7; 6:4ff.), only of the Lord (11:17–18). Thus it is through his exposition of the kerygmatic text as the basis of his apostleship that he confronts the Corinthians once again with the word of reconciliation, in such a way that their seeing of the Christ, the Apostle, themselves, is probed by a fresh hearing of the word. If Paul now appears *tapeinos* to them (10:1), it is not because he is without authority or power, nor because he cannot stand up to powerful opposition (13:2ff., 10),[39] but because his weakness should lead to their strength (13:9).[40] This manner of speaking can be understood, of course, only in relation to the Apostle's power vis-à-vis his churches: he does not and cannot lord it over their faith (1:24), since if he did, faith would not depend solely on their hearing. For the same reason it is of no consequence that he is poor in extempore discourse, or that he refuses to boast of his visions and ecstasies, or that he offers signs and wonders of dubious character. His opponents demand what he cannot deliver: legitimizing evidence *ex ergōn nomou* (Gal 3:5). Such visions, ecstatic experiences, and the like as he has had do not concern the Corinthians at all, they concern only his relation with God. What does concern the Corinthians is his con-

---

37. Bornkamm, *Die Vorgeschichte des sogenannten Zweiten Korintherbriefes*, 12.

38. 1:3ff. is not to be psychologized, as the reference to *sōtēria* in 1:6 shows. 1:3–11 as a whole has a soteriological reference.

39. It may well be that the "vacillation" that appears to be the subject of 1:15ff. (the explanation for which continues through 1:23–2:13; 7:5–16!) arises out of his threat to visit them a third time and exercise his power (13:1ff.; cf. 10:2), in which case his decision not to come in order to spare them would be open to further misinterpretation as weakness.

40. In 10:1 his entreaty is by the meekness and gentleness of Christ; cf. 4:11–12.

scious day-to-day conduct of his ministry (5:13).[41] He must refrain from boasting of private experiences so that no one may think more of him than what he sees in him or heard from him (12:6b). Moreover, he is not inferior in knowledge (*gnōsis*) (11:6), which, however, will appear as foolishness apart from faith.[42]

Paul's refusal to accept support from the Corinthians is grounded in 11:7 in an interesting kerygmatic formulation: he abased himself in order that they might be exalted (*tapeinoō/hypsoō*), i.e., he accepted support from other churches to serve them. One is reminded of the language of the Christ hymn in Phil 2:6–11.[43] It has often been noted that a similar formulation, utilizing a different pair of terms (*ptōcheia/plousios*), is employed in 8:9 as the basis for the Apostle's appeal for the relief offering. The latter is connected, on the one hand, with the "proof" (*endeixis*) of their love (8:24), and the "test" (*dokimē*) of their service (*diakonia*), which attests their obedience in confessing (*homologia*) the gospel of Christ (9:13), and, on the other hand, with Paul's characterization of his own ministry (6:10). We have, then, a clear case of the kerygma coming to expression as the norm of Paul's financial relation to the Corinthians and of their financial relation to the Jerusalem church. In both instances its language is adapted to the specific terms of the situation.

Finally, Paul cannot offer letters of recommendation because the Corinthians themselves are all the recommendation he requires: they are a letter from Christ ministered[44] by Paul and his co-laborers (3:1–3). He may boast of them only as God has allotted them to his ministry, and hence he cannot, like the intruders, boast in another man's labors (10:13ff.). But insofar as God has used him as an ambassador of Christ, they are his boast just as he ought to be theirs (1:14). In the last analysis, the proof of his legitimacy as apostle is dependent upon whether or not he has communicated to them the word of reconciliation so that it evokes faith. Aside from this, the question is idle.

---

41. Bultmann, *Exegetische Probleme des zweiten Korintherbriefes*, 14.

42. Note the catchword *aphrosynē* (and cognates) in 11:1–12:11 and cf. 1 Cor 1:18ff., esp. 2:6ff.

43. And of the Synoptic sayings found in Luke 14:11 and elsewhere. The fact that it is attested in the rabbinic literature (J. Jeremias, *The Parables of Jesus* [New York: Scribner's Sons, 1955], 82–83) does not alter the case that it is used by Paul with a christological reference. Cf. the kerygmatic use of *hypsoō* in John (3:14; 8:28; 12:32, 34).

44. Play on *diakoneō*.

Just as the Corinthians, under the provocation of wandering apostles, have put Paul to the test (13:13), having missed the signs of a true apostle (12:12), so Paul must put them to the test (13:5) by a fresh exposition of the kerygma. He must, in this instance, achieve the latter by submitting himself to the test. If the Corinthians fail to find Christ in themselves (13:5), Paul himself will have failed (13:6), even though it matters little whether he *appears* to meet the test if the Corinthians do what is right (13:7). His *apparent* failure may in fact serve for their improvement (13:9). Thus it appears that Paul's case must ultimately rest on a fresh hearing of the word of reconciliation, a hearing in which both he who speaks and they who listen participate, thereby giving rise to common understanding. The word must be heard within the spectrum of Corinthian individual and community, and if it is heard in the language of their own existence, then they themselves have vindicated Paul—and the hermeneutical function of the word has achieved its fulfillment.

2. The Word as Self- and Community-Probing and Historical Criticism

Two factors in the theological development since the Reformation can be said to have converged to raise the hermeneutical problem to the center of the discussion. Heiko Oberman has summed them up with these words: "It [the ongoing effort to translate the Scriptures] unfolds under the abiding tension of a dual freedom: the freedom obediently to conform to the apostolic witness, and the freedom creatively to translate that witness for the experiences and thought patterns of successive generations. This is a task of freedom because it is the Holy Spirit who leads the Church into new responses to the unique historic revelation in Christ."[45] Broadly speaking, these two factors can be referred respectively to orthodoxy, which insists on obedient conformity, and to liberalism, which seeks above all to make the gospel relevant. With the theological renaissance in this century the question of what transpires when these two meet became a burning issue.

If it can be said that Barth won back the legitimate demand of the word of God for obedient conformity, it may also be said that this victory brought with it a potential if not real threat to the critical historical method with which the so-called liberal theology had fought with so

---

45. Heiko Oberman, *Christianity Divided: Protestant and Roman Catholic Theological Issues*, ed. D. J. Callahan, Heiko Oberman, and D. J. O'Hanlon (New York: Sheed & Ward, 1961), 76.

much success against old orthodoxy. The danger that presented itself had consequences for both sides of the hermeneutical problem: The text cannot speak for itself if it is not painstakingly exegeted in its own context, and it cannot be interpreted if it cannot be brought into intimate relation with contemporary modes of thought and experience. As a defense against this threat Ebeling has set out a series of propositions concerning the function of the Bible in theological work. We may quote a portion of proposition 7: "Criticism is an integral element in the effort to understand the text. It is directed *to* that which the Biblical text wants to bring to understanding and *against* anything and everything that stands as a hindrance in the way of the hermeneutical function of the text."[46] As set out here, the two sides of criticism, which are really one, correspond to the dual freedom of faith (Oberman): The possibility of obedience depends on access to what the text intends to bring to understanding, and creative translation depends on the effective removal of impediments to the hermeneutical function of the text. It is clear that these two sides are interdependent and form a circle.[47]

The affirmation that historical (biblical) criticism is an integral element in the effort to understand the text does not, however, answer the question of *how* it functions. The *how* remains a crucial problem because the so-called scientific study of the Bible, especially on this side of the Atlantic, has developed a splendid isolation from the theological task. Its isolation is due in no small measure to the effective disappearance of the thing against which it fought in an earlier period.[48] It stands in need, therefore, of a basic reorientation to the current theological situation.

Before proceeding to this question, however, it is necessary to recognize a basic premise without which the historical method is simply irrelevant. That premise is the radical historicity of the word of God. The rise of historical criticism brought with it the acknowledgment of the con-

---

46. Emphasis added. "Diskussionsthesen für eine Vorlesung zur Einführung in das Studium der Theologie," in *Wort und Glaube*, 451. English translation: "Discussion Theses for a Course of Introductory Lectures on the Study of Theology," in *Word and Faith*, 428 [editorial note: subsequent references to English version].

47. This is to say, that when one side is lost, both are lost. Herein lies the irony of the denouement of both orthodoxy and liberalism. Cf. Ebeling, "Discussion Theses for a Course of Introductory Lectures on the Study of Theology," 428, proposition 6.

48. One certainly has to take note of local differences in this respect. Nevertheless, even in those places which regard themselves as bastions of conservatism, liberalism has had a silent, if empty, victory.

tingency of the word, and therefore of the relativity of every expression of the word. It is this proposition which must be affirmed over against theologies of transcendence which emphasize the givenness of the word.[49] Only if the word is regarded as a fully human and therefore historically conditioned word can historical criticism be of service.

Historical criticism is not inappropriately named. It is criticism in the generic sense developed out of and against historical perspectives. Its circular movement is thus a constitutive element in its program. So understood, how can it function effectively with respect to the text? We may set out our answer in a series of propositions accompanied by brief expositions.

(1) Historical criticism is the means of gaining authentic access to the intention of the text. Authentic access is achieved by removing obstacles that impede the hermeneutical function of the text. To this removal of obstacles we now turn.

(2) Historical criticism is designed to preserve the distance between text and interpreter.[50] As commonly understood this means reading the text in its own context, with regard for its full historicity. It goes without saying that the recognized tools of the historical method are entirely appropriate and indispensable to this purpose. Historical criticism strives to understand the historical as the particular, which means, in the case of the New Testament, as something that is strange and alien, given the distance of the twentieth from the first century. But it is not always recognized that this distancing function serves also to thwart the tyranny of the question; i.e., it pushes the past away as that which cannot, without further

---

49. This is a way of saying that the labor of putting the New Testament in its context has not been wasted. On the other hand, it needs to be recognized that to reduce the New Testament to its context is to *deny* the full historicity of the word, since every historical phenomenon is also absolute, i.e., not repeatable, unique. This refers, for example, to the language of the New Testament; although New Testament Greek has been referred to its position in the history of the language and within Koine, an achievement that is not to be gainsaid, there is nevertheless justification for treating New Testament Greek, as the language of the community of faith, as a special phenomenon. Cf. F. Blass and A. Debrunner, *A Greek Grammar of the New Testament and Other Early Christian Literature*, translated and revised by Robert W. Funk (Chicago: University of Chicago Press, 1961), para. 1. This observation does not call for a revival of the question in what way the New Testament is unique, i.e., on the basis of invidious comparison, but demands a regard for every historical phenomenon as something to be encountered in its own right, a demand to "let the thing be."

50. Ebeling, "Significance of the Critical Historical Method," 46–47, 49.

consideration, be brought into relation to the present. The history of historical criticism itself provides the clue to this understanding of its task.[51] As the antidote to the tyranny of dogmatic theology, historical criticism held up the dogmatic appropriation of the text against the integrity of the text and found the former to be wanting. As a result, dogmatics was denied the right, at least in principle, to base its claims on the text. Therewith was decreed the divorce between dogmatic theology and biblical studies that has had its disastrous effects down to the present time.[52] Viewed as a means of thwarting the tyranny of the question, historical criticism does not function merely as the opposition party; on the contrary, preserving the distance between text and interpreter is another way of saying that the sole means of legitimate access to the text is the understanding of the historical event in its particularity, and if in its particularity, in those modes of thought and experience which come to expression therein. As it attempts to illuminate such modes, it clears away the obstacles that hinder the hermeneutical function of the text.

(3) Historical criticism, moreover, attempts to establish chronology. This does not refer primarily to the determination of absolute dates (although these may be helpful, even indispensable), but to the ordering of events. Such ordering at its most profound level has to do with observing the vicissitudes of tradition, i.e., with the mutation of the appropriation of past events. It is concerned, therefore, with the way the past is taken up into the present, and thus not only with the immanental causative factors that are operative in a given epoch or locale, but also with the fresh appropriation of the past for which the past itself provides the stimulus. In this regard, too, historical criticism is endeavoring to conserve the particularity of the historical at those points where proximity in time and/or space invites the reductionist fallacy. Reductionism in this sense is called harmonizing when applied to the Old or New Testament. It can be seen that the effort to preserve the distance between the text and its interpreter is directed toward a more flagrant form of the same error that is being resisted here.

As applied to historical theology, the ordering function of criticism will seek to read New Testament theology as the history of the theological appropriation of the Christ event in the New Testament period, and

---

51. Cf. Ebeling, "Meaning of 'Biblical Theology,'" 79–97.

52. This point currently applies more generally to Anglo-American theology than to Continental theology.

church history/history of dogma as the history of the theological appropriation of the text.[53] This view of historical theology as the history of hermeneutic is based on the assumption that the way the Christian community appropriates a particular segment of its past; i.e., the originating events, is determinative for its life as the body of Christ. This is not to say, however, that historical theology will confine itself to the history of the interpretation of specific texts; it will also interrogate the community concerning the way in which the word that comes to expression in the New Testament comes to expression in various periods in the community.

To the preceding must now be added a fourth: (4) historical criticism exposes the word of God as a fully human word by exposing the human situation into which it is received as radically human. This procedure may be termed "unmasking." Unmasking is used here in the sense suggested by Peter Berger[54] and involves calling in question all human claims to access to the divine. It is important to grasp the connection of this formulation with Bultmann's repeated emphasis on history as a closed causal continuum as the presupposition of the historical method,[55] an emphasis shared by Fuchs.[56] The historian cannot presuppose supernatural intervention in the causal nexus as the basis for his work any more than the interpreter of the biblical text can presuppose the Holy Spirit as the basis for his. This assertion, however, is not forced upon theology from the outside, but is connected internally with the basis of faith. *Sola fide* means the rejection "of all secret revelational docetism by means of which the historicity of revelation is sidestepped and which turns revelation into a history *sui generis*."[57] Authentic faith is therefore compelled to accept the full historicity of the word since it denies to itself any extrinsic basis. For this reason "faith is at the mercy of the complete questionableness and ambiguity of the historical."[58]

If the historian or exegete is engaged in the ruthless exposure of the text as a human word, he is opening the way for a fresh appropriation

---

53. Ebeling, *Die Geschichtlichkeit der Kirche und ihrer Verkündigung als theologisches Problem*, 78–79, 81ff.

54. Peter Berger, *The Precarious Vision* (Garden City, NY: Doubleday, 1961), esp. 152ff.

55. E.g., Bultmann, *Glauben und Verstehen*, 3:144–45.

56. Fuchs, *Zur Frage nach dem historischen Jesus*, 227ff., 230.

57. Ebeling, "Significance of the Critical Historical Method," 56.

58. Ebeling, "Significance of the Critical Historical Method," 56.

of the intention of the text because he is helping to let faith be what it is by exposing human pretension in all forms, and also because he is directing his criticism against the text from a locus occupied by himself. Apart from such exposure a genuinely historical appropriation of the past is rendered impossible with the result that the past degenerates into a kind of fate[59] which dominates the present to the degree that social and personal fictions are left unexposed.[60] The Bible no less than other documents is subject to such distortion. If it is understood that the church must renew its life at its source, historical criticism in this sense is not an option but a necessity.

(5) Under the aegis of its presupposition that history is a closed unity and prompted by its methodological aim not to presuppose its results, historical criticism is *blind*.[61] It is blind in that it strives for objectivity; it attempts to posit the past as something discrete from the present and thus release it from every relative appropriation. It can explain every historical event by reducing it to cause and effect on the immanent level. It debunks all human achievement by exposing it as enmeshed in the skein of natural, social, and psychological causes. It recognizes no sacred precincts. This blindness is characterized also by disinterestedness, which means that the question of the existential meaning of an event or document for the present is not the *first* order of business. Even though the subject-object schema, on the analogy of the natural sciences, is not valid for historical investigation, historical criticism presupposes that a free decision with respect to the past is itself subject to historical causality.[62] Its blindness, therefore, stands in conscious opposition to the historicity of the historian and makes it possible for the critic to take his historical work seriously. That these are methodological aims and not achievements goes without saying. Nevertheless, the virtue in this blindness is not to be overlooked.

---

59. I have borrowed this formulation from my colleague, Gordon Harland, whose perceptive analysis "The American Protestant Heritage and the Theological Task," *Drew Gateway* (Winter 1962): 71–93, as well as many conversations, has helped shape this essay.

60. One thinks, e.g., of various forms of nationalism that tend to idealize the past and hence lose their self-transcending and thus their self-correcting power. The result is invariably disastrous.

61. Cf. the remark of Georges Rouault: "Subjective artists are one-eyed, but objective artists are blind" (quoted in Jacques Maritain, *Rouault*, Pocket Library of Great Art [New York: Abrams, 1954], under the caption "Rouault on His Art" in an appendix).

62. Bultmann, *Glauben und Verstehen*, 3:144.

If the historicity of the interpreter makes historical criticism necessary, the blindness of the historian makes it possible. For—and with this we return to proposition (1)—authentic access to the text arises out of the blind exposure of the full historicity of the text in conjunction with the exposure of the historicity of the interpreter. By means of historical criticism, then, an opening occurs for a new hearing of the text, a hearing in which the text gives rise to the future as its own, i.e., the intention of the text is executed. Such an opening occurs only at the point where the function of historical criticism, understood as letting the text be by pushing it away, ordering it and exposing it as human, is related to the hearing. It is this dialectic of letting be/hearing which brings historical criticism to its fulfillment, since it is here that the world as self- and community-probing becomes effective.

The problem that now arises, however, is that because historical criticism is blind it tends to become irrelevant. And if irrelevant, then it suffers reduction to techniques preoccupied with bits of knowledge. When it thus loses its effectiveness, the temptation to make the ahistorical leap from text to biblical theology arises and is put down only with difficulty.[63] It may be concluded, therefore, that if historical criticism continued relentlessly on its independent course, it stands in danger of sacrificing its relationship to theological work altogether, and its position in theological faculties becomes an anomaly.[64] Its critical power vis-à-vis the theological appropriation of the text consequently depend on its capacity to readjust itself to the unfolding situation. This problem will be the concern of the following section.

3. Proclamation as Hearing Anew and Exegesis of the Text

Proclamation may be defined as the occurring word of God, i.e., word of God as word event.[65] As such it is dependent upon a fresh *hearing* of the word. The relation between text and interpreter needs now to be opened up

---

63. Cf. Ebeling, "Significance of the Critical Historical Method," esp. 42–43, 48–49, 57ff. The whole essay is concerned with this problem.

64. This is not to say that biblical criticism cannot be carried on outside the theological faculty, either with or without reference to the theological situation.

65. Fuchs, e.g., *Zum hermeneutischen Problem in der Theologie*, 281–305; Fuchs, *Zur Frage nach dem historischen Jesus*, 424–30.

from the side of the interpreter, i.e., from the side of the hearing through which the text comes to expression as proclamation.

Bultmann has mediated to the contemporary discussion the view that one can interrogate history meaningfully only with "some specific way of raising questions, some specific perspective."[66] Posing relevant questions to a text depends, according to Bultmann, on a prior life relationship to the subject under consideration.[67] This notion is embodied in his concept of preunderstanding. Although Bultmann has illustrated this concept in relation to subject matter suggested by various types of texts, e.g., those whose subject matter is music, mathematics, philosophy, religion, etc.,[68] his entire program has been worked out in relation to the existentialist analysis of Heidegger, which he accepts as a viable basis from which to raise relevant questions.[69] He is careful to make the distinction between existential and existentialist,[70] and points out that the latter, as a philosophical analysis of existence from which he proceeds, is a formal analysis that has to do with the structure of existence as such.[71]

It will be observed that Bultmann proceeds from an analysis of the human situation as such.[72] But the structural analysis of the human situ-

---

66. Bultmann, *Glauben und Verstehen*, 3:146.

67. E.g., Bultmann, *Glauben und Verstehen*, 2:216ff.; 3:146–47, 149.

68. E.g., in his essay on hermeneutic, Bultmann, *Glauben und Verstehen*, 2:217ff.; cf. 3:146.

69. E.g., Rudolf Bultmann, *Jesus Christ and Mythology* (New York: Scribner's Son, 1958), 54–55, 66–67, 74; cf. 45–59; Bultmann, *Existence and Faith*, 92–110; S. M. Ogden, *Christ without Myth* (New York: Harper & Row, 1961), 45ff., 56–57.

70. E.g., Bultmann, *Jesus Christ and Mythology*, 74.

71. E.g., Rudolf Bultmann, *Kerygma und Mythos*, vol. 2 (Hamburg-Volksdorf: Herbert Reich, 1952), 192; English translation *Kerygma and Myth*, trans. R. H. Fuller (New York: Harper & Row, 1957), 195; Bultmann, *Jesus Christ and Mythology*, 74; Bultmann, *Existence and Faith*, 93ff.

72. Emil L. Fackenheim, *Metaphysics and Historicity* (Milwaukee: Marquette University Press, 1961), distinguishes the human from the natural and historical situations: "This concept is additional to those of natural and historical situation. But the human situation is not a source of additional limitations. Rather, it is the ontological ground of both the natural and the historical situation, and is in turn individuated only in these. Correspondingly, the recognition of the human situation cannot be divorced from that of the natural and the historical situation; it is achieved when the natural and the historical situation are understood radically, as specific manifestations of a universal condition. It is the radicalization of the natural and of the historical situation which discloses the human situation" (76).

ation, while it aids in understanding the subject matter given expression in historical documents, is deficient in mediating an interpretation of those documents in that it produces an interpretation that is universally applicable. An interpretation that is universally applicable cannot, without further consideration, be brought into relation to the specific existence of a given period or individual. That is to say, the human situation must be *interpreted* in terms of the concrete existence of a particular community or person.[73]

It follows that the questions that arise out of the preunderstanding must themselves have historical body if they are to bear fruit in the interrogation of the text. This is required in order that the text can be *heard* in relation to the realities of present historical existence. What is at issue is the dialectic between the human situation (*existentialist*) and the historical situation (*existential*).[74] If the human situation is the situation of man *qua* man and the historical situation is the situation of man *qua* historically individuated, the two must stand in dialectical relationship to each other; man never wholly transcends the context of his historical situation, yet he cannot be reduced without residue to his historical situation without losing his character as man.[75] The point to be made here is that the human situation is always individuated in the historical situation, though, of course, it remains in dialectical relation to it. And if such individuation is characteristic of the human situation, the historical situation must enter into the constitution of the pre-understanding as well as serve as the matrix of interpretation.

The circularity of preunderstanding and understanding, which Bultmann correctly urges, is still deficient in that it proceeds *from* the human situation *to* the human situation without entering seriously into dialectic with the historical situation on the side of the interpreter. To put it succinctly, the circle on the interpreter's side is lacking in fullness—a fullness that is taken as axiomatic on the side of the text. What is objectionable in the existentialist analysis is that its framing of the questions tends to

---

73. See §1, above.

74. Fackenheim, *Metaphysics and Historicity*, 48ff., provides a discussion of the concept "historical situation." Man is historically situated (1) by his own past acting and (2) by the acting of other men (50–51). "The historical situation both limits and augments what it situates; and it is the togetherness of both which alone can constitute a situation as historical" (53).

75. Cf. Fackenheim, *Metaphysics and Historicity*, 76ff.

be undertaken in isolation from the prehistory of the situation. In other words, existentialist analysis is likely to be a snapshot which arrests man in his history, cuts across it, and exposes the skeleton. Bultmann's "now," the moment of decision, is thus open to the danger of becoming an empty abstraction.[76] There is the disposition in this type of analysis, moreover, to ignore the social character of existence. Although it is doubtless correct to saddle the individual with the decision that goes with faith, such decisions are never made in a vacuum, as Bultmann himself repeatedly emphasizes. Furthermore, while theology cannot dictate the specific *existential* content of faith in a given instance, neither can it fulfill its vocation without raising such content into a theological key and thereby proving it. In short, the existentialist analysis converts the particular into an abstraction, thereby cutting it out of its historical nexus. Such analyses, while indispensable, are inadequate for the same reason that sociology that is confined to one generation is myopic, and psychological analysis that is not based on the history of the individual and/or culture is a distorted fragment.

It can be allowed, however, that Bultmann's way of posing the question, i.e., his own preunderstanding, has more historical body than the above criticism suggests. His own theological work is often explicitly informed by an analysis of the prehistory of the present situation,[77] and his participation in the theological upheaval of the twenties indicates that he is acutely aware of the historical dimensions of his work. Furthermore, his dependence upon Heidegger can be justified in this connection by understanding the letter's work as historical in distinction from metaphysical. The existentialist analytic may be interpreted as belonging specifically to our own period.[78] The estimate of Bultmann's work in this respect will

---

76. It should be made clear that Bultmann's intention is not being called into question: "Indeed, the questioning itself grows out of the historical situation, out of the claim of the now, out of the problem that is given in the now" (*Glauben und Verstehen*, 3:148). Nor his insistence that theology cannot proceed apart from the help of philosophical analysis being contested.

77. Note the appendix to Bultmann's *Theology of the New Testament*, 2:241–51, and his essays in Bultmann, *Glauben und Verstehen*, 1:1–25, 114–33. Cf. also his remarks on pneuma in *Glauben und Verstehen*, 3:144, and his treatment of the problem of revelation in *Glauben und Verstehen*, 3:1–14. One thinks also of his concept of demythologizing in relation to the man to whom the gospel is to be preached; cf. Kendrick Grobel, "Bultmann's Problem of New Testament 'Mythology,'" *JBL* 70 (1951): 99–103; Grobel, "The Practice of Demythologizing," *JBR* 27 (1959): 28–31.

78. Martin Heidegger, *Sein und Zeit*, 9th ed. (Tübingen: Niemeyer Verlag, 1960),

depend in part on whether one thinks he has correctly read the way in which the present is determined by the past, and in part on whether he speaks to the present situation. The two, of course, are interrelated.

It is nevertheless the case that special histories, personal and collective, operate in us too, and these must be exposed before the word can be heard anew. The problem, then, is the unexamined past as fate involved in the preunderstanding in relation to the formulation of questions.

A pair of propositions pertain to biblical criticism, both of which are double-edged: (1) historical criticism in the preceding period was shaped by that with reference to which it was critical; and (2) historical criticism was channeled into the service of its own presuppositions.

The characteristics of biblical criticism to which these two propositions point can be regarded either as its vitality and relevance or as its undoing. They may be regarded as the former if the object against which criticism is directed remains a viable option (better: *the* option), and if the presuppositions which underlie its positive work are conceived historically and can be recalled and critically re-examined at crucial points in the development. They are to be taken as debilitating if the object of criticism is retained only as a straw man, and the presuppositions lost to view so that they operate as a fate. The two sides in each case go inevitably together.

Now, of course, a judgment with respect to the stage of the development in a given period is itself a historical judgment. There is no escape from the circularity of the problem. Nor can there be if historical criticism is to function critically, for to function critically means also to function

---

20–21; English translation *Being and Time*, trans. J. Macquarrie and E. Robinson (London: SCM, 1962), 42: "The ownmost meaning of Being which belongs to the inquiry into Being as an historical inquiry, gives us the assignment [*Anweisung*] of inquiring into the history of that inquiry itself, that is, of becoming historiological. In working out the question of Being, we must heed this assignment, so that by positively making the past our own, we may bring ourselves into full possession of the ownmost possibilities of such inquiry." Cf. Fackenheim, *Metaphysics and Historicity*, 77ff., n. 44; 80, n. 45; Thomas Langan, *The Meaning of Heidegger* (New York: Columbia University Press, 1959), 143–51. I do not propose, either here or elsewhere in this essay, to engage the question of whether philosophical inquiry is to be subsumed wholly under the historical question or not. That Heidegger's work may be so understood is one way of justifying Bultmann's dependence on his analysis vis-à-vis the historical situation.

historically. The hermeneutical circle, consequently, applies to the interpreter and his past as well as to the interpreter and the text.[79]

In carrying this analysis forward, there is the initial handicap, which needs sorely to be remedied, that biblical criticism has not been sufficiently interrogated with respect to its wider historical and epochal nexus, and further that it has not developed sufficient transcendence to be able to read its own internal development historically for the period just ended.[80] This deficiency notwithstanding, it is necessary to probe that development tentatively as a means of elucidating the point.

Biblical theology[81] began by having to challenge the very basis in which it rested, *viz.*, the orthodox doctrine of verbal inspiration.[82] The

---

79. The hermeneutical circle as defined by Erich Dinkler, "Existentialist Interpretation of the New Testament," *JR* 32 (1952): 87–96, and "Principles of Biblical Interpretation," *Journal of Religious Thought* 13 (1955–1956): 20–30, refers to the relationship between interpreter and text: the interpreter brings a question to the text, listens to what the text has to say, corrects his question, and begins again. To this circle is added the historical circle, i.e., setting the text in its historical nexus. While acknowledged in principle by Bultmann and Dinkler, the correction that is being urged here appears to be a widespread deficiency in existentialist hermeneutic in that it merely assumes the relevance and body of the question arising from the existentialist analysis.

80. Bultmann's appendix to his *New Testament Theology*; Ebeling's programmatic essay, "Significance of the Critical Historical Method," 17–61; his essay on biblical theology, "Meaning of 'Biblical Theology,'" 79–97; and the article "Hermeneutik," *RGG* 3:242–62, provide broad internal assessments. Cf. Emil Kraeling, *The Old Testament Since the Reformation* (New York: Harper & Row, 1955). The American development has received very little attention. Amos N. Wilder has opened up the question of the difference in Continental and American traditions for the development of biblical theology in a pair of essays: Wilder, "New Testament Theology in Transition," in *The Study of Bible Today and Tomorrow*, ed. H. R. Willoughby (Chicago: University of Chicago Press, 1947), 419–36; Wilder, "Biblical Hermeneutic and American Scholarship," in *Neutestamentliche Studien für Rudolf Bultmann*, ed. Walther Eltester (Berlin: Töpelmann, 1954), 24–32. Cf. C. T. Craig, "Biblical Theology and the Rise of Historicism," *JBL* 72 (1953): 281–94. J. Coert Rylaarsdam has written a provocative essay, "The Problem of Faith and History in Biblical Interpretation," *JBL* 77 (1958): 26–32, in which he raises the question of the destiny of biblical criticism. Of particular interest is the suggestion that certain historical disciplines were developed in the service of orthodoxy, while others appear to have been the outcome of certain liberal perspectives. He identifies the vitality of biblical scholarship as its ability to transcend theological systems (31).

81. It is not necessary here to distinguish between biblical theology as a historical discipline and historical criticism.

82. Ebeling, "Meaning of 'Biblical Theology,'" 89.

challenge was necessitated by the desire to break the effective control of dogmatics over the interpretation of Scripture and thus to establish biblical theology as a historical discipline. Having abandoned its fundamental connection to dogmatics, it could now pursue its own course independently as biblical criticism. Nevertheless, that course was determined in no small measure by its repeated need to justify itself by producing new and more devastating criticisms of the orthodox view.[83] In America at the turn of the century this need was still operative, for example, in the program of the Chicago School.[84] The writings of S. J. Case illustrate very well the tenacity with which biblical criticism has remained true to its initial thrust.[85] In the course of the development, however, biblical criticism

---

83. Ebeling, "Meaning of 'Biblical Theology,'" 88–89.

84. It may be conceded that there was good reason to revitalize the attack in reaction against fundamentalism.

85. In *The Historicity of Jesus* (Chicago: University of Chicago Press, 1912; 2nd ed., 1928), Shirley Jackson Case makes the observation that liberal theology believes that religious knowledge is no longer supernaturally acquired, which means it can no longer rely "upon some record of a supposedly supernatural revelation...." (7). Reason and human experience have been made fundamental (7ff.). This point is made again, this time on his own authority, in Case, *The Evolution of Early Christianity* (Chicago: University of Chicago Press, 1914), e.g., 4–5, and then expanded in *The Social Origins of Christianity* (Chicago: University of Chicago Press, 1923) in a chapter entitled "The 'New' New Testament Study," 1–37. The upshot of liberal criticism is that "the quest for a normative result was gradually abandoned, and the past was allowed to go its own way independently of present-day needs and interest" (35–36). The programmatic essay which introduced the new *Journal of Religion*, "The Historical Study of Religion," *JR* 1 (1921): 1–17, strikes the note that "belief in the normative function of history rests ultimately up on that pessimistic philosophy of life which interprets the present as a deterioration of humanity, a condition to be remedied only by the restoration of an idealized past.... But when history is viewed scientifically, as an evolutionary process in human living, the past inevitably loses its authoritative character" (14). The same note has grown stronger by 1943 in *The Christian Philosophy of History* (Chicago: University of Chicago Press, 1943) partially in reaction to dialectical theology which Case believes is not primarily interested in history (94). It is of interest to compare Case's 1921 essay in *JR* with essays by F. C. Porter, "The Historical and the Spiritual Understanding of the Bible," and B. W. Bacon, "New Testament Science as a Historical Discipline," in the Yale memorial volume, *Education for Christian Service* (New Haven: Yale University Press, 1922), 19–48, 77–79. Bacon, for example, affirms that "the development of criticism has been quite as truly under divine direction as the fixation of the canon" (95), and "the New Testament ... is a book which *enforces* criticism" (99), yet he is concerned to show, as the title of his chair indicates (New Tes-

tended to obscure its critical function vis-à-vis itself and became, as a result, increasingly dogmatic at those points where it thought it was least dogmatic.[86] In the struggle against the doctrine of the verbal inspiration of Scripture the question of the function of Scripture got misplaced and then lost in the equally dogmatic proposition that the past can have no normative function for the present.[87] When this question is reopened, e.g., by Barth and Bultmann, the biblical criticism that was shaped by the older conflict cannot help but misunderstand the new form of the question, and hence finds itself critically sterile.

To return to the question with which we began, the interpreter must interrogate the text from a particular locus in history, i.e., from his own present as it is in formed and shaped by the past. Historical criticism as an integral element in the interpretation of the text is subject to preunderstanding. But the preunderstanding that is brought to the text is itself (both humanly and) historically situated and must itself be submitted to historical criticism. The full circularity of question/text has to be

---

tament Criticism and Interpretation), that historical criticism may be utilized to bring men "into vital contact with the eternal Word" (107). E. F. Scott, too, is concerned to expose the limitations of the historical method in "The Limitations of the Historical Method," in *Studies in Early Christianity*, ed. S. J. Case (New York: Century, 1928), 3–18, but he implies that it may well be invoked against false notions of revelation (3ff.). There is also the possibility that it may provide a kind of apologetic in reverse (5). The differences between Chicago and New England are significant in illuminating the shape of the opponent in the struggle of historical criticism for ascendancy. It may be said that Chicago has the better of the debate in carrying through the radical historicity of the text, while the Easterners are concerned not to let the question of revelation get lost. Under the duress of orthodoxy and fundamentalism it was perhaps impossible for the hermeneutical question to emerge.

86. Ebeling, "Meaning of 'Biblical Theology,'" 88–89.

87. Cf. Case, *Christian Philosophy of History*: "Revelation is thus only what every sincere religious man believes to be divine truth, and it is capable of as much variation as marks the life and thinking of different persons living under different conditions in the various periods of history" (170); "... heritages from the past will justify their right to survive only by the measure of their functional value in the experience of the continuing Christian society" (183). What is at stake for Case is the ideality of the past as opposed to the ideality of the future (see 158ff.). Attention has been called to the strange similarity of "modernism" and fundamentalism in rejecting the historical basis of the Christian faith, the former deliberately, the latter unconsciously. Cf. John Dillenberger and Claude Welch, *Protestant Christianity* (New York: Scribner's Sons, 1954), 226–27.

taken with seriousness and not circumvented by the attempt to derive a preunderstanding from outside of history. In relation to biblical criticism, it can be said that every critical effort must presuppose the history of its own development.[88] The exposition of its own history is subject to the same principles that apply to the biblical text. At this juncture the intimate relation between biblical criticism and the history of theology becomes evident.

Bultmann and Fuchs have rightly insisted that the subjectobject schema is invalid for historical knowledge, that the latter is never closed because a historical event is known only by its future.[89] If the meaning of historical events is disclosed ever anew in the future by the way in which they are reappropriated, it becomes all the more apparent that historical criticism has as its primary function the thwarting of the tyranny of the question. But what does this mean in view of the assertion that it is only by means of some question that the interpreter can interrogate history at all? The interrogation of history would be a deceptive mental exercise unless the past is encountered in its own integrity, and this means unless the preunderstanding that is brought to it is subject to criticism from the standpoint of that past. But the past is not something "out there" which can be confronted, say, as a tree or a mountain; it is embodied in historical texts and monuments, in the individual and collective memory both conscious and unconscious, in the way it functions in the present either as a fate or as a creative possibility for the future. Historical criticism must, therefore, function as the probing of the present in such a way that the past is released from its appropriation by the present in distorted form. For every appropriation of the past, while it may lay hold of truth, effects at the same time the exclusion of other possibilities. The fresh appropriation of the past, therefore, is a recurring task in the service of which historical criticism must be placed. Historical criticism, then, can function only in relation to a particular appropriation of the past, and it must always function critically in relation to that appropriation if it is to

---

88. There is regrettable deficiency in this respect in the majority of modern works. Even where such histories are provided, as often in older studies, they are descriptive rather than analytical, and far too narrowly conceived. There are, of course, instances where the assessment of the development is obvious though not set out explicitly.

89. Rudolf Bultmann, *History and Eschatology* (Edinburgh: Edinburgh University Press, 1957), 120ff.; Bultmann, *Glauben und Verstehen*, 2:1, 148, 149–50; Fuchs, *Zur Frage nach dem historischen Jesus*, 227ff., 283–84.

fulfill its vocation. To let history speak for itself means to let it speak critically with reference to the present grasp of history, and thus in a way that is relevant to the present.

Bibliography

Bacon, B. W. "New Testament Science as a Historical Discipline." Pages 77–109 in *Education for Christian Service*. New Haven: Yale University Press, 1922.

Berger, Peter. *The Precarious Vision*. Garden City, NY: Doubleday, 1961.

Blass, Friedrich, and Albert Debrunner. *A Greek Grammar of the New Testament and Other Early Christian Literature*. Translated and revised by Robert W. Funk. Chicago: University of Chicago Press, 1961.

Bornkamm, G. *Die Vorgeschichte des sogenannten Zweiten Korintherbriefes*. Heidelberg: Winter, 1961.

Bultmann, Rudolf. *Exegetische Probleme des zweiten Korintherbriefes*. SymBU 9. Darmstadt: Wissenschaftliche Buchgesellschaft, 1947.

———. *Glauben und Verstehen*. Vol. 1. Tübingen: Mohr Siebeck, 1933. 2nd ed., 1954.

———. *Glauben und Verstehen*. Vol. 2. Tübingen: Mohr Siebeck, 1952. 3rd ed., 1961. English translation in *Essays Philosophical and Theological*. Translated by C. G. Grieg. New York: Macmillan Company, 1955.

———. *Glauben und Verstehen*. Vol. 3. Tübingen: Mohr Siebeck, 1960. 2nd ed., 1962. English translation in *Existence and Faith: Shorter Writings of Rudolf Bultmann*. Translated by S. M. Ogden. New York: Meridian Books, 1960.

———. *History and Eschatology*. Edinburgh: Edinburgh University Press, 1957.

———. *Jesus Christ and Mythology*. New York: Scribner's Son, 1958.

———. *Kerygma und Mythos*. Vol. 2. Hamburg-Volksdorf: Herbert Reich, 1952. English translation: *Kerygma and Myth*. Translated by R. H. Fuller. New York: Harper & Row, 1957.

———. *Theology of the New Testament*. 3 vols. New York: Scribner's Sons, 1951–1953.

Case, Shirley Jackson. *The Christian Philosophy of History*. Chicago: University of Chicago Press, 1943.

———. *The Evolution of Early Christianity*. Chicago: University of Chicago Press, 1914.

———. "The Historical Study of Religion." *JR* 1 (1921): 1–17.

———. *The Historicity of Jesus*. Chicago: University of Chicago Press, 1912. 2nd ed., 1928.

———. "The 'New' New Testament Study." Pages 1–37 in *The Social Origins of Christianity*. Chicago: University of Chicago Press, 1923.

Craig, C. T. "Biblical Theology and the Rise of Historicism." *JBL* 72 (1953): 281–94.

Dillenberger, John, and Claude Welch. *Protestant Christianity*. New York: Scribner's Sons, 1954.

Dinkler, Erich. "Existentialist Interpretation of the New Testament." *JR* 32 (1952): 87–96.

———. "Principles of Biblical Interpretation." *Journal of Religious Thought* 13 (1955–1956): 20–30.

Ebeling, Gerhard. "Die Bedeutung der historisch-kritischen Methode für die protestantische Theologie und Kirche," *ZTK* 47 (1950): 1–46. Repr. as pages 1–49 in *Wort und Glaube*. Tübingen: Mohr Siebeck, 1960. English translation: "The Significance of the Critical Historical Method for Church and Theology in Protestantism." Pages 17–61 in *Word and Faith*. Translated by James W. Leitch. Philadelphia: Fortress, 1963.

———. "Diskussionsthesen für eine Vorlesung zur Einführung in das Studium der Theologie." Pages 447–57 in *Wort und Glaube*. Tübingen: Mohr Siebeck, 1960. English translation: "Discussion Theses for a Course of Introductory Lectures on the Study of Theology." Pages 424–33 in *Word and Faith*. Translated by James W. Leitch. Philadelphia: Fortress, 1963.

———. *Die Geschichtlichkeit der Kirche und ihrer Verkündigung als theologisches Problem*. Tübingen: Mohr Siebeck, 1954.

———. "Hauptprobleme der protestantischen Theologie in der Gegenwart." *ZTK* 58 (1961): 224–51.

———. "Hermeneutik." *RGG* 3:242–62.

———. "Jesus und Glaube." Pages 205–54 in *Wort und Glaube*. Tübingen: Mohr Siebeck, 1960. English translation: "Jesus and Faith." Pages 201–46 in *Word and Faith*. Translated by James W. Leitch. Philadelphia: Fortress, 1963.

———. "The Meaning of 'Biblical Theology.'" *JTS* 6 (1955): 210–25. Repr. pages 49–67 in *On the Authority of the Bible: Some Recent Studies by L. Hodgson, C. F. Evans, J. Burnaby, C. Ebeling and D. E. Nineham*. London: SPCK, 1960. German translation: "Was heißt 'Biblische Theologie'?" Pages 69–89 in *Wort und Glaube*. Tübingen: Mohr Siebeck,

1960. English translation: "The Meaning of 'Biblical Theology.'" Pages 79–97 in *Word and Faith*. Translated by James W. Leitch. Philadelphia: Fortress, 1963.

———. "Die 'nicht-religiöse Interpretation biblischer Begriffe.'" Pages 90–160 in *Wort und Glaube*. Tübingen: Mohr Siebeck, 1960. English translation: "The 'Non-religious Interpretation of Biblical Concepts.'" Pages 98–161 in *Word and Faith*. Translated by James W. Leitch. Philadelphia: Fortress, 1963.

———. *Theologie und Verkündigung: Hermeneutische Untersuchungen zur Theologie*. Vol. 1. Tübingen: Mohr Siebeck, 1962.

———. *Das Wesen des Christlichen Glaubens*. Tübingen: Mohr Siebeck, 1959. English translation by R. G. Smith. *The Nature of Faith*. London: Collins, 1961.

Fackenheim, Emil L. *Metaphysics and Historicity*. Milwaukee: Marquette University Press, 1961.

Fuchs, D. Ernst. *Hermeneutik*. Bad Cannstatt: Müllerschön Verlag, 1954. 2nd ed., 1958.

———. *Zum hermeneutischen Problem in der Theologie: Die existentiale Interpretation*. Tübingen: Mohr Siebeck, 1959.

———. *Zur Frage nach dem historischen Jesus*. Tübingen: Mohr Siebeck, 1960.

Grobel, Kendrick. "Bultmann's Problem of New Testament 'Mythology.'" *JBL* 70 (1951): 99–103.

———. "The Practice of Demythologizing." *JBR* 27 (1959): 28–31.

Harland, Gordon. "The American Protestant Heritage and the Theological Task." *Drew Gateway* (Winter 1962): 71–93.

Heidegger, M. *Sein und Zeit*. 9th ed. Tübingen: Niemeyer Verlag, 1960. English translation: *Being and Time*. Translated by J. Macquarrie and E. Robinson. London: SCM, 1962.

Jeremias, J. *The Parables of Jesus*. New York: Scribner's Sons, 1955.

Kasernann, Ernst. "Die Legitimität des Apostels: Eine Untersuchung zu II Korinther 10–13." *ZNW* 41 (1942): 33–71.

Kraeling, Emil. *The Old Testament Since the Reformation*. New York: Harper & Row, 1955.

Langan, Thomas. *The Meaning of Heidegger*. New York: Columbia University Press, 1959.

Maritain, Jacques. *Rouault*. Pocket Library of Great Art. New York: Abrams, 1954.

Oberman, Heiko. *Christianity Divided: Protestant and Roman Catholic Theological Issues.* Edited by D. J. Callahan, Heiko Oberman, and D. J. O'Hanlon. New York: Sheed & Ward, 1961.

Ogden, S. M. *Christ without Myth.* New York: Harper & Row, 1961.

Porter, F. C. "The Historical and the Spiritual Understanding of the Bible." Pages 19–48 in *Education for Christian Service.* New Haven: Yale University Press, 1922.

Robinson, James M. "Basic Shifts in German Theology." *Int* 16 (1962): 76–97.

———. "The Historicality of Biblical Language." Pages 150–58 in *The Old Testament and the Christian Faith.* Edited by Bernhard W. Anderson. New York: Harper & Row, 1963.

Rylaarsdam, J. Coert, "The Problem of Faith and History in Biblical Interpretation." *JBL* 77 (1958): 26–32.

Schmithals, W. *Die Gnosis in Korinth: Eine Untersuchung zu den Korintherbriefen.* Göttingen: Vandenhoeck & Ruprecht, 1956.

Schweizer, Eduard. *Lordship and Discipleship.* London: SCM, 1960. Translation of *Erniedrigung und Erhöhung bei Jesus und seinen Nachfolgern.* Zürich: Zwingli, 1955.

Scott, E. F. "The Limitations of the Historical Method." Pages 3–18 in *Studies in Early Christianity.* Edited by S. J. Case. New York: Century, 1928.

Stendahl, K. "Kerygma und kerygmatisch." *ThLZ* 77 (1952): 715–20.

Wilckens, U. *Weisheit und Torheit: Eine exegetisch-religionsgeschichtliche Untersuchung zu I Kor. I und 2.* Tübingen: Mohr Siebeck, 1959.

Wilder, Amos N. "Biblical Hermeneutic and American Scholarship." Pages 24–32 in *Neutestamentliche Studien für Rudolf Bultmann.* Edited by Walther Eltester. Berlin: Töpelmann, 1954.

———. "New Testament Theology in Transition." Pages 419–36 in *The Study of Bible Today and Tomorrow.* Edited by H. R. Willoughby. Chicago: University of Chicago Press, 1947.

Language, Hermeneutic, and the Vocation of the Word

Robert W. Funk

> You brood of vipers! how can you speak good, when you are evil? For out of the abundance of the heart the mouth speaks. The good man out of his good treasure brings forth good, and the evil man out of his evil treasure brings forth evil. I tell you, on the day of judgment men will render account for every careless word they utter for by your words you will be judged, and by your words you will be condemned.
>
> —Matt 12:34–37 (RSV)

The text gives warrant for taking speech seriously. It commends care in the use of words. It makes language the basis upon which men are called to account. Such deference for speech may be understood as aimed at the thoughtless and reprehensible use of unseemly and profane expressions. It may be taken as a call to avoid offensive language of all kinds, to make judicious use of words in every relationship between man and man. It may be interpreted more formally, as the concern for premeditation and precision in discourse. While one or all of these may be implied in the text, it is a question whether observing the proprieties and consulting the dictionary will in themselves constitute a satisfactory accounting for the use of language.

The text indicates that speech is linked with the abundance of the heart or lack of it, with the vision of truth or blindness of spirit out of which speech proceeds. Care for language is thus not a matter merely of the propitious use of words. Furthermore, speech itself involves the ear upon which speech falls. Because speech is something which is heard as well as spoken it is possible to call its articulator to account for words carelessly uttered. Language enters into the history, personal and collective, of man and shapes it for better or for worse; it simultaneously creates understanding and incomprehension, it binds together and it rends asunder. The constellation to which speech belongs, then, invariably has two poles, enunciation and audition, each of which sustains its own relation to language and bears, at the same time, responsibility for the other through speech.

Since the ear and the mouth, which are the two parties to speech, normally belong to different persons, language is understood as communication. One person seeks, through language, to convey something to another. The minimal condition for communication, therefore, is language that is already understood: understanding can take place only where language is previously understood. And so editors and advertisers, journalists and politicians, teachers and popular poets endeavor to confine experience and thought to domesticated language. Use comprehensible language, we are told, and communication must follow as the night the day.

It is doubtless the case that language sets the limits for understanding. Is it not possible, nevertheless, that experience and thought occasionally press the limits of conventional speech and spill over? That language already understood is sometimes inadequate to what is to be understood? In that case the language that sets the limits for understanding is not common parlance, but an idiosyncratic language or even a language as yet unborn. The authentic poet, for example, may be understood as one who has crossed the frontier of conventional parlance into uncharted linguistic terrain: he is seeking to hear, as it were, and to articulate for himself that which has not yet come to expression. In his case ear and mouth are united in the same person, but the responsibility of enunciation and audition to each other is no less for that.

When language is pressed to its limits, it is discovered that speech is more than words or even content of words, that it is more than sentences composed of subject and predicate. If the problem of communication lay only in words and sentences, the speaker or writer, if he wished to be understood, could provide a glossary and a grammar. Or another person, who understood what was being said, could translate. Perhaps there could be several translations from one into the same or different languages. But what would translation achieve if the subject matter spoken about were not understood? And how can understanding take place without understandable language? And if there is understandable language as a means of understanding, then is translation necessary at all? Does this not suggest that without previously understood language no understanding could take place?

Common parlance appears to presuppose a common, view of reality: two people can talk with understanding about the same thing because they share the reality being talked about. Communication presupposes understanding, however imperfectly, of a common subject matter. Non-understanding and misunderstanding therefore arise where language does not refer to a common subject matter—where speaker and hearer, writer and reader, do not participate in a common reality with reference to which meaningful discourse can be created. The problem posed by language may thus turn finally on whether common understanding precedes and makes meaningful speech possible. Put this way, it would seem that language is an epiphenomenon dependent on shared experience and joint understanding. This formulation obviously converts the previous suggestion that understanding depends upon language.

These considerations, then, suggest that the problem to be resolved is whether a common, understandable language depends upon a prior joint understanding, or whether joint understanding is dependent upon a previously understood language. To formulate the problem as a question of priority is to make evident that resolution is impossible. Such a formulation, moreover, obscures the root issue. In pressing the question, consequently, these two ways of putting the matter should be juxtaposed as a means of discovering what bearing they have on each other.

The initial difficulty is that the problem to be spoken *about*, namely, speech, is bound up *with* the mode of language that must be employed in speaking about it. The problem of language can apparently be addressed only by means of more language. The problem of language has to be raised out of language as it is used and understood, into language as it is not used and understood. So long as that further language does not break out of the plane of language which constitutes the locus of the problem, the discussion will fall prey to itself—that is, to language as already understood. At the same time, any discussion of language must proceed from and in relation to language as it is known, used, experienced. The old house of language is to be dismantled and its materials used to build the new. Meanwhile, there is no place to dwell, no place to carry on the conversation, except in the old house.

Consider the artist who has before him a blank canvas. He has at his disposal the technical skills requisite to his craft and a tradition which stretches as far back as the Stone Age. The picture in his mind—the one he aspires to put on canvas—will not be the product merely of skills plus tradition. Skills and tradition are the basis of his work, but in the execution of the painting he is placing his skills and his knowledge of the tradition in the service of a tradition which is yet to be. The picture is there, in his mind, only by anticipation; the painting itself, if successful, will disclose to his own mind what he aspired to paint. It is this *out of* what is at one's disposal *into* what is not at one's disposal that constitutes the trajectory of creative art.

The "language of language" is analogous to the "language" of art. In confronting the problem of language one has to aspire to what is *not* at his disposal (an understanding, a language) on the basis of what *is* at his disposal (an understanding, a language). Out of language as it is understood, out of joint understanding, is to be won new language and new understanding. The new has to be projected onto possibilities which lie beyond the frontiers of common language and joint understanding. Only so can the new be genuinely new.

It has been noticed that common language and joint understanding go together in such a way that it is impossible to determine which is prior. This is because language conceals a commonly understood way of looking at things, and a commonly understood way of looking at things fosters sedimentation in language. Language and understanding give birth to each other; they also hold each other captive. A tradition is a common language and a joint understanding held in solution. A tradition falters when language and understanding are divorced.

It may be said, then, that the common reality which makes meaningful speech possible precedes speech in the sense that it is the reference, as yet unavailable to the common understanding, upon which creative speech is projected. It is the picture which is in the artist's mind only by anticipation. This common reality follows speech, however, in the sense that it becomes audible only as meaningful discourse is created. The picture in the artist's mind becomes visible, to himself and to others, only as it is put on canvas. The before-after relationship, since it must be taken both ways around, can best be expressed as simultaneity or reciprocity. Language and understanding arise together, are reciprocal. The common reality to which they refer both precedes and follows. It makes them possible, and yet the common reality does not become audible without language and understanding. Language and understanding both arise out of and invoke shared reality.

These reflections have now and then touched upon the subject of "reality." It was said, for example, that nonunderstanding and misunderstanding arise when speaker and hearer do not participate in a common reality. Is there any reality other than that which all men have in common? Is it not necessary to affirm a single, univocal reality, which is "out there," external to language and thought? However this may be, it is indisputable that reality can be and is disputed. Rational beings disagree about what is "really real."

If language and understanding are taken to be fully reciprocal, if they arise together, to what shall their rise (and decline) be attributed? To language invented on a whim? To capricious understanding? To the willful creation of rational thought? In any case, language and understanding are taken to be the product of human artifice. Some means must then be contrived in order to test whether language and understanding do in fact have reference to reality, whether they are "true." T. R. Miles has argued that philosophy, when properly understood has the task of contriving just such tests. On this view philosophy is a second-order activity which comes into play only when someone has already made a first-order assertion.[1] The philosopher waits on somebody to say something, and then he endeavors to decide whether what has been said is true or false. Philosophy, of course, does not depend upon a single criterion, or even a set of criteria, but endeavors to discover criteria appropriate to various forms of discourse. This type of philosophy is known as functional linguistic analysis.

The point to be made over against functional linguistic analysis is that a second-order linguistic activity does not have adequate resources to enable it to arbitrate over first-order linguistic activity so long as it (1) confines itself to the "logic" already implicit in the language it is submitting to analysis, or (2) refers that language to the "logic" of some other order of discourse in order to determine the issue. Philosophy must itself investigate the grounds of first-order language if it wishes to dispute language and/or reality.

To put the matter abruptly, language and understanding have to be made to recoil upon the reality to which they allegedly refer. If common language and joint understanding presuppose a shared reality, the failure of language and understanding betoken the failure of that reality. Tradition fails because the reality, which has supported it fails. In such a time, it is incumbent upon those who care for language and understanding to attend to the disjuncture between them and reality, and to attend to the reality that is striving to impress itself upon language and understanding.

---

1. T. R. Miles, *Religion and the Scientific Outlook* (London: Allen & Unwin, 1959), 63.

The reciprocity of language and understanding has to be grasped in relation to the question of the "real."

It was remarked that a tradition fails when language and understanding are divorced. A divorce of this order follows upon the disintegration of the reality to which understanding refers, while conventional language lags behind experience. "Understanding" in that case is a kind of not-knowing and not-having what language promises. Language goes dead when it forecloses rather than discloses understanding. On the other hand, understanding remains a not-knowing until language comes to its rescue. And both of them linger in limbo until the "real" breaks through the limitations set by the reciprocal dependence of language and understanding. Who knows what "worlds" lie buried behind our very eyes, under the rubble of countless language traditions!

* * *

Since the essays that follow are about language and written in language, the foregoing considerations have some bearing on how they are written and how they are to be read. These several studies are attempts to enter upon possibilities arising out of a disposition toward language as it is experienced and used today. This disposition is itself informed by various analyses of language, which are trained on both contemporary (part 1) and biblical (parts 2 and 3) language. Disposition and analysis from a circle, hopefully a spiraling and not a vicious one.

The problem language presents is keenly sensed in many quarters in contemporary theology. Because it has become problematical whether the Christian message can be addressed to contemporary man in meaningful terms, the language of theology has itself come into dispute. The bearing which word of God and theological language have on each other will be the underlying theme of part 1. The justification for attending to biblical language is that the disposition to language reflected in biblical language may afford some perspective on the problem of language as it is experienced today. It is possible that biblical language, if interrogated properly, will also shed some light on the relation of language to the question of the "real."

[Cross-references in this essay are to parts 1, 2, and 3 of Robert W Funk, *Language, Hermeneutic, and Word of God: The Problem of Language in the New Testament and Contemporary Theology* (New York: Harper & Row, 1966). —Ed.]

The essays presented here doubtless lack overt and "logical" coherence. While each may be read by itself, without reference to the others, the collection turns on a center as yet unfocalized. An element in the disposition, mentioned above, is a "soft focus" on the problem. A "soft focus" requires that the circumference and contours of the issue be permitted to emerge along with its center. The effort is made to allow the problem to present itself—to listen aggressively to what various modes of language are saying with reference to themselves. It will come as no surprise that the work lacks a definitive conclusion. My aim has been to uncover the problem and some clues pointing to its resolution by attempting to sketch a picture, or rather a series of pictures, I know only by anticipation.

Much of what is written doubtless stands in need of translation. Did it not require translation, it would not, perhaps, have had to be written. But into what can it be translated? It can be fairly demanded only that other pictures be drawn—perhaps an endless succession—each of which would suffer from the same deficiency, but the total impact of which might evoke understanding. In that event translation would become superfluous because translation would have taken place. The reader may bear in mind that other pictures have been and are being drawn by litterateurs, philosophers, and theologians, pictures which have founded and already considerably extended the series. To this series the present work aspires only to make a modest contribution.

These essays invite the reader not to founder on the words and sentences. The "logic" does not aspire to a rigid dialectic. What is to be listened for is what is struggling to come to expression. If it is borne in mind that something is being talked about which requires a deformation of our common speech, and thus our way of looking at reality it may be possible to accord imprecise language a certain latitude. In any case, it is a curious not-knowing and not-having that is seeking its way into the clarity of expression.

It has already been intimated that this work has the vocation of the word ultimately in view. Vocation of the word may be understood either as the call of the word, its summons (subjective genitive), or as the task (vocation as calling) of articulating, proclaiming the word that summons (objective genitive). The reader may take it in either way, since hearing and speaking, attending and articulating, are taken to be coconstitutive: they are reciprocally enabling. He who aspires to the enunciation of the word must first learn to hear it; and he who hears the word will have found the means to articulate it.

It is not, however, to the hearing of the word nor its enunciation that these studies are immediately devoted. They reflect, rather, on language and hermeneutic as they enter into hearing and speaking. Such reflection makes it necessary to draw near hearing and speaking in order to "listen in" on the process to participate, as it were, with a side glance at what is going on.

The word that is heard and spoken, spoken and heard, in the context of Christian theology, is called word of God. The subject matter of these essays is thus the Christian gospel. It is to the articulation of this word that the ministry of the church is called, and the pulpit is understood as the place where its enunciation takes place. Since the subject matter is word of God, it is appropriate to begin with some preliminary reflections on language, hermeneutic, and word of God as they bear directly on the vocation of the church's ministry. In this way the diverse perspectives from which the matter is subsequently viewed can be focused at the outset on the concrete issue of the proclamation of the word. This procedure may be welcomed by those to whom the terrain of contemporary hermeneutic is still largely unexplored, since these brief remarks bring together, in a practical way, themes which are later elaborated in a maze of detail. It is to be hoped that a practical introduction to a more abstruse discussion will not disappoint those who prefer a concise theoretical introduction to a more extended practical treatment.

1.

This has been described as a time of the death of God.[2] The affirmation of the death of God is neither a scientific nor a philosophical assertion, but a *confession*, a confession that God is no longer "there," no longer available. It is useless to contest the point unless it is understood that the affirmation of the existence of God is not the contradiction of the death of God. The religious affirmation of God's reality, from the point of view of the death of God, is neither here nor there: it is simply irrelevant.

The testimony to the death of God bears witness to a correlative tragedy, namely, the failure of language. It is possible to claim that God has withdrawn only because man can no longer speak authentically of him.

---

2. Cf. Rudolf Bultmann, "The Idea of God and Modern Man," *JThC* 2 (1965): 83–95, where further references may be found.

When God disappears, man falls silent. He falls silent in spite of the fact that he may even talk more. His talk, under the circumstances, becomes mere verbalization, vain prattle without ultimate reference. One may talk of God, to be sure, even affirm his existence or speak of his attributes, but such talk, if prattle, betrays its own emptiness and becomes inverted testimony to the death of God. This is the basis on which the observation is made that the religious affirmation of God's existence is at least irrelevant, at most testimony against itself.

If our specific concern is with the language of faith, with the message of reconciliation, with the proclamation of the gospel, it is not too much to say that the question of reality and language has everything to do with that concern. It is averred by those from whom one has a right to expect more than idle opinions that the preaching of the gospel has taken on the character of prattle. This means that the preached word no longer proceeds out of the reality to which it is supposed to give expression. "How can you speak good, when you are evil?" When preaching consists of words split off from the reality of grace, it has been reduced to talk. Under such circumstances, not only is God dead, but Christ, too, remains an inert figure in the tomb. It may therefore be said: the gospel is not really being preached because its claim is not being heard. If that sounds as though it has the matter backward, it is an intentional reversal: the articulation of the gospel depends upon the reality to which it refers becoming audible in language. The failure of language is commensurate with the disappearance of the reality to which it refers. To put it succinctly, when the language of faith fails, it is because faith itself has failed. Or, conversely, when the word of God invokes faith, man responds in the language that bears the reality of faith. When God is silent, man becomes a gossip; when God speaks and man hears, kerygmatic language is born, and the gospel is preached.

There is no intention to argue the case for the failure of preaching in our time. Such an argument would itself be idle. The failure of preaching will not and cannot be demonstrated or even discovered until the gospel is apprehended afresh, in which case the need for argument will have ceased. In short, the only course ever open to those who are concerned with the proclamation of the gospel, whether or not they believe this is a time of the failure of the word of faith, is to learn to listen as never before, with ears sharply tuned for the tones that are suspected of having fallen on deaf ears; to seek to hear the silent tolling of grace as it echoes faintly from the traditional language of the church. Perhaps then, by some miracle, the sacred trust of the gospel, which comes not according to man nor from man, but through a revelation of Jesus Christ (Gal 1:2), may be granted to this time and place.

The vital nerve of the hermeneutical problem—to introduce now the catchword—is therefore the failure of language. The failure of language as it relates to preaching, is correlative with deafness, with insensibility to the word which God has spoken in Christ. If this fundamental connection between hearing and speaking, between reality and language, can be made clear, the relation of the hermeneutical problem to the minister's task will have been grasped. It will have been understood that the minister's work is essentially hermeneutical.

2.

It is perhaps advisable to clear away some of the common misunderstandings which attach to the term hermeneutics, if indeed that term is any longer comprehensible at all.[3] Hermeneutics is traditionally conceived as the theory of which exegesis is the practice, i.e., has to do with the rules for the interpretation of scripture. Of the elements involved in the interpretation of a text—i.e., the text, the interpreter, the interpretation, and the rules governing interpretation—hermeneutics in its classical form concentrates on the last. With the rise of modern scientific biblical study, hermeneutics was gradually replaced by the critical historical method, now nearly universally known and practiced, and hermeneutics as a special subdivision of theology dropped out of sight.

Historical criticism as the modern counterpart to hermeneutics insisted, and rightly so, on applying to the biblical text the same rules that were used in the interpretation of other documents. It was under the tutelage of the historical method that the integrity of the text was discovered, and it is by this method that the victory over rigid allegedly literalistic orthodoxies was achieved. Nevertheless, the historical method was seriously deficient at one point: it failed to take into account the limitations and biases of the interpreter. It was to remedy this deficiency that Rudolf

---

3. For an extensive and illuminating discussion of the history and components of hermeneutics, see James M. Robinson and John B. Cobb, eds., *New Frontiers in Theology: The New Hermeneutic*, vol. 2. (New York: Harper & Row, 1964), 1–77. *Hermeneutics* (plural) is used to refer to the traditional discipline, *hermeneutic* (singular) to the subject as it has been reintroduced into the current discussion, in accordance with Robinson's practice (x).

Bultmann taking his lead from Schleiermacher and Dilthey, added the existential dimension to the historical-critical method. Under Bultmann hermeneutic came to embrace all the elements involved in the interpretation of a text.

The presupposition that underlies the whole development from the rise of modern biblical criticism to Bultmann is that when one does exegesis one is interpreting the *text*. That is, it is the text that requires interpretation. Yet from historical criticism it had already been learned that the biblical text, like any other text, is composed of human language and is therefore culturally conditioned. It was but a short step to the conclusion that the New Testament is only a relative statement of the word of God. It was not until Barth's commentary on Romans that the force of this discovery began to be felt: if the text is a human word and therefore historically conditioned, it is not the text that is the word of God but the text itself is already the *interpretation* of the word of God. Barth's methodology, as he describes it in the preface to the second edition of the *Römerbrief*, is to live with the text until it disappears and one is confronted with the divine word itself. One sees emerging here the view that it is not the text that is to be interpreted—the text is already interpretation—but the word of God itself, which, of course, cannot be equated with any human formulation.

If it is God's word that is the object of exegetical endeavors, the process is at a dead end, for this word is not accessible to the exegete as an object for scrutiny. Yet this blind alley is precisely what led Gerhard Ebeling and Ernst Fuchs to the conclusion, remarkable as it may sound, that the word of God is not interpreted—it interprets. That is to say, it is indeed the word rather than the words with which exegetes have ultimately to do, but since they are in the embarrassing position of being unable to lay hold of that word they can only permit it to lay hold of them. With this startling insight the direction of the flow between interpreter and text that has dominated modern biblical criticism from its inception is reversed, and hermeneutics in its traditional sense becomes hermeneutic, now understood as the effort to allow God to address man through the medium of the text.

It is precisely the assumption, endemic to the modern period, that man is the subject to which all things, including the word of God, must give account that led to the failure of language, and thus to disintegration of the language of faith. Implicit in the broader phenomenon is the assumption that the text is the object of interpretation; as "object" the text simply falls silent. The consequence has been the debilitation if not the collapse of preaching.

With man as the filter through which the word must pass, or, if you like, arbiter of the meaning of the word, it is inevitable that he will censor out what he does not wish to hear and audit only what he is predisposed to hear. Yet the word of God, like a great work of art, is not on trial. The work of art exists in its own right, to be viewed and contemplated, received or dismissed, but not reconstructed. The text, too, although shaped by human hands, stands there to be read and pondered, but not manipulated. With respect to the edifices in which men dwell, the late Winston Churchill once remarked, "We shape our buildings, and thereafter they shape us."[4] The view of hermeneutics which begins with the assumption that the text requires interpretation, that it is, so to speak, on trial, has the matter backward. It is not the text that requires interpretation, but—if the text is called forth by what it says—the interpreter! This reversal is what makes sense of the affirmation that the gospel is not being preached because it is not being heard.

Such an understanding of hermeneutic by no means vitiates the affirmation that the only authentic access to the true word which God has spoken in Christ is through the New Testament. Nor does it undercut the crucial function of the critical-historical method. On the contrary, this view allows both to come into their own.

It may be rejoined that the affirmation that the gospel is not being preached because it is not being heard scarcely needs elaboration. It is a matter which every conscientious minister understands well, and which the church has never forgotten. A look into the textbooks on homiletics, the church papers, and best sermons of the year is ample demonstration. But the issue cannot be contested in this way. The question being posed is not about what one says he does or ought to do, but about whether the language of the proclamation goes together with the reality of faith like new wine and fresh skins (Mark 2:22). It is the question whether the words spoken from the pulpit and in the counseling chamber carry with them the reality of God's redemptive grace. It is the question whether the sermon gives presence to the Christ for both speaker and hearer. It is a matter of determining whether preaching any longer refers to anything real, or whether it merely continues to traffic in words and concepts which have long since been dashed to pieces on the rocks of a profane world.

The threat to the preaching ministry of the church is that it *thinks* it has not forgotten that hearing and speaking are correlative, that it *thinks* it

---

4. Quoted by Roy W. Larson in the *Christian Advocate* 9.3 (February 11, 1965): 15.

has not forgotten what word of God says when heard. Those who mount the pulpit Sunday in and Sunday out before a sea of people are inclined to sail their ships into the harbor of Pharisaic intransigence. They do so, of course, in the interest of a firm anchorage. It is there, however, that one can forget and then forget that one has forgotten. One cannot remember because one cannot remember forgetting. The horizon of the sea has become the mouth of the harbor.

Only as the memory is refreshed by the silent tolling of a largely vacuous language is it possible to recall that at one time, somewhere in the collective past, one ceased to hear. Therein lies the subtlety of the dilemma: those concerned for the renewal of the world cannot remind each other until someone is himself reminded, until someone is again addressed by the text of faith in such a way that hearing is restored.

3.

It has been assumed that the vocation of the minister is to "preach Christ crucified, a stumbling-block to Jews and folly to Gentiles, but to those who are called, both Jews and Greeks, Christ the power of God and the wisdom of God" (1 Cor 1:23–24 RSV). That the minister as the servant of Christ is "the aroma of Christ among those who are being saved and among those who are perishing, to one a fragrance from death to death, to the other a fragrance from life to life" (2 Cor 2:15–16 RSV). The Pauline formulation may well meet some resistance in the American tradition with its strong activist leanings. If so, it is because the relation between word and deed has not been properly understood. The word to be spoken is not mere word, but the word that creates, brings into being. Like the word spoken in creation, it is the word that brings man from death to life or the word that condemns. By it men are lost, and by it men are saved. It is the word spoken in the name and therefore in the authority of God.

Such a word need not, of course, be phonetic. It may be a gesture, a deed, or even silence.[5] It is by no means limited to formal occasions on which ministers speak. Its essential characteristic is that it gives expression

---

5. The current use of the term *language* by one school of thought to cover more than vocables, i.e., more than the spoken or written word, is a metaphorical (nonliteral) use of the term. It is so used in order to call attention to a dimension of language long lost to view, viz., its event-character. On the word-character of deeds, cf. Gerhard Ebeling, "Theology and the Evidentness of the Ethical," *JThC 2* (1965): 119.

to God's Word in Christ, that it speaks or interprets or translates the meaning of the saying, "The word became flesh" (John 1:14). Such speaking, interpreting, or translating is always life-giving or death-bringing because it is the word of God coming to speech, the word which cannot fail.

This is hermeneutic as it is now understood. The hermeneut—the one who practices hermeneutic—is he who, having been addressed by the word of God and having heard, is enabled to speak, interpret, or translate what he has heard into the human, vernacular so that its power is transmitted through speech. If the minister is not a hermeneut, he has missed his vocation.

4.

Is this understanding of language and hermeneutic related in any way to the New Testament? Part 2 of this volume is devoted to a detailed examination of this question in connection with the parable of Jesus, and part 3 in connection with the letter of Paul. It will suffice here to set out briefly, the hearing of the text from which the preceding understanding of hermeneutic is derived. The concern will not be with hermeneutical theories, but with the substance of the gospel, for hermeneutic has now become the doctrine of the word of God.

The larger text for this preliminary sketch is the parables and parabolic deeds of grace to be found in the Synoptic Gospels.[6] These would include such parables as the prodigal son, the laborers in the vineyard, the great supper, the lost sheep and lost coin, the two sons, and others; among the parabolic deeds of grace the story of Zacchaeus is typical.

Parables and parabolic deeds of grace are sprinkled liberally throughout the gospel tradition. Considered as a group they reveal certain more or less constant features: (1) they are regularly addressed to, or acted out for the benefit of, Jesus's opponents; (2) they invariably cause offense to these opponents (usually designated as scribes and Pharisees); (3) they are also addressed to sinners, and normally produce joy and/or thanksgiving, either on the part of God and the angels, or on the part of the sinner who receives grace, or both.[7]

---

6. On parabolic actions, cf. J. Jeremias, *The Parables of Jesus* (New York: Scribner's Sons, 1955), 227ff.

7. On the question of audience, see ch. 5, 143ff.; ch. 6, 176–82. [Cross-references to chapters in Funk, *Language, Hermeneutic, and Word of God*. —Ed.]

All three of these features are present in the parabolic deed of grace represented by the story of Zacchaeus (Luke 19:1–10). That the context of this drama is the opposition to Jesus is indicated by the anonymous chorus of v. 7: "And when they saw it they all murmured." Making oneself a guest in the home of a chief tax collector who was rich could not help but evoke criticism. So the chorus says: "He has gone in to be the guest of a man who is a sinner." That is an exclamation of incredulity with a sharp edge of reproach. But Zacchaeus, we are told, jumped down from his perch and received him joyfully.

These three features provoke three questions: (1) Who really hears the parable of grace, or really understands the act of grace? (2) What is the affront of grace which regularly induces deafness in righteous auditors? And (3) what is the courage which joy brings that enables the sinner to overcome the affront of grace and so to hear the word spoken for him? In answering these questions we may draw on the larger tradition.

With his diverse audience in view, Jesus aims the parables of grace in three different directions: (1) he sometimes directs attention to the poor and the sinners ("I came not to call the righteous, but sinners" Mark 2:17 and parallels); (2) he sometimes invites the righteous and wealthy to consider themselves ("You brood of vipers" Matt12:34); or, (3), he may draw attention indirectly, to God ("there will be more joy in heaven over one sinner who repents than over ninety-nine righteous persons who need no repentance" Luke 15:7). But these distinctions are purely formal and tend to obscure the basic question: Who hears these parables? In the parable of the prodigal son, as it is called, there are the speaker, the father, and the three auditors: (1) the servants, (2) the elder son, and (3) the younger son. When the father sees the younger son approaching, he runs to meet him (an unbecoming act for an older Oriental), embraces him, orders a robe, ring, and shoes for him, and then crowns his welcome with a merry feast.[8] (All these eloquent deeds, incidentally, are in effect words!) Who in this circle of hearers understands these gracious and forgiving acts? Who now understands the meaning of the father's love? To ask the question borders on the trite. Nevertheless, the question pulls one up short when he understands what is being asked. For on this question the whole gospel turns.

Well then, the younger son heard. To be sure. He hears and understands the father's love. But who is the younger son? The younger son, of

---

8. For the details, see Jeremias, *Parables*, 130f.

course, is the prodigal, and that means that he is the offender, the sinner. It is the sinner who hears and understands the parables of grace. The tax collectors and harlots hear and rejoice because this grace is for them.

But is that all? Does not the older son also hear? Does he not grasp that it is *his* father whose love is reaching out to the prodigal? Does he not recall that it is *his* brother who was lost and is found? The reply is unequivocal: indeed, he does hear, and that is just the difficulty. Such grace as this, which is blind to merit, can only provoke anger. Who among elder sons can tolerate a father who is utterly without discrimination?

It has to be said that, in the primary sense, it is the sinner who hears and understands. Zacchaeus jumps down and receives Jesus with joy; the laborers hired in the eleventh hour gratefully receive the wages which they did not earn; the tax collectors and prostitutes hear him gladly. It is the sinner who hears, for he alone understands grace. But the understanding of grace is not something brought to the parables or to Jesus either by squandering oneself morally or physically or by having the right theology. No, it is something one gains from meeting grace itself. The Apostle Paul learned the meaning of grace from his status as blameless before the law! It may be said, then, that from an encounter with grace one learns what grace is by learning that he is a sinner. One cannot be grasped without the other.

Consequently, it is all the same whether Jesus points to outcasts, to the righteous, or to God: those who stand in his audience will be able to identify themselves only as they understand his word of grace. And when they hear that word they will know. They will know not only who they are but who God is. They will understand themselves as sinners claimed by grace only when they know what God is; they will know what God is only when they understand themselves as sinners claimed by grace.

But the elder son also hears. The chorus at Jericho murmurs; the laborers hired in the first hour cry out for justice; the Pharisees are incensed because he goes in and eats with sinners. So the elder son, too, learns who he is when he learns what God is. Only he refuses to be identified as a sinner because he is righteous and so has no need for the grace of God. The word of grace and the deed of grace divide the audience into younger sons and elder sons—into sinners and Pharisees.

This is what Ernst Fuchs means when he says that we do not interpret the parables; *the parables interpret us.* The auditors are not invited to consider their response; they either rejoice because as sinners they are glad to be dependent on grace, or they are offended because they want justice on top of grace. They cannot go away and come back another day to give their decision. When man has been addressed by the word of grace, he has already been interpreted.

With this note one already strikes upon the affront of grace which turns so many listeners into elder sons. Such listeners are simply outraged that something so insubstantial as a word, even a word of forgiveness and acceptance, should be made the touchstone of their relation to God. They are horrified at the kind of undiscriminating and even irresponsible God that is coming to expression in such a word. But most important of all, they find it incredible that Jesus cannot see what they themselves see so clearly, namely, that the commandments and religion provide a handy means of discriminating between righteous and sinner. If he sees it, he has turned the criteria quite upside down.

In the parable of the laborers in the vineyard (Matt 20:1–15)[9] those hired early in the day protest because (1) they are paid last, and (2) they are paid the same amount as those who worked only one hour. One is not to think here of labor problems. One is to think of the householder who says, "Is your vision evil because I am generous?" (v. 15: completely obscured in RSV!) In the parable of the two sons (Matt 21:28–32), one of whom says he will but doesn't, while the other says he won't but does, Jesus draws this conclusion: "Truly I say to you, the tax collectors and the harlots go into the kingdom of God and you do not." (Verse 31: comparison expressing exclusion, also obscured in RSV!) What could be clearer? The word that turns the righteousness (not hypocrisy!) of the Pharisee out, that cancels the loyalty of the elder son, that overlooks the perseverance of the early laborers in the vineyard, has something drastically wrong with it. And one does well to reject such a word and him who speaks it, in order to save the church and religion!

There is nothing wrong with such logic except that it fails to discern that it is man and not God who is on trial. It refuses to let God be God. *The Pharisees are those who insist on interpreting the word of grace rather than letting themselves be interpreted by it.* The elder son is he who insists that his loyalty counts for something: his loyalty must be the basis of interpretation, i.e., the condition of any view of grace acceptable to him. For that

---

9. Cf. Ernst Fuchs, *Zur Frage nach dem historischen Jesus* (Tübingen: Mohr Siebeck, 1960). English translation: *Studies of the Historical Jesus*, trans. A. Scobie, SBT 42 (London: SCM, 1964), 219–26, 361–64 [32–38, 154–56]. References to the English version are given in brackets.

reason the grace in the parable strikes him as rejection. And so it is with the righteous—the term need not be self-righteous, merely righteous— who resist being exposed as sinners and are therefore constrained to hear the word of grace as blasphemy.

It is not so with the tax collectors and harlots. They hear the word gladly because it is the word for them. They hear it with the joy that attends the discovery of a priceless treasure. Out of that joy arises the courage to sell all they have in order to acquire it.

The word of grace is therefore the word of the cross. Jesus goes to the cross because he clings to the word of grace: that is at once the offense to the elder son and the hope of the younger. It is an offense to the elder son because he, unlike Jesus, cannot give up his claim; it is the hope of the younger because he knows he has no claim. He who hears the word of grace as a word addressed to him knows the meaning of the cross. For just as Jesus invests everything, including whatever title he had a right to claim, as well as his life, in the certainty of that word of grace, so he who hears the word will know what it requires of him. By hearing he has been claimed as a vessel of grace and plunged into the way of the cross.

Who has ears to hear let him hear.

Theses Concerning the Deeds and Parables of Grace

1. Grace always wounds from behind, at the point where man thinks he is least vulnerable.
2. Grace is harder than man thinks: he moralizes judgment in order to take the edge off it.
3. Grace is more indulgent than man thinks: but it is never indulgent at the point where he thinks it ought to be indulgent.
4. Grace is not something man can have at all.
5. Grace remains a mystery: it unveils itself as the ground of faith, but evaporates like a mist before the acquisitive eyes of belief.

Bibliography

Bultmann, Rudolf. "The Idea of God and Modern Man." *JThC* 2 (1965): 83–95.

Ebeling, Gerhard. "Theology and the Evidentness of the Ethical." *JThC* 2 (1965): 95–129.

Fuchs, Ernst. *Zur Frage nach dem historischen Jesus.* Tübingen: Mohr Sie-
    beck, 1960. English translation: *Studies of the Historical Jesus.* Trans-
    lated by A. Scobie. SBT 42. London: SCM, 1964.
Miles, T. R. *Religion and the Scientific Outlook.* London: Allen & Unwin,
    1959.
Robinson, James M., and John B. Cobb, eds. *New Frontiers in Theology:
    The New Hermeneutic.* Vol. 2. New York: Harper & Row, 1964.

Part 4
Parables

The Seismic Shift: A Major Moment in the History of Parable Interpretation

Bernard Brandon Scott

Between 1966 and 1975, Robert W. Funk published three essays that have influenced the study of the parables of Jesus more than any other development in the twentieth century. In "Parable as Metaphor" and "The Old Testament in Parable: The Good Samaritan," published in *Language, Hermeneutic, and Word of God* (1966), and in "The Parable of the Leaven: Away-from-Here as Destination," from *Jesus as Precursor* (1975), Funk initiated a seismic shift in parable scholarship, one that has reverberated throughout the study of the historical Jesus and with which scholars are still coming to terms.[1]

Parable as Metaphor

Funk understood himself as standing in and moving forward a tradition of parable interpretation that began with the monumental work Adolf Jülicher, *Die Gleichnisreden Jesu* (1889, 1899).[2] Jülicher had challenged the

---

1. Robert W. Funk, "Parable as Metaphor," in *Language, Hermeneutic, and Word of God: The Problem of Language in the New Testament and in Contemporary Theology* (New York: Harper & Row, 1966), 133–62; Funk, "The Parable of the Leaven: Away-from-Here as Destination," in *Jesus as Precursor*, SemeiaSt 2 (Philadelphia: Fortress; Missoula, MT: Scholars Press, 1975), 51–72; Funk, "The Old Testament in Parable: The Good Samaritan," in *Language, Hermeneutic, and Word of God*, 199–223. These three essays are available in Bernard Brandon Scott, ed, *Funk on Parables: Collected Essays* (Santa Rosa, CA: Polebridge, 2006), 25–50, 89–110, and 63–82, respectively. The present article is adapted from the introduction to that book. Unless otherwise noted, all page numbers are references to *Funk on Parables*.

2. Adolf Jülicher, *Die Gleichnisreden Jesu*, 2 vols. (Freiburg im Breisgau: Mohr Siebeck, 1889, 1899; 3rd ed. Darmstadt: Wissenschaftliche Buchgesellschaft, 1969).

understanding of the parables as allegories, a pervasive view that had been in place at least since the Gospel of Mark allegorized the parable of the sower (see Mark 4:13–20). The tree of allegory had grown wildly since Mark's modest effort. Jülicher did not simply trim this tree of its luxuriant growth; he attempted to cut it down. His strategy was to reduce the parable to a single moral point. In this rejection of allegory Funk recognized a permanent gain for scholarship—one that he strove to advance and one that has remained controversial.

Along the same line, Funk gratefully recognized the work of two mid-twentieth-century scholars, C. H. Dodd and Joachim Jeremias, both of whom sharply criticized Jülicher on the issue of a single *moral* point.[3] Dodd and Jeremias agreed that a parable has a single point, but they argued that it had to be a single *historical* point. While acknowledging the importance of Jeremias's work and agreeing with much of Dodd's, Funk nonetheless attacked both for their insistence that a parable has one and only one point.

Funk opens not with this attack, however, but by turning to the issue of "Parable as Metaphor." His approach appears simple. After all, a parable is a *mashal*, the Hebrew word for "comparison." He begins, then, by quoting with approval Dodd's definition of parable, which had begun, "at its simplest the parable is a metaphor or simile";[4] but then he starts to dismantle the definition as a way to gain leverage on parable itself. He applies this dismantling operation not only to the history of scholarship but also to the historical tradition of each parable. One must "dismantle the tradition in order to reach its source."[5] Neither hostile nor even essentially destructive, this analysis is an effort to make careful note of where the tradition cannot account for the evidence or the text. Dismantling is not a peeling away, a separation of the kernel from the husk, but rather a careful observation of where the tradition betrays itself, where it masks or covers over its own fissures or fault lines.

Funk distinguishes metaphoric discourse from the logical or dictionary language in which the meanings of words are presumed to be fixed.

The title means "Parables of Jesus." Unfortunately, this superb book has never been translated into English.

3. C. H. Dodd, *The Parables of the Kingdom* (New York: Scribner's Sons, 1935); Joachim Jeremias, *The Parables of Jesus* (New York: Scribner's Sons, 1972).

4. Funk, "Parable as Metaphor," 29.

5. Funk, "Parable as Metaphor," 38.

The logic of metaphor is quite different from the logic of everyday language. It is about the discovery and creation of new meaning. "Metaphor shatters the conventions of predication in the interests of a new vision, one which grasps the 'thing' in relation to a new 'field,' and thus in relation to a fresh experience of reality."[6] The traditional definition of metaphor argues that *A is B*, in which *A* is the unknown term and *B* is the known term. "Hercules is a lion" is an example of metaphor used in Aristotle's discussion. But Funk goes deeper. "The maker of a metaphor, like the maker of a parable, utilizes *B* [the known term] in such a way as to (a) break the grip of tradition on the language , and (b) discover new meaning."[7] In this twofold move we see Funk's key methodological insight stripped to its bare essentials.

- Since Funk equates metaphor and parable, Jesus, the maker of parables, needs to be understood as a poet.
- Since metaphor must operate within language, it must dismantle its language tradition. This implies that in his parables Jesus was stripping away his language tradition. Thus Funk insists that the historical Jesus must primarily be understood by *contrasting* him with his tradition.
- To get at a parable's root metaphor, its ultimate source, the interpreter must likewise dismantle the interpretive tradition in which the parable has been encased or ossified. Ossification is a metaphor Funk often uses to describe the effect of traditions—those of scholarship, the church, and especially the gospels. We will see more of this below.
- Because *A* and *B* are bound together in metaphor:
  - Their relationship creates meaning. There is no single point, as Jülicher argued, but a multiplicity of points as each person makes that metaphorical relationship.
  - The relationship is historically determined. The metaphor must always be understood in its own historical context because language is historically conditioned.
  - Finally, the metaphor/parable cannot be dispensed with. It is the only way to uncover mystery. Without the parable, mystery is lost and meaning is at the mercy of lexicographers.

---

6. Funk, "Parable as Metaphor," 33.
7. Funk, "Parable as Metaphor," 35.

Funk uses this understanding of metaphor/parable to take on some of the important issues in parable criticism. Not only had Dodd and Jeremias understood the parables as argumentative, but to refute Jülicher's notion of a single moral point Jeremias had emphasized the argumentative context, seeing in Jesus's recurring debates with his opponents—notably the Pharisees—what amounted to a single historical point. Funk argues that Jeremias is reducing the parable to ideas and thus its dictionary meaning, and insists that what the parable means can never replace the parable. "The emphasis on one point over against the allegorization of the parables was a necessary corrective, but one point understood as an idea valid for all times is as erroneous as Jülicher's moral maxims."[8] The parable remains primary: it is never mere ornament; it does not stand for something else; it provides a necessary vehicle for the reality it opens onto.

Against Jeremias, Funk points out that since the original context of the parable is lost, so must be the original meaning. And if that is the case, how can the parable be understood—and in what sense is it "historical"? When understood as metaphor, the parable creates its own meaning and can convey "as many points as there are situations into which it is spoken."[9] The historical context—and hence any historical understanding of the parable—has as its referent not a specific historical incident in the ministry of Jesus, but the parable's everydayness, a quality rooted in the realism of first-century Galilean village life. This everydayness is a key issue for Funk, because it means that one must pay attention to the parable's details. Here he faces two traditional opponents. At one hand stands allegory, which pays such close attention to the specifics of the story that "every detail or most details are conceptual ciphers."[10] The result is that the parable's details disappear, overwhelmed by their supposed meanings. At the other hand stands Jeremias, who restricted the parable's reference to a single historical moment and thus causes the parable to disappear into an expression of eternal meaning extracted from that moment. For Funk the parable is always a metaphor, ever ready to create new meaning. An historical understanding of the parable comes about from setting the details of its everydayness within the context of first-century Galilean village life. These historically understood elements of secularity then become

---

8. Funk, "Parable as Metaphor," 43.
9. Funk, "Parable as Metaphor," 42.
10. Funk, "Parable as Metaphor," 43.

the vehicle that enables the parable-as-image to project the new vision of reality that the parable-as-metaphor discloses and invites.

The everydayness of the parable "tempts the hearer to substitute another meaning, i.e., to disregard the literal and thus to allegorize."[11] This temptation arises because "the hearer or reader assumes that the literal subject matter could not possibly be the real subject matter." Allegory is then a temptation to go against the parable's literal image and thus towards a reduction of the parable's real intention. "In the parable of the Sower, for example, the equations seed = word and soils = people can be made and the literal meaning quietly abandoned."[12] Funk sees the temptation to allegorize a parable built into the very everydayness of its imagery.

Yet the everyday is not just everyday. Carefully dismantling the tradition of the parable, paying close historical attention to its everydayness and its secularity, prompts a hearer to ask "What's wrong with this picture?" Funk is here moving beyond those interpreters who had accented the parable's everydayness as a perfect picture of ancient life. He sees that everydayness is somehow eschewed. "Distortions of everydayness, exaggerated realism, distended concreteness, incompatible elements—often subtly drawn—are what prohibit the parable from coming to rest in the literal sense."[13] Ignoring the off-centeredness of the literal enables allegorization and all the other strategies of interpretation that substitute abstract meaning for the parable's concrete image; paying careful attention to the parable's literal content raises the question of the interplay between its literal and metaphorical levels. "The literal and the metaphorical meanings of the parable have to be grasped concomitantly."[14] Forfeit either one and the interpretation devolves into allegory.

The Good Samaritan as Parable

Jülicher had proposed three forms for parables: similitude (the leaven), parable proper (the sower), and example story (good Samaritan). An example story "has no figurative element at all.... The Samaritan is just an example of a true neighbor,... nothing more."[15] But Funk's careful dismantling of

---

11. Funk, "Parable as Metaphor," 48.
12. Funk, "Parable as Metaphor," 48.
13. Funk, "Parable as Metaphor," 48.
14. Funk, "Parable as Metaphor," 48.
15. Funk, "Old Testament in Parable," 76.

the interpretive history that began with Luke's moralizing contextualization demonstrates that the tradition fails to account for the details: it does not even address the basic question of why the protagonist is a Samaritan!

Since a hearer completes the parable's meaning by weighing its literal and metaphorical elements at the same time, Funk begins his analysis by asking, "From what perspective is the parable told?" Clearly perspective makes all the difference in hearing a narrative. He argues that this story presupposes the point of view of a traveler going down the road from Jerusalem to Jericho. Its picture of life is violent, but neither shocking nor even unusual. Funk underlines the Jewish sensibilities of the parable's audience: the traveler who was mugged and left in the ditch is a Jew, as are the priest and the Levite. Funk even suggests the listener's uniquely Jewish anticlerical response to the unfolding scenario.

As the narrative develops, hearers observe its everydayness: yes, this is the way things are. But then, "to the utter amazement and chagrin of every listener as Jew ..., a hated enemy, a half-breed, a perverter of true religion comes into view and ministers to the helpless victim when he is powerless to prevent him."[16] The Samaritan's actions shatter everyday expectation.

Funk continues to pursue the question, Why the Samaritan? If one responds that the Samaritan is an example of neighborliness, "in that case the parable is reduced to a commonplace and its bite completely vitiated." He drives home the point that the Samaritan is "he whom the victim does not, could not expect would help, indeed does not want help from."[17] It is "the literal, i.e., the historical, significance" of the Samaritan that smashes the everydayness and shocks the listener.

A narrative begun with all the traits of an experience about which everyone knows, or thinks he knows, is ruptured at the crucial juncture by a factor which does not square with everyday experience. The logic of everydayness is broken upon the logic of the parable. It is the juxtaposition of the two logics that turns the Samaritan, and hence the parable, into a metaphor.[18]

Here we have in a nutshell Funk's seismic shift. To be sure, Jülicher had initiated the tectonic movement with his decisive rejection of allegory, but Funk's move here represents much more than just an interpretive or methodological advance beyond Jülicher—something that Dodd, Jeremias,

---

16. Funk, "Old Testament in Parable," 76.
17. Funk, "Old Testament in Parable," 77.
18. Funk, "Old Testament in Parable," 77.

and others had already accomplished. Rather Funk makes the case that all parables are metaphors and operate by means of the same dynamic: "The literal and the metaphorical meanings of the parable have to be grasped concomitantly."[19] By demonstrating that the good Samaritan operates this way, he shows that it is a true parable and that example story is not a separate form of the parable, as Jülicher and the subsequent tradition in his wake had maintained; it is simply an interpretive method, just like allegory. Actually, the example story is shown to be only an extension of allegory, and all of Jülicher's terms are now turned on their heads.

◆   Parables do not have a single point but multiple points.
◆   Parables are metaphors that disclose a new way of construing or envisioning reality.
◆   The parable does not present some lesson or idea, because its literal and metaphorical aspects must be held in a creative tension.
◆   The parable is not to be interpreted; rather, it interprets the hearer.
◆   The parable is not just the everyday on display but the everyday torn asunder by the unexpected.

The Leaven as Parable

Earlier we noted Jülicher's three parable forms: similitude, parable proper, and example story, as well as Funk's demonstration that the second and third categories were the same. Now he turns his attention to the similitude, a form characterized by the preposition "like": "The Kingdom of God is like …." As such it seems to present an illustration; but Funk sets out to show that the similitude is likewise a parabolic metaphor.

In this third essay, "The Parable of the Leaven: Away-from-Here as Destination," Funk's rejection of Jülicher, Dodd, and Jeremias is more forthright and bold. He argues that for Jülicher and all his successors "the parables score a didactic point that can readily be reduced to discursive language."[20] Despite their efforts to reject and escape allegory, Jülicher's single point strategy has trapped them. They have made parable interpretation "a form of reduced allegory."[21]

Funk returns to his tried and true method: he dismantles by paying attention to details that the tradition cannot interpret. He begins by

---

19. Funk, "Parable as Metaphor," 48.
20. Funk, "Leaven," 97.
21. Funk, "Leaven," 98.

noticing that the parable of the leaven presents a common enough scene, the baking of bread, a piece of everydayness. But then, if one looks closely at the details within Jesus's own tradition, the everydayness comes unglued. One example of this disturbance of the everyday will suffice, although this briefest of parables provides at least five or six such dissonances with the everyday expectation of its listeners.

Funk notes "the curious choice of the central figure of the parable," namely, leaven. Just as formerly he had asked, "Why a Samaritan?," now he asks, "Why leaven?" He quotes Hebrew Bible and New Testament texts to show that leaven "was apparently universally regarded as a symbol of corruption." Only a few scholars had noted this negative implication of leaven, but even those who did had set it aside because it did not comport with the positive meaning of the kingdom of God. Funk issues a sharp challenge to their blithe disregard: "did Jesus allow his understanding of God's rule to be determined by the received tradition regarding that rule?"[22] Thus the parable of the leaven forces open a new window on God's rule and thereby undermines and indeed overturns the sedimented understanding of the kingdom. The parable is "a wrecking bar … designed to precipitate the loss of the received world of traditional religion in favor of the gain of the world of God's imperial rule."[23]

But as the parable was handed on, it became resedimented and its metaphorical meaning lost. By being paired with the parable of the mustard seed, it became an illustration of the "infectiousness of God's imperial rule."[24] This loss of metaphor by resedimentation seems to be an inevitable trajectory. The new construal of the world revealed by the parable is always at risk of being overwhelmed by the everyday. As Kafka had noted, "many complain that the words of the wise are … of no use in our everyday lives."[25] When the parable is yoked to the everyday, the ordinary, the secular, it is at risk of trivialization and thus the forfeiture of the kingdom's fabulous yonder that is available only in metaphor.

For Funk the parable of the leaven "parsimoniously encapsulates the horizons of the message of Jesus."[26] As such the clues to its foundational meaning lie strewn about, awaiting to be discovered.

---

22. Funk, "Leaven," 103.
23. Funk, "Leaven," 107.
24. Funk, "Leaven," 108.
25. Franz Kafka, *Parables and Paradoxes* (New York: Schocken Books, 1935), 11.
26. Funk, "Leaven," 107.

It is for this reason the secondary analysis, like that undertaken in biblical interpretation, may rediscover the wavelength of foundational language, as it were, by "listening in" on that language and its sedimentations, as though from a great distance. In stumbling around for clues in the texts of the Jesus tradition and the history of interpretation, the interpreter is endeavoring to locate the trajectory of the original language by attending to the ways in which that language has "fallen out" in its subsequent history. Once on the right wave length, the alert interpreter may hope to recover something of its original horizon.[27]

No more succinct summary of his method is available. Parsimony has distilled method to its penetrating essentials.

Jülicher's drive to reject allegory is maintained and reinforced. However, Funk has initiated a seismic shift. Gone is the single point methodology and in its place is parable as metaphor. The parable opens out onto a fabulous yonder and invites the hearer to cross over. It is now up the imagination of the hearer to find the kingdom in the here and now.

Bibliography

Dodd, C. H. *The Parables of the Kingdom.* New York: Scribner's Sons, 1935.

Funk, Robert W. "The Old Testament in Parable: The Good Samaritan." Pages 199–223 in *Language, Hermeneutic, and Word of God: The Problem of Language in the New Testament and in Contemporary Theology.* New York: Harper & Row, 1966. Repr. as pages 63–82 in *Funk on Parables: Collected Essays.* Edited by Bernard Brandon Scott. Santa Rosa, CA: Polebridge, 2006.

———. "Parable as Metaphor." Pages 133–62 in *Language, Hermeneutic, and Word of God: The Problem of Language in the New Testament and in Contemporary Theology.* New York: Harper & Row, 1966. Repr. as pages 25–50 in *Funk on Parables: Collected Essays.* Edited by Bernard Brandon Scott. Santa Rosa, CA: Polebridge, 2006.

———. "The Parable of the Leaven: Away-from-Here as Destination." Pages 51–72 in *Jesus as Precursor.* SemeiaSt 2. Philadelphia: Fortress; Missoula, MT: Scholars Press, 1975. Repr. as pages 89–110 in *Funk on Parables: Collected Essays.* Edited by Bernard Brandon Scott. Santa Rosa, CA: Polebridge, 2006.

---

27. Funk, "Leaven," 109.

Jeremias, Joachim. *The Parables of Jesus*. New York: Scribner's Sons, 1972.

Jülicher, Adolf. *Die Gleichnisreden Jesu*. 2 vols. Freiburg im Breisgau: Mohr Siebeck, 1889, 1899. 3rd ed. Darmstadt: Wissenschaftliche Buchgesellschaft, 1969.

Kafka, Franz. *Parables and Paradoxes*. New York: Schocken Books, 1935.

Scott, Bernard Brandon. Introduction to *Funk on Parables: Collected Essays*. Santa Rosa, CA: Polebridge, 2006.

The Old Testament in Parable: A Study of Luke 10:25–37

Robert W. Funk

The Old Testament is posed as a problem initially for the church by its own constitution of the canon: it embraced the two Testaments in a single canon, but drew a line between them and marked by the discontinuity by designating one the *Old* in contrast to the *New*. The Old Testament is also a problem by virtue of the conflict between Jewish and Christian interpretation. This tension has been heightened, furthermore, by the rise of the critical-historical method. This method, which endeavors to let the Old Testament speak for itself, points back to but is not identical with Jewish interpretation.[1] How the Old Testament may be appropriated by the Christian faith has consequently reappeared as a theological problem of the first magnitude.[2] This essay is a modest effort to approach the question from a New Testament perspective without losing sight of its theological dimensions.

Some justification is to be expected for selecting the parable as a locus of inquiry. One might stipulate that with the parables we are in particularly close contact with the historical Jesus;[3] it was in this domain that the original quest of the historical Jesus is held to have been the most successful, and that may be the reason the "new hermeneutic" has taken the parables as its point of departure.[4] But in the interest of the new hermeneutic in the parables has, I think, other grounds.

---

1. T. W. Nakarai, to whom this essay is dedicated, took this tension with utmost seriousness, as his philological and historical work shows. We do well not to relax it.

2. Cf., e.g., Bernhard W. Anderson, ed., *The Old Testament and the Christian Faith* (New York: Harper & Row, 1963); Claus Westermann, ed., *Essays on Old Testament Hermeneutics* (Richmond: John Knox, 1963).

3. Joachim Jeremias, *The Parables of Jesus*, trans. S. H. Hooke, rev. ed. (New York: Scribner's Sons, 1963), 12.

4. James M. Robinson, "The New Hermeneutic at Work," *Interpretation* 18 (1964): 351–52.

Gerhard Ebeling has remarked, "The parable is the form of the language of Jesus which corresponds to the incarnation."[5] Eberhard Jüngel, following the lead of his teacher, Ernst Fuchs, has attempted to work out an explication of this thesis in his recent book, *Paulus und Jesus*.[6] To put it briefly, the parable "collects" Jesus, his relation to God, his eschatology, his ethic *and* the hearer into a language event which is the kingdom;[7] the kingdom comes to speech in the parable as parable.[8] The kingdom comes to speech as parable because it is in this way that the *nearness* of the kingdom as God's future can be brought into relation to man's present without the loss of distinction, yet in parable the former can qualify the latter.[9] Günther Bornkamm, in an excellent brief sketch of the parable as used by Jesus, puts the same point in a different way.[10] Bornkamm identifies the parable as a not fortuitous medium of giving expression to the mystery of the kingdom. In the parable a mystery lies hidden, and that "mystery is nothing but the hidden dawn of the kingdom of God itself amidst a world which to human eyes gives no sign of it."[11] Hence, "the parables are the preaching itself" and do not merely serve "the purpose of a lesson which is quite independent of them."[12]

These formulations assert and attempt to justify the view that the parable is the mode of language most appropriate to the incarnation. One could even say, they postulate that the parable is the linguistic incarnation. If in the parable we are close to the heart and mind of Jesus, to use the older formulation, or if in the parable we encounter *logos* incarnate, we may expect some light on Jesus's relation to the Old Testament as tradition to emanate from his use of the parable.

---

5. Gerhard Ebeling, *Evangelische Evangelienauslegung: Eine Untersuchung zu Luther's Hermeneutik*, 2nd ed. (Darmstadt: Wissenschaftliche Buchgesellschaft, 1962), 108.

6. Eberhard Jüngel, *Paulus und Jesus: Eine Untersuchung zur Präzisierung der Frage nach dem Ursprung der Christologie* (Tübingen: Mohr Siebeck, 1962), 87–174.

7. See, his "Leitsätze," in Jüngel, *Paulus und Jesus*, 173–74.

8. Jüngel, *Paulus und Jesus*, 135.

9. Jüngel, *Paulus und Jesus*, 159.

10. Günther Bornkamm, *Jesus of Nazareth* (New York: Harper & Brothers, 1960), 69ff.

11. Bornkamm, *Jesus of Nazareth*, 71.

12. Bornkamm, *Jesus of Nazareth*, 69.

1.

Scripture may be said to function in relation to the parable (including the rabbinic parables) in three ways: (1) as the test for which the parable is exposition; (2) as the source of the basic image or figure utilized in the construction of the parable; or (3) as the means of elucidating or enlivening the parable.

According to Jeremias, the primitive church introduced scriptural references and allusions in the parables of Jesus, usually in support of allegorizing tendencies (e.g., the parable of the wicked tenants), but there is scant evidence that Jesus cited scripture explicitly to any significant degree in the body of his parables. Hence, if only for the reason that the parable makes little or no overt and explicit use of scripture, it would be particularly illuminating to examine the role of scripture and scriptural allusion in the narrative body of the parable.[13]

It is a different matter to assert that Jesus drew upon Old Testament imagery in the construction of his parables, for in this case it is not a matter of scriptural quotation or allusion, but of dependence upon a common reservoir of images, of reference to a system of interlocking images and figures, known and meaningful in and of themselves to the hearer. The parable would then depend for its significance on the ability of the hearer to catch the overtones, to supply, as it were, out of his own heritage the

---

13. In his survey of the influence of the Old Testament on the parables, Jeremias (*Parables of Jesus*, 31–32) notes that there is a remarkably small number of references to scripture. Luke 13:24–30 is a mosaic; the conclusion of one parable (Matt 25:10–12) is merged with three related similes (Matt 7:13–14, 22–23, 8:11–12), two of which involve scriptural references (Luke 13:27 // Matt 7:23 = Ps 6:8; Luke 13:29 // Matt 8:11 = Ps 107:3) (*Parables of Jesus*, 95–96). Matthew 25:31, 46 may be editorial (*Parables of Jesus*, 31 n. 27, 84 n 83, 206). The allusions to Isa 5:1ff. and Ps 118:22–23 in the parable of the wicked tenants (Mark 12:1–12 parr.) are seen to be secondary by a comparison of the three Synoptic versions and Thomas (logion 65): Luke and Thomas lack the former, and Thomas reports the latter as an independent logion (66) (*Parables of Jesus*, 31. Mark 4:32 parr. (the mustard seed), Matt 13:33 parr. (the leaven), and Mark 4:29 (seed growing secretly) may contain original scriptural allusions; in the first two instances, however, Jesus employs the Old Testament images in their opposite sense! (*Parables of Jesus*, 31–32, 149). In addition, Jeremias thinks the publican's prayer in Luke 18:13 may reflect the opening words of Ps 51 (*Parables of Jesus*, 144). While there appears to have been a tendency in the tradition to elucidate the parables by means of scripture, the instance in which scripture was utilized by Jesus in the elaboration of the parable seem to have been small indeed (*Parables of Jesus*, 32).

body of the image, which alone has the power to let the parable speak. Harald Riesenfeld has argued that the parables make use of the repertory of the Old Testament images and motifs in a quasi-allegorical way,[14] with the consequence that the parables of Jesus are not really intelligible to someone immersed in Old Testament lore. Riesenfeld's student, Birger Gerhardsson, has attempted to make the case for the parable of the good Samaritan in particular, not only that Jesus draws upon Old Testament imagery, but that he employs well-known rabbinic techniques of interpretation.[15] It is our intention to examine this effort more close in due course.

It should be noted that the view advocated by Riesenfeld and Gerhardsson apparently runs counter to the widely held view that the parables are realistic in essence, that they reflect the everyday world. C. H. Dodd has put the matter well:

> Each similitude or story is a perfect picture of something that can be observed in the world of our experience. The processes of nature are accurately observed and recorded; the actions of person in the stories are in character; they are either such as anyone would recognize as natural in the circumstances, or, if they are surprising, the point of the parable is that such actions *are* surprising.[16]

Neither Dodd[17] nor Amos Wilder[18] wishes to press this characteristic too far: it is possible, both would allow, that now and then there are allegorical overtones in what is otherwise a completely human and realistic picture or narrative. Nevertheless, Wilder insists, "the impact of the parables lay in their immediate realistic authenticity," and to press the concrete, realistic

---

14. Harald Riesenfeld, "The Parables in the Synoptic and the Johannine Traditions," *Svensk Exegetisk Arsbok* 25 (1960): 37–61, cited by Amos Wilder, *The Language of the Gospel: Early Christian Rhetoric* (New York: Harper & Row, 1964), 81; cf. Edwyn C. Hoskyns and Noel Davey, *The Riddle of the New Testament* (London: Faber & Faber, 1931), 182–88.

15. Birger Gerhardsson, *The Good Samaritan—The Good Shepherd?*, ConBNT 16 (Land: Gleerup, 1958).

16. C. H. Dodd, *The Parables of the Kingdom*, 2nd ed. (London: Nisbet, 1952), 20–21.

17. Dodd, *Parables of the Kingdom*, 21; cf. his remarks on the symbol of the heavenly banquet (121), which Jesus alludes to merely as a banquet.

18. Wilder, *Language of the Gospel*, 81–82.

images in the direction of allegorical ciphers "is to pull the stories out of shape and to weaken their thrust."[19]

If realism and allegory are occasionally compatible (extended allegory tends, as a rule, to weaken realism[20]), it is to be wondered whether secularity and allegory dependent upon the Old Testament stock of images can be reconciled, even occasionally. Lucetta Mowry, has noted that the subject matter of the parables, with four exceptions, is secular,[21] and Wilder suggests that the naturalness and secularity of the parables point to something very significant about Jesus and the gospel, viz., that for Jesus man's destiny is at stake precisely in "his ordinary creaturely existence."[22] Ernst Fuchs puts it pointedly: "Jesus does not use the details of this world only as a kind of 'point of contact'; instead, *he has in mind precisely this* 'world.' "[23] If the secular world is the "field" intended by the parable, does the Old Testament stock images belong to this world as part of its secular landscape? If so, what are the consequences for Jesus's use of the Old Testament?

This matter can be viewed from still another perspective. Assuming that Jesus is drawing upon a repertory of images belonging to the common Jewish heritage, is there anything determinative in this fact for his relation to the Old Testament? Could Jesus, for example, have drawn upon the Homeric metaphors with equal effectiveness, has his audiences been steeped in the *Iliad* and *Odyssey*? Or is the Old Testament the necessary linguistic school for the Christian faith? We are here touching upon the root problem of the relation of the New Testament to the Old Testament, which could be specified, to take one example, as the problem of typology. Even if it were established that there is *some* inner relation between

---

19. Wilder, *Language of the Gospel*, 81. Cf. his further remark on the same page: "In the parable of the Lost Sheep the shepherd is an actual shepherd and not a flashback to God as the Shepherd of Israel or to the hoped-for Messiah who will shepherd Israel."

20. Dodd, *Parables of the Kingdom*, 19–20.

21. Lucetta Mowry, "Parable," *IDB* 3:650. The exceptions are: the rich fool, the rich man and Lazarus, the publican and the Pharisee, and the good Samaritan. It might be inquired whether the "religious" content of these four parables is really religious, or whether it is religion viewed as a secular phenomenon.

22. Wilder, *Language of the Gospel*, 82.

23. Ernst Fuchs, "The New Testament and the Hermeneutical Problem," in *The New Hermeneutic*, ed. James M. Robinson and John B. Cobb (New York: Harper & Row, 1964), 126.

the Old Testament images and the parable, it would still be necessary to inquire *what* this relation is.

This line of reflection may be arbitrarily terminated in order to note the first way, mentioned above, in which scripture may be related to the parable. The rabbinic parables are characteristically used in the exposition of scripture.[24] Gerhardsson is certainly justified in saying that one might antecedently expect Jesus to use the parable for this purpose also.[25] This is not often assumed to be the case, and indeed there is little evidence to indicate that Jesus did employ the parable in the exposition of scripture. One ostensible exception is the parable of the good Samaritan in its Lukan context (Luke 10:25–37). It is just this point which is felt to provide the sharpest contrast between the rabbinic and Jesus's use of parables. Let Bornkamm summarize:

> The rabbis also relate parables in abundance, to clarify a point in their teaching and explain the sense of a written passage, but always as an aid to the teaching and an instrument in the exegesis of an authoritatively prescribed text. But this is just what they are not in the mouth of Jesus, although they often come very close to those of the Jewish teachers in their content, and though Jesus makes free use of traditional and familiar topics.[26]

It will now be clear that the relation of the parables to scripture in Jesus's usage is entirely problematic. Were it not for the position which the parables occupy in the tradition and the importance they are accorded by those of varying persuasions, one would be inclined to look elsewhere for light on Jesus's relation to the Old Testament. It would be possible, of course, to proceed *via negative* and eliminate all possible contact between the parable and scripture. A detailed demonstration of this order would only be a *tour de force*, were it successful. It remains to examine with care those cases where the tradition has reported a connection between scripture and the parable, or where there is reason to suspect a connection not explicitly

---

24. Paul Fiebig, *Die Gleichnisreden Jesu im Lichte der rabbinischen Gleichnisse* (Tübingen: Mohr Siebeck, 1912), 239–40; Mowry, "Parable," 81 n. 1, rightly warns against overemphasizing this point: the rabbinic parables are occasionally prophetic and noncasuistic in character; cf. b. Ber. 28b, m. Pirke Avot 3.17, b. Shabb. 153a.

25. Gerhardsson, *Good Samaritan*, 25.

26. Bornkamm, *Jesus of Nazareth*, 69. Cf. Fiebig, *Die Gleichnisreden Jesu*, 239–40, 260.

recorded. Attention in this study will be devoted exclusively to the parable of the good Samaritan.

The reasons for selecting the parable of the good Samaritan have already been suggested. In the first place, the Lukan context connects the parable with the lawyer's question about eternal life (Luke 10:25–28), which is initially answered out of the law. The parable would appear to be a midrash on the second part of the commandment. In the second place, starting out from the patristic tradition that the parable is a christological allegory, Gerhardsson has argued that Jesus draws upon the Old Testament imagery of the good shepherd (with its constellation of meaning) and employs well-known rabbinic techniques in debating the interpretation of the commandment with the lawyer in question. Together or singly, these could afford valuable clues to Jesus's use of the Old Testament and specifically to his hermeneutic. The balance of this essay will in effect be a study of the parable, and of Gerhardsson's interpretation of it.

2.

Gerhardsson first considers the parable apart from its context.[27] The parable is not concerned with the injured man but with the three persons who come across him, as the concluding question (Luke 10:36) shows. The challenge to the hearer is to identify the true neighbor: he is, of course, the Samaritan.[28] Adopting Jeremias's view that the parables of Jesus are marked by a polemic directed against the Jews, particularly the Pharisees and their scribes,[29] Gerhardsson reasons that the parable is intended as a criticism of the Jewish leaders.[30] It cannot be accidental, furthermore, that the parable exhibits such striking affinities with the shepherd motif found in the Old Testament, particularly Ezek 34. The elements are the same: "The defenseless flock, abandoned by the false shepherds, given over to wild beasts, receiving the promise of the true shepherd."[31] The

---

27. I.e., omitting Luke 10:25–28, 37b (the imperative), but including vv. 29, 36–37a (Gerhardsson, *Good Samaritan*, 9–10).

28. Gerhardsson, *Good Samaritan*, 10.

29. Jeremias, *Parables of Jesus*, 21–22, 123, 145–46, 166–67, et passim.

30. The priest and the Levite do not represent a Jewish party, but the religious leaders as a whole (Gerhardsson, *Good Samaritan*, 11 n. 2).

31. Gerhardsson, *Good Samaritan*, 14. On 11–14 he analyzes John 10:1–16 and Ezek 34 as a basis of these judgments; he concludes that Ezek 34 lies behind John 10.

interpretation which suggests itself is therefore the following: the injured man represents Israel, the priest and Levite the religious leaders, and the Samaritan is the true shepherd (*r'h ysr'l*).[32]

Is there any other support for this understanding of the parable? Indeed there is. It is to be found in the significance of the name Samaritan (the significance of names is utilized in patristic exegesis as well as in the Jewish, including Old Testament, and early Christian tradition),[33] and in the double meaning of the root, *r'* or *r'h*.[34] *Samaritēs* represents *šwrwny*, derived from *šmr*, which means to "watch over" and "to keep, observe." The intransitive verb can mean "to be a shepherd" (e.g., Hos 12:12), the present active participle "shepherd" (e.g., 1 Sam 17:20). Like *rō'eh*, *šōmēr* is used to designate God and his anointed. The Samaritan in the parable thus stands for the true shepherd, who is the true keeper of the law.[35] In patristic exegesis it was a common place, beginning with Origen, to note that Samaritan meant *watchman*.[36] The patristic tradition, then, which universally interpreted the parable christologically,[37] has preserved under its "florid allegorizing" the original sense of the parable, viz., that the subject was Christ himself.[38]

Similarly, the Greek word *plēsion*, "neighbor," represents the Hebrew word *rea'*. The Hebrew word for shepherd is *rō'eh*. These words are graphically quite similar and even their phonetic difference is slight in many forms; moreover, they derive from a single verb, *rā'āh*.[39] "It is not too rash to suggest," says Gerhardsson, "that this parable did not originally deal with who is the true neighbor, *rea'* (*rē'eh*), but who is the true shepherd, *rō'eh*.[40] Such an interpretation is possible on the basis of the rabbinic rule that a word may be interpreted in its double significance.[41] The lawyer asked a question concerning the commandment (who is my neighbor?)

32. Gerhardsson, *Good Samaritan*, 14–15.
33. Gerhardsson, *Good Samaritan*, 15–18.
34. Gerhardsson, *Good Samaritan*, 19–21, 25–29.
35. Gerhardsson, *Good Samaritan*, 17.
36. Gerhardsson, *Good Samaritan*, 15.
37. Gerhardsson, *Good Samaritan*, 3–5. He summarizes: "The 20th century exegetes seem as united in their opposition to a christological interpretation as the early fathers in their support of it" (5).
38. Gerhardsson, *Good Samaritan*, 18.
39. Gerhardsson, *Good Samaritan*, 19–20.
40. Gerhardsson, *Good Samaritan*, 20.
41. Gerhardsson, *Good Samaritan*, 27.

and received an answer about the true shepherd.[42] Such wordplay strikes the modern reader as grotesque, but it is quite in accord with the techniques of Jewish midrash, as exemplified, for example, at Qumran.[43]

The shift in meaning must have taken place before the parable took its canonical form, for the Greek word *plēsion* preserves the secondary interpretation, which accords with the proclivity of the church to transform the parables into didactic and paraenetical vehicles for its own situation;[44] the church would not need reminding of who the true shepherd was, hut they would be interested in the lawyer's question! The secondary meaning was secured by the final imperative: "Go and do likewise."[45]

The Lukan context, in Gerhardsson's judgment, supports his analysis of the parable.[46] There is depicted a learned discussion of the law between Jesus (a *didaskalos*, rby) and a lawyer (a *nomikos*).[47] The discussion proceeds according to custom, including the use of rabbinic formulae and Hebrew. Since the rabbis were fond of the parable in the exposition of scripture, it is not surprising that the lawyer's question, which has to do with an *exegetical* point (what is the meaning of re'ªkha in the text?), evokes a parable as a midrash on the text. The transcript abbreviates the discussion (customary in the rabbinic literature), but the parable gives evidence that Jesus knew and used rabbinic techniques of interpretation (see above). The conclusion is that the pericope, Luke 10:25–37, was a unity from the first.

The original significance of the parable, Gerhardsson believes, accords with the meaning of the pericope of the rich young man (Mark 10:17–21

---

42. Gerhardsson, *Good Samaritan*, 29.

43. Gerhardsson, *Good Samaritan*, 26–28. Cf. Krister Stendahl, *The School of St. Matthew and Its Use of the Old Testament*, Acta Seminarii Neotestamentici Upsaliensis 20 (Uppsala: Almqvist & Wiksell, 1954), 185ff.; W. H. Brownlee, "Biblical Interpretation among the Sectaries of the Dead Sea Scrolls," *BA* 14 (1951): 54–76.

44. Cf. Jeremias, *Parables of Jesus*, 33–66.

45. Gerhardsson, *Good Samaritan*, 21. Gerhardsson thinks this injunction, however, may not be wholly secondary (21 n. 4); it is a set phrase from the language of the Jewish schools (10 and n. 1), and it is suitable to the Lukan context (23–24).

46. Gerhardsson, *Good Samaritan*, 22–29, makes the following points.

47. It does not matter that a precise Hebrew equivalent for nomikos cannot he established; the lawyer in any case was a learned student of the law (Gerhardsson, *Good Samaritan*, 23). Thomas Walter Manson, *The Sayings of Jesus* (London: SCM, 1949), 260 surmises that Luke uses "lawyer" rather than "scribe" because the latter would he misunderstood by gentile readers. Cf. W. Gutbrod, "νομικός," *TDNT* 4:1088.

parr.), with which it has certain formal parallelisms:[48] the answer of the law as traditionally expounded is not sufficient; Jesus refers to scripture as the Messiah, i.e., gives his own interpretation, which means in the end that he interprets scripture messianically or christologically.[49] It is by no means clear how Gerhardsson gets from the former to the latter: Does the authority of the Messiah to reinterpret scripture imply that such reinterpretation, *eo ipso*, will be christological interpretation?

The formal proximity of Gerhardsson's view to that of Ernst Fuchs, who regards the parables as (veiled) self-attestations of Jesus himself,[50] and to the patristic view[51] requires that these tendencies in contemporary scholarship be carefully distinguished from each other and from the patristic tradition. The differences are correlative with how one understands Jesus's understanding and use of scripture. It is not possible here to embark upon a systematic examination. It will be necessary, as a consequence, to restrict ourselves to a reexamination of the parable of the good Samaritan with the problem of scripture in view.

3.

The discrepancy between the formulation of the question ("Who is my neighbor?," Luke 10:29) and the question answered by the parable ("Which of these three proved neighbor?," Luke 10:36) is regularly noted.

---

48. The two are introduced with the same initial question, which is answered out of the law.

49. Gerhardsson, *Good Samaritan*, 29. One might have expected Gerhardsson to draw a parallel also between the good Samaritan and the parable of the lost sheep (Luke 14:4–7 // Matt 18:12–13), but he does not seem to notice this possibility.

50. Ernst Fuchs, *Hermeneutik*, 2nd ed. (Bad Canstatt: Müllerschön Verlag, 1958), 223ff.; Fuchs, "Bermerkungen zur Gleichnisauslegung," in *Zur Frage nach dem historischen Jesus* (Tübingen: Mohr Siebeck, 1960), 136–42; cf. Jüngel, *Paulus und Jesus*, 87, 87–88 n. 3; Jeremias, *Parables of Jesus*, 230.

51. Gerhardsson wants to distinguish his understanding of the parable as an *allegoric parable* from the patristic understanding of it as a *timeless allegory* (*Good Samaritan*, 22). Here he parts company with J. Daniélou, "Le Bon Samaritain," in *Mélanges Bibliques rédigés en l'honneur de André Robert* (Paris: Bloud & Gay 1957), 457ff., who wants to reinstate the patristic allegory (*Good Samaritan*, 31, additional note). If the patristic view is that the parable is a timeless allegory of the history of the human race or soul, Gerhardsson's view is that it contains a timeless christological didache; in his own judgment it is a difference between two types of universality and timelessness.

The disjuncture may be epitomized as *"Quis diligendus?"* (the lawyer's question) and *"Quis diligens?"* (the question answered by the parable).[52] This hiatus has been advanced as an argument for divorcing the parable from its Lukan context,[53] but it has also been explained or minimized.[54] What is not often noticed is that the prevailing modem interpretation of the parable, i.e., that the parable defines neighbor as he who needs my help, is as much in conflict with the parable as the lawyer's question.[55] The lawyer's question still tends to dominate the parable!

Without a reformulation of the leading question or a recasting of the parable, the incongruity stands. It could even be said that the discrepancy is not alleviated by disengaging the parable from the lawyer's question. For his question continues to be the hearer's question. It should be asked, furthermore, whether the parable really deals with the subject of love as opposed to the object of love. Or are these options—subject or object—simply misleading?

It is methodologically sound to follow Gerhardsson in considering the parable initially in and of itself.[56] Quite apart from the Lukan framework it appears that the parable is devoted to the question of neighbor.[57] On the other hand, it is doubtful that a moralistic interpretation does more than reflect the later interest of the church, which happens, in this case, to coincide with modern interests.[58] Jeremias has demonstrated the pronounced

---

52. Adolf Jülicher, *Die Gleichnisreden Jesu* (Tübingen: Mohr Siebeck, 1910; repr. 2 vols. in 1; Darmstadt: Wissenschaftliche Buchgesellschaft, 1963), 2:596; Gerhardsson, *Good Samaritan*, 6; Jeremias, *Parables of Jesus*, 205.

53. E.g., Jülicher, *Die Gleichnisreden Jesu*, 2:596; Rudolf Bultmann, *History of the Synoptic Tradition*, trans. John Marsh (New York: Harper & Row, 1963), 178; Jüngel, *Paulus und Jesus*, 169–70, decides that vv. 25–28 are secondary but leaves the question open whether vv. 29, 36–37 are also.

54. E.g., by Thomas Walter Manson, *The Teachings of Jesus* (Cambridge: Cambridge University Press, 1951), 301; Jeremias, *Parables of Jesus*, 205; Gerhardsson, *Good Samaritan*, 28–29.

55. Gerhardsson, *Good Samaritan*, 19, correctly emphasizes this point. Manson, *Sayings of Jesus*, 261, does not follow the dominant view but holds that the parable does not define neighbor at all.

56. Gerhardsson, *Good Samaritan*, 9; cf. Jüngel, *Paulus und Jesus*, 170.

57. Wilhelm Michaelis, *Die Gleichnisse Jesu: Eine Einführung*, 3rd ed. (Hamburg: Furche, 1956), 205; Rudolf Bultmann, *Jesus and the Word*, trans. Louise Pettibone Smith, Erminie Huntress Lantero (New York: Scribner's Sons, 1958), 96; Jüngel, *Paulus und Jesus*, 170.

58. Gerhardsson (*Good Samaritan*, 8–9) notes the situation with respect to the

tendency of the tradition to convert parables with eschatological horizons into hortatory material.[59] Going together with a moralizing interpretation is the definition of the good Samaritan as a *Beispielerzählungen* (exemplary story). An exemplary story does not draw its pictorial element from a sphere other than the one to which its *Sache* belongs; it has no figurative element at all. "The 'exemplary stories' [*Beispielerzählungen*] offer examples = models of right behaviour."[60] The exemplary story does not, therefore, call for a transference of judgment as do the parables proper.[61] The Samaritan is just an example of a true neighbor (or, to follow the prevailing view, of the true love of one's neighbor), nothing more. Gerhardsson, in my judgment, has rightly challenged the validity of this designation,[62] although for what strike me as the wrong reasons.[63]

In comprehending the parable it is important to grasp how the hearer is drawn into the story. From what perspective is the parable told?[64] Initially at least, the account compels the hearer to put himself in the place of that nameless fellow jogging along the wild and dangerous road.[65] Straightway he finds himself the brunt of a murderous attack which leaves him stripped, beaten, and half dead. While lying helpless in the ditch, he perceives the priest and Levite pass by with only an apprehensive glance. It does not much matter to him whether their callousness can be excused or

---

message of Jesus has changed materially since Jülicher formulated his views. It is strange that Jülicher's reading of the good Samaritan as a *Beispielerzählung* has gone virtually unchallenged. The Lukan tradition has given support, however, to a moralistic reading, terminating as it does with the exhortation, "Go and do likewise."

59. Jeremias, *Parables of Jesus*, 42–48 et passim.

60. Bultmann, *History of the Synoptic Tradition*, 178 n. 1; cf. 177–78; Jülicher, *Die Gleichnisreden Jesu*, 1:112; 2:585; Eta Linnemann, *Gleichnisse Jesu: Einführung und Auslegung*, 2nd ed. (Göttingen: Vandenhoeck & Ruprecht, 1962), 55; Jüngel, *Paulus und Jesus*, 170–71.

61. Bultmann, *History of the Synoptic Tradition*, 198.

62. Gerhardsson, *Good Samaritan*, 5 n. 6, 9.

63. The other parables identified as exemplary stories are: the rich fool, the Pharisee and the publican, the rich man and Lazarus, the wedding guest (Luke 14:7–11), the proper guests (Luke 14:12–14): Jülicher, *Die Gleichnisreden Jesu*, 1:112; 2:585–641; Bultmann, *History of the Synoptic Tradition*, 178–79. Naturally we are not considering here whether the designation is appropriate in these other cases, but it is interesting to note that the exemplary stories are also those identified as having religious content (see n. 21), except for the two Lukan examples added by Bultmann.

64. Bornkamm, *Jesus of Nazareth*, 112–13, thinks this point is crucial and I agree.

65. Bornkamm, *Jesus of Nazareth*; Jeremias, *Parables of Jesus*, 205.

justified, and, if that victim (as auditor) is a layman, his secret anticlerical-ism is confirmed. The priest or Levite as hearer will, of course, be incensed. At this juncture the lay hearer will anticipate a benign layman to appear on the scene;[66] the ecclesiastical auditor, muttering under his breath, will expect no less. In the teeth of just such anticipations, to the utter amaze-ment and chagrin of every listener as Jew[67] (the previous dichotomy is bridged in an instant), a hated enemy, a half-breed, a perverter of true religion comes into view and ministers to the helpless victim when he is powerless to prevent him.[68] While still in inner turmoil over this unex-pected turn of events, the hearer is snatched back into reality: "Which of these three, do you think, proved neighbor…?" It is a question on which the Jew chokes. The lawyer in the Lukan account cannot bring himself to pronounce the name of that hated "neighbor," but he can hardly avoid the answer which the parable demands.

The Samaritan is undoubtedly the primary shock, although the behavior of the priest and Levite will raise preliminary resistance in cer-tain quarters, nodding approval in others. The first sentences of the story evoke a silent "Yes, that's how it is" from everyone, but the clerics will already have begun their retreat with their own appearance. Neverthe-less, the subsequent development overwhelms first reactions and brings the Jewish audience together again in a common crisis. Only the destitute and outcasts weather the second onslaught; they alone are untouched by the attack.[69]

---

66. Jeremias, *Parables of Jesus*, 204.

67. Manson, *Sayings of Jesus*, 263: we may suppose that the man who fell among thieves was a Jew. According to rabbinic teaching, an Israelite was not to accept alms or a work of love from a non-Jew, since Israel's redemption is thereby delayed: Jüngel, *Paulus und Jesus*, 172, quoting Walter Grundmann, *Die Geschichte Jesu Christi*, 2nd ed. (Berlin: Evangelische Verlagsanstalt, 1959), 90; cf. Paul Billerbeck, *Kommentar zum Neuen Testament aus Talmud und Midrasch* (Münich: Beck, 1922–1928), 4:538, 543–44.

68. Jeremias, *Parables of Jesus*, 204.

69. The Pharisees excluded non-Pharisees from their definition of neighbor; the Essenes were to hate all sons of darkness; and a rabbinical saying ruled that heretics, informers, and renegades should be pushed (into the ditch) and not pulled out. Per-sonal enemies were also excluded from the circle (Matt 5:43): Jeremias, *Parables of Jesus*, 202–3. The victim in the ditch could also belong to one of these categories: every listener becomes victim. The parable would not have been offensive to listeners of this type.

When it is asked why Jesus chose the Samaritan as the central figure in the parable, it is simply not satisfactory to answer that the Samaritan is merely a model of neighborliness. For in that case the parable is reduced to a commonplace[70] and its bite completely vitiated. Rather, the Samaritan is he whom the victim does not, could not expect to help, indeed does not want to help. The literal, i.e., historical, significance of the Samaritan is what gives the parable its edge. In this respect the Samaritan is a *secular* figure; he functions not as an esoteric cipher for a religious factor as Gerhardsson thinks, but in his concrete, everyday significance. On the other hand, the Samaritan is brought into a constellation in which he cannot be anticipated. It is this surprising, odd tum which shatters the realism, the everydayness of the story. A narrative begun with all the traits of an experience about which everyone knows, or thinks he knows, is ruptured at the crucial juncture by a factor which does not square with everyday experience. The "logic" of everydayness is broken upon the "logic" of the parable. It is the juxtaposition of the two "logics" which turns the Samaritan, and hence the parable, into a metaphor.

Metaphor directs the hearer's attention, not to this or that, but to the whole background and foreground of the event by means of imaginative shock; it does so by virtue of the fact that it does not allow the figure or narrative picture to come to rest in the literal meaning. Metaphor seizes a focal actuality which it loosens from its moorings in everydayness in order to descry its penumbral actuality or field;[71] the latter metaphor discovers to the imagination. If it is the literal meaning of Samaritan which provides the initial jolt to the everyday mentality embodied in the story, it is the nonliteral meaning which triggers, through the parable, a whole new vista, i.e., the penumbral field. In sum, comprehending the figure and the parable depends upon grasping the literal and nonliteral meanings concomitantly.[72]

---

70. Dodd, *Parables of the Kingdom*, 24ff.

71. I am indebted to Ray L. Hart ("The Imagination and the Scale of Mental Acts," 1964, unpublished) for the elements of this formulation.

72. It is not possible in this context to develop the category of the parabolic metaphor as a mode of language beyond these and the following suggestive remarks. I have attempted to do so in another essay to be published in a forthcoming work with the tentative title "Language, Hermeneutic and the Word of God" (New York: Harper & Row, 1965). In the meantime, the reader is referred to Wilder's illuminating remarks, *Language of the Gospel*, 79–96; Owen Barfield, *Poetic Diction, A Study in Meaning*, rev. ed. (London: Faber & Faber, 1952); Jüngel, *Paulus und Jesus*, especially 88ff.; and

The nonliteral or metaphorical horizon of the figure of the Samaritan and of the parable is suggested by the literal meaning and depends upon it. In this case, the Samaritan is both just a Samaritan and he whom we could not expect and do not wish to see on that road. The parable is both just a story of a good Samaritan and a parabolic metaphor opening onto a referential totality which is informed by a new vision of reality that shatters the everyday view.

As a means of advancing this concept it may be said that metaphorically the parable has an existential and a temporal tenor, the one because of the other. Existentially the metaphor gives itself to unfinished reality, so to speak, so that the narrative is not complete until the hearer is drawn into it as participant. This is the reason the parables are often said to be argumentative, calling for a transference of judgment. The hearer is confronted with a situation in relation to which he must decide how to comport himself: is he willing to allow himself to be the victim, to smile at the affront to the priest and Levite, to be served by an enemy? The parable invites, nay, compels him to make some response, and it is this response that is decisive for him. Temporally the metaphor resists specificity for itself, refuses ideational crystallization.[73] What it says is minimal; what it intends is maximal. It therefore opens onto a plurality of situations, a diversity of audiences, and consequently the future. Every hearer has to hear it in his own way. The parable as metaphor does not foreclose but discloses the future.

These considerations have prepared the way for a brief characterization of the other figures in the narrative. The victim is faceless and nameless, perhaps intentionally so, since every auditor finds himself in the ditch. The poor traveler is literally the victim of a ruthless robber. So were the poor, the lame, the blind, and the others whom Jesus drew to his side. In fact, one has to understand himself as the victim, i.e., sinner, in order to be eligible. Furthermore, the victim is given his true identity in relation to the three figures who come along the road. *How* he views them

---

a recent article by H. Jack Forstman, "Samuel Taylor Coleridge's Notes toward the Understanding of Doctrine," *JR* 44 (1964): 310–27, esp. 319ff.

73. It is for this reason that the parables should not be allegorized (allegory: reduction to a congeries of ideas or concepts, for which the narrative elements are ciphers), but it is also the reason why the parables cannot be reduced to a leading idea (Jeremias, *Parables of Jesus*, 115) or understood to teach "spiritual truths." Rationalization in any form maims the parabolic image.

determines who he is! The priest and the Levite, on the other hand, are those from whom the victim might have expected more. But they should also be considered from their own point of view. The priests and Levites in the audience can almost be heard either protesting that they want to deliberate the situation as the narrative pushes them by, or justifying or excusing themselves. They have the option, of course, of moving to the place of the victim or the Samaritan! In both cases the literal and metaphorical meanings must again he grasped concomitantly.

The parable has been considered thus far without raising the christological question. Gerhardsson's thesis compels us to ask whether Jesus appears in the narrative picture. Certainly not explicitly. The question can be rephrased: does Jesus appear in the *field* of the narrative picture? It would be a mistake to hasten to a positive answer. It should first be noticed that the question is restricted to Jesus, i.e., without reference to his messiahship. One is led to think, as Gerhardsson does, of Jesus as the physician, healer, shepherd who moves to the side of the destitute, tax-collectors, prostitutes, sinners. The Samaritan is one who does not consider whether he has any business helping an enemy (it cuts both ways!); he does not cast an apprehensive glance around for the robbers; he does not calculate the cost or the consequences, anticipate a reward, or contemplate a result. To this extent Jesus stands behind the Samaritan. He is there in Samaritan not as a messianic figure, but as one who lives in the "world," or under the "logic," drawn by the parable. It can of course be said that in this Jesus moves to God's side in relation to mundane reality, that he acts out of the vision of a world under the jurisdiction of God's righteousness.[74] But to do so is to affirm that Jesus is declaring who God is, and that he is looking at the in-breaking of a kingdom nobody else sees.

If the latter is allowed to stand, then it could also be said that Jesus hovers behind the Samaritan also in the sense that he is the one whom his hearers could not expect and from whom they wanted no help, that is, so long as they refuse to be victims and allow themselves to be helped by the alien. In that case the parable is christological, but not in the sense Gerhardsson takes it to be.

---

74. Cf. Ernst Käsemann, "Gottesgerechtigkeit bei Paulus," *ZTK* 58 (1961): 377–78 (translated as "The 'Righteousness of God' in Paul," in *New Testament Questions of Today* [Philadelphia: Fortress, 1969], 168–82), who uses the phrase in a formulation from the Pauline perspective.

It should he recalled at this point that the parable ends by calling upon the hearer to pass judgment on the performance. He is no longer victim, priest or Levite, or even Samaritan, but judge. From the point of view of the conclusion, the parable invites the auditor to take up a new position, this time in relation to the three named actors. He knows the answer to the question posed and suspects that he has walked into the trap. Indeed he has. The parable is an invitation to comport oneself with reality in the way in which the Samaritan does. This should not be understood exclusively or even primarily as a moral demand to love neighbor; it is rather permission to live in the "world" of the parable, in a "world" under the jurisdiction of God's righteousness. That has drastic consequences, needless to say. If, then, the hearer is invited to "see" what the Samaritan "sees" and embark upon his "way," he is also invited to follow Jesus, for Jesus, as we saw, "appears" in the penumbral field of the parable as the one who qualifies the situation. Indeed, the parable bodies forth Jesus's "world," opening metaphorically as it does onto a "world" under the aegis of love. To put it succinctly, the parable is permission on the part of Jesus to follow him, to launch out onto a future that is God's own. In this sense, too, it is christological.

A final observation is necessary, for on it depends the "logic" set out in the preceding. The hearer is able to affirm the Samaritan and enter into his "world" only because he has first been victim: "We love because he first loved us" (1 John 4:19).

4.

It is evident from the foregoing analysis that the parable cannot be rightly understood as a punning exegesis[75] of the Old Testament text as Gerhardsson proposes. While I would concur in his intuition that the parable requires a more adequate interpretation than modern exegetes generally have given it, and that the patristic tradition preserves, albeit in distorted form, the correct horizon of the parable, his own thesis is too ingenious, not to say palpably in contradiction to the mode of language of the parable as Jesus employs it. The real question is not the extent to which Jesus was influenced by his time and age,[76] but whether the language of Jesus,

---

75. Gerhardsson, *Good Samaritan*, 27.
76. Gerhardsson, *Good Samaritan*, 31.

and hence his hermeneutic, is amenable to or shatters rabbinic categories[77] The answer does depend, of course, on how one understands Jesus of Nazareth.[78]

More specifically, the everydayness (or realism) of the parable inveighs against Gerhardsson's view. On his view the narrative elements are merely ciphers. To the contrary, the metaphorical value of the narrative elements depends, paradoxically, on their everyday meaning for cogency. Gerhardsson is simply unable to cope with this aspect of the parable.

It is still possible, nevertheless, to inquire whether the parable is an interpretation of the Old Testament text (as in the Lukan context). In seeking an answer, it is necessary to begin again with the parable itself.

What is the prior question to which the parable addresses itself? Even without Luke 10:29, 36–37, it was noted, modern interpreters agree that the parable is devoted to the question of neighbor.[79] According to Bultmann, the point of the story lies in the contrast between the loveless Jew and the loving Samaritan.[80] Jüngel rightly points out that this contrast by itself does not yield the point, but rather the relation of the two to the anonymous man in need of compassion.[81] The priest and Levite represent the Jew who interprets the law correctly,[82] the Samaritan the unexpected one who misunderstands (*sic*) the law but understands the call of love.

---

77. That is to say, one cannot allow the common tradition to dominate the question of Jesus's own mode of discourse. That the latter is to be determined in relation to the former is true enough, but the particularity of the historical relativizes the significance of correlative modes and structures. The crucial item is what Jesus does with the common tradition.

78. Cf. Amos Wilder, "Eschatology and the Speech-Modes of the Gospel," in *Zeit und Geschichte: Dankesgabe an Rudolf Bultmann zum 80. Geburtstag*, ed. Erich Dinkier (Tübingen: Mohr Siebeck, 1964), 27. Wilder's criticisms in this article and another ("Form-History and the Oldest Tradition," in *Neotestamentica et Patristica*, ed. W. C. van Unnik [Leiden: Brill, 1962], 3–13) of Gerhardsson's broader thesis with respect to tradition and interpretation in the early church, fully articulated in *Memory and Manuscript: Oral Tradition and Written Transmission in Rabbinic Judaism and Early Christianity*, ASNU 22 (Uppsala: Gleerup, 1961), serve as background for my criticisms of Gerhardsson's treatment of the parable of the good Samaritan in particular.

79. Above, n. 57.

80. Bultmann, *History of the Synoptic Tradition*, 178.

81. Bultmann, *History of the Synoptic Tradition*, 171.

82. Jeremias (*Parables of Jesus*, 203–4) carefully considers this point and finds it dubious on two grounds: (1) Did the priest and Levite consider the man to be dead (v. 30, "half dead")? (2) Was the Levite governed by ritual considerations? It is perhaps

The parable therefore presents itself as a reinterpretation of the law on the authority of him who speaks the parable (cf. the "But I say to you," "I tell you" of the great sermon). The Lukan context is consequently not inappropriate to the parable.[83]

We may now consider the Lukan context. In contrast to Matthew (22:34–40) and Mark (12:28–31), who have Jesus answer the question of the first commandment, Luke puts the summary of the law in the mouth of the lawyer. Bornkamm thinks that such a summary of the essence of the law is alien to the rabbinic understanding of the law.[84] However that may be, the reduction of the law to the double commandment (cf. Matt 22:40) may well derive from Jesus. By attributing the summary to the lawyer, however, the possibility of relating the parable of the good Samaritan to the commandment is opened up.[85] Whether or not the Lukan complex is original, the combination "brings the original sense of the double commandment of Jesus and thereby his understanding of what 'neighbor' means to expression in an incomparable way."[86] The question of the authenticity of the Lukan context is thus not decisive for a correct understanding of Jesus's intention with respect to the interrelation of commandment and parable. Luke or the tradition before him holds fast to the thrust of the parable by providing this context.[87]

It is appropriate, consequently, to consider the parable as an interpretation of an Old Testament text, specifically, of the double commandment.

---

the ambiguity of the situation which gives the parable its pinch: the priest and Levite want to debate the issue (see above).

83. Bultmann, *Jesus and the Word*, 96; Günther Bornkamm, "Das Doppelgebot der Liebe," in *Neutestamentliche Studien für Rudolf Bultmann*, 2nd ed., BZNW 21 (Berlin: Töpelmann, 1957), 85; Jüngel, *Paulus und Jesus*, 172.

84. Bomkamm, "Das Doppelgebot der Liebe," 86. The rabbis, of course, occasionally gave brief synopses of the law but would have been opposed to a reduction in principle.

85. Bornkamm, "Das Doppelgebot der Liebe," 92. Bornkamm thinks Matthew and Luke had variants of the Markan text before them; Manson, *Sayings of Jesus*, 259, thinks the Lukan story is independent of Mark.

86. Bornkamm, "Das Doppelgehot der Liebe," 93.

87. Manson, *Sayings of Jesus*, 260, suggests that the Lukan account presupposes, so to speak, the Markan account in that the lawyer gives what he knows to be Jesus's answer in order to raise the further question. The Lukan version begins in earnest where the Markan account leaves off. One can reach this conclusion by inference from the parable itself rather than by attempting to establish first the authenticity of the Lukan context as Manson does.

As an interpretation, the parable must be grasped with respect to its metaphorical field. The love of God or God's love (subjective or objective genitive) do not figure explicitly in the picture. The Samaritan does not love with side glances at God.[88] The need of neighbor alone is made self-evident, and the Samaritan responds without other motivation. At the same time, the narrative picture forces the hearer to take up the position of one in need of compassion. In so doing he learns what "as thyself" means.[89] The hearer himself becomes the object of unconstrained, unmotivated mercy, at the point where he could not expect, perhaps was not willing to accept, it. The narrative picture is therefore secular; God does not "appear."

While the need of neighbor is self-evident, the priest and Levite, as custodians of the law, pass by. Only the Samaritan answers the call of neighbor's need. What frees him to do so, while the other two are constrained to look away? The field intended by the parable, as was suggested, is qualified by the one speaking, by Jesus as the incarnate word. This word must be love as event. Thus, while Jesus (or God) does not "appear," he is the off-stage qualifier of the situation, a decisive factor in the penumbral field. One would have to say, then, that it is God's love as event which gives the Samaritan in the narrative picture this freedom, the freedom to risk all, to proceed with his love unhurried, deliberately. As Jüngel puts the announcement of the parable, "The reign of God is as near to you as the Samaritan to the one threatened by death."[90] But God has drawn near the Samaritan, too, as the one who is half-conscious in the ditch knows. There is forged here the eschatological unity of promise and demand.[91]

With respect to the Lukan context, it follows that Jesus does not allow the lawyer's question (and ours) to dominate the parable, for the lawyer's question is an effort to hold the question of neighbor at arm's length, and hence the force of the commandment. From the perspective of the parable the question "Who is my neighbor?" is an impossible question.[92] The disjuncture between question and answer, considered so grievous by Jülicher and those who have followed him, far from being inimical to the parable, is

---

88. Bornkamm, *Jesus of Nazareth*, 110.
89. Bornkamm, *Jesus of Nazareth*, 113.
90. Jüngel, *Paulus und Jesus*, 173.
91. Jüngel, *Paulus und Jesus*, 173.
92. Bornkamm, *Jesus of Nazareth*, 113.

necessary to the point.[93] This means also that Jesus does not allow the law to dominate love as God's drawing near. Rather, Jesus proclaims the law in a context qualified by the event of divine love and interprets it with the help of the concrete instance of love's needfulness.[94] Jesus thus brings the question of neighbor near in its own right, i.e., as a self-evident question,[95] but makes it impossible to give the right answer except out of the event of grace in his own person and word. "The law now says [in the proclamation of Jesus], with your permission, look, I stand on the side of *love*! I allow you *your* righteousness. That is the sense, e.g., of the double command-ment of love of God and neighbor (Mark 12:28–34 par.)."[96]

For Jesus the law labored under severe handicaps. It had been con-fined to a field in which God was ostensibly present but from which he was actually remote. The scribes and Pharisees sought to relate it to every-day existence in countless ways, but it grew less relevant with each step. Rabbinic interpretation of the law sought to engage the Jew, but ended by disengaging him from reality. Jesus attempted nothing less than to shatter the whole tradition that had obscured the law. To put it in a way that is still enigmatic but in the way the parable suggests, Jesus had to interpret the law in parable.[97]

Bibliography

Anderson, Bernhard W., ed. *The Old Testament and the Christian Faith.* New York: Harper & Row, 1963.

Barfield, Owen. *Poetic Diction, A Study in Meaning.* Rev. ed. London: Faber & Faber, 1952.

Billerbeck, Paul. *Kommentar zum Neuen Testament aus Talmud und Midr-asch.* München: Beck, 1922–1928.

---

93. Contra Jeremias, *Parables of Jesus*, 205: "The alteration in the form of the question hardly conceals a deeper meaning."

94. Ernst Fuchs, *Zum hermeneutischen Problem in der Theologie* (Tübingen: Mohr Siebeck, 1959), 286–87, 290.

95. Cf. Gerhard Ebeling, "Die Evidenz des Ethischen und die Theologie," *ZTK* 58 (1960): 318–56 (English translation to appear in: *JThC* 1 [1965]).

96. Fuchs, *Zum hermeneutischen Problem in der Theologie*, 287.

97. The reader may wish to compare my earlier reading of the parable in "How Do You Read?," *Int* 18 (1964): 56–61.

Bornkamm, Günther. "Das Doppelgebot der Liebe." Pages 85–93 in *Neutestamentliche Studien für Rudolf Bultmann*. 2nd ed. BZNW 21. Berlin: Töpelmann, 1957.

———. *Jesus of Nazareth*. New York: Harper & Brothers, 1960.

Brownlee, W. H. "Biblical Interpretation among the Sectaries of the Dead Sea Scrolls." *BA* 14 (1951): 54–76.

Bultmann, Rudolf. *History of the Synoptic Tradition*. Translated by John Marsh. New York: Harper & Row, 1963.

———. *Jesus and the Word*. Translated by Louise Pettibone Smith and Erminie Huntress Lantero. New York: Scribner's Sons, 1958.

Daniélou, J. "Le Bon Samaritain." Pages 457–65 in *Mélanges Bibliques rédigés en l'honeur de André Robert*. Paris: Bloud & Gay 1957.

Dodd, C. H. *The Parables of the Kingdom*. 2nd ed. London: Nisbet, 1952.

Ebeling, Gerhard. *Evangelische Evangelienauslegung: Eine Untersuchung zu Luther's Hermeneutik*. 2nd ed. Darmstadt: Wissenschaftliche Buchgesellschaft, 1962.

———. "Die Evidenz des Ethischen und die Theologie." *ZTK* 58 (1960): 318–56.

Fiebig, Paul. *Die Gleichnisreden Jesu im Lichte der rabbinischen Gleichnisse*. Tübingen: Mohr Siebeck, 1912.

Forstman, H. Jack. "Samuel Taylor Coleridge's Notes toward the Understanding of Doctrine." *JR* 44 (1964): 310–27.

Fuchs, Ernst. "Bermerkungen zur Gleichnisauslegung." Pages 136–42 in *Zur Frage nach dem historischen Jesus*. Tübingen: Mohr Siebeck, 1960.

———. *Hermeneutik*. 2nd ed. Bad Canstatt: Müllerschön Verlag, 1958.

———. "The New Testament and the Hermeneutical Problem." Pages 111–45 in *The New Hermeneutic*. Edited by James M. Robinson and John B. Cobb. New York: Harper & Row, 1964.

———. *Zum hermeneutischen Problem in der Theologie*. Tübingen: Mohr Siebeck, 1959.

Funk, Robert W. "How Do You Read?" *Int* 18 (1964): 56–61.

Gerhardsson, Birger. *The Good Samaritan—The Good Shepherd?* ConBNT 16. Land: Gleerup, 1958.

———. *Memory and Manuscript: Oral Tradition and Written Transmission in Rabbinic Judaism and Early Christianity*. ASNU 22. Uppsala: Gleerup, 1961.

Grundmann, Walter. *Die Geschichte Jesu Christi*. 2nd ed. Berlin: Evangelische Verlagsanstalt, 1959.

Hoskyns, Edwyn C., and Noel Davey. *The Riddle of the New Testament.* London: Faber & Faber, 1931.

Jeremias, Joachim. *The Parables of Jesus.* Translated by S. H. Hooke. Rev. ed. New York: Scribner's Sons, 1963.

Jülicher, Adolf. *Die Gleichnisreden Jesu.* Tübingen: Mohr Siebeck, 1910. Repr. 2 vols. in 1. Darmstadt: Wissenschaftliche Buchgesellschaft, 1963.

Jüngel, Eberhard. *Paulus und Jesus: Eine Untersuchung zur Präzisierung der Frage nach dem Ursprung der Christologie.* Tübingen: Mohr Siebeck, 1962.

Käsemann, Ernst. "Gottesgerechtigkeit bei Paulus." *ZTK* 58 (1961): 367–78. Translated as "The 'Righteousness of God' in Paul." Pages 168–82 in *New Testament Questions of Today.* Philadelphia: Fortress, 1969.

Linnemann, Eta. *Gleichnisse Jesu: Einführung und Auslegung.* 2nd ed. Göttingen: Vandenhoeck & Ruprecht, 1962.

Manson, Thomas Walter. *The Sayings of Jesus.* London: SCM, 1949.

———. *The Teachings of Jesus.* Cambridge: Cambridge University Press, 1951.

Michaelis, Wilhelm. *Die Gleichnisse Jesu: Eine Einführung.* 3rd ed. Hamburg: Furche, 1956.

Riesenfeld, Harald. "The Parables in the Synoptic and the Johannine Traditions." *SEÅ* 25 (1960): 37–61.

Robinson, James M. "The New Hermeneutic at Work." *Int* 18 (1964): 346–59.

Stendahl, Krister. *The School of St. Matthew and Its Use of the Old Testament.* ASNU 20. Uppsala: Almqvist & Wiksell, 1954.

Westermann, Claus, ed. *Essays on Old Testament Hermeneutics.* Richmond: John Knox, 1963.

Wilder, Amos. "Eschatology and the Speech-Modes of the Gospel." Pages 19–30 in *Zeit und Geschichte: Dankesgabe an Rudolf Bultmann zum 80. Geburtstag.* Edited by Erich Dinkier. Tübingen: Mohr Siebeck, 1964.

———. "Form-History and the Oldest Tradition." Pages 3–13 in *Neotestamentica et Patristica.* Edited by W. C. van Unnik. Leiden: Brill, 1962.

———. *The Language of the Gospel: Early Christian Rhetoric.* New York: Harper & Row, 1964.

Beyond Criticism in Quest of Literacy: The Parable of the Leaven

Robert W. Funk

> The fundamental question for the interpreter who addresses himself to the Jesus-tradition today is this: Is it possible any longer to recover the parable as parable?

Biblical criticism is a species of literary criticism. If the range and function of literary criticism were clear, that remark would be more illuminating than it is. Yet in spite of the ambiguity of terms, the correlation is suggestive.

Literary criticism, on minimal terms, ought to instruct the uninitiated in what to read and how to read it. A guide to what is worthy of attention amidst the deluge of printed matter assaulting the optical nerves is alone worth the price of admission. Even after the sorting has been made, it may not be immediately evident to all why a particular piece merits close reading and reflection. All of which is to say, how a piece is to be read and whether it is worth reading in the first place are not unrelated questions.

The literary critic, according to George Steiner, has these two functions: his task is to "prepare the context of future recognition" and to widen and complicate the map of sensibility.[1] The present reader is taught to see what is really there to be seen; failing the adequate transformation of present sensibility, the critic must lay the ground for delayed recognition. Criticism is a second-order enterprise, but the poet could not survive without it.

The biblical corpus is large enough to warrant, even require, selective attention. And because it has suffered overattention, its language has been overlayed with tons of obfuscating debris. To change the metaphor, few lit-

---

1. George Steiner, *Language and Silence: Essays on Language, Literature, and the Inhuman* (New York: Atheneum, 1967), 8–9.

erary compendia in the Western tradition have been so completely washed clean of resonances by the waters of common repetition and interpretation.

My assignment is to give some account of the usefulness of phenomenological analysis in clearing away the obfuscating debris spoken of above that overlies the biblical text or to suggest how this method might restore some resonance to a text now cold by nearly two millennia.

An exhaustive programmatic statement is out of the question, were the full contours of such a statement already clear to me. They are not. Much theoretical groundwork needs yet to be laid in a discipline, scarcely a half-century old, which concerns language, currently the problem child also of linguistics, analytic philosophy, and literary criticism. In spite of theoretical deficiencies, the phenomenology of language appears to have made considerable progress in practice. Progress is possible, it seems, even where, or perhaps especially where, the practitioner does not know exactly what he is doing. I therefore propose to exhibit certain aspects of the phenomenological method by analyzing a biblical text; my analysis will offer some generalizations, which may or may not illuminate what I am doing.

1. Away-from-Here: The Point of Departure

The first question that naturally arises in connection with the interpretation of any text is: Where does one begin? The student learning to do exegesis finds getting started the most difficult task of all. Once a start has been made, however, he is able, as a rule, to proceed to a conclusion without faltering.

There is a point in the last remark: the way in which the task of interpretation is *undertaken* is determinative for the whole process. The *undertaking* anticipates what is to be *overtaken*. Methodology is not an indifferent net; it catches only what it is designed to catch. For this reason, phenomenology has been preoccupied with the methodology, but not as an enterprise independent of the subject matter. The slogan, "to the things themselves," suggests that the thing itself should be permitted to propose the terms of its unconcealment.

Permit me to leave the matter vague for the moment and return to the initial question: Where does one begin? The phenomenologist will reply: Let us begin where we must. But where must we begin? *We must set out from where we are.* Where we are is, of course, our particular time and place in history in relation to the text under scrutiny.

The naiveté of this common-sense reply should not deceive. In the first place, it is no easy matter to determine precisely where we are. Writing the history of the last fifty years is always the most hazardous task. The future of these years has not yet fallen out into the sunlight of historical distance. In the second place, the advice presupposes that where we are in relation to the interpretation of a given text is in some sense (as yet undefined) a misinterpretation, a misunderstanding, or a nonunderstanding of that text. There would be no need for fresh interpretation were it not assumed that previous interpretation was in some respects deficient.

To put the difficulties concisely: We are to set out from where we are as a place that cannot be located with precision and move away from some unspecified misunderstanding or nonunderstanding in the direction of some unspecified understanding to a future that comports authentically with both the subject matter of the text we are interpreting and with the context in which the text is to be interpreted.

To mark the way to this elusive destination the map has not yet been drawn. When the knowledge requisite to the map is in hand, there will no longer be any need for the map. Meanwhile, only the direction of the quest is certain: it is away-from-here, away from established understanding which also entails misunderstanding and nonunderstanding.

We are now in a position to discern the real gravity of our dilemma: How can the text propose the terms of its unconcealment when the terms themselves are dependent upon a glimpse of the text already unconcealed? *Mis*understanding and *non*understanding can give way to understanding only when the *mis* and the *non* are exposed by some understanding.

Getting underway, consequently, is of crucial importance. A phenomenological analysis will proceed circumspectly; it will endeavor to coax the text into betraying its own intentionality by pressing the issue with the text, all the while looking for the stray clue dropped inadvertently along the path of violent wrestling with the tradition.

It may prove lucrative to advance these preliminary abstractions as a down payment on the analysis of a concrete text. I would prefer to address a biblical text that is relatively free of ambiguities; but, alas, such a text is not to be found. Since ambiguity and complexity is our lot, we may settle for brevity. I have chosen as my *pièce de résistance* the parable or similitude of the leaven, taken from the Jesus tradition.

The parable of the leaven is reported by Matthew and Luke in a form without significant variation: "The kingdom of heaven is like leaven which a woman took and hid in three measures of meal, till it was all leavened"

(Matt 13:33; cf. Luke 13:20–21). The parable is presumably derived from Q and is reported in both cases as a twin to the parable of the mustard seed.

The Gospel of Thomas preserves a slightly different version: "The kingdom of the father is like a woman who has taken a little leaven and has hidden it in dough and has made large loaves of it" (Gos. Thom. 96). Most interpreters of Thomas hold that this version does not represent a significant alternative to the Synoptic tradition.

In accordance with sound scholarly practice, and as a means of locating approximately where we are, the history of recent interpretation may be briefly sampled. Joachim Jeremias, the oracle of modern parable interpretation, avers that the meaning of this parable, like that of the mustard seed, is that "out of the most insignificant beginnings, invisible to human eye, God creates his mighty kingdom, which embraces all the peoples of the world."[2] For Jeremias the parable is a parable of contrast: The "tiny morsel of leaven" is "absurdly small in comparison with the great mass of more than a bushel of meal."[3] The parable is aimed at the doubts of those who hesitated to believe that the kingdom of God could issue from the insignificant beginnings of Jesus's ministry. It is therefore a parable of assurance.[4]

Jeremias interprets the leaven jointly with the mustard seed because, he says, the two are closely linked by content. He admits that their juxtaposition in Q may derive from a collector or redactor.[5] One may wonder whether the compiler of Q has not in fact skewed the interpretation of one or both of the parables by placing them together. In any case, Jeremias appears to have determined that the connection is valid.

C. H. Dodd in a somewhat earlier work toys with the idea that the leaven should be interpreted without reference to the mustard seed. If taken independently, he claims, it means that Jesus's ministry is comparable to leaven working in dough: It works from within, without external coercion, "mightily permeating the dead lump of religious Judaism...."[6] If it goes with the mustard seed, then "the emphasis must lie upon the com-

---

2. Joachim Jeremias, *The Parables of Jesus*, trans. S. H. Hoake, rev. ed. (New York: Scribner's Sons, 1965), 149.

3. Jeremias, *Parables of Jesus*, 148.

4. Jeremias, *Parables of Jesus*, 149.

5. Jeremias, *Parables of Jesus*, 146.

6. C. H. Dodd, *The Parables of the Kingdom*, rev. ed. (New York: Scribner's Sons, 1961), 155–56.

pletion of the process of fermentation. The period of obscure development is over; ... the Kingdom ... has now come."[7] In either case, Dodd's thesis that the kingdom is here and now present and effective is substantiated.

Space does not permit expansion of this sample of opinion. For our purposes, notice of one other giant may suffice.

Adolph Jülicher is the father of all recent parable interpretation. In his mammoth two-part work, published in 1899 and 1910, he not only reviews the history of interpretation but establishes the guidelines that parables are to be stripped of all allegorical overlay and interpreted in accordance with one point of the broadest possible (moral) application.[8] For Jülicher's one generalized moral, A. T. Cadoux, Dodd, and Jeremias propose to substitute one particular point of historical application, namely, the point that suits Jesus's historical setting. In other respects, however, they agree with Jülicher that the parables score a didactic point that can be readily reduced to more discursive language. Jülicher thus launched modern interpretation on its course, and the search for that one elusive point of particular historical application has gone on relentlessly, but largely without decisive resolution.

With the rejection of allegory, the details of the picture or narrative were reduced to incidental features of the parable. Determine the point, we are told, and the details fall into place. But how is one to determine the point without first ascertaining what detail or which details are the vehicle of the point? According to Jeremias, the parable contrasts insignificant beginnings with great issue. The tiny morsel of leaven is thus contrasted with the huge mass of dough. How do we know that it is just these two details which convey the point, while the leaven and the dough themselves are incidental? Dodd, again, fastens on the process of fermentation as the clue to the point: like leaven working in dough, the kingdom works in the world or in Judaism. Dodd has elected quite a different detail from which to adduce his point, and, one might suppose, with equal justification, since the process of selection appears to be arbitrary. Alternately, Dodd can fix on the leavened lump of dough as a sign of the kingdom's arrival. In either case, he is following Jülicher's fundamental maxim: one point corresponding more or less to one detail of the narrative or picture.

---

7. Dodd, *Parables of the Kingdom*, 154.
8. Dodd, *Parables of the Kingdom*, 24ff., and Jeremias, *Parables of Jesus*, 18ff.

Jeremias, by contrast, often sneaks in two or more details in order to win his single point.

Dodd and Jeremias are struggling with Jülicher's legacy without realizing they have been trapped by it. Instead of recovering the parable by discarding allegory, they have been thrown into anarchy: choose a detail, any detail, and draw your point. The point drawn is as reliable as the choice of the detail, or as reliable as the theology informing the point that prompts the choice of detail.

Jülicher's legacy is a trap because he was never able to escape from the allegory he so fervently rejected. For him and his successors parable interpretation is a form of reduced allegory; instead of many points corresponding to a variety of details, there is only one point corresponding to one, or a pair of details.

Parable interpretation is at an impasse. The way forward is away-from-here.

2. Away-from-There: Sedimented and Refracted Language

The ultimate point of departure in addressing a text is away-fromhere, as the interpreter's locus within the history of interpretation. The penultimate point of departure is away-from-there, as the writer or speaker's locus within his own linguistic tradition The former I have already endeavored to justify. To the justification and exposition of the latter we must now give brief attention.

As a tradition matures, its myths, symbols and lexical stock, its semantic logic, are crystallized. The meanings evoked by the terms of a culture are sedimented. The crystallization and sedimentation of a tradition constitute the immediate background within which and against which one speaks or writes the language. If one merely traffics in the sedimented tradition, he merely repeats what is already contained in the language. Under these circumstances, the text produced is rightly interpreted within the framework of the sedimented or dictionary meanings of the terms.

The dictionary represents a tacit social compact to which every speaker must subscribe if he wishes to speak intelligibly. Yet even the poorest speaker or writer, because he has learned to manipulate a finite system of grammatical and semantic variables, so as to be able to produce, potentially, an infinite string of novel sentences, never simply repeats what is already contained in the language. As a matter of fact, the semiliterate and illiterate constantly produce novel sentences in daily parlance that infringe the established grammatical and semantic conventions. Only the fully literate has any real prospect of trading in fully sedimented speech because only he is sufficiently familiar with the conventions to be able to rehearse them.

This point should be kept in mind as a rejoinder to those who hold that Jesus trafficked in the sedimented language of late Judaism *because he was unliterary.*

There is another reason sedimented speech is essentially unstable. A pure recapitulation of the tradition is a task of herculean, if not divine, proportions, as any good historian can attest. History does not pause sufficiently long to allow one to repeat even the same string of linguistic symbols without the temporal passage taking its modifying toll. What is said in one moment is modified when reiterated in the next by the same speaker just because the "I" of the speaker has shifted its temporal locus.

The unrepeatability of the tradition is a limiting concept of no little significance, but it is not the immediate issue.

The creative writer, in contrast to the hack or gossip, employs language as a means of refracting language. If he aspires to say something new, he must seek some exit from the vicious circle of sedimented meaning, and this exit is provided for a deformation of the tradition. He cannot begin with new language. He must begin with the habituated language at hand, with the language he learned at his mother's knee. But he may succeed in moving away from those sedimentations and finding his own voice. The measure of his success is commensurate with the degree to which he has infringed the semantic compact represented by the dictionary.

Away-from-there as the penultimate point of departure means, consequently, that the interpreter must work out of the sedimented tradition as received by the author of a given text, and into the refraction or deformation of that tradition, as the author in question brings the tradition to speech afresh.

The assumption of lexicographers, grammarians, and philologians who ply their trades in relation to biblical texts, is that the language of the Bible is fully, or nearly fully, sedimented: Meaning can be determined on a comparative basis. The historical range of the assumption, of course, varies from the homogeneity of the entire length and breadth of the biblical tradition, to the homogeneity of a testament, period, or writer.

The theory of language advocated by at least one branch of modem, descriptive linguistics would appear to support this assumption. The transformationalist Jerrold J. Katz writes: "Linguistic description can be no more concerned per se with the speech performance of members of a language community than a physicist is concerned per se with meter readings or a biologist is concerned with individual specimens of various sorts. Like other scientists, the linguist idealizes away from the heterogeneous phenomena that directly face him in nature. Thus, the linguist makes no effort to describe actual speech, the linguistic behavior resulting from the speaker's performance, but concentrates on language, the mental structure that constitutes the speaker's competence in the language."[9] Whatever else may be said of this linguistic program, one important difference between the linguist and the interpreter of a biblical text is immediately evident: the latter is concerned with the heterogeneous phenomena that face him in the texts. He ignores the heterogeneity on the pain of ignoring the texts.

Nevertheless, the assumption reflects sound methodology *when it is correctly understood as the point of departure.* The fallacy lies in assuming that a text can be understood, exhaustively, in relation to received tradition. The matter may now be put in the round: The matrix of historical interpretation is comparative philology and *Traditionsgeschichte*, but the interpreter must emerge from this matrix into the spiral of refracted language as encountered in the concrete text.

The reference to descriptive linguistics bears expansion for the wider bearing the conception of this discipline may have on the way in which the problem language is being posed the days.

In a provocative article on recent phenomenology in France, Paul Riceour points out that for descriptive linguistics, language is conceived as having neither speaking subject nor referent about which something is said. Rather, language is a constellation of internal dependencies, a structure, that is considered in and of itself. The ultimate presupposition of this view is that language is an *object*, like other objects, which may be analyzed into a system of internal dependencies.[10] The corollary, as Heidegger has noticed, is language regarded as a tool at hand, to be used in expressing a sense that is arrived at, experienced, taken possession of, by some other means. On this view both the speaker and the thing, the referent, that about which something is said, disappear behind the homogeneity of

---

9. Jerrold J. Katz, *The Philosophy of Language* (New York: Harper & Row, 1966), 116–17.

10. Paul Riceour, "New Developments in Phenomenology in France: The Phenomenology of Language," *Social Research* 34 (1967):15ff.

sedimented speech, of language idealized away from the heterogeneity of the phenomena.

Phenomenology, to be sure, aspires to challenge such a reduction. Riceour affirms: "Language is no more foundation than it is object: it is mediation; it is the *medium*, the 'milieu' in which and through which the subject poses himself and the world shows itself."[11] The concrete phenomenon of language is thus something quite different from the abstraction siphoned off by linguistics. Any account of language, empirical or theoretical, must take into consideration the full range of linguistic phenomena. Nevertheless, phenomenology of language can no longer succeed without the complicity of descriptive linguistics, for it is the latter that has brought to the surface the pervasive syntactical system that dominates every natural language, and has shown that sedimented lexical stock is so interwoven with the grammatical system that tradition has again taken on the contours of innate ideas. In fine, linguistics has shown how stubborn language tradition really is. At the same time, it has given us fresh purchase on the problematic: It is now possible to broach the problem of language on a variety of models, much as modern mathematics has a variety of theoretical constructs at its disposal for explaining its own operation. Somewhere in this recently unearthed labyrinth of possibilities lies the key or keys to adequate linguistic theory.

From our distance, the parable of the leaven looks flat. It does not strike us as poignant; in fact, it probably docs not strike us at all. We may conclude that the parable is trite and let it go at that. It is just possible that our sensitivities have gone dead—a possibility we are initially inclined to regard as remote since the parable has been domesticated in our language tradition. As historians we may nevertheless persist and indulge in a course of sensitivity training. But how are we to go about enlivening the senses?

Two procedures are immediately open to us. First, we may bury ourselves in the primary literature, read parables of all kinds, read texts on leaven, baking, and the like, and even read texts that have no apparent connection with the subject matter of this parable. Our object will be to reacclimate ourselves to the sedimented tradition of that time and place, with a view to "listening in" on the lost resonances of our text. Secondly,

---

11. Riceour, "New Developments in Phenomenology in France," 27, emphasis original.

we may scan the secondary literature for items which show up, "appear," but do not converge with the interpreters view of the parable. Such items may prove to be important as clues to both away-from-here and away-from-there on the grounds that they have not been assimilated to what the parable is taken to mean. Ideally, we should combine the two procedures.

Consider the parable sentence once again: "The kingdom is like leaven which a woman took and hid in three measures of meal until all was leavened." What items in the sentence stand out against the background of language sedimented "there"? Which items attract attention "here"? Which items show up as residual problems in the history of interpretation?

The scene is common enough. Anyone who has observed bread made, here or in the Near East, recognizes the scene for what it is: a piece of everydayness.

Well, then, have we any clues beyond an undifferentiated common picture of a woman kneading dough for bread?

(1) Even to the English reader the word "hid" may sound odd in the context of putting yeast into dough. In what sense does she "hide" the leaven? Jülicher is of the opinion that "hide" may have struck Matthew as appropriate to the situation of the kingdom in the world at the time he wrote: it is hidden to the eyes of most men. However, Jülicher goes on to say that *kruptō* may also have been employed in a completely faded sense, meaning merely *to put* or *place in*. But the evidence he cites is slender.[12] The word normally conveyed the nuance of *conceal, secret, cover*. Other scholars avoid the question by averring that leaven is hidden in dough in the sense of disappearing in it, of becoming one with the dough it leavens. Dodd proposes that leaven is hidden in that, at first, nothing appears to happen;[13] it is there, no longer with its own identity, but without apparent effect. This view is perhaps supported by the final phrase: "until the whole was leavened."

We hear elsewhere in the language of Jesus of things pertaining to the kingdom being "hidden": the Father has *hidden* things from the wise and understanding (Matt 11:25; Luke 10:21); the kingdom is likened to a trea-

---

12. Adolph Jülicher, *Die Gleichnisreden Jesu: Zweiter Tell; Auslegung der Gleichnisreden der drei ersten Evangelion* (Darmstadt: Wissenschaftliche Buchgesellschaft, 1963), 578.

13. Dodd, *Parables of the Kingdom*, 192; cf. Ernst Lohmeyer, *Das Evangelium des Matheus*, ed. Werner Schmauch, 2nd ed. (Göttingen: Vandenhoeck & Ruprecht, 1958), 220.

sure *hidden* in a field (Matt 13:44); indeed, the mystery of the kingdom is hidden in the parables themselves (cf. Mark 4:11–12). If hiddenness belongs to the essence of the kingdom, as Gunther Bornkamm maintains,[14] it is not surprising that the suggestion turns up in various contexts. In this case, we may have to do with a word deliberately chosen so as to vibrate in its context and thus attract attention, obliquely because metaphorically, to some horizon of the subject matter.

(2) Although lost on the reader of the English translation, the unusual amount of meal involved in "three measures" would not have been lost on the original audience. The exaggerated amount has been a constant irritant to modern scholarship, especially to those who wish to affirm the everyday realism of the parables.

The precise value of the *saton* (Hebrew *səʾāh*), translated "measure," is not known. It may have amounted to as much as one and one-half pecks, or as little as two-tenths of a bushel.[15] The total amount may then have been slightly more than a half-bushel, or slightly more than a full bushel. Jeremias estimates 3 seahs as about 50 pounds of flour, or enough to make bread for more than a hundred persons.[16] In any case, we have to do with a "party" baking, as C. W. F. Smith puts it,[17] or with preparations for a festive occasion of significant proportions.

Jeremias takes advantage of the large amount of dough in contrasting it with the "tiny morsel of leaven," yet he suggests that the number three may be an eschatological touch added by Matthew and Luke[18] (more exactly, the redactor of Q?). Support for the omission is afforded by the Gospel of Thomas, where the amount of meal is not specified. Perhaps the strongest argument for regarding the number as a gloss is that it constitutes a parallel to the "tree" in the mustard seed, which is almost certainly a modification of an original "shrub" or "bush" under the influence of the figure of the towering cedar in Ezek 17, 31, and Dan 4.

---

14. Gunther Bornkamm, *Jesus of Nazareth*, trans. Irene and Fraser McLuskey with J. M. Robinson (New York: Harper & Brothers, 1960), 71ff.

15. O. R. Sellers, "Weights and Measures," *IDB* 4:834–35.

16. Jeremias, *Parables of Jesus*, 147 and n. 7.

17. C. W. F. Smith, *The Jesus of the Parables* (Philadelphia: Westminster Press, 1948), 72.

18. Jeremias, *Parables of Jesus*, 147.

These arguments are not without force. Nevertheless, there are even better reasons, in my judgment, for retaining "three measures" as part of the original parable. These may be stated succinctly.

In the mustard seed, the smallness of the seed is emphasized, but not the size of the mature tree. The mustard plant constitutes a burlesque of the mighty cedar of Lebanon, a symbol for the mighty kingdoms of the earth. If the leaven were precisely parallel, we would expect the smallness of the leaven to be emphasized. But that is not in fact the case. "Leaven" is not qualified at all. What is qualified is the unusual amount of dough, and this comports well with Jesus's tendency elsewhere to indulge in comic exaggeration (e.g., hiring laborers at the eleventh hour, the celebration for the lost son, the size of the forgiven debt). That is to say, the parable of the leaven is devoid of comic exaggeration if the amount of flour is a secondary expansion.

Jeremias's suspicions were raised initially in this connection because of an Old Testament parallel. In Gen 18, Yahweh visits Abraham by the oaks of Mamre in the form of three men. Abraham wishes to entertain his visitors with a "morsel of bread" on the occasion of this epiphany. He instructs Sarah to knead "three measures of fine meal" and from it to make cakes (Gen 18:6). A three-measure baking is thus suitable as an offering for an epiphany.

Gideon's experience at the oak of Ophrah parallels Abraham's at the oaks of Mamre.[19] Gideon prepares a kid (Abraham, a calf, Gen 18:7) and unleavened cakes from an ephah of flour (Judg 6:19). An ephah is is made up of 3 seahs or three measures. Again, the amount is suitable for the celebration of an epiphany.

It may also be noted in passing that when Hannah dedicates Samuel at the house of the Lord at Shiloh, she offers, among other things, an ephah or three measures of flour (1 Sam 1:24).

The everyday realism of the parable of the leaven appears to be shattered, then, the gross amount of dough—about as much as a woman could knead at one time[20]—and the specific amount is intended to suggest that the occasion is no ordinary one, perhaps even an epiphany.[21]

---

19. The tree as the locus of a divine epiphany in these accounts is faintly suggestive of the juxtaposition of the mustard (tree) and leaven in the synoptic tradition, but the concatenation is, I think, merely fortuitous. The mustard is linked with the mighty cedar rather than the oak.

20. Jülicher, *Die Gleichnisreden Jesu*, 577.

21. Cf. Jeremias, *Parables of Jesus*, 147.

(3) It has been remarked that three measures of meal is associated with the epiphany or with a thank-offering to the Lord. If we take this overtone as a clue to the horizon of the parable, we are brought back abruptly to the curious choice of the central figure of the parable. In this connection, we may recall two texts:

> And you shall observe the feast of unleavened bread, for on this very day I brought your hosts out of the land of Egypt: ... For seven days no leaven shall be found in your houses; for if any one eats what is leavened, that person shall be cut off from the congregation of Israel. (Exod 12:17–20)

This injunction was joined by a more general injunction to the effect that leaven was prohibited in connection with sacrifices and meal offerings (Exod 23:18, 34:25; Lev 2:11, 6:17).

The second text reflects the annotations the symbol of leaven conjured up in the New Testament period (1 Cor 5:6–8). Leaven was apparently universally regarded as a symbol of corruption.[22] So pervasive was this understanding of leaven, in fact, that a number of commentators have remarked of the parable of the leaven: "an unexpected application of a familiar illustration."[23]

The difficulty of taking a figure predominantly associated with the "infectious power of evil" in a positive sense has often enough been observed by modern interpreters. C. W. F. Smith insists that leaven cannot be reinterpreted in a positive sense, given the sedimented understanding of the figure. And for Jesus to refract the sedimented understanding of the term in his own disposition to the kingdom, would be to expect too much of Jesus's hearers![24] I reply: did Jesus allow his understanding of the kingdom to be determined by the received tradition regarding the kingdom?

But Smith and others are unaware of the real difficulty attached to reading the leaven in a positive sense because they have taken only perfunctory note of the sacramental overtones of the three measures of flour. To my knowledge only Ernst Lohmeyer has grasped the real tension inherent in the juxtaposition. For Lohmeyer the inseparable connec-

---

22. Even among the Greeks, to judge by Plutarch and Persius (Heinrich F. Beck, "Leaven," *IDB* 3:105).

23. B. T. D. Smith, *The Parables of the Synoptic Gospels: A Critical Study* (Cambridge: Cambridge University Press, 1937), 122–23.

24. Smith, *Jesus of the Parables*, 71.

tion between unleaven and the holy was so intense that the parable of the leaven could be understood only as part of an attack on temple and cult, an attack that comports with Jesus's displacement of the righteous and pious in Israel with the poor and destitute, the tax collectors and harlots: "the tax collectors and prostitutes go into the kingdom, but you (the Pharisees) do not" (Matt 21:31).[25] Such an attack represents an inversion of the symbol of the unleavened and thus a refraction of the sedimented language tradition: The kingdom arrives as a negation of the established temple and cult and replaces them with a sacrament of its own—a new and leavened bread.

It is just possible that this horizon is preserved less obliquely in the version in Thomas, where the woman makes large loaves (leavened?) out of the dough.

The proximity of the three terms, "leaven," "hide," "three measures of meal": within the confines of the brief sentence that comprises the parable, thus reverberate against each other and against the sedimented language tradition in such a way that the parable as a whole becomes plurisignificative. The terms are so subtly arranged that the unwary may well read it as a commonplace illustration of a commonplace bit of wisdom. But for the alert the parable triggers the imagination: The terms and the whole are set free to play against one another and against the tradition. Those who have ears hear strange voices.

3. Mode and Meaning

Listening in on the language opens the way for a consideration of mode and meaning. The words and sentences, when allowed to have their own say—against our preconceived notions of what they mean—put us on the track of the subject matter, so to speak. But the subject matter is not something else, to be divorced entirely from the words. *What* the parable says cannot be simply divorced from the *way* it says. Form and content are wedded.

These assertions can be generalized in a phenomenology of language, but we must here confine our observations to the case of the parable itself.

The kingdom may be compared to: leaven which a woman took and hid in three measures of meal, until all was leavened. The leaven suggests

---

25. Lohmeyer, *Das Evangelium*, 220–21.

an inversion of the locus of the sacred: there unleavened; in the kingdom, leavened. *Hidden* hints that the presence of the kingdom is not overtly discernible. Three measures of meal points to the sacramental power of the kingdom, to the festive occasion of an epiphany. Over against the religious tradition into which Jesus was speaking, the kingdom arrives as an inversion, as a mystery, and as power.

If the subject matter is characterized as mystery, then the mode of communication, if it is to be faithful to the subject matter, must convey that mystery as mystery. It may be put more strongly: the proclamation of the kingdom cannot very well dispel the hiddenness without at the same time eroding the essence of the kingdom. The mode of communication must be commensurate with the thing to be communicated.

The kingdom is hidden. It does not arrive with observable signs, so that people can say, "Lo, here it is! or There! for behold" (Luke 17:21). And the kingdom is proclaimed in parables, riddles, and dark sayings so that hearing, people hear not, and seeing they see not (cf. Mark 4:12).

Furthermore, if the kingdom comes as an inversion of what everybody takes to be the case with the sacred, then the terms of its proclamation will of necessity represent a refraction of sacred tradition. The last shall be first and the first last; the tax collectors and harlots go into the kingdom but the righteous Pharisees do not. The mighty cedar becomes a lowly mustard shrub, the long-awaited Messiah arrives incognito. The unleavened is leavened; the holy becomes profane and the profane, holy. In sum, the kingdom inverts the terms of the sacred and the profane.

If the mode and meaning of Jesus's language converge in both inversion and mystery, it may be anticipated that they will converge in power also. It is this convergence that has given rise to all the talk about language event. The conjunction of mode and meaning in power may be put concisely and provisionally this way: In the parables of Jesus the kingdom is offered only for what it is, namely, a venture of faith undertaken on the authority of the parable, in the power of the parable. The parable authorizes the kingdom into which it invites the hearer, and it empowers the hearer to cross over into that fabulous yonder.

4. World-Loss and World-Gain

What does the parable authorize? In traditional language but with deliberate ambiguity, it can be said that the parable authorizes the arrival of the kingdom of God. More precisely, the parable announces a kingdom that is on its way, much as the imperial message in Kafka's parable is on its way.[26] For Kafka, the imperial messenger never arrives; in Jesus he has arrived, but his person and message lack the court credentials for which everyone looks. The kingdom is therefore heralded by a messenger and in a mode that are unaccredited, or accredited only on their own authority.

Messenger, mode, and message, consequently, are conjoined. If one is prepared to perceive the arrival of the one, he is prepared to perceive all three. For this reason, it would be quite possible to speak of the kingdom authorized by the parable in terms of any one of its aspects. Owing to the need for brevity, however, we shall single out the message as our focal point.

Gunther Bornkamm, in the work already cited, gives this interesting summary of the message: "To make the reality of God present: this is the essential mystery of Jesus. This making-present of the reality of God signifies the end of the world in which it takes place."[27] Observe three features of this summary: (1) Jesus makes the reality of God present; (2) this making-present is a mystery; (3) the presence of God, or the arrival of the kingdom, brings an end to the world in which it arrives. We shall concentrate on the last, but in so doing, something shall be said about the first two as well.

In what sense does the kingdom's rival bring an end to the world in which it arrives? We are wont to think of the apocalyptic pictures drawn so fancifully by Daniel, Revelation, and the little apocalypse in the Synoptic Gospels. It is probably not possible for us any longer to understand the apocalyptic mode in anything like its original sense. However, a phenomenology of the language of Jesus directs attention to a different dimension of the question and provides fresh perspective on the problem.

What was the world into which Jesus came? To say that it was a world of sticks and stones, like our own, is accurate but not very revealing. It is more illuminating to observe what lived world dominated the scene; to inquire after the way in which the Jews of Jesus's time and place experienced reality; to ask what referential nexus constituted the horizon of all possible experience, including the experience of God's reign.

In posing the question in this form, we are posing a phenomenological question. When Husserl stated that the world is "always already there,"

---

26. Franz Kafka, *Parables and Paradoxes* (New York, Schocken Books, 1961), 13ff.
27. Bornkamm, *Jesus of Nazareth*, 62.

he meant that no me experiences an object without at the same time experiencing the horizon within which the object is located; the object is the focal point of a backlying referential nexus to which it belongs as object. As Ray Hart has put it, it is the shift in horizons that prompts me to "perceive a cow as so many pounds of beef rather than as something to be worshipped."[28] But Husserl also meant that the perceiving consciousness is also "historically constituted: what is there is there in part as the history of consciousness has programmed it to apprehend.[29] The term "world," in a phenomenological sense, refers to the fundamental horizon or referential nexus within which consciousness apprehends and things are apprehended.

The religious world into which Jesus came—to confine ourselves to me aspect of that world—was a world dominated by the law and the traditions of the fathers. The received world of Judaism in late antiquity was programmed to guard the deposit of tradition once for all delivered to Moses and the prophets, and to preserve this tradition against the day when Yahweh would restore his people to their rightful place within the economy of world history. In the meantime, Yahweh was taken to have withdrawn into the confines of sacred scripture and its interpretation by the fathers into the temple and its cultus, into its latter day surrogate, the synagogue, and into those customs which overtly set the people of God off from their fellows. Within these confines Israel was to await, by faithful and patient observance of the law, the renewal of the ancient glory; to come, it was widely anticipated, in the near future.

It was into this world that Jesus burst with his herculean wrecking bar. His message can only be understood as something designed to precipitate the loss of the received world of Judaism in favor of the gain of the world of the kingdom. The world in which the scribes and Pharisees were at home was shattered upon a new world designed for the poor and destitute, the tax collectors and sinners. The righteousness, of the Pharisees was devalued as confederate paper. The temple and cultus were swallowed up in new forms of celebration: eating, drinking, and dancing in profane style. Sacred scripture was either ignored or criticized, and the traditions of the fathers were set down as milestones about the neck. In short, the home

---

28. Ray L. Hart, "The American Home-World: Reality and Imagination" (lecture in a series "Imagination and Contemporary Sensibility" series, University of Montana, 25 March 1970).

29. Hart, "American Home-World."

world of Judaism was turned upside down in the face of the new reality of the kingdom.

The trauma produced by Jesus's message for those whose home world was Judaism is difficult to exaggerate; the hostility of the scribes and Pharisees, for whom the loss of this world was nothing short of apocalyptic, is readily appreciated. On the other hand, the joy of the religiously disinherited, the destitute, the maimed and the blind was spontaneous. They had been invited to inhabit a strange, new, and alien world that demanded only that they celebrate its arrival as redemption from the past and openness to the future.

Meanwhile the world of sticks and stones had not vanished in a cloud of apocalyptic smoke. To those who participated in the kingdom, however, the world took a new shape, its objects hung together in a new way, and the things themselves were transformed as by a miracle. Reality itself underwent a metamorphosis. To those who refused this new reality, the world was very much the same though perhaps less secure. These looked in vain to see what Jesus saw; what all the shouting was about they took to be a senseless mystery—and from their point of view, rightly so.

In the message of Jesus, the loss of received world, the mystery of the kingdom, and the making-present of the reality of God are coincident. In the parable of the leaven the coincidence is marked by the juxtaposition of "leaven" (loss of received world), "hide" (mystery), and "three measures of meal" (the presence of God). The parable thus parsimoniously encapsulates the horizons of the message of Jesus. World-gain is made concrete, is particularized, "instantiated" by the parable, as a passage for all who care to follow him.

5. Resedimentation: Handing the Tradition Around and On

According to B. T. D. Smith, the parable of the leaven probably owes its preservation to the fact that Christians saw in it a prophecy of the spread of the gospel and the extension of the church.[30] The parable is not provided with a generalizing conclusion, as is the case with a number of other parables, so that we must infer how the later church understood it from some other premise. If the leaven was joined in the mustard seed subsequent to Jesus, there is basis for the inference that the metaphorical

---

30. Smith, *Parables of Synoptic Gospels*, 123.

overtones of the parable were soon lost and its meaning reduced to an illustration of the infectiousness of the kingdom. By the time of Ignatius, the figure of the leaven appears to have stood for the contrast between Judaism and Christianity. In his Letter to the Magnesians, he writes: "Put aside then the evil leaven, which has grown old and sour, and turn to the new leaven, which is Jesus Christ. Be salted in him, that none among you may be corrupted, since by your savor you shall be tested. It is monstrous to talk of Jesus Christ and to practice Judaism" (10:2–3). In this case, the fuller range of overtones, the plurisignificative character of the parable has been lost, but the interpretation has preserved in ossified form the original contrast between the new faith and Judaism.

In the case of the mustard seed, we may observe how the burlesque of the mighty cedar of Israel in the original parable had faded, and the mustard plant converted back into a tree. This conversion may have been accompanied by additional emphasis on the smallness of the seed, as many interpreters, including Jeremias, believe. The mustard seed thus became at the hands of the church a parable of contrast, contrary to the opinion of Jeremias, who attributes this meaning to Jesus. In any case, the church "reinstitutionalized" the mustard plant, just as Ignatius "reinstitutional-izes" the leaven. "Institutionalizing" in this context means that the trauma of world-loss and world-gain has receded, and world, albeit in a new sense, is once again taken for granted.

It is inevitable that world-gain be freshly institutionalized or sedimented as it becomes established as tradition. In phenomenological parlance, tradition houses "received world," the circumspective horizon of all interpretation.

The emergence of world-gain is concomitant with what Ernst Fuchs calls language-gain. That is to say, new language is generated at the threshold of any new world as the means of access to and habitation in that world. Such foundational language, as it may be termed, grants the rights of passage, but it also tends to linger on in sedimented form to become the instrument of eviction. The rights of passage must perpetually be renewed at the price of a recovery of foundational language or the creation of yet another new language.

The sedimentation of foundational language has as its antidote one or more modes of secondary discourse, the function of which is to cast sedimentations, or tradition, back upon primary language and the experience of world-gain concomitant therewith. Failing appropriate modes of secondary language, primary or foundational language withers away in the dungeon of sedimented meanings until its pristine power is completely eroded by the vicious winds of common parlance. There is another possibility however: foundational language may die a historical death, given a radical shift in sensibility, in spite of all appropriate efforts to recover its horizon.

Foundational language is never totally lost to view within the continuity of a tradition. If the original language of a tradition has been forgotten, then the continuity of the tradition has been broken. The memory of an original tongue may grow extremely weak; as though its call were like the pealing of a distant bell. But the sedimentations will preserve that memory, though perhaps in a petrified form. It is for this reason that secondary analysis, like that undertaken in exegesis may rediscover the wave length of foundational language, as it were, by "listening in" on that language and its sedimentations, as though from a great distance. In stumbling around for clues in the texts of the Jesus tradition and the history of interpretation, we are endeavoring to locate the trajectory of the original language by attending to the ways in which that language has "fallen out" in its subsequent history. Once on the right wave length, we may hope to recover something of its original horizon.

As the parables were sedimented in the Jesus tradition, their potential as parables was stopped down. The potential of the parable to evoke a fresh circumspective apprehension of the totality of what is there—a new world—was reduced to a specified meaning, a point, a teaching. This meaning or teaching could then be attached to the parable as a generalizing conclusion or be divorced from the parable and transmitted as a "truth." The point drawn from the parable diverts attention from the parable itself to what it teaches, and thus from the world onto which the parable opens to an idea in an ideological constellation, or, as we might also say, in a theology.

The loss of the parable as parable means the loss also of the cardinal points on the horizon onto which the parable originally opened. The inversion is lost and is replaced by contrast: it is no longer a matter of passage from world-loss to world-gain, but of the contrast between one world (e.g., pagan, Jewish) and another (Christian). The mystery is decoded as teaching or truth. And the making-present of the reality of God is exchanged for belief in God. Conversely, the recovery of the parable as parable restores the original horizon, namely, the inversion, the mystery, and the power.

The fundamental question for the interpreter who addresses himself to the Jesus tradition today is this: Is it possible any longer to recover the parable as parable? Or has there been such a radical shift in world-gain?

The answer depends upon whether the foundational language of Jesus is any longer living tradition.

6. Technical and Essential Literacy

The analysis has come full circle. If the circuit has not been shorted, the return to the starting point will have occurred in another plane, and the circle will have become a spiral. Even so, success may not be imminent: phenomenological analysis may turn out to be just one more opinion in the pantheon of opinions, unless or until it throws us back upon the text and leaves us there in solitude to confront the text without benefit of conceptual comforts.

Whether the parable of the leaven, or any part of the Jesus tradition, is living tradition cannot be answered in advance. The line between the life and death of symbols is too fine for certainty. A death certificate may make demise legal, but it does not make it irreversible.

Such metaphors, if resonant, suggest that the Jesus tradition has taken on the appearance of death. What George Steiner says of the classics can be said also of the Christian tradition: it is not possible to edit classical texts or write commentaries on Scripture within a few kilometers of Buchenwald without some premonition that these languages no longer speak.[31] Steiner puts it in another way: "He who has read Kafka's *Metamorphosis* and can look into his mirror unflinching may technically be able to read print, but is illiterate in the only sense that matters."[32] It is a live question whether proverbial modem man, within or without the church, is any longer literate in the only sense that matters with respect to the foundational language of the Christian faith.

Phenomenology can teach one to read texts with larger eyes, but it cannot mate literate. The text alone has that power. Biblical criticism, like literary criticism, comes anon to the end of its way: from that point he who aspires to literacy must go on alone.

Bibliography

Bornkamm, Gunther. *Jesus of Nazareth*. Translated by Irene and Fraser McLuskey with J. M. Robinson. New York: Harper & Brothers, 1960.

---

31. Steiner, *Language and Silence*, 54.
32. Steiner, *Language and Silence*, 11.

Dodd, C. H. *The Parables of the Kingdom.* Rev. ed. New York: Scribner's Sons, 1961.

Hart, Ray L. "The American Home-World: Reality and Imagination" Lecture in the "Imagination and Contemporary Sensibility" series, University of Montana, 25 March 1970.

Jeremias, Joachim. *The Parables of Jesus.* Translated S. H. Hoake. Rev. ed. New York: Scribner's Sons, 1965.

Jülicher, Adolph. *Die Gleichnisreden Jesu: Zweiter Tell; Auslegung der Gleichnisreden der drei ersten Evangelion.* Darmstadt: Wissenschaftliche Buchgesellschaft, 1963.

Kafka, Franz. *Parables and Paradoxes.* New York: Schocken Books, 1961.

Katz, Jerrold J. *The Philosophy of Language.* New York: Harper & Row, 1966.

Lohmeyer, Ernst. *Das Evangelium des Matheus.* Edited by Werner Schmauch. 2nd ed. Gottingen: Vandenhoeck & Ruprecht, 1958.

Riceour, Paul. "New Developments in Phenomenology in France: The Phenomenology of Language." *Social Research* 34 (1967): 1–30.

Smith, B. T. D. *The Parables of the Synoptic Gospels: A Critical Study.* Cambridge: Cambridge University Press, 1937.

Smith, C. W. F. *The Jesus of the Parables.* Philadelphia: Westminster Press, 1948.

Steiner, George. *Language and Silence: Essays on Language, Literature, and the Inhuman.* New York: Atheneum, 1967.

Theoretical Frame of Parables

Robert W. Funk

This is an email that Robert Funk sent to Westar leaders summarizing his view of parables. In it he refers to Charles ("Charlie") Hedrick's book, *Many Things in Parables*, as what prompted him to summarize his view of parables. Hedrick had written an earlier work on parables, *Parables as Poetic Fictions*, in which he agreed with Funk that parables are metaphors, but argued, against Funk, that the metaphors were created by the early church as a way of making sense of Jesus's teaching. This "post" is Funk's last, retrospective definition of parables.—Ed.

5 November 2004
Colleagues:

Forgive the length of this post. It has been a long time since I wrote specifically about parables, so I thought I should hone my responses. I thought we needed a theoretic frame for our conversations just to clarify some issues. I have chosen the one I developed in the *Poetics of Biblical Narrative* as my frame.

A narrative text consists of two parts: the part that is written and the part that is unwritten. Let me explain.

The first sense in which the narrative is unwritten is the story. A story may defined as a continuous sequence of events, into which descriptions (time, place, characters) are interspersed. The narrative text is merely a selection of items that suggests the story but does not spell it out.

The narrative text also implies a frame of reference (fr, for short). The frame of reference for the parables as poetic fictions, as Charlie says, is the Galilean village, plus other things not strictly belonging to the village. (I think we have read the fr of the parables too narrowly as Jewish defined by Rabbinic Judaism and omitted the Hellenistic aspects of Jesus's social world.) The fr is also unwritten in the sense that we have to infer the frame from what is said in the narrative text and implied in the story.

There is also Field of Reference (FR, for short, capitalized, to distinguish it from the fr), which in the case of the parables is the larger frame of Galilee, the whole of the region, the Roman empire, etc. The FR can extend in all directions, depending on how rich the narrative text is.

Another name for the FR is the term "world." At least, that is how I use the term in my essays, including the *Poetics of Biblical Narrative* (ch. 12).

Now to simplify, the narrative parables and the picture parables both have frs, which consist of scenes set in Galilee, as Charlie avers. But the parables also imply a story, part of which is unwritten and a fr, which is only implied in these brief accounts, which are extremely parsimonious in the use of language. But rich in the use of provocative overtones.

Now to quote Charlie quoting himself, the parables "subverted, affirmed, and confronted the broader views of reality on the basis of which first-century humans conducted their lives." The parables have "the potential of igniting the imaginations of those who consent to enter [Jesus's] fictional world."[1]

Precisely: The parables open onto an alternative reality, or altered frame of reference, or Field of Reference, to which we have customarily given the term Kingdom of God. They constitute an invitation to enter that world and live in it. (Even if the gospel frame is secondary, the real subject is implied in the body of the texts themselves and appears elsewhere in the tradition, i.e., Thomas.)

The point about the parables being nonliteral (I avoid the term *metaphorical*, since it seems to confuse) is that they are not merely descriptive. They exaggerate, poke fun at, employ irony and other devices in order to reshape the lived world of his listeners. That world is a social world and is socially constructed, so he employs the poetic fiction as a way of deforming the everyday world of Galileans.

I would and do describe them as realistic, but a more accurate term is surrealistic, owing to the proclivity to deform or subvert the everyday world of Galilee. On the other hand, the parables are not realistic in the sociological sense, or even in the historical sense. They are on the fringe of fantasy. They are just plausible enough to work as a way to undermine

---

1. Charles W. Hedrick, *Many Things in Parables* (Louisville: Westminster John Knox, 2004), 84.

the received reality. Or, as Amos Wilder used to say, they are sufficiently plausible (read: realistic) to get initially under the guard of the listener.

Stories that are wholly plausible are realistic without remainder. It is very difficult to create a fiction that belongs wholly to this category. Think how difficult it is to describe a thing or event without adding or subtracting from a close description, without interpretation, without adding or subtracting one's own sensibilities. Plausibility at the next level conforms to public opinion, what we may call the "they say" mentality: this is what everybody takes to be case (but of course not everybody does). The parables begin with that initial "they say" plausibility. The third form of plausibility is the narrative frame of reference: it is the world that has already been storied, that is taken for granted by the culture, by the living myth, so that this narrative version is immediately plausible and convincing. The fourth kind of plausibility is the use of strategies and ploys the author employs to convince us that the story is accurate, realistic, plausible, even though she is making it all up or most of it all up. And finally, authors may interrupt their own narrative to comment on, in case we are missing what is going on. When we say things that are ironic or exaggerated, in oral presentations, we can wink at the audience, so to speak, to let them know that we are kidding. Rhetorical strategies are the means by which writers wink at the reader.

The parable movement that Charlie thinks has misled us attempted to show that Jesus consistently, in the authentic parables, undermines or subverts the "they say" mentality of his Galilean neighbors in order to get them to see that he is talking about an alternative world into which he is inviting them. The parables and aphorisms are full of tropes that provide hints but do not spell that world out. So Charlie is right that the parables do not tell us what they "mean," if by that is meant what to believe and how to act, beyond the intention to undermine the way we usually construe reality. It is only in that sense that the parables are "apocalyptic," i.e., have a temporal horizon: the parables are open to a different future. The gospel tradition, on the other hand, immediately set to work to moralize the parables and aphorisms, i.e., to supply them with specific courses of action or thought. And scholars have trotted right along in the footsteps of the evangelists. Nevertheless, some innocence readers and listeners got it right away and never let it go. Fortunately, the evangelists did not erase all the clues from the narrative and aphoristic texts, so we see also see through the interpretive overlay back toward the original horizon of the stories and tropes.

Dare I risk an example? The prodigal is not just the story of a dysfunctional family. It has both syntagmatic and paradigmatic elements. The syntagmatic plot is the story of departure and return, leaving home and returning home. It is also the story of someone who forsook his patrimony and threw it away in a "foreign" land. I say "foreign" to indicate that passing through the alien is one way to discover who we are, to discover our own identify. Quite a number of the fairy tales collected by Grimm are of this type. The paradigmatic aspects of the parable have to do with the relationship between parent and two siblings, who take opposite sides of the family equation. Neither is right and neither wrong. But in the kingdom of God, or the divine domain, as I now prefer to term it, generosity is the rule, because God is generous. But I have not drawn any rules about behavior from the story, other than to indicate the horizon of the world as Jesus imagined it.

If this analysis is not wide of the mark, we have to say that the parables, both narrative and picture, contain clues that prompts us to read them in this imaginative way.

Another way to putting the matter is to say that Jesus is describing life in Galilee as it may be seen through God's eyes.

This is the theoretic frame within which I read both the parables and the aphorisms.

Bibliography

Hedrick, Charles W. *Many Things in Parables*. Louisville: Westminster John Knox, 2004.

Part 5
Historical Jesus

Honest to Jesus and Honest to Bob

John Dominic Crossan

Prologue

The session for which this essay was originally prepared asked us not just to describe but to *assess* the legacy of Bob Funk under various headings; mine is "The Historical Jesus." In doing so, I distinguish between Bob's legacy in terms of academic debate—an *interesting* subject—but also in terms of public discourse—an *important* subject.

Internal scholarly interest and external public importance should always be in tensive dialectic, like two sides of a coin that can be distinguished but not separated. I emphasize that distinction between the interesting and the important because the formal purpose of the Society of Biblical Literature is to "foster biblical scholarship," but Bob (and many of us) think it should be to "promote (internally) and publicize (externally) biblical scholarship" and not just to foster it like an exotic plant or hothouse orchid. I return to that point in the last part of this presentation.

Part 1. Honest to Jesus

I begin with where I think historical Jesus scholarship is at the moment, and here, of course, I am personally and professionally involved and cannot speak from any neutral—that is, irrelevant—viewpoint.

It is often said that we are now in the third stage of historical Jesus research and the standard way of describing the three stages is something like this: before Schweitzer, during Bultmann, Schweitzer revisited. By the way and as an aside, am I alone in thinking that twentieth-century theology would have been vastly enriched had it taken seriously not only Schweitzer's 1906 *From Reimarus to Wrede* but also—or even more so—Ramsay's 1907 *The Cities of St. Paul* and Deissmann's 1908 book *Light from the Ancient East*? Those latter authors recognized that, whatever about that modern transition from Reimarus to Wrede, even more fundamental was the ancient transition from Caesar to Christ. If they had been put together for the twentieth century, Albert Schweitzer, William Mitchell Ramsay, and Gustav Adolf Deissmann might have been used for public eschatological anti-imperialism rather than for private eschatological existentialism.

Be that as it may, I also think in terms of three stages up to the present time but I base them on matrix and matrix-appropriate method: stage 1 is historical Jesus research *within Christianity*; stage 2 is historical Jesus research *within Christianity within Judaism*; stage 3 is historical Jesus research *within Christianity within Judaism within the Roman Empire*. We are now at stage 3, but I have no presumption—despite ancient triadic law—that we are now at climax and consummation. There will no doubt be further stages—maybe, for instance, a stage 4 for all of that within human evolution.

One further point about present location. Cutting across those three stages are three visions of Jesus. One is the *literal Jesus*: what you get by a simple amalgamation of the four intracanonical gospel versions. Another is the *historical Jesus*: what you get by interpreting that data within standard historical constraint and discipline. By the way, when Bob and I started our own work on the historical Jesus in the late 1960s and codirected the Jesus Seminar from the mid-1980s to the mid-1990s our personal and collective reconstructions were considered as the far-left alternative to the relatively standard literal Jesus.

Lately, however, a third option has opened up on the left wing that makes the Jesus Seminar downright center-of-the-road. We now have—besides a *literal* or an *historical* Jesus—a *fictional Jesus*. This Jesus never existed, or, if he existed, was not crucified, or if he was crucified, never died. He married Mary Magdalene and went off to live in France.

Granted those presuppositions, how do I assess the strength and weaknesses of Bob's vision of the historical Jesus?

Three weaknesses. First, I locate Bob's own Jesus-reconstruction work within my stage 1, within Christianity rather than within Judaism or within the Roman Empire. But he is located there negatively—among the great deniers within the post-Enlightenment world. He was an unchanged and undeveloped anti-fundamentalist, but he was also trapped in the negativity of anti-fundamentalist fundamentalism.

Second, his emphasis was almost exclusively on the words rather than on the deeds of Jesus: he reconstructed Jesus as a superb gadfly philosopher. His Jesus points—like Kafka—"away from here" but Bob never reconstructed any "to where" for Jesus. It was as if any "to where"—however tentative, relative, and time-place conditioned in word, deed, or vision—would be a betrayal of Jesus's own vision.

Third, within those words, the parables received pride of place, but Bob never moved—at least not positively—from parables about God *by Jesus* to parables *about Jesus* by the evangelists (i.e., realistic fiction with a theological point, in both cases). Neither did he ever recognize that, if Jesus proclaimed a present but bilateral eschaton of divine-human cooperation rather than an imminent but unilateral one of divine-alone action, then the interactive, collaborative, participatory genre of parable was its most appropriate linguistic genre. Because of that, he never moved convincingly from Jesus life to Jesus's death, from word to execution. Jesus, after all, was not crucified as king of the parables but as king of the Jews.

Three strengths. First, as founder and leader of the Jesus Seminar Bob never imposed his own views on our discussions. Therefore, any assessment of his own Jesus-reconstruction must also take into account the creative, communal, and collaborative reconstructions of that seminar itself. That too is legacy.

Second, there is probably a general consensus today that the Jesus materials in the New Testament—both words said by and to Jesus as well as deeds done by and to Jesus—fall into three general categories: data from Jesus, data from the tradition, data from the evangelists—along with all the intricate difficulties of an interwoven tapestry. Bob insisted that, granted acceptance of that distinction, historical Jesus scholars should be prepared to say *what was and was not* in each category and how they made those decisions. He was especially aware of how many scholars made that general threefold distinction but never gave any full and divided inventory thereafter. He thought that at least disingenuous and possibly dishonest.

Third, he insisted that Jesus reconstructions should not only assert their conclusions but also assess their certainties. As one decided whether a given unit came from the historical Jesus, one had to grade one's surety, one's security, one's certainty in that judgment as: yes, maybe yes, maybe no, no (or some such expressions). And those categories were visually transferred into red, pink, grey, black for color-coding the gospel-text in print.

By the way, I found it rather dismaying that the many scholars who mocked that as trying to establish *truth by vote* never explained that we had simply copied those four categories from the scholarly seminar that had established the United Bible Societies' *Greek New Testament*. In disputed cases, they graded their surety on the proper Greek text as: "{A} = virtually certain; {B} = some degree of doubt; {C} = considerable degree of doubt, {D} = a very high degree of doubt."[1] And I found it rather disgusting when one scholar described our color-coding as "black-balling" certain texts and called it a white-racist action.

Part 2. Honest to Bob

I became a member of the Society of Biblical Literature in 1964, which means that my first experience of the Annual Meeting was sitting in classrooms at Union Theological Seminary—one for Old Testament papers and one for New Testament papers—staying at a nearby hotel, and doing all of that between Christmas Day and New Year's Day. I was then still a monk and would have preferred to stay in my Chicago monastery than in a New York hotel under those conditions. If that was to be the future of my life in the Society of Biblical Literature, I dreaded even to think about it.

Between 1968 and 1973, Bob was Executive Secretary of the Society of Biblical Literature, and under his brilliant leadership the Annual Meeting changed forever into what most of us now experience every year. The venue became a hotel rather than a seminary, and the program diversified into sections, consultations, and seminars. Then in 1974 Bob created Scholars Press and was its director until 1980. That represented a total remake of the Society of Biblical Literature, and I for one am eternally grateful to Bob for that extreme makeover.

It would, however, be very inaccurate and inadequate to think that Bob's purpose in those changes was simply to make the Society of Biblical Literature more like most other learned societies or simply to improve the society's annual meetings, research programs, or publication options. All of that was intended, to be sure, but there was something even more fundamental driving Bob in wrenching the Society of Biblical Literature (kicking and screaming?) into the late twentieth century.

In that same period, Bob left Vanderbilt Divinity School, where he had been from 1966 to 1969, to found along with Ray Hart the Department of Religious Studies at the University of Montana, where he remained until his retirement in 1986. That deliberate move from divinity school to state

---

1. Bruce M. Metzger, *A Textual Commentary on the Greek New Testament* (New York: United Bible Societies, 1970), xxviii.

university revealed much more clearly what was behind all those Society of Biblical Literature changes as far as Bob himself was concerned.

I first came to know Bob by working fairly closely with him during those 1970s—years vitally important for the Society of Biblical Literature's future and for Bob's career. Between 1972 and 1976 I was chair of the Parables Seminar, a seminar proposed not by me but by Bob and Norman Perrin. Between 1974 and 1980 I was, along with other colleagues, an associate editor as Bob founded the journal *Semeia*. It was only then that I slowly realized that Bob's vision for the future of biblical studies was a breakout from the closed world of academic scholarship toward a lay audience eager to understand what was happening. That is my understanding of Bob's basic intention and fundamental purpose. He believed that the Bible and its interpretation were too important to be nothing more than a playing field for academic scholarship (as a possibly Freudian slip, I first typed "acidic scholarship" in mistake for "academic scholarship").

In theory, of course, the seminaries and divinity schools were supposed to train ministers and pastors in biblical scholarship, and they, in turn, were supposed to teach and put into parish practice the implications of all that research. But, like all other trickle-down theories, it was not working. Maybe the professors could not teach or the ministers could not preach, but, for whatever reason, the power of the biblical vision was not reaching the laity—except maybe as literalism or fundamentalism.

In 1980 Bob was fired as director of Scholars Press, and he broke completely with the Society of Biblical Literature. I have never heard the full story of that breach from either side, and I never heard Bob speak about either Scholars Press or the Society of Biblical Literature again (that is just my own experience). In founding the Westar Institute, Polebridge Press, and eventually the Jesus Seminar in 1986, Bob was re-creating in microcosm what he had helped create in macrocosm with the Society of Biblical Literature itself. He once told me that, before the break, he had imagined a Jesus Seminar inside the Society of Biblical Literature just as another of its standard seminars. I do not know when that would have been or whether there are any documents about it in the Society of Biblical Literature files.

With that triple creation, Bob's hope to break biblical studies out into the lay world was triumphantly successful. Our colleagues who said the Jesus Seminar was after publicity were, of course, absolutely correct. That was our purpose. Bob's argument was that it was not ethically correct to kept saying and discussing in scholarship what we were not willing to state in public discourse. To my mind, that was the single theme on which we all agreed in starting the Jesus Seminar.

I conclude with two points that return to the start of this paper. An extremely literalist and fundamentalist understanding of the Christian Bible is presently dominant not just in many American denominations and churches but as the basis of matters from medicine through education to foreign policy. Bob's vision of a laity schooled in biblical scholarship—schooled, that is, in an alternative understanding of the Bible based on historical context—is even more desperately needed right now than when Bob created the Jesus Seminar in 1986. But, it is his abiding success to have informed a laity inside and outside churches all over this country about that alternative vision.

My second point is why I called this section "Honest to Bob" and why that subtitle is especially important in speaking of Bob in any Society of Biblical Literature context. I am not concerned here with the pros and cons of the breach between Bob and the Society of Biblical Literature in 1980. I want to ask, in the name of Bob, what the Society of Biblical Literature is going to do as an institution with regard to the abuse of the Bible in our current American situation. Should our mission be to "foster biblical scholarship" or to "publicize biblical scholarship"? As I understand the logic of Bob's professional life, it was to infuse biblical scholarship—especially critical historical scholarship—into American public discourse. To assess Bob fully and honestly, we should *either* say he was quite wrong in that vision *or*, if he was right, ask what the Society of Biblical Literature—as an institution—is going to do about it.

Bibliography

Deissmann, Gustav Adolf. *Light from the Ancient East: The New Testament Illustrated by Recently Discovered Texts of the Graeco-Roman World.* Translated by Lionel R. M. Strachan. 4th ed. Grand Rapids, MI: Baker Book House, 1965. English translation of *Licht vom Osten: Das Neue Testament und die neuentdeckten Texte der hellenistisch-römischen Welt.* Tübingen: Mohr Siebeck, 1908.

Metzger, Bruce M. *A Textual Commentary on the Greek New Testament.* New York, NY: United Bible Societies, 1970.

Ramsay, William Mitchell. *The Cities of St. Paul: Their Influence on His Life and Thought; The Cities of Eastern Asia Minor.* New York, NY: Hodder & Staughton, 1907.

Schweitzer, Albert. *The Quest of the Historical Jesus: A Critical Study of Its Progress from Reimarus to Wrede.* Translated by William Montgomery. New York, NY: Macmillan, 1969. English translation of *Von Reimarus zu Wrede: Eine Geschichte der Leben-Jesu-Forschung.* Tübingen: Mohr Siebeck, 1906. Repr., *The Quest of the Historical Jesus.* Translated by W. Montgomery, J. R. Coates, Susan Cupitt, and John Bowden. 1st complete ed. Minneapolis, MN: Fortress, 2001. English translation of *Von Reimarus zu Wrede: Eine Geschichte der Leben-Jesu-Forschung.* 2nd ed. Tübingen: Mohr Siebeck, 1913.

The Looking-Glass Tree Is for the Birds:
Ezekiel 17:22–24; Mark 4:30–32

Robert W. Funk

> The kingdom as Jesus sees it breaking in will arrive in disenchanting and disarming form: not as a mighty cedar astride the lofty mountain height but as a lowly garden herb.... It will erupt out of the power of weakness and refuse to perpetuate itself by the weakness of power.

1.

The mighty cedars of Lebanon crown a magnificent spine of mountains strung casually along the shores of the eastern Mediterranean. The snow-clad peaks fall away proudly and precipitously into the azure waters of the sea on the one side, and into the flat, burning mirror of the desert on the other. Riding this haughty crest, sandwiched in between water and waste, the muscle-bound trunk of the cedar silently announces its stately grandeur. The cedar does not want for nourishment or for admiration, nor does it want for those who, like Solomon, covet its splendid timber.

Few Israelites could fail to be impressed by the towering height and bulk of the Lebanese cedar. Ezekiel was no exception. So impressive did he find it that it inspired one of his rich metaphors.

From the lofty top of the cedar—so Ezekiel's vision runs—Yahweh will take a tender twig, which he will plant on a high and lofty mountain on the mountain height of Israel. Under the surveillance of the Lord God, the young cedar will wax and mature, will put forth boughs and bear fruit. It will furnish a haven for beasts of every kind, and the birds of the heaven will make their nests in the shade of its branches.

The noble cedar, seemingly immovable, from a human perspective apparently eternal, symbolizes the secular powers of the earth. From among the tender shoots of its majestic imperturbability, Yahweh will take the tenderest and from it produce a new cedar to be the glory of Israel. The cedar of Israel, which will form the locus of eschatological rest for all the peoples of the earth, will stem from the lineage of the secular powers: Yahweh will create his cedar out of the stock of the secular cedar, but will make it serve his own redemptive purposes.

Since the cedar of Israel will exceed the secular cedars in nobility and grandeur, in strength and longevity, all the trees of the field shall know that Yahweh brings the high tree low and exalts the low tree, that he dries up the green tree and causes the withered tree to flourish. The lone cedar of Israel will displace the secular cedars, which will pale, by comparison, into insignificance.

Thus the word of the Lord God in the mouth of Ezekiel: the Lord has spoken, and he will do it.

2.

The parable of the mustard seed is undoubtedly to be read against the background of the history of the symbol of the mighty cedar, a symbol utilized not only by Ezekiel, but found also in Dan 4 and elsewhere in the Old Testament. The interplay of Jesus's parable and the tradition has to be considered initially, however, in connection with the history of recent interpretation. Only in this way can the full range of metaphorical overtones be discerned by ears atuned to prespecified wave lengths.

The emphasis on the smallness of the seed—"the smallest seed in the world"—found in parentheses in Mark (4:31b) and echoed by Matthew (13:32) and the Gospel of Thomas (20) is taken by C. H. Dodd to be a secondary expansion of the parable. Luke's version, which omits this emphasis and is to derive from Q, is held to be original. The parable has nothing to do with the contrast between insignificant beginnings and great issue, according to Dodd, but with the capacity of the shrub to afford shelter to the birds of the heavens. The parable therefore announces that the time has come when the multitudes of Israel, perhaps even of the gentiles, will flock to the kingdom as birds flock to the shelter of the tree.[1]

It is quite possible that Mark's parenthesis, and thus the emphasis on the minute size of the seed, is secondary, as Dodd thinks. However, Dodd

---

1. C. H. Dodd, *The Parables of the Kingdom* (London: Religious Book Club, 1942), 191.

fails to notice that the seed in question is the mustard seed in every form of the tradition, and the microscopic size of this seed, with or without emphasis, was already proverbial.

The oversight of Dodd coincides with an aberration of the original parable to be found already in the New Testament itself: in Mark (4:32) the seed grows into the greatest of all *shrubs*, but in Matthew (13:32) and Luke (13:19) it becomes a *tree*. It is hardly speculation to say that the eschatological tree of Ezekiel and Daniel has influenced the transmission of the parable in the New Testament period and that it has also shaped Dodd's perspective.

The theological interest in making the parable conform to the prophetic and apocalyptic tradition has thus been at work on the one side, in the tendency to play down the smallness of the seed and play up the size of the mature plant.

Modem botanical interests have joined the game, on the other side, in an attempt to salvage the "realism" of the parable. Rather than have the birds come and *make their nests* in the branches of a shrub, the botanizers want the birds to "light upon" or "roost" in its branches. It is of course the case that only Matthew and Luke speak of birds dwelling in the *branches*; in Mark's version the birds are able to make their nests in the shade of the shrub, while Thomas has it that a large branch becomes a shelter for birds. The botanists know that mustard does not grow to tree size, although it may reach a height of 8 or 10 feet. It is an annual plant, moreover, which, although fast growing, and consequently mostly hollow, would hardly provide nesting places for birds in the early spring. It seems more reasonable, then, from a botanical point of view, to say, that birds come and "roost" in the mustard plant during summer, attracted seasonally, as they are, to its shade and to its seed.

The text, however, is everywhere clear: birds come and *dwell* in or under the shrub. Whether preferred or not, the parable indulges in a bit of exaggeration, hyperbole if you will, which every common hearer, who might have been expected to know something of the mustard plant first hand, would scarcely have missed: foolish birds to take up their abode in the short-lived mustard!

The difficulties inherent in the parable merely illustrate how poorly suited the figure is to the old cedar imagery on the one hand and to modem botanical exactness on the other. The botanists are interested of course, in saving the everyday literalness of the parable. Modern theological interpreters, under the spell of Dan 4, Ezek 17, and 31, are interested in asserting the figurative literalness of the parable. The interpretation of Joachim Jeremias illustrates the second position well, when he writes of the parables of the mustard seed and leaven as parables of contrast:

> Their meaning is that out of the most insignificant beginning, invisible to human eye, God creates his mighty Kingdom, which embraces all the peoples of the world.[2]

The mighty kingdom is symbolized by the "mighty" mustard plant, which provides a haven for birds from the four corners of the heavens! Jeremias has recapitulated Ezekiel's allegory of the cedar of Israel, with hardly a glance in the direction of the parable of the mustard seed.

3.

Dodd sees the parable as depicting the growth of the tree up to the point where it can shelter birds.[3] It is therefore an announcement that the period of obscurity for Jesus is at an end. Jeremias thinks that the parable sets out the fundamental contrast between the beginning and end of a process, which, he claims, is the oriental way of viewing a story. He therefore takes the parable to affirm the miraculous power of God in the face of doubts that the kingdom could issue from the mission of Jesus and his disreputable band.

Of the two, Jeremias more nearly seizes the parable as a whole, but he, too, finally comes to rest in the shade of the noble cedar.

The metaphorical meanings assigned by Dodd and Jeremias to the parable represent what might be called first octave metaphorical overtones. It is not so much that these overtones are false notes in themselves, as it is that they are not being heard in concert with second and third octave metaphorical overtones, which is to say that the parable is not being heard as a whole in relation to the history of the imagery.

When the parable of Jesus is set alongside the vision of Ezekiel (17:22–24), the first impression one gains by the juxtaposition is that Jesus has created a light-hearted burlesque of Ezekiel's figure: The noble cedar, which provides a haven for the beasts and birds of the earth, is caricatured

---

2. Joachim Jeremias, *The Parables of Jesus*, rev. ed. (New York: Scribner's Sons, 1963), 149.

3. Dodd, *Parables of the Kingdom*, 190.

as a lowly mustard plant! And the first impression is not entirely wide of the mark. At second glance, however, the parable takes on the character of serious satire. Jesus appears to have grasped the final injunction of Ezekiel's oracle radically, "The Lord will bring the high tree low and make the low tree high"! The noble cedar of Israel as the hope of Israel will be quite comparable, on Ezekiel's view, to the secular cedars of the world. But when Jesus takes up the figure, it is to conform Ezekiel's new cedar—precisely Israel's future—to Yahweh's final dictum. That is only to say that all cedars, including Israel's proud hope, will be brought low; and the insignificant tree, indeed the ephemeral mustard plant, will be made to bear Israel's true destiny.

The kingdom as Jesus sees it breaking in will arrive in disenchanting and disarming form: not as a mighty cedar astride the lofty mountain height but as a lowly garden herb. The kingdom is asserted with comic relief: what it is and what it will do, it will be and do, appearances to the contrary notwithstanding. It will erupt out of the power of weakness and refuse to perpetuate itself by the weakness of power.

The mustard plant does offer a refuge to the birds of heaven, but what a modest refuge it is—in the eyes of the world! The contrast between insignificant beginning and glorious end is a pittance paid to the grandiose pretensions of human hope. Man asks for a continent as the paradisiacal sanctuary of his final rest and is given a clump of earth. The birds, too, have their metaphorical wings clipped: What odd birds they are to flock—in modest numbers—to the shade of a seasonal plant, thinking it to be their eternal home.

If the kingdom is extended in the parable with comic relief, it is in order to offer the kingdom only for what it is. It is not a towering empire, but an unpretentious venture of faith. As a venture of faith, however, it is of course potentially world-transforming: "if you have faith as a grain of mustard seed, you will say to this mountain, 'Move hence to yonder place,' and it will move" (Matt 17:20). It is faith which, in its unostentatious way, reorders the face of the world.

The parable relocates the power of the kingdom where the world cannot have access to it apart from faith. The parable is full of promise and assurance, but these become available only in the context of what the kingdom really is, namely, the faith to dwell in the kingdom.

4.

The parable of the mustard seed intends nothing less than to transform the face of Israel's hope. The transformation of a tradition is much like moving mountains by word of command: both are equally difficult to effect because both are dependent upon the power of words. Hope and mountains belong to the map of reality which man takes to be fixed and unalterable. Because of his god-like tenacity in clinging to what presents itself as stubborn reality, man finds world-transforming faith difficult to negotiate: He prefers a literal world, the order of which is immutable, to a world subject to the linguistic whims of the poet and prophet and thus open to the future.

Among those to whom the parable of the mustard seed was addressed were those who reckoned their chances of participating in Israel's hope, as traditionally understood, to be good. It was too much to expect them to abandon a reasonably certain future for themselves, even if they had to purchase that future at the expense of most other men. The risk was too great for them to be lured away by the ludicrous vision of an idle blasphemer. Those who had no future and no prospect of one, on the other hand, were doubtless favorably disposed to a fresh pack of cards and a new deal if not a new frontier. Any prospect at all was better than none. Yet they, too, found it difficult to risk the future, such as it was, on such a hazardous gamble. It must have been like inviting them to flee the debtor's prison and gallows by taking a leaky, short-masted, poorly provisioned frigate for the new world, on the condition that they would welcome aboard all and sundry who wanted to go and face the prospect of an endless voyage at sea. There were few, even among the destitute, who were desperate enough to set out. Such is the power of the old hope that besets the human breast, even when that hope is certainly beyond reach.

The church, like Israel, is wont to stumble over its hope. It seizes, solidifies, and then takes possession of its hope in the name of divinely certified reality. In so doing, it merely converts the mustard plant back into a towering cedar. As regards that hope and its encapsulation in the tradition the parable suggests the following items for reflection:

1. Whatever the Christian hope is, the form of its realization will come as a surprise to all who think they know what it ought to be.
2. The coming of the kingdom will disappoint the righteous, but be a source of joy to the religiously disinherited.

3. The certainty of our hope is inversely proportionate to the certainty with which we hold the resurrection of Jesus to be paradigmatic of our future.

4. The promise of the future is directly proportionate to the degree we make no claim upon the future at all.

5. The gift of the future is the gift of language: The mystery of the divine promise is tendered in and through language, and it is seized and lived into as the salvific word occurring between and among men.

Jesus advances the parable as an invitation to pass through the looking glass: On the other side the mighty cedar is brought low and the humble herb exalted. On the other side—that is to say, in the world mirrored in the looking-glass of the parable.

Who has ears to hear, let him hear.

Bibliography

Dodd, C. H. *The Parables of the Kingdom*. London: Religious Book Club, 1942.

Jeremias, Joachim. *The Parables of Jesus*. Rev. ed. New York: Scribner's Sons, 1963.

Introduction to *The Five Gospels:*
The Search for the Authentic Words of Jesus

The Search for the Real Jesus: Darwin, Scopes, and All That

Robert W. Funk

The Five Gospels represents a dramatic exit from windowless studies and the beginning of a new venture for gospel scholarship. Leading scholars—Fellows of the Jesus Seminar—have decided to update and then make the legacy of two hundred years of research and debate a matter of public record.

In the aftermath of the controversy over Darwin's *The Origin of Species* (published in 1859) and the ensuing Scopes "monkey" trial in 1925, American biblical scholarship retreated into the closet. The fundamentalist mentality generated a climate of inquisition that made honest scholarly judgments dangerous. Numerous biblical scholars were subjected to heresy trials and suffered the loss of academic posts. They learned it was safer to keep their critical judgments private. However, the intellectual ferment of the century soon reasserted itself in colleges, universities, and seminaries. By the end of World War II, critical scholars again quietly dominated the academic scene from one end of the continent to the other. Critical biblical scholarship was supported, of course, by other university disciplines which wanted to ensure that dogmatic considerations not be permitted to intrude into scientific and historical research. The fundamentalists were forced, as a consequence, to found their own Bible colleges and seminaries in order to propagate their point of view. In launching new institutions, the fundamentalists even refused accommodation with the older, established church-related schools that dotted the land.

One focal point of the raging controversies was who Jesus was and what he had said. Jesus has always been a controversial figure. In the gospels he is represented as being at odds with his religious environment in matters like fasting and sabbath observance. He seems not to have gotten along with his own family. Even his disciples are pictured as stubborn, dense, and self-serving—unable to fathom what he was about. Herod Antipas, in whose territory he ranged as a traveling sage, had him pegged as a troublemaker, much like John the Baptist and the Romans regarded him as a mild political threat. Yet much about him remains obscure. We do not even know for sure what language he usually spoke—Aramaic or Greek—when instructing his followers. It is not surprising that this enigmatic figure should be perpetually at the center of storms of controversy.

The contemporary religious controversy, epitomized in the Scopes trial and the continuing clamor for creationism as a viable alternative to the theory of evolution, turns on whether the worldview reflected in the Bible can be carried forward into this scientific age and retained as an article of faith. Jesus figures prominently in this debate. The Christ of creed and dogma, who had been firmly in place in the Middle Ages, can no longer command the assent of those who have seen the heavens through Galileo's telescope. The old deities and demons were swept from the skies by that remarkable glass. Copernicus, Kepler, and Galileo have dismantled the mythological abodes of the gods and Satan, and bequeathed us secular heavens.

The profound change in astronomy was a part of the rise of experimental science, which sought to put all knowledge to the test of close and repeated observation. At the same time and as part of the same impulse, the advent of historical reason meant distinguishing the factual from the fictional in accounts of the past. For biblical interpretation that distinction required scholars to probe the relation between faith and history. In this boiling cauldron the quest of the historical Jesus was conceived.

Historical knowledge became an indispensable part of the modern world's basic "reality toolkit." Apart from this instrument, the modern inquirer could not learn the difference between an imagined world and "the real world" of human experience. To know the truth about Jesus, the real Jesus, one had to find the Jesus of history. The refuge offered by the cloistered precincts of faith gradually became a battered and beleaguered position. In the wake of the Enlightenment, the dawn of the Age of Reason, in the seventeenth and eighteenth centuries, biblical scholars rose to the challenge and launched a tumultuous search for the Jesus behind the Christian façade of the Christ.

The Seven Pillars of Scholarly Wisdom

The question of the historical Jesus was stimulated by the prospect of viewing Jesus through the new lens of historical reason and research rather than through the perspective of theology and traditional creedal formulations.

The search for the Jesus of history began with Hermann Samuel Reimarus (1694–1768), a professor of oriental languages in Hamburg, Germany. A close study of the New Testament gospels convinced Reimarus that what the authors of the gospels said about Jesus could be distinguished from what Jesus himself said. It was with this basic distinction between the man Jesus and the Christ of the creeds that the quest of the historical Jesus began.

Most late twentieth-century Americans do not know that one of our own sons of the Enlightenment, Thomas Jefferson (1743–1826), scrutinized the gospels with a similar intent: to separate the real teachings of Jesus, the figure of history, from the encrustations of Christian doctrine. He gathered his findings in *The Life and Morals of Jesus of Nazareth, Extracted Textually from the Gospels in Greek, Latin, French, and English*, a little volume that was first published in 1904 and is still in print.

Meanwhile, back in Germany the views of Reimarus and his successors were greatly furthered in the monumental *Life of Jesus Critically Examined* by David Friedrich Strauss (first edition, 1835). Strauss distinguished what he called the "mythical" (defined by him as anything legendary or supernatural) in the gospels from the historical. The storm that broke over the 1,400 pages of minute analysis cost him his first teaching post at the seminary at Tübingen. Critics hounded him up to the time of his death in 1874.

The choice Strauss posed in his assessment of the gospels was between the supernatural Jesus—the Christ of faith—and the historical Jesus. Other scholars in the German tradition developed a safer, but no less crucial, contrast between the Jesus of the synoptic gospels—Matthew, Mark, Luke—and the Jesus of the Gospel of John. Two pillars of modern biblical criticism were now in place. The first was the distinction between the historical Jesus, to be uncovered by historical excavation, and the Christ of faith encapsulated in the first creeds. The second pillar consisted of recognizing the synoptic gospels as much closer to the historical Jesus than the Fourth Gospel, which presented a "spiritual" Jesus.

By 1900 the third and fourth pillars of modern critical scholarship were also in place. The recognition of the Gospel of Mark as prior to Matthew and Luke, and the basis for them both, is the third pillar. A fourth pillar was the identification of the hypothetical source Q as the explanation for the "double tradition"—the material Matthew and Luke have in common beyond their dependence on Mark. Both of these pillars will be discussed below.

The tragic and heroic story of those who endeavored to break the church's stranglehold over learning has been chronicled by Albert Schweitzer in his famous *The Quest of the Historical Jesus* (1906). Schweitzer himself contributed to that revolt in a major way, following the breakthrough of Johannes Weiss in his *Jesus' Proclamation of the Kingdom of God* (1892). For Weiss and Schweitzer, the basic decision that had to be made about Jesus was whether he thought the age was about to end in a cataclysmic event, known as the "eschaton" (Greek for the "last event"), or whether he took a longer view of things. Weiss and Schweitzer opted for an eschatological Jesus. Consequently, Schweitzer saw Jesus's ethic as only an "interim ethic" (a way of life good only for the brief period before the cataclysmic end, the eschaton). As such he found it no longer relevant or valid. Acting on his own conclusion, in 1913 Schweitzer abandoned a brilliant career in theology, turned to medicine, and went out to Africa where he founded the famous hospital at Lambaréné out of respect for all forms of life.

The eschatological Jesus reigned supreme among gospel scholars from the time of Weiss and Schweitzer to the end of World War II. Slowly but surely the evidence began to erode that view, which, after all, had been prompted by the revolt, towards the close of the nineteenth century, against the optimistic theology of progress that then prevailed. Meanwhile, neo-orthodoxy under the tutelage of Karl Barth and Rudolf Bultmann suppressed any real interest in the historical Jesus for the better part of five decades (1920–1970). Barth and Bultmann dismissed the quest of the historical Jesus as an illegitimate attempt to secure a factual basis for faith—an attempt to "prove" Christian claims made on behalf of Jesus. Even today historical studies of Christian origins still labor under that theological interdiction.

The creation of the Jesus Seminar coincides with the reemergence of interest in the Jesus of history, which was made possible by the wholesale shift of biblical scholarship away from its earlier academic home in the church, seminaries, and isolated theological enclaves. While biblical scholarship has not lost its interest in and concern for the Jewish and Christian traditions, it has finally won its liberty. As that interest came back to life in the 1970s and 1980s, scholars were surprised to learn that they no longer labored under the tyranny of either neoorthodoxy or an eschatological Jesus. John the Baptist, not Jesus, was the chief advocate of an impending cataclysm, a view that Jesus's first disciples had acquired from the Baptist movement. Jesus himself rejected that mentality in its crass form, quit the ascetic desert, and returned to urban Galilee. He took up eating and drinking and consorting with toll collectors and sinners, and developed a different point of view, expressed in the major parables and root metaphors for God's imperial rule, as the kingdom of God has now come to be known. The liberation of the noneschatological Jesus of the aphorisms and parables from Schweitzer's eschatological Jesus is the fifth pillar of contemporary scholarship.

Jesus's followers did not grasp the subtleties of his position and reverted, once Jesus was not there to remind them, to the view they had learned from John the Baptist. As a consequence of this reversion, and in the aura of the emerging view of Jesus as a cult figure analogous to others in the Hellenistic mystery religions, the gospel writers overlaid the tradition of sayings and parables with their own "memories" of Jesus. They constructed their memories out of common lore, drawn in large part from the Greek Bible, the message of John the Baptist, and their own emerging convictions about Jesus as the expected messiah—the Anointed. The Jesus of the gospels is an imaginative theological construct, into which has been woven traces of that enigmatic sage from Nazareth—traces that cry out for recognition and liberation from the firm grip of those whose faith overpowered their memories. The search for the authentic words of Jesus is a search for the forgotten Jesus.

A sixth pillar of modern gospel scholarship, to be explored subsequently, consists of the recognition of the fundamental contrast between the oral culture (in which Jesus was at home) and a print culture (like our own). The Jesus whom historians seek will be found in those fragments of tradition that bear the imprint of orality: short, provocative, memorable, oft-repeated phrases, sentences, and stories.

The seventh and final pillar that supports the edifice of contemporary gospel scholarship is the reversal that has taken place regarding who bears the burden of proof. It was once assumed that scholars had to prove that details in the synoptic gospels were *not* historical. D. F. Strauss undertook proof of this nature in his controversial work. As a consequence, his work was viewed as negative and destructive. The current assumption is more nearly the opposite and indicates how far scholarship has come since Strauss: the gospels are now assumed to be narratives in which the memory of Jesus is embellished by mythic elements that express the church's faith in him, and by plausible fictions that enhance the telling of the gospel story for first-century listeners who knew about divine men and miracle workers firsthand. Supposedly historical elements in these narratives must therefore be demonstrated to be so. The Jesus Seminar has accordingly assumed the burden of proof: the seminar is investigating in minute detail the data preserved by the gospels and is also identifying those that have some claim to historical veracity. For this reason, the work of the seminar has drawn criticism from the skeptical left wing in scholarship—those who deny the possibility of isolating any historical memories in the gospels at all. Of course, it has also drawn fire from the fundamentalist right for not crediting the gospels with one hundred percent historical reliability.

These seven pillars of scholarly "wisdom," useful and necessary as they have proven to be, are no guarantee of the results. There are no final guarantees. Not even the fundamentalists on the far right can produce a credible Jesus out of allegedly inerrant canonical gospels. Their reading of who Jesus was rests on the shifting sands of their own theological constructions.

In addition to the safeguards offered by the historical methodologies practiced by all responsible scholars and the protection from idiosyncrasies afforded by peer review and open debate, the final test is to ask whether the Jesus we have found is the Jesus we wanted to find. The last temptation is to create Jesus in our own image, to marshal the facts to support preconceived convictions. This fatal pitfall has prompted the Jesus Seminar to adopt as its final general rule of evidence:

- Beware of finding a Jesus entirely congenial to you.

The Jesus of History and the Christ of Faith

Eighty-two percent of the words ascribed to Jesus in the gospels were not actually spoken by him, according to the Jesus Seminar. How do scholars account for this pronounced discrepancy? Is it realistic to think that his disciples remembered so little of what he said, or that they remembered his words so inaccurately?

Before sketching the answer that gospel specialists in the Jesus Seminar give, it is necessary to address an issue that invariably—and inevitably—comes up for those whose views of the Bible are held captive by prior theological commitments. This issue is the alleged verbal inspiration and inerrancy of the Bible.

Inspiration and Inerrancy

If the spirit dictated gospels that are inerrant, or at least inspired, why is it that those who hold this view are unable to agree on the picture of Jesus found in those same gospels? Why are there about as many Jesuses as there are interpreters of writings taken to be divinely dictated? The endless proliferation of views of Jesus on the part of those who claim infallibility for the documents erodes confidence in that theological point of view and in the devotion to the Bible it supports.

An inspired, or inerrant, set of gospels seems to require an equally inspired interpreter or body of interpretation. Interpretation must be equally inspired if we are to be sure we have the right understanding of the inerrant but variously understood originals. There seems to be no other way to ascertain the truth. It is for this reason that some churches were moved to claim infallibility for their interpretation. And it is for the same reason that televangelists and other strident voices have made equally extravagant claims.

For critical scholars no such claims are possible or desirable. Scholars make the most of the fragmentary and belated texts they have, utilizing the rigors of investigation and peer review, and offering no more than tentative claims based on historical probability. True scholarship aspires to no more. But that is the nature of historical knowledge: it is limited by the character and extent of the evidence, and can be altered by the discovery of new evidence or by the development of new methods in analyzing data. Even the more exact knowledge of the physical sciences must settle for something less than absolute certainty. Human knowledge is finite: there is always something more to be learned from the vast and complex workings of the universe. And this view makes room for faith, which seems to be in short supply for those who think they have the absolute truth.

There is this further question for the inerrant view: Why, if God took such pains to preserve an inerrant text for posterity, did the spirit not provide for the preservation of original copies of the gospels? It seems little enough to ask of a God who creates absolutely reliable reporters. In fact, we do not have original copies of any of the gospels. We do not possess autographs of any of the books of the entire Bible. The oldest surviving copies of the gospels date from about one hundred and seventy-five years after the death of Jesus, and no two copies are precisely alike. And hand-made manuscripts have almost always been "corrected" here and there, often by more than one hand. Further, this gap of almost two centuries means that the original Greek (or Aramaic?) text was copied more than once, by hand, before reaching the stage in which it has come down to us. Even careful copyists make some mistakes, as every proofreader knows. So we will never be able to claim certain knowledge of exactly what the original text of any biblical writing was.

The temporal gap that separates Jesus from the first surviving copies of the gospels—about one hundred and seventy-five years—corresponds to the lapse in time from 1776—the writing of the Declaration of Independence—to 1950. What if the oldest copies of the founding document dated only from 1950?

Part 6
The Jesus Seminar

Robert W. Funk and the Jesus Seminar

Harold W. Attridge

Robert W. Funk was, without a doubt, one of the leading American New Testament scholars of the twentieth century. He helped to reshape the Society of Biblical Literature into the organization it is today, publishing as well as providing a venue for new scholarship. His own scholarly contributions embraced Greek grammar and literary and historical research, making original contributions in each area. It is a privilege to participate in this remembrance of Bob's life and work.

My initial contact with Bob came at second hand, when I was a doctoral student at Harvard in 1969. The Harvard New Testament faculty at the time included Helmut Koester and George MacRae, S.J., both of whom collaborated with Bob in the modernization of the Society of Biblical Literature. They also worked with Bob and other scholars such as Jim Robinson and Eldon Epp to found the Hermeneia commentary series, which started its illustrious publication history in the mid 1970s.

In the next decade Bob organized a group of scholars into the Jesus Seminar, the first meeting of which was held on March 21–24, 1985, in Berkeley. Bob's opening remarks at that meeting, published in the first number of *Forum* as "The Issue of Jesus," record his aspirations for the seminar.[1] It was, he boldly claimed, "a momentous enterprise" that would "provoke hostility," as indeed it did.[2] The seminar's goal was clear, to "determine what [Jesus really said]—not his literal words, perhaps, but the substance and style of his utterances." Bob also made clear an important commitment of the seminar to "carry out our work in full public view." This was not to be an enterprise by and for scholars alone. It was designed to

---

1. Robert W. Funk, "The Issue of Jesus," *Forum* 1.1 (1985): 7–12. [Reproduced as pages 207–13 in this volume; subsequent references are to the pages in this volume.]
2. Funk, "Issue of Jesus," 207.

bring to a wider public the results of serious historical critical research and to have an impact on a subject of "widespread and passionate interest."[3]

Bob's vision for the seminar built upon his work of reforming the Society of Biblical Literature. Through the seminar he celebrated the fact that American New Testament scholarship, an heir to lengthy traditions of German and French learning, "threaten[ed] to come of age."[4] It aimed to do so on the basis of path-breaking work by scholars whom Bob celebrated, the "patron saints" of the seminar, Amos Wilder, Norman Perrin, Fred Francis, and by some of its leading members, John Dominic Crossan, M. Eugene Boring. The new scholarly enterprise would not be confined to the database of the past but would take into account the array of new materials, such as the Gospel of Thomas, that had come onto the scholarly stage in the twentieth century.

The insistence that the seminar was to be conducted in the view and for the benefit of a wider public brought with it a kind of evangelical fervor. The gospel to be proclaimed was not the traditional one, but a rational analysis that challenged important elements of contemporary evangelicalism, particularly of an apocalyptic variety. The cardinal elements of a familiar Christian narrative, bounded by creation and the apocalypse and centered on the figure of the Messiah, were all dubious at best and in need of reformation. A new narrative, a new "fiction," was required and the seminar would provide it. Such a narrative would among other things counter the "fiction of Revelation" which "keeps many common folk in bondage to ignorance and fear."[5] So the seminar and its quest for liberation began.

Although I was not there for the inauguration of the seminar, I accepted Bob's invitation to join the merry band and attended many of its meetings in the late 1980s until becoming a dean at Notre Dame forced me to cut back some of my scholarly engagements. The sessions of the seminar involved serious scholarly papers and lively exchanges on the authenticity of the sayings of Jesus.

One prominent and widely mocked feature of the seminar, voting with colored beads, was not part of its operating procedure from the start. It was introduced, at Bob's suggestion, to move the conversation along, enabling the seminar to identify broad areas of consensus, thus allow-

---

3. Funk, "Issue of Jesus," 208.

4. Funk, "Issue of Jesus," 209.

5. Funk, "Issue of Jesus," 212.

ing for more careful attention to controversial sayings. The famous color pattern, red, pink, grey, and black, emerged as a feature of the seminar's publications, and it certainly catches one's attention. Some readers of the seminar's results were astounded that scholars did not think Jesus uttered the beatitudes in their Matthean form. Equally disturbing to many was the idea that Jesus did not compose the Lord's Prayer as Matthew reports it. Yet these and other such judgments were hardly radical innovations by members of the seminar.

Perhaps the most controversial result of the seminar's deliberations was the judgment that the historical Jesus was not, as Albert Schweizer had famously characterized him, convinced of an apocalyptic eschatology. The voice of Jesus that the seminar heard and popularized was the voice that spoke provocative parables and issued challenges to the political and religious status quo. My own judgment on that issue differs from the consensus that finally prevailed in the seminar. I think that Jesus probably did exploit apocalyptic tropes, although not in a naive or all consuming way, but debate about that issue will no doubt continue as long as scholars worry about the historical Jesus.

More than fifteen years after its start, Bob Funk looked back on the Jesus Seminar, summarized how it worked, and reflected on its significance.[6] He laid out its premises, that:

> The quest of the historical Jesus is the pursuit of the discrepancy between the historical figure and the representations of him in the gospels The quest of the historical Jesus is the search for reliable data. The quest of the historical Jesus assumes that some reliable historical data are recoverable. Knowledge of the historical Jesus matters for faith.[7]

Those premises, which guided the work of the seminar, remain alive today in the work of many scholars, even when they disagree with the results that Bob and the seminar produced.

In the same article Bob celebrated the achievement of the seminar, particularly its publication *The Five Gospels*,[8] and responded to some of

---

6. Robert W. Funk, "The Jesus Seminar and the Quest," in *Jesus Then and Now: Images of Jesus in History and Christology*, ed. Marvin Meyer and Charles Hughes (Harrisburg, PA: Trinity Press International, 2001), 130–39.

7. Funk, "Jesus Seminar and the Quest," 133.

8. Robert W. Funk, *The Five Gospels: The Search for the Authentic Words of Jesus*, with Roy W. Hoover and the Jesus Seminar (New York: Macmillan, 1993).

the seminar's critics, whose work, he noted, was often characterized by "rancor, vituperation, name calling, and scathing satire." Bob suggested that underlying the harshest criticism was a conviction that "the old symbols are still in place and functional" because "the credibility of the apocalyptic worldview requires it."[9]

Bob clearly disliked millenarian views and their secular counterparts—he would no doubt have a field day in critiquing the current political scene. He also continued to believe in the powerful relevance of the historical Jesus, a figure who did not request belief in himself but trusted God and invited his followers to share his trust in the kingdom of God.[10] Bob summarized the work of the seminar in glowing terms:

> Even a partial recovery of Jesus of Nazareth will serve to purge the clogged arteries of the institutional churches, arteries blocked with self-perpetuating bureaucracies and theological litmus tests designed to maintain the status quo. His voice will redefine the nature and parameters of the Christian life.[11]

Bob Funk's immense contributions to the work of New Testament scholarship resonate to this day. His approach to a central problem of that scholarly tradition, with its elaborate communal dimension and its commitment to engaging a wider public with the results of critical analysis, remains an ideal to be emulated in new and creative ways.

Bibliography

Funk, Robert W. *The Five Gospels: The Search for the Authentic Words of Jesus.* With Roy W. Hoover and the Jesus Seminar. New York: Macmillan, 1993.

———. "The Issue of Jesus." *Forum* 1.1 (1985): 7–12.

———. "The Jesus Seminar and the Quest." Pages 130–39 in *Jesus Then and Now: Images of Jesus in History and Christology.* Edited by Marvin Meyer and Charles Hughes. Harrisburg, PA: Trinity Press International, 2001.

---

9. Funk, *Five Gospels*, 137.
10. Funk, *Five Gospels*, 138.
11. Funk, *Five Gospels*, 139.

The Issue of Jesus

Robert W. Funk

The opening remarks of Jesus Seminar Chairman Funk, presented at the first meeting held 21–24 March 1985 in Berkeley, California.

We are about to embark on a momentous enterprise. We are going to inquire simply, rigorously after the *voice* of Jesus, after what he really said.

In this process, we will be asking a question that borders the sacred, that even abuts blasphemy, for many in our society. As a consequence, the course we shall follow may prove hazardous. We may well provoke hostility. But we will set out, in spite of the dangers, because we are professionals and because the issue of Jesus is there to be faced, much as Mount Everest confronts the team of climbers.

We are not embarking on this venture in a corner. We are going to carry out our work in full public view; we will not only honor the freedom of information; we will insist on the public disclosure of our work, and, insofar as it lies within our power, we shall see to it that the public is informed of our judgments. We shall do so, not because our wisdom is superior, but because we are committed to public accountability.

Our basic plan is simple. We intend to examine every fragment of the traditions attached to the name of Jesus in order to determine what he really said—not his literal words, perhaps, but the substance and style of his utterances. We are in quest of his *voice*, insofar as it can be distinguished from many other voices also preserved in the tradition. We are prepared to bring to bear everything we know and can learn about the form and content, about the formation and transmission, of aphorisms and parables, dialogues and debates, attributed or attributable to Jesus, in order to carry out our task.

There are profound and more obvious reasons we have decided to undertake this work. The more profound and complex reasons may be deferred until a subsequent session of the seminar. A statement of the more patent motivations will serve this occasion adequately.

We are launching these collective investigations in the first instance in response to our students, past, present, and future. Once our students learn to discern the traditions of the New Testament and other early Christian literature—and they all do to a greater or lesser extent under out tutelage—they want to know the ultimate truth: what did Jesus really say? Who was this man to whom the tradition steadily refers itself? For a change, we will be answering a question that is really being asked.

Make no mistake: there is widespread and passionate interest in the issue, even among those uninitiated in the higher mysteries of gospel scholarship. The religious establishment has not allowed the intelligence of high scholarship to pass through to pastors and priests to a hungry laity, and the radio and TV counterparts of educated clergy have traded in platitudes and pieties and played on ignorance of the uniformed. A rude and rancorous awakening lies ahead.

What we are about takes courage, as I said. We are probing what is most sacred to millions, and hence we will constantly border on blasphemy. We must be prepared to forebear the hostility we shall provoke. At the same time, our work, if carefully and thoughtfully wrought, will spell liberty for other millions. It is the latter that we labor.

We are forming this seminar in the second place because we are entering an exciting new period of biblical, especially New Testament scholarship.

We have new and tantalizing primary sources with which to work, such as the Gospel of Thomas, the Apocryphon of James, the Dialogue of the Savior, and we stand on the verge of new study instruments, such as the *New Gospel Parallels*, the new *Sayings Parallels*, and perhaps even a new and more tolerable translation of other New Testament apocrypha.

Beyond these advances, we have learned to transcend the paradigms of scholarship set for us early in this century. We have learned our textual criticism, our source and form and redaction criticism, we have taken in the best—and some of the worst—of our German and English and French predecessors. But we are now moving on to different paradigms: to parables and aphorisms as metaphors and poetry, to narratology, to reader-response criticism, to social description and analysis, and to many other promising ventures. We are laying new foundations in editing and publishing primary source materials, new and old, and are building new edifices of interpretations on those foundations.

Perhaps most important of all, these developments have taken place predominantly, though not exclusively, in American scholarship. We need not promote chauvinism; we need only recognize that American biblical scholarship threatens to come of age, and that in itself is a startling new stage in our academic history. We may even be approaching the time when Europeans, if they know what they are about will come to North America on sabbaticals to catch up, rather than the other way around. It is already clear that Europeans who do not read American scholarship are falling steadily behind.

The acknowledgment that a bonafide tradition of American New Testament scholarship is aborning brings me to the second large point of these introductory remarks. Creating a tradition of scholarship means that our work must finally and firmly become cumulative.

Cumulative is defined in law as evidence that gives greater weight to evidence previously introduces. In banking, cumulative interest is interest on both principal and accumulated interest. Scholarship is cumulative that lays down successive layers of evidence and interpretation of preceding layers.

I invite you to ponder the more than sixty books written by fellows of this seminar and its patron saints (Amons N. Wilder, Norman Perrin, Fred O. Francis). In some important respects these books represent cumulative effort: in and through these works a new tradition of scholarship is being formed. But in many respects, our work remains fragmented and isolated. We too often set about reinventing the wheel for each new vehicle we attempt to design and build. We are too often ignorant of each other's achievements. As a consequence, we tend to repeat the same major projects. Yet this phase of our history is coming to an end, as the emergence of this seminar will attest.

In order to abet cumulative scholarship, I want to propose two preliminary steps. First, I am requesting fellows of the seminar to prepare prose account of their careers to be published in *Foundations and Facets Forum* (*FFF*). These autobiographical sketches should indicate something of one's intellectual odyssey as well as the principal stations of endeavor along the way. In other words, we need to know the movements and pauses of our colleagues, in order better to understand how we got where we are. And it would make these sketches more interesting reading were they to include hints of the human.

As a second step, I am requesting that each fellow provide a comprehensive bibliography of his or her publications for *FFF*. With the appearance of these bibliographies, fellows need no longer be ignorant of the work of colleagues.

Beyond these two items, I am further suggesting that we review, in some depth, works of fellows that are relevant for the seminar. We have begun with Crossan's *In Fragments* and *Four Other Gospels*. These reviews will be published in *FFF*, of course. We should proceed to other works. I am subsequently going to propose that we tackle M. Eugene Boring's *Sayings of the Risen Jesus* and the recent work of Werner Kelber. But that will be only the beginning. I am herewith inviting fellows to submit reviews of any works published by other fellows for publication in *FFF*. If our work is to become genuinely cumulative, we must become acquainted with everything that has been produced.

These are only provisional steps that should lead up to the work of the seminar itself. In making an inventory of the Jesus tradition and evaluating the items in that inventory, we must lay the foundations carefully. And we must then build painstakingly on those foundations. Only so will our work stand the tests of consensus and time.

Our endeavors must be cumulative and reciprocal in the last analysis in order to frame our individual proclivities and eccentricities by the highest degree of scholarly objectivity. My idiosyncrasies will be counterbalanced by your peculiarities. Our common finitude will be baptized in collective wisdom. (That does not make us gods, but it does obscure the consequences of original sin.) The result will be a compromise: not a sacrificing of integrity, but an acquiescence in the best informed common judgment. Our end product may look like a horse designed by a committee, that is, like a camel, but at least it will be a beast of burden tough enough to withstand the desert heat of powerful adverse criticism.

To heighten the risk of our program, I am proposing that we conduct our work in full public view. If we are to survive as scholars of the humanities, as well as theologians, we must quit the academic closet. And we must begin to sell a product that has some utilitarian value to someone—or which at least appears to have utilitarian value to someone. We could begin with our students—not a bad place to begin—but we could also undertake to advise our president, who regards himself as a Koine Kowboy, about the perils of apocalyptic foreign policy. And we might conceivably do so on the basis of this seminar, to the extent that he is willing, not to just cite, but to actually heed, the words of Jesus. At all events, we must begin earnestly to report on our work to a wider public and then engage that public in conversation and conference.

I come now to the final point. It is a rather large one and can be made here only in the skimpiest outline. It lies central to all the other points I have made or will try to make in the course of our investigation together.

Since we are Bible scholars, let us begin with the Bible as whole. The Bible begins, we are wont to say, at the Beginning and concludes with a vision of the heavenly city, the ultimate End. Traditionally, the Bible is taken as a coherent structure: the Apocalypse is thought to bring things around again to their original state; the evil introduced into the garden in the first instance is eradicated in the last. And the beginning and end are viewed as wholly constant with the *real* events that occur between them. Thus, the Christian savior figure is interpreted as belonging to the primeval innocence of the garden and yet predicting and precipitating the final outcome.

There are two things to be said about this scheme. First, we are having increasing difficulty these days in accepting the biblical account of the creation and of the apocalyptic conclusion in anything like a literal sense. The difficulty just mentioned is connected with a second feature: we now know that narrative accounts of ourselves, our nations, the Western tradition, and the history of the world, are fictions.

Narrative fictions, aside from recent experiments in "structureless" novels, must have a beginning and an end and be located in space. They must involve a finite number of participants and obviously depict a limited number of events. Moreover, it is required of narrative that there be some fundamental continuity in participants and some connections between and among events that form a narrative chain. It is in this formal sense that the Bible is said to form a narrative and to embrace in its several parts a coherent and continuous structure. And it is also this same sense that the Bible, along with all our histories, is a fiction.

A fiction is thus a selection—arbitrary in nature—of participants and events arranged in a connected chain and on a chronological line with an arbitrary beginning and ending. In sum, we make up all our "stories"—out of real enough material, of course—in relation to imaginary constructs, within temporal limits.

Our fictions, although deliberately fictive, are nevertheless not subject to proof or falsification. We do not abandon them because they are demonstrably false, but because they lose their "operational effectiveness,"[1]

---

1. Frank Kermode, *The Sense of an Ending* (Oxford: Oxford University Press, 1967), 40.

because they fail to account for enough of what we take to be real in the everyday course of events. Fictions of the sciences or of law are discarded when they no longer match our living experience of things. But religious fictions, like those found in the Bible, are more tenacious because they "are harder to free from mythological 'deposit,'" as Frank Kermode puts it.[2] "If we forget that fictions are fictive we regress to myth."[3] The Bible has become mostly myth in Kermode's sense of the term, since the majority in our society do not hold that the fictions of the Bible are indeed fictive.

Our dilemma is becoming acute: just as the beginning of the created world is receding in geological time before our very eyes, so the future no long presents itself as naive imminence. Many of us believe that the world may be turned into cinder one day soon without an accompanying conviction that Armageddon is upon us. But our crisis goes beyond these terminal points: it affects the middle as well. Those of us who work with that hypothetical middle—Jesus of Nazareth—are hard pressed to concoct any form of coherence that will unite beginning, middle and end in some grand new fiction that will meet all the requirements of narrative. To put the matter bluntly, we are having as much trouble with the middle—the messiah—as we are with the terminal points. What we need is a new fiction that takes as its starting point the central event in the Judeo-Christian drama and reconciles that middle with a new story that reach beyond old beginnings and endings. In sum, we need a new narrative of Jesus, a new gospel if you will, that places Jesus differently in the grand scheme, the epic story.

Not any fiction will do. The fiction of the superiority of the Aryan race let the extermination of six million Jews. The fiction of American superiority prompted the massacre of thousands of Native Americans and the Vietnam War. The fiction of Revelation keeps many common folk in bondage to ignorance and fear. We require a new, liberating fiction, one that squares with the best knowledge we can now accumulate and one that transcends self-serving ideologies. And we need a fiction that we recognize to be fictive.

Satisfaction will come hard. Antihistoricist criticism, now rampant among us, will impugn every fact we seek to establish. Every positive attribution will be challenged again and again. All of this owes, of course, to

---

2. Kermode, *Sense of an Ending*, 40.

3. Kermode, *Sense of an Ending*, 41.

what Oscar Wilde called "the decay of lying"; we have fallen, he says, into "careless habit of accuracy."[4] And yet, as Kermode reminds us, "the survival of paradigms is as much our business as their erosion."[5] Our stories are eroding under the acids of historical criticism. We must retell our stories. And there is one epic story that has Jesus in it.

Bibliography

Boring, M. Eugene. *Sayings of the Risen Jesus*. SNTSMS 46. Cambridge: Cambridge University Press, 1982.

Crossan, John Dominic. *Four Other Gospels: Shadows on the Contours of Canon*. Minneapolis: Winston Press, 1985.

———. *In Fragments: The Aphorisms of Jesus*. San Francisco: Harper & Row, 1983.

Kermode, Frank. *The Sense of an Ending: Studies in the Theory of Fiction*. Oxford: Oxford University Press, 1967.

---

4. Quoted by Kermode, *Sense of an Ending*, 43.

5. Kermode, *Sense of an Ending*, 43.

On Distinguishing Historical from Fictive Narrative

Robert W. Funk

0. Introduction

1. Fiction and Nonfiction

The whole of the literary world is divided into two parts: fiction and non-fiction. The task of the Jesus Seminar is to determine to which of these categories the gospels belong.

The narrative text may have as its referents, its signified, some imagined series of events, in which case its story lacks an objective basis in the world of lived experience. This kind of story is called fiction. Or, the narrative may be about "real" events—events taken actually to have occurred, apart from particular memories and records of them. In that case, the story has history as its referent.

Native speakers of English tend to distinguish story as fiction from the kind of story called history. Every bookstore, library, and publisher of my acquaintance makes that fundamental distinction in the classification of books.

Biblical scholars have not been able to make up their minds whether the biblical narratives are about real or fictive events. Or, if they are about both, which is which. The test is a simple one: did the events depicted as having taken place actually take place? Are the gospels essentially fiction or biography?

This elementary problem has been at the center of historical criticism since its rise in the Enlightenment. Nevertheless, a tendency has recently emerged to dismiss the issue peremptorily and take the canonical texts in their received form as the object of investigation. This move, practiced under the heading of redaction criticism, relieves the pressures of piety by substituting the implied author, the subtleties of plot, and reader response for the hard empirical question of fact or fiction. It also gets scholars off the ecclesiastical hook. But in so doing it also muddles the categories and obscures the issue: fantasy and fact are lumped together with the result that neither is accorded its rightful place in the life of the mind and the spirit. My concern is as much the liberation of fantasy from literalist control as it is to distinguish fact from fantasy. We must inquire after the real story, but we must also pursue the mythologies that hold cosmic chaos at bay and provide the basis for an ordered society.

Structuralists and deconstructionists, on the other hand, have also belittled the historical issue as false, for something like the opposite reasons. They hold that narrative texts, historical as well as fictive, are ensnared in the endless play of differences of which language consists and so can tell us nothing about their referents: signifier and signified are both imprisoned in language.

Biblical critics of more traditional persuasions have been at an understandable loss in these cross currents, since their methodological paradigm is being discredited on both fronts. In spite of these trends, the problem will not go away. Scholars may vacate their responsibility out of a false sense of piety, or out of a beleaguered cynicism, or out of a smug elitism. But the constituency they are losing, both inside and outside the circle of faith, deserves and will demand a clear scholarly assessment of the nature of the texts. Humankind, moreover, cannot afford to do without the distinction between fact and fiction. To attempt to do so is to open society to demonic stories, such as the one on which Nazism was based, or to the fantasies of various fundamentalisms, which will certainly lead to the kind of tragic experiment attempted by Jim Jones.

To be sure, our venerable discipline, historical, critical scholarship, has been inclined to go in exclusive quest of the holy land of historical fact and leave everything aside that does not fall under that literalism. I do not propose to return to that stage of our innocence, as significant as it was. Yet the more sophisticated distinctions we aspire to make involve assessing texts for their historical underpinnings that are predominantly mythical and symbolic, if only in order to clear the air. Recovering the historical Jesus, or any other historical person or event, will not solve our problems. Yet an assault on the fundamental issues may help produce the new methodological paradigms we need in order to let fantasy have its rightful place in our scholarship, alongside the more venerable search for the facts. After all, there is nothing wrong with myth. But when myth is misunderstood as history it becomes demonic. And the demonic is on a rampage in the public we seek to serve.

2. Narratology and a Theory of Tradition

Basic preparation for the Jesus Seminar II: the search for the authentic acts of Jesus includes the investigation of narratology for its bearing on the analysis and evaluation of narrated events. Narratology embraces both the theory and the criticism of narrative texts. Narratology is both inductive and deductive. In other words, narratology is the development of a theory or theories of narrative, in conjunction with the close analysis of actual narrative texts.

In addition to narratology, the seminar needs to invoke or develop a theory of tradition. Tradition includes the received world that has been socially constructed, its roots in previous tradition, and the transmission and modification of that world in specific strands of oral and written tradition. Access to the early Christian world is provided principally by biblical and related texts, together with relevant artifacts. At the moment, biblical scholarship lacks a coherent theory of tradition, so it must make do with elements of a theory as they have been conceived, often haphazardly, in practice.

To ward off disappointment at the conclusion of this essay, I should advance this caveat: there are no infallible markers in narrative texts that will point the way unerringly to fact. What we may hope to achieve is to begin gathering the elements of new procedures that will enable us to study narrative texts with a greater degree of precision and hence confidence than has heretofore been the case. Since I will be breaking relatively new ground—much of what I will propose was advanced in my *Poetics of Biblical Narrative* (1988)[1]—you will need to allow for a certain latitude in the description of theoretical constructs, nomenclature, and conclusions based on a limited sampling of the data. We will be exploring new ground.

In part 1, I propose to lay out the procedures for analyzing narrative texts in order to isolate the kind of information we will want to evaluate. I propose to do so under the following heads:

1. Narrative statements
2. Types of narrative statements

---

1. Robert W. Funk, *The Poetics of Biblical Narrative* (Sonoma: Polebridge, 1988).

3. Action statements and event
4. Status statements
5. Levels of generality
6. Rules of procedure
7. Segments and their structure
8. Sequences of segments
9. The narrator: point of view and narration
10. Showing and telling: focused and unfocused segments
11. Memory and literacy
12. The social construction of reality

After all, the first step is to determine what the texts claim for themselves and what they do not.

A second, correlative step is to advance a theory of tradition, based on psychological and sociological data, that identifies how tradition is formed and how it is transmitted. The last two segments listed above are devoted to this issue.

Part 2 consists of an analysis of the first synoptic pericope, which introduces John the Baptist to the reader. This text and its parallels will function as the basis for additional procedural observations under the following heads:

13. Introduction
14. Status statements
15. Action statements
16. Iteratives
17. Direct and indirect discourse
18. Conclusions

We begin with a consideration of the poetics of biblical narrative.

1. Narratology and a Theory of Tradition

1. Narrative Statements

The recommended combination of theory and empirical data can be observed in the analysis of a simple narrative segment drawn from the gospels. I propose to examine Mark 2:14, which narrates the call of Levi, for the kind of information we may expect to derive from narrative reports. This simple exercise will focus on the procedures that must precede our attempts at historical evaluation.

The first step is to resolve the continuous text into narrative statements:

(1)   As Jesus was walking along,

(2)   he saw Levi, the son of Alphaeus,

(2.1)   sitting at the toll booth,

(3)   and Jesus said to him,

(3.1)   "Follow me."

(4)   And Levi got up

(5)   and followed him.

This pericope has been divided into five (seven) narrative statements, each of which is determined by a verb. In other words, there is one narrative statement for each verb in the text.

The verbs in (2.1) and (3.1) are embedded in larger grammatical structures. In isolating narrative statements, embedded sentences are resolved as independent sentences for the purpose of the analysis.

It is not always necessary, of course, to carry out this formal exercise on paper. Yet precision is a desirable feature in narrative analysis.

An even greater degree of precision can be achieved by two additional steps: (a) We can rewrite each statement as a fully explicit, independent sentence; and (b) we can extract implied statements from the narrative text and rewrite them as fully explicit, independent sentences.

Once again utilizing our simple text as the basis, we may resolve the five narrative statements as follows:

(1)   Jesus was walking along.

(2a)   Jesus saw Levi.

(2b)   Levi was the son of Alphaeus.

(2.1)   Levi was sitting at the toll booth.

(3)   Jesus said (x) to Levi.

(3.1)   [Levi, you] follow me.

(4)   Levi got up.

(5)   Levi followed him.

We have again stayed as close to the language of the text as possible. We have substituted explicit subjects and objects for pronouns. However, we have had to supply the copula (the verb "to be") in (2b), where it is only implied. This step means that the number of narrative statements will not necessarily correspond to the number of verbs in the primary text. The result: each narrative statement is now a fully explicit independent sentence.

2. Types of Narrative Statements

Narrative statements fall into two broad categories: they are termed is-statements and do-statements. The first is also known as status statements, the second as action statements.[2] It is not always possible to distinguish sharply between the two, and we often find status statements embedded in or implied by action statements and the reverse.

Do-statements express either an action or a happening. An action is performed by an agent:

    (i) John baptized Jesus.

    (ii) John preached repentance.

A happening is a change of status affecting a patient:

    (iii) The fever left her.

    (iv) His ankles were made strong.

A patient is the one to whom something happens. Compare the following statements:

    (v) Fortna raised the sails on his boat.

    (vi) Fortna sailed out to sea.

In (v) Fortna is the agent of the action; in (vi) he is the patient, although he is also the grammatical subject of the sentence. This difference calls attention to the fact that the resolved narrative statement may differ from the surface grammatical structure of actual sentences in the text.

In the analysis of gospel texts we will want to ask whether statements like (iv) above has an implied agent, viz. God, or whether it is simply an observation of empirical fact. A decision might well affect how we assess such statements as "history."

3. Action Statements and Event

A cluster of narrative statements constitutes an event. In the call of Levi, we have seven narrative statements. If we were to reduce the account to its bare essentials, we could say that this story consists of two narrative statements that together constitute an event:

    (a) Jesus calls Levi (3) + (3.1)

    (b) Levi follows Jesus (5)

---

2. Funk, *Poetics of Biblical Narrative*, 18–19.

These two actions are the key actions performed by each of the two actors or participants in this narrative segment. They are the actions in "focus." The focus of a narrative segment is customarily determined by that action or complex of actions that constitutes a change in status. In this instance, before the event Levi was not a follower of Jesus; after the event he is a follower of Jesus. The event is Levi's change in status.

The other action statements are incidental to the event. Put differently, the other statements contribute only indirectly to the event. The incidental action statements provide the setting. In this narrative segment, the incidental action statements belong to the "framework" of narration:

    (1) Jesus is walking along (spatial setting)
    (2) Jesus sees Levi (the focalizer)
    (3) Levi is sitting at the toll booth (spatial setting)
    (4) Levi gets up (preparation for the defocalizer)

(The technical terms, focalizer and defocalizer, will be defined subsequently.) It would be pointless for the historian to try to determine whether incidental statements such as these are historical or not. Our work will be more efficient and better focused if we limit ourselves to a consideration of the event as such-to that action or complex of actions that constitutes the focus of a narrative segment.

4. Status Statements

Is-statements are marked, of course, by some form of the copula or equivalent, expressed or implied.

    (a) There was a person named Jesus.*
    (b) There was a person named Levi.*
    (c) Levi was the son of Alphaeus*
    (d) Levi was a toll collector*
    (e) Levi was a disciple of Jesus*, OR
        Jesus had a disciple named Levi*

Then, based on this and other stories in the gospels, we could formulate this generalization:

    (f) Jesus had disciples (students)*

If we affirm that there was a historical person named Jesus in connection with one statement, it will be unnecessary to repeat that affirmation each

---

* These are derivative status statements: they are inferred from other statements in the text.

time we meet it in the text. In the case of secondary participants, such as Levi, I suggest we take them one at a time as we meet them.

5. Levels of Generality

We have already raised the question of levels of generality in connection with the two types of narrative statements. In the case of action statements, the three levels would be:

(a) Jesus calls (a) disciple(s).
(b) Jesus calls Levi to discipleship; Levi accepts.
(c) Jesus calls Levi to discipleship one day while he is sitting at a toll booth; Levi leaves his booth and follows Jesus.

In (c) we have included the incidental narrative statements as a part of the summary. In (b) we have omitted details of the setting and focused exclusively on the two event statements. In (a) we have raised the narrative to another level of abstraction: on the basis of this report, can we conclude that Jesus called disciples (at least one)?

We have already suggested that level (c) embraces too much detail to warrant consideration. Level (b) is the highest level of generality specific to this pericope. Level (a) is an even higher level of generalization that applies to this and all other narratives about Jesus that tell of his recruiting or having disciples. Since we will often be considering a group of narrative forms or genres, we will just as often have to inquire about level (a).

In the case of status statements, the highest level of generality simply affirms the existence of particular participants (level a) at a time and place relevant to the narrative. At a second level, generalizations are based on data derived from more than one narrative segment or sources. We will need to make a distinction in level (b) affirmations between those that rest on multiple evidence from the same source and those that rest on data derived from two or more independent sources. This distinction involves rule of evidence (A1). Finally, specific elements of participant identification or setting will have to be assessed separately at a third level (c).

It is not difficult to see that the action statements and status statements in this one tiny pericope branch out into other pericopes and questions, some at a more specific level, others at a higher level of abstraction. The foundation of our work will have to be to analyze the gospel narratives for kinds of evidence and then assess that evidence on the broadest possible basis in the sources.

6. Rules of Procedure

We are now in a position to formulate the first set of procedural guidelines (let P stand for procedure):

(P1) Reduce each narrative segment to narrative statements.

(P2) Determine the action or complex of actions that constitutes the event—the change in status—narrated in that segment.

(P3) Assess for fact or fiction the action or complex of actions that constitutes the event.

(P4) Assess for fact or fiction action statements at the highest level of generality.

(P5) Assess for fact or fiction status statements at the highest level of generality, as in the case of action statements.

(P6) At the second highest level of generality, status statements attested by two or more segments or sources should be assessed separately as fact or fiction.

Additional rules of procedure will be developed below. Some of the rules of evidence developed for the sayings tradition will be relevant to action statements. Others will either require modification or have to be dropped.

7. Segments and Their Structure

A narrative of any length consists of a series of segments, each with a more or less discrete beginning and end. A narrative segment has a formal structure of three parts: introduction, nucleus, conclusion. The *nucleus* customarily contains the action statements that constitute the event in focus: an event in focus is what advances the "plot" (we must be cautious in applying modern literary terms to ancient narratives without observing possible differences). The introduction functions to bring the participants together in a specific time and place so something can happen. Because the introduction brings the story into focus on particular persons, times, places, I have called it the *focalizer*. The conclusion rounds the narrative segment off in the same way that a musical composition returns to its tonic at the end. Because the conclusion reverses the focalizing process, I have termed it the *defocalizer*.

The structure of the narrative segment may be represented graphically as:

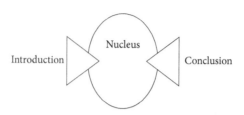

In the graphic, the two facing triangles represent the focalizer and defocalizer; the egg represents the nucleus. These features are sketched in detail in *Poetics*, 59–132.

In the account of the call of Levi sketched earlier, statements (1)–(2.1) constitute the focalizer, statements (3)–(3.1) the nucleus, and statements (4)–(5) the defocalizer. In this instance, the focal event narrated in this segment comes to expression in both the nucleus and the defocalizer, unlike the typical structure. It is, of course, always possible for the narrator to relegate focal actions either to the introduction or the conclusion as an exception to the general rule.

It is undoubtedly significant to distinguish the introduction and conclusion from the nucleus in most narrative segments in the gospels. If we compare parallel narrative segments in the gospels-such comparisons substitute for native informants-we can observe that the nucleus of many narrative segments tends to be more stable that either the introduction (focalizer) or conclusion (defocalizer). This suggests that the authors took greater liberties with introductory and concluding elements than they did with focal elements.

This observation goes together with another commonplace of synoptic criticism. As E. P. Sanders puts it,

> It is especially noteworthy that agreement between Matthew and Luke begins where Mark begins and ends where Mark ends. Mark's gospel starts with John the Baptist. Matthew and Luke both have birth narratives before the appearance and preaching of John, but they do not agree. They begin to agree with the first passage about the Baptist. Similarly Mark ends with the women fleeing from the empty tomb. Matthew and Luke have resurrection accounts after the discovery of the empty tomb, but they do not agree with each other.
>
> The same phenomenon occurs within individual pericopes.[3]

---

3. E. P. Sanders and Margaret Davies, *Studying the Synoptic Gospels* (Philadelphia: Trinity Press International, 1989), 54.

To these two observations, I would like to venture a third, which I cannot in this context support in detail: the words ascribed to Jesus, even in narrative segments where those words are context-bound, tend to be more stable than the surrounding narrative statements.

This brings us to another rule of procedure:

(P7) We should distinguish introductions and conclusions from nuclei in narrative segments and sequences of segments and give closer attention to the nuclei.

8. Sequences of Segments

The observations in the preceding paragraph regarding the connective and transitional elements between and among narrative segments (introductions and conclusions) merely confirms a commonplace in gospel criticism: the syntagmatic thread of the gospels (the sequence of events) is mostly fictive. It is a fiction of the ancient storyteller, who did not know how particular events were actually connected or even the order in which they occurred. More than that, the ancient storyteller did not have an interest in chronological and causal relationships in the modern sense. The "plot" discovered by recent biblical scholars seeking to employ the categories developed in literary criticism is mostly the figment of the scholarly imagination as it seeks to find its own sense of order in the sequence of events.

Connective devices in the gospels are more often than not purely grammatical, or mnemonic (story type, keyword, and so on), or the result of rhetorical compendia, such as the parable complex in Mark 4:1–34. Connectives may also involve the repetition of themes or the use of the prophecy/fulfillment schema. Accordingly, we should expect the plot structure of the gospels to be relatively weak, if by plot structure we mean the before/after or cause/effect sequence of narrative segments. Plot in the modern literary-critical sense does not appear in Western literature, strictly speaking, until the rise of the modern novel. The gospel narratives, like the *Iliad* and the *Odyssey*, and other extended narratives in the ancient world, are strung on the artificial story line of travel narratives.

Court raconteurs in the Middle Ages also narrated episodically: they related events in almost any order since they employed the travel adventure as the framework. Cervantes's (1547–1616) treatment of Don Quixote, although sometimes designated the first modern novel, is still nothing more than a series of adventures linked by a journey. Even Daniel Defoe (1660–1731), who started writing as a journalist, sketches his novels as journeys to strange parts of the world. According to Walter Ong, "the novel-length climactic linear plot" begins with Jane Austen (1775–1817) and reaches its modern height in Edgar Allan Poe's *Murders in the Rue Morgue* (1841).[4] For this reason, Ong can state: an oral culture "cannot organize even shorter narrative in the studious, relentless climactic way that readers of literature for the past 200 years have learned more and more to expect-and, in recent decades, self-consciously to depreciate."[5] The reasons for this, Ong continues, are:

> A narrator in an oral culture, as has been seen, normally and naturally operated in episodic patterning, and the elimination of narrative voice appears to have been essential at first to rid the story line of such patterning. We must not forget that episodic structure was the natural way to talk out a lengthy story line if only because the experience of real life is more like a string of episodes than it is like a Freytag pyramid. Careful selectivity produces the tight pyramidal plot, and this selectivity is implemented as never before by the distance that writing establishes between expression and real life.[6]

The narrative unity of the gospels is therefore to be understood as largely paradigmatic rather than syntagmatic, and the excessive claims for "plot" in the gospels by recent critics are based on modern concepts quite alien to the oral narrators of the gospel tradition.

These considerations produce the next rule of procedure:

(PB) We should isolate data derived from the order of segments and sequences in the gospel narratives and evaluate such data very circumspectly: the connectives provided by the evangelists are largely fictive and vary frequently from performance to performance, from source to source.

9. The Narrator: Point of View and Narration

Every story is told by someone. That someone is called the narrator. The narrator does the narrating. The first question to be asked, accordingly, is: who is speaking?

---

4. Walter J. Ong, *Orality and Literacy: The Technologizing of the* Word (London: Methuen, 1982).

5. Ong, *Orality and Literacy*, 143.

6. Ong, *Orality and Literacy*, 148.

Every story is also told from some particular point of view or perspective. Point of view may of course shift from segment to segment. The second question to be asked is: who does the seeing (or hearing)?

The one narrating and the one seeing may be two different persons. For example, Pip in Dickens's *Great Expectations* tells the story, but he relates events as seen through the eyes of himself as a youngster. Further, the narrator may also employ a participant in the story as a sub-narrator and allow that participant to tell things as he or she sees them.

We need not belabor the numerous fine distinctions possible on the subject· of narrators and points of view. We need review only those relevant to the gospels.

9.1. Intra- and extradiegetic narrators. Materials in the gospels may be divided broadly into two categories:

    (1) Jesus sees and narrates (intradiegetic narrator)

    (2) The evangelist sees and narrates (extradiegetic narrator)

In the first, the perspective is that of Jesus—at least it is so represented. In the second, the perspective is that of the storyteller.

With regard to the first: When Jesus speaks, we must decide whether he is really the speaker and the perspective is his own, or whether the narrator is putting words in his mouth and the perspective is that of the narrator. We have attempted to make these decisions in the first phase of the seminar.

With regard to the second, there is a whole battery of considerations to be taken into account.

1. What is the proximity of the narrator to the event being narrated? Was the narrator an eyewitness? Is the narrator's perspective close to events and his knowledge therefore limited; or is the narrator at some remove from events, which makes possible a panoramic view of things?

2. Is the narrator's perspective temporally external to the story: does he or she have all temporal dimensions simultaneously available—past, present, and future? Or is the temporal perspective internal, in which case only the immediate events are accessible? An internal perspective is, to a certain extent, always artificial, since by definition a story is told in the present about events in the past and the perspective is therefore external. Yet the distinction is worth making.

The spatial and temporal perspectives of (1) and (2) are of course correlative.

3. What is the cognitive perspective of the narrator? Does the narrator have unrestricted knowledge of events or is that knowledge restricted?

4. What is the emotive perspective of the narrator? Is the story colored because the narrator is emotionally involved, or is the narrator's emotional relation to the story purely external, in which case the perspective is neutral and uninvolved?

5. Does the narrator tell the story from the perspective of a single, monolithic lived world, or does the narrator admit a plurality of ideological positions?

Clear and unequivocal answers to these questions will help determine whether we are dealing with narrators that can be classified as historians, or whether the evangelists are predominantly writers of fiction. The following is a summary:

1. The evangelists were not eyewitnesses of the events they narrate.

2. The evangelists have considerable spatial distance from the events they narrate and their knowledge seems to be unlimited.

3. The evangelists have a complete panorama of the story—past, present, and future, including how events will turn out in their own futures. They thus have unrestricted temporal knowledge as well.

4. The evangelists are omniscient: they know states of mind, emotions, what happened when no observers were present, what God wants and does, and the like.

5. The evangelists are emotionally involved: they believe fervently in the story they are telling, which means they are not impartial observers.

6. The evangelists have assimilated their stories to the lived worlds of themselves and their communities, which means that their perspectives tend to be monolithic: they have thus filtered the data in large measure through a single perspective.

Conclusion: These observations suggest that the evangelists do not qualify as historians in the modern sense of the term.

9.2. Marks of the narrator's presence. Narrators either announce their presence and make it evident in the telling of the story or they hide their presence as effectively as they can. Yet every narrative has a narrator whose presence can be detected to a greater or lesser degree. According to Chatman, the marks of the narrator's presence in the narrative are as follows, arranged from the strongest to the weakest evidence:[7]

---

7. Seymour Chatman, *Story and Discourse: Narrative Structure in Fiction and Film* (Ithaca, NY: Cornell University Press, 1978), 219–51.

8. Description of the setting: no one can be assumed to provide descriptive statements other than the narrator, unless of course the narrator works them into the observations of one or the other of the participants.

7. Identification of characters: we have to rely on the narrator to identify the participants, to tell us who does and says what. There is no way to verify that information apart from the narrator's assertions.

6. Narrative summaries: when the narrator summarizes a series of events or provides linking devices, we know that we are dependent on the narrator for this information.

5. Definition of character: it is the narrator's judgment that the scholars were scoundrels and the disciples were stupid in the Gospel of Mark, even though stories are told to justify that judgment. Yet the reader is not permitted to make those judgments on the basis of the evidence.

4. Reports of what the characters say or think: such information can only have been provided by the narrator.

3. Narrative commentary: narrative asides and commentary of course betray the narrator directly.

2. The arrangement of the narrative elements is the work of the narrator, to be sure, although this fact is often ignored by the listener or reader.

1. The selection of events to be narrated is also the responsibility of the narrator and obliquely betrays the narrator's presence to a certain degree.

These and still other subtleties are clues to the narrator's presence. These clues should be correlated with the perspectives sketched in §9.1 in order to evaluate the narrator's contributions to the story.

(P9)   The seminar should identify the role of the narrator by determining voice and perspective and by noting marks of the narrator's presence. In assessing the historical basis of particular segments, the seminar should calculate the effect of limiting factors—factors based on voice, perspective, and presence—on what is narrated.

10. Showing and Telling: Focused and Unfocused Segments

Narration falls into two broad types: focused and unfocused. In the unfocused type, the narrator "reports" what has transpired without permitting the reader (auditor) to witness events directly or immediately: the narrator intervenes, so to speak, between the story and the reader and overtly mediates the story.

In the focused type, in contrast, the narrator transports the listener or reader, by means of words, to a specific time and place, with participants present, and allows the reader to observe and listen in on what transpires. Actions and settings are portrayed with sufficient "objectivity" to give the illusion that the reader is present. Accordingly, there is a minimum of narrator intervention.

In the focused scene, events are enacted; in the unfocused segment, they are recounted. In the first, events are shown; in the second, we say they are told. The classical terms of these two types of narration are mimesis and diegesis. In tabular form the pairs of contrasting terms are:

focused scene	unfocused segment
showing	telling
enactment	recounting
mimesis	diegesis

10.1. The unfocused segment. The unfocused segment takes two forms: in one form, the events reported are singular (what happened once is reported once); in the second form, the events reported happen more than once, often repeatedly or habitually. The first form may be termed recounting in the singulative mode; the second form we will refer to as recounting in the iterative mode.

Recounting in the iterative mode is characteristic of the narrative summary, which may occupy an entire narrative segment or segments, and of introductions and conclusions to segments and sequences. In summaries, or descriptive passages, the character of participants is being established by what they (typically) do and how they (typically) look.

10.2. The focused scene. In the enacted scene, time, place, and participants must be definite and particular. Actions must also be particular and thus singulative. In the focused scene, the narrator invokes the reader's senses directly, to the extent that words permit the approximation of that illusion. Enacted scenes tend to be more vivid and dramatic, since they are analogous to the scene in the stage drama. Enacted scenes are marked by direct discourse—directly quoted speech—rather than by indirect discourse.

To all the generalizations about focused and unfocused scenes there are, of course, exceptions. There is one generalization that is valid, however: most segments in the gospels are a mixture of recounted and enacted narration. What is of interest at the moment is not the exceptions—since we are not, in this context, pursuing the elements of a narrative grammar-but what these generalizations may mean for distinguishing fact from fiction.

(P10) The seminar should distinguish showing from telling in each narrative segment.

11. Memory and literacy

Recent research in reading and memory theory has shed some light on the problems we face in understanding ancient texts. A brief sketch of some of the salient features of this research will assist us in evaluating what and how the first disciples of Jesus remembered.

Psychologists distinguish between short-term and long-term memory. Short-term memory is a special function of the mind that lasts only a matter of milliseconds. Its ability to retain random items presented to it is severely restricted. It can manage only four to seven items before it is subject to overload.

The limitations of short-term memory account for the fact that language use and retention involve seizing word-groups rather than individual words or phonemes. A clause or a sentence counts as one, apparently, rather than as many, so far as the short-term memory is concerned. However, the long-term memory imposes some restrictions even on this possibility.

In the transfer of individual clauses and sentences to long-term memory, the mind apparently does not work with words, but makes use of "meanings" or the gist of the words instead. On the basis of numerous experiments,

> we could predict that our memories for the literal words of sentences would be poor, whereas our long-term memories for their gists would be quite reliable.[8]

The surface forms of sentences are lost to memory within a few seconds, while what those sentences mean can be retained for much longer periods. The reason the mind is able to retain meaning is that it seems able to distribute the meaning of words into pre-acquired schemata, which are employed to organize knowledge and to store it for quick retrieval. The mind is equipped with such schemata as a result of its acculturation. It

---

8. E. P. Hirsch Jr., *Cultural Literacy: What Every American Needs to Know* (New York: Vintage Books, 1988), 36.

employs these schemata to screen information it is attempting to process: what it can adapt to the categories it has available can be retained and retrieved; what it cannot fit into one or the other of its pigeonholes is lost to memory immediately.

Such experiments as underlie these generalizations have led to another very significant observation. When we hear speech or read a text, we process the words and sense by comparing the new information with information we have already stored away, as already indicated. In so doing, we also bring that prior knowledge to bear on the new information, in fact supplying much of the knowledge needed to understand the new information. Put differently, what stands written in a text suggests to the mind a much larger pool of background information to which the mind refers as it processes new data. Without that background knowledge, the listener or reader would have difficulty in processing the new information or at least would be forced to process it much more slowly. This background knowledge is what constitutes "cultural literacy" in a particular society: it enables literate persons to understand statements and process information rapidly.

While we may expect the oral mind to have a larger capacity for long-term memory than the average mind in a print culture, there is no reason to assume that the basic process differs materially in the two cultures. What does this mean for storytelling? In narrating an historical event,

> Our memories are always introducing elements from our normal schemata that weren't in an original event, and, by the same token, they are always suppressing some elements of the original event that don't exist in our normal schemata.[9]

In general, describing an actual event we have witnessed is an extremely difficult exercise. We don't normally take up the event detail by detail and then frame it in words. Rather, we process the incoming information as outlined above, referring our impressions to the schemata already in place, and slough off what does not fit those categories. Then, as memory ages and we repeat our accounts, we adapt our memories more and more to our habitual schemata. It is possible, to be sure, to be sufficiently well trained to circumvent these normal procedures to a certain extent, but in general practice this is the way the mind functions.

---

9. Hirsch, *Cultural Literacy*, 55.

(P11) With regard to the relation of the evangelists to Jesus of Nazareth, the seminar should assume that the purveyors of the Jesus
tradition, upon which the evangelists drew, have preserved no
more than the gist of what Jesus said and did, and that this gist
would have been filtered through the typifications regnant in
the communities creating the gospels.

12. The Social Construction of Reality

The mental schemata of which psychologists speak and with which they
experiment are socially constructed, according to sociologists and anthropologists. Berger and Luckmann refer to the schemata and typifications in
their ground-breaking study of the sociology of knowledge.[10]

Typifications are built up out of the face-to-face situation in which
one person encounters another. The immediate presence of the other
introduces an element of flexibility into the categories under which the
other is apprehended: If I typify and stereotype my friend, the presence
and activity of that friend will exert subtle pressure on me to modify those
typifications if they do not match the reality. It is less so with typifications
of the other at a greater remove: the anonymous other is known to me
only by way of hearsay, and so my typifications tend to be more rigid, less
susceptible to correction by incoming evidence.

We should bear this distinction in mind in evaluating the gospel materials, since the stories that are recorded in the gospels are based on hearsay
evidence, so far as we can tell. The typifications would therefore have
undergone a process of crystallization and have become more or less fixed.

Typifications are of three temporal types:
(1) we typify things as they used to be-the way we remember them;
(2) we typify things as they are, currently, in the face-to-face situation;
(3) we typify things as we want them to be (future oriented: wishful
     thinking).
In actual practice, all three temporal types are intermixed in our schemata or network of typifications, although the first and the third tend to
overpower the second: our immediate present carries less weight than the
tradition and our hopes for the future-at least in most instances.

---

10. Peter L. Berger and Thomas Luckmann, *The Social Construction of Reality: A
Treatise in the Sociology of Knowledge* (New York: Doubleday, 1966).

This observation should give pause to the view that the gospels are predominantly indices to their own times. They are actually better indices to the immediately preceding social world out of which typificatory schemata arise, and even to the future to which those communities aspire, than to the actual present of their composition.

Our typificatory schemata are derived from various loci. They stem initially from the tradition we inherit as individuals, tradition that is transmitted through parents, schools, peers, and our cultural context in general. But tradition is supplemented at an early stage by typifications arising out of the face-to-face situation. In addition to these loci, our cultural milieu in the wider sense provides us with categories of understanding and interpretation; the American cultural context for American interpreters of the Bible, the Near Eastern Mediterranean for first-century Palestine. Since language is the vehicle used to carry much of this network, we must pay close attention to the constraints of language and, in the case of storytelling, to the constraints of narrative. Linguistic conventions have a profound effect on what we can remember and what we can tell.

Institutions arise out of habitualization: we create a social world out of our habits and, by repeating those habits and developing actors to whom they are assigned, institutionalize them. Once they are institutionalized, they can be transmitted to new generations. And if transmitted, they can be enacted by ritual and legitimized by myth and logic. They are then subject to enforcement through a system of rewards and sanctions. This process, however, is not clean: it is beset by deviants who refuse to accept, or adhere to, the received social world and refract or revolutionize it in various ways, large and small. Deviations that win acceptance by a significant number of people become new habits that in turn become institutionalized. It is important, of course, to recognize the role of the deviant in the rise of new religious traditions, such as Judaism, Christianity, and Islam.

We never encounter a tradition that does not consist of mixed elements: some are in the process of decaying and will ultimately be lost, others are aborning and will eventually enter the mainstream of social existence. Since the actual state of affairs is always mixed, we should expect any particular tradition to carry along on its tide—think of it as a river of tradition—debris from dying traditions and debris from traditions on the rise. Although institutions tend to insist on a monolithic account of the way things are, the lore in the public domain will invariably contain elements that do not "fit."

What is the status of tradition in the gospels, generally speaking? New communities were in the process of formation—communities that would eventually emerge, in the fourth century, as a monolithic institution. However, in the gospels the development is only in an intermediate stage: the gospels come at that stage in which deviant Jesus is being domesticated in these new communities in the framework of the everyday world known to Judeans and new foreign converts living in proximity to each other. We should therefore anticipate, a priori, that the traditions being embodied in the gospels will represent, in their dominant aspects, that domestication, but that they will also retain traces of the deviations that propelled the new movement to separate from the Judaism of the second temple.

In sociological terms, this means that the typifications that dominate the everyday life of these new communities are being employed as categories into which to pour the lore about Jesus. At the same time, debris from earlier memories will linger on in the tradition in spite of their incompatibility with the new social formations. These earlier memories will betray the typifications of the founder, or those in his immediate company—typifications that will represent some departures from the received world of that earlier social world. One fact compels us to come to this conclusion: the Christian movement did spawn new social enclaves and institutions.

By definition, then, Jesus must have been a deviant who set this process in motion, assuming that he sustained some relation to the budding Christian movement. Yet deviants do not live entirely out of their deviations: they also project new modes of behavior and form or inspire incipient groups to enact them. As a consequence, deviants inspire tradition formation that is designed to refract or modify received tradition in the process of launching a new tradition. The social reconstruction of reality always involves employing the materials of the old house out of which to construct the new. Meanwhile, it is necessary to live in the old house while the new one is being built.

In looking back on this process from the distance of the written gospels, we are prompted to conclude, from various pieces of evidence in the gospels, that Jesus did refract the tradition of his received Judean context. The primary evidence for that, in my judgment, lies in the narrative parables and in the root metaphors Jesus used. Yet precisely this deviation from the typifications that controlled the lived world of his disciples would be hard to remember: they lacked the categories with which to carry such new knowledge. However, they could learn figures of speech, cliches, and stories, since their repertoire already contained such items.

They could even remember the gist of some of the things Jesus said or did—when they grasped the meaning of those words or acts. But the newness of it all—new only in the sense that it represented a departure from their everyday knowledge—prevented them holding on to more than a fraction of the information.

Two large conclusions are to be drawn from this sketch. First, we will find the Jesus of history in the gospels only in that "debris" which has not been assimilated to—domesticated in—the new societies emerging under Christian mandate. The second is correlative: the multiple traditions preserved by the gospels are more of an index to what the evangelists and the social reality that immediately preceded them took to be typical, rather than to what Jesus regarded as his world. There is not much historical comfort in numbers if we are looking for a particular face in a Galilean crowd.

If these conclusions are sound, two final rules of procedure are in order:

(P12) The seminar should seek the Jesus of history in the unassimilated "debris" preserved in the gospels.

(P13) The seminar should be especially wary of traditions that are often repeated in the gospels: they tend to be elements that fit the typifications of emerging Christian communities.

2. John the Baptist: Fact or Fiction?
Mark 1:1–8 // Matt 3:1–12 // Luke 3:1–20

13. Introduction

13.1. The sketch of a narrative poetics and theory of tradition advanced in part 1 should now be put to the test to see what relevance they have for the work of phase 2 of the Jesus Seminar. The first step is to reduce the three parallel texts to narrative statements and to identify each statement as either an action or a status statement or as a combination of the two. This step has been carried out and appears as appendix 1 (the reader will need this appendix at hand for ready reference in the second half of this essay).

I have organized my comments around the major categories in part 1 wherever possible; within those categories I have endeavored to follow the order in which items appear in the texts.

13.2. We may ignore Mark 1:1–3; Matt 3:3; Luke 3:l–2a, which are either not immediately relevant to John the Baptist (hereafter JB) or involve the prophecy/fulfillment schema, which requires separate treatment.

13.3. Mark 1:1–8 is part of the introduction to the Gospel of Mark, which extends through 1:13; 1:14–15 opens the body of the narrative and functions as the immediate introduction to the first sequence.[11]

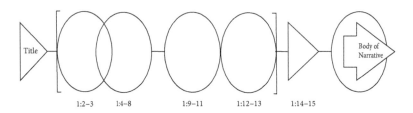

Since Mark 1:1–8 is an introduction, the segment is unfocused and the entire segment is recounted. There are several status statements which introduce and identify participants. Action statements are iterative: they depict characteristic or habitual action and thus contribute to the narrative setting of the story. In spite of these features, the evangelists employ direct discourse frequently, which is an earmark of the mimetic or enacted scene. We will take this anomaly up in detail subsequently.

Matthew 3:1–12 and Luke 3:1–20 are also general introductions having the same characteristics as the introduction in Mark. Matthew and Luke thus have two introductions to their gospels, one beginning with the birth and childhood of Jesus, the second beginning where Mark begins. This confirms the scholarly judgment that the birth narratives in both Matthew and Luke are secondary formations attached belatedly to the narrative of Mark.

In pursuing these observations on the nature of narrative statements, it would be helpful if we could consult native informants to instruct us whether two similar statements with modified wording signal differences in meaning and function or whether they are essentially synonymous. In the absence of native informants for Hellenistic Greek, we must rely on written texts. One way to measure native responses and proclivities is to

---

11. Funk, *Poetics of Biblical Narrative*, 218–26.

see how those reading and copying or reading and commenting on other texts treat their sources. The Synoptic Gospels offer a particularly fertile ground for such comparative data, since nearly all critical scholars agree that at least two of the Synoptic writers are dependent on one or more written texts. The introductory passage in Mark and its parallels offer material for an instructive exercise in this regard.

14. Status Statements

14.1. The following is a list of status statements derived from these pericopes arranged by level in accordance with (P6):

Level 1

(s1)   There was a person named John the Baptizer (Baptist): Mark 1:4 +

(s5)   There were Jerusalemites and Judahites (Judeans): Mark 1:5 +

(a12)   There were Pharisees and Sadducees: Matt 3:7a +

(a14)   There were toll collectors: Luke 3:12a +

(a15)   There were soldiers: Luke 3:14a +

(a27)   There was a tetrarch named Herod: Luke 3:19 +

(a27)   There was a woman named Herodias, who was married to Herod's brother: Luke 3:19 +

Level 2

(s2)   JB was the son of Zechariah: Luke 3:2 +

(a3)   JB appeared in the wilderness (of Judea): Luke 3:3 +

(a3)   JB moved about in the region around the Jordan: Luke 3:3; cf. John 1:23, 28; 3:23, and Josephus, *Ant.* 18.5.2, a variety of locales

Level 3

(s8)   JB dressed in camel hair: Mark 1:6 +

(s9)   JB wore a leather belt around his waist: Mark 1:6 +

(s10)   JB lived on locusts and wild honey: Mark 1:6 +

14.2. Status statements at level 1. There are several status statements of the highest level of generality in this pericope and its parallels.

(s1): There was a person named John the Baptizer (Baptist). There are approximately eighty references to this John in the canonical gospels, plus two references in Thomas, eight in Acts, and the additional references in Josephus, *Ant.* 18.109–119. It goes without saying that should the seminar decide negatively about the existence of John the Baptizer, all the other items of which he is agent or patient are automatically negated, unless, of course, we posit a different subject (someone with a different name) for these statements. This observation is also relevant to status statements about the Pharisees and perhaps other subjects of the period.

(s5): This narrative statement posits the existence of Jerusalemites and Judahites (Judeans), the existence of which, I take it, is beyond dispute.

(a12): In this context, Matthew identifies Pharisees and Sadducees among those who come out to JB in the wilderness. The seminar will need to determine whether it wishes to admit the existence of these groups as contemporaries of JB. This is an issue of high generality, since there are many references to both groups in the gospel tradition. And, if one or both of these names prove to be fictive for the period, the question still remains whether John had listeners and Jesus critics with different names who served this function. In other words, the names could be historical errors, but the events themselves historical.

(a15): That there were soldiers at this period in this place is beyond dispute.

(a27): Herod the tetrarch is mentioned in this statement.

(a27): Herodias, wife of Herod's brother, is referred to in this statement. Since the existence of these groups and persons is attested in a wide variety of texts, their existence for this narrative should be affirmed (or denied) at the highest level of generality. If they are affirmed, it is then possible to consider particular statements that depict them.

14.3. Status statements at level 2.

(a3): This statement asserts the locus of JB's principal activity: the wilderness. The question arises whether the wilderness is the same as "the region around the Jordan" mentioned in (a3) and (a5) and whether this locus is fact or fiction. In this connection, the question arises whether JB was an itinerant, if we take Luke's statement in (a3) at face value.

14.4. Status statements at level 3.

(s8)–(s10) are descriptive statements depicting JB's habitual dress and diet. The match between descriptions of Elijah and JB raises an interesting question: were the descriptions invented to match the model of Elijah (fiction), or had John in fact modelled his behavior on Elijah (fact)?

15. Action Statements

15.1. Events. The action statements in this narrative introduction, taken as a whole, may be construed as two events. The first consists of actions in the iterative mode: they happened more than once, or repeatedly, or habitually, according to the narrators. As a consequence, the event itself is also iterative. The second event consists of a single event.

Event 1
- (a4)   JB called on people [cf. (all), (a25), (a26)] to repent and be baptized
- (a5)   People came (to hear him)
- (a6)   People were baptized
- (a7)   People acknowledged their sins

We can reduce this outline to two statements, of which the second narrates a change in status:
- (1)   JB called on people to repent and be baptized
- (2)   People repented and were baptized

Event 2
The second event also consists of two statements:
- (a27) JB denounces Herod
- (a28) Herod puts JB in prison

The first statement (a27) is probably iterative (JB did it more than once: present participle); the second (a28) is singulative.

15.2. Actions at a higher level of generality. In addition to the two events narrated in this segment, we should consider three statements at a higher level of generality:
- (a3)   JB carried out his work in the region around the Jordan (the wilderness)
- (a4)   JB preached (this was his typical activity)
- (a6)   JB baptized with water: cf. (11.3), John 1:26, 28, 31 +

15.3. Words ascribed to JB. As in the case of Jesus, John, too, is represented as proclaiming a particular message. We should determine whether the words ascribed to JB in the following statements represent him:
(a4); (a11); (a16); (a18); (a20); (a22)

Our assessment of these ascriptions will depend in part on how we interpret the iterative verbs to be considered in §16.

15.4. Incidental action statements. The other action statements in this segment are incidental and do not, in my judgment, warrant separate consideration:

(a5)   Crowds came out to JB: cf. (a13)
(a12)   Pharisees and Sadducees came out to JB
(a14)   Toll collectors came out to JB
(a15)   Soldiers came out to JB
(a17)   Crowds asked: What should we do?
(a19)   Toll collectors asked: What should we do?
(a21)   Soldiers asked: What should we do?
(a29)   Herod committed other crimes

These actions are either embraced in a general way by the events outlined above, or they are too trivial (too specific, too generalizing) to warrant separate assessment.

16. Iteratives

16.1. In the process of creating the Scholars Version of the gospels and in working on a complete revision of Blass-Debrunner-Funk, it has become apparent that we need a new assessment of the function of tense and aspect in the Greek verb. This is not the place to sketch out a new theory of Greek aspect and tense. However, it is appropriate to make some observations on the iterative in the narrative segment under analysis. These observations will affect how we understand action and status statements and how we assess direct and indirect discourse.

16.2. Aspect and tense. In a preliminary way, it may be said that the Greek verb exhibits the following aspects:

(1)   Occurrence of an action = dynamic
(1a)   Punctiliar: kick, tap, strike
(1b)   Extended: eat, drink, read, sleep
(2)   Existence of a state: stative
(3)   Action in progress: progressive
(4)   Action repeated: iterative
(4a)   Action repeated
(4b)   Action customary or habitual

(4c)   Action continuous
(4d)   Pseudo-iterative
(5) Action continued or resumed
(6) Action resisted or refused
(7) Action attempted: conative
(8) Action begun: inceptive
(9) Action completed

The tenses of the Greek verb include:

(1) Universal time
(2) Habitual time
(3) Present
(3a)   Instantaneous present
(3b)   Various combinations of present and past, future
(4) Past
(4a)   Simple past
(4b)   Past from some standpoint in the past
(5) Future
(5a)   Simple future
(5b)   Future from some standpoint in the future

By observing some of these distinctions, particularly those not found in older grammars, we hope to sharpen our reading of tense and aspect especially in narrative texts.

16.3. Iteratives (not verbs of saying).

(s1) Mark 1:4 // Matt 3:1. I understand the word (ἐγένετο) (Matt: παραγίνεται) to be a status statement indicating locale rather than an action statement: JB makes his public appearance in the wilderness (of Judah). It is a generalized statement: it does not refer to a particular incident, but to the general locale of JB's activity. While it is not an iterative, it is a generalized status statement that corresponds to the iterative. It contributes the spatial notice to the setting of the narrative segment. It appears to be a matter of indifference whether such status statements are expressed in the aorist or present (or imperfect).

(a4) Mark 1:4 //Matt 3:1 // Luke 3:3. JB's principal form of activity is κηρύσσων: calling out, preaching, proclaiming. The present participle suggests repeated action (the tense of participles presumably denotes aspect but not time). Luke makes this nuance unmistakable: he interprets by having the word of God come to JB in the wilderness (locale is confirmed) and then has JB moving about in "the whole region around the Jordan," which may or may not denote the same area. In any case, JB's movement indicates that Luke understands this activity to be characteristic of JB as he moves about in his locale; it is therefore typical. The action is repeated, and it takes place in multiple locales: these are two marks of the iterative.

We will return in a moment to the content of JB's proclamation.

(a5) Mark 1:5 // Matt 3:5–6 (cf. John 3:23–24). There are three subjects in statement (a5) and they are all plural. Indeed, Luke subsequently refers to them as "crowds" (3:7, 10). Many people did a similar thing at different times. Plural subjects and plural occasions are two marks of the iterative. The tenses are imperfects (twice), linked to a present participle (likewise iterative). The report is unfocused. The activity is thus a typification or generalization on the part of the storyteller. Of course, the narrator will particularize this activity shortly in having one person, Jesus, follow suit. Matthew simply copies Mark; Luke has no parallel.

(a11) Mark 1:7 // Luke 3:16a [// Matt 3:7]. Then, in v. 7, Mark continues: καὶ ἐκήρυσσεν λέγων..., which SV translates, "And he began his proclamation by saying...." What warrant is there for interpreting this imperfect as inceptive? None that I can see, other than the fact that this report comes near the beginning of Mark's narrative. In accordance with everything else in this passage, particularly v. 5, it should have been represented as a full iterative: "He used to call out in these words," or, "He would proclaim by saying."

Note: a full iterative is one that is indefinitely iterative, rather than one that refers to the beginning of a series, or an attempted action, or the end of a series. A full iterative refers to repeated, habitual, or continuous action.

The parallel in Luke is 3:15–16a: the plural subject and the present participles in 3:15 reinforce the fully iterative character of the segment. Note ἀπεκρίνατο λέγων πᾶσιν in v. 16. SV translates: "John's answer was the same to everyone." The translation reinforces the Greek: JB gives this answer on more than one occasion. On the other hand, does the phrase "the same" give the false impression that John said exactly the same words, which are quoted directly, on every single occasion? John probably did not do that. Accordingly, this would be an example of the pseudo-iterative: the representation of a single action or quotation is made to stand for what took place on several or many occasions. We shall return to this important topic again.

Matthew's parallel to these verbs of saying is found in 3:7, to which we will return below.

(25.1): The present tense in Matt 3:11, "I baptize you with water" (ὑμᾶς βαπτίζω ἐν ὕδατι = Luke 3:16) is also iterative: John performs this act repeatedly. John 1:26 has the same construction. However, Mark 1:8, which is the parallel, reads: ἐγὼ ἐβάπτισα ὑμᾶς ὕδατι, "I baptized you with water." The aorist is certainly as iterative as the present tense, since ὑμᾶς (the object) is plural: John baptized more than one person. An aorist embracing a series of actions is comprehensive. Matthew and Luke may have derived their version from Q.

(25.4): In the contrasting statement, the verb is βαπτίσει (future) in Mark 1:8 // Matt 3:11 // Luke 3:16. The object is again plural, so the aspect must once again be iterative.

In the two preceding observations, we have noted an iterative present, an iterative aorist, and an iterative future. The initial clue to these iteratives is, of course, the character of the narrative passage: it is recounting in the iterative mode. Yet there are ample additional markers to reinforce this grammatical observation.

(11.1): It is worth noting in passing that in Mark 1:7 the present tense (ἔρχεται) is replaced by a participle in Matt 3:11 (ἐρχόμενος), while Luke reproduces Mark's present tense. But the temporal reference is future. We thus have an instance of the present referring to the future. The action is singulative.

(16.6): The present tense in Matt 3:9 // Luke 3:8, λέγω γὰρ ὑμῖν (SV: "Let me tell you") can be interpreted as an instantaneous present: it could refer to a singulative event located in the narrative "now." However, several present tenses follow in Matt 3:10 // Luke 3:9: κεῖται, ποιοῦν, ἐκκόπτεται, βάλλεται, all of which are gnomic presents: the time is universal time and the action is continuous. Once again we have iteratives in aphoristic statements of John; elsewhere they are found repeatedly in maxims attributed to Jesus.

(a26) Luke 3:18. We may skip now to Luke's conclusion to this segment and consider v. 18, which is part of the defocalizer.

Luke concludes the segment with an action expander, or defocalizer: "And so, with many other exhortations he preached to the people." "Exhortations" here translates a present participle, and εὐηγγελίζετο is imperfect. SV could have translated: "And so, he continued to preach to the people and exhort them in many other ways." At all events, the actions are clearly iterative: the statement is unfocused: JB's activity takes place on different occasions.

In this short stretch of text we have encountered a variety of tenses employed to express iterative action in past, universal, and future times.

16.4. Iteratives (verbs of saying). I have sketched the segment as a whole to establish the character of the narration as recounting in the iterative mode. I want now to examine the verbs of saying used as the framework for direct discourse.

(a16) Luke 3:7. At the beginning of JB's exhortation in Luke, Luke writes (3:7) ἔλεγεν οὖν τοῖς ἐκπορευμένοις ὄχλοις: "So (John) would say to the crowds that came out to be baptized by him...." Luke thus continues the segment in the iterative mode. And he sustains this mode in 3:10: "the crowds would ask him" (ἐπηρώτων: imperfect); "and he would answer" (ἀποκριθεὶς δὲ ἔλεγεν).

(a19)–(a20): But in 3:12–13 he apparently makes a departure from this narrative strategy: Toll collectors came (ἦλθον) to be baptized, and they said (εἶπαν) to him ... And JB told them ... The switch to the aorist is striking. Although it is perfectly clear that the aorist can comprehend a series of actions (perhaps we should call this phenomenon the comprehensive aorist), it does look as though Luke switches from a clearly marked iterative mode to a singulative mode. Without the surrounding context, vv. 2–13 would be taken as a singular event: on one occasion toll collectors came and asked, etc.

(a21)–(a22): Luke 3:14 is even more curious: soldiers "would ask" (ἐπηρώτων), but then JB "said" (εἶπεν). This subscene appears to be a mixture of the iterative and singulative.

(a16): Matthew, on the other hand, attributes only one set of admonitions to JB (3:7–10). Matthew introduces the scene with two aorists (ἰδών, εἶπεν). The switch to the verb "see" in itself suggests a singulative event (JB saw many Pharisees and Sadducees corning) and the aorist εἶπεν ("he said") seems to confirm that impression. Indeed there are many instances in the triple and double tradition where Matthew appears to "historicize."

I use *historicize* here with some hesitation. Yet the tendency seems to be for Matthew to turn iterative segments into singulative scenes, thus turning what is unfocused and recounted into scenes that are focused and enacted. As a result, a typical, recurring or customary event is turned into a specific scene. That, I think, may fairly be called historicizing.

The apparent inconsistency in this matter may derive in large part from the role of direct discourse. As we all know, the New Testament writers were not adept at indirect discourse. They much prefer the direct, simpler form. Direct discourse goes together, of course, with the focused, singulative scene, indirect discourse with unfocused, recounted, and iterative segments. Yet in the gospels we seem to have direct discourse often combined with iterative segments, as in the pericope under consideration. Oral narrators apparently had no difficulty combining direct discourse with recounting in the iterative mode. When these stories were reduced to writing, the chirographic narrators were prompted by the presence of direct discourse to slide over into the singulative aorist, even when they were narrating in an iterative segment.

16.5. Pseudo-iterative. When we encounter direct discourse with plural subjects not acting as a chorus, we have what Genette has termed the pseudo-iterative.[12] The construction is a logical anomaly: one cannot quote plural subjects collectively unless they speak in unison; one can, of course, quote them typically—"they all said something like the following"—in which case what is put down as a direct quotation is really an invention of the narrator. In this instance, the combination results in plural speakers being linked to a single statement directly quoted.

A counterpart to this phenomenon is the solitary speaker, a single direct quotation, and multiple occasions. One cannot logically provide a single direct quotation for one speaker on multiple occasions without creating a comparable anomaly: speakers are not robots, and they rarely repeat themselves in precisely the same words, aside from well-worn phrases and clichés.

These are both examples of the pseudo-iterative: all the speakers did not actually say the same thing, or a single speaker did not actually say exactly the same thing on different occasions.

It is for these reasons that the SV translators have taken a new tack in treating Greek tenses in narrative. Traditional translations ignore or suppress the differences in the tenses. Is that really our best grammatical judgment? The requirements of narrative grammar have forced us to differentiate focused from unfocused segments, the singulative from the iterative, and yet to recognize that narrators do not employ abstract distinctions consistently. Yet they employ them consistently enough to enable us to read

---

12. Gerard Genette, *Narrative Discourse: An Essay in Method*, trans. Jane E. Lewin (Ithaca: Cornell University Press, 1980).

them more accurately, especially when taken together with what we now know of narrative grammar.

The ordinary narrative tense is the aorist (past from the standpoint of the narrator; aspect comprehensive: it may represent a single event or comprehend a series of events). The imperfect and the present are used to achieve some particular nuances: the imperfect indicates iteration in past time; the present is employed when the narrator pretends to be present at the event, whether singulative or iterative, although by the nature of the case, the narrative present will be singulative (a narrator cannot be present at several events at one time). However, when the present refers to universal or habitual time, it is the equivalent, in certain narrative contexts, of an iterative imperfect.

The apparent contradictions in these generalizations about the temporal element in tense arise from the following consideration. When narrating, the narrator may elect to look back on events from some point in the narrator's present; or, the narrator may elect to narrate from some immediate temporal point in the narrative itself; or, finally, the narrator may theoretically narrate events in the past from some temporal point in a hypothetical future. The first two temporal perspectives are often confused in narration. This same confusion lies at the base of the switch from past to present and from present to past in the work of biblical scholars when commenting on the text: the text was composed long ago and so it belongs to the past; but it lies right here in front of the scholar so it belongs to the present as well.

16.6. Harvesting grain on the sabbath. The account of the disciples eating grain on a sabbath day provides some interesting comparative observations (Mark 2:23–28 // Matt 12:1–8 // Luke 6:1–5).

The sequence of framework verbs in Mark is:

2:23	ἤρξαντο ὁδὸν ποιεῖν	("began to make way")
	τίλλοντες (participle)	("stripping")
24	ἔλεγον (imperfect)	("started to argue")
25	λέγει (present)	("says")
27	ἔλεγεν (imperfect)	("would say")

Framework verbs are those that carry the action, including those employed to introduce direct and indirect discourse. Non-framework verbs are those employed in embedded constructions, principally those in quoted speech.

The subjects of the first two verbs are plural: disciples and Pharisees. The disciples are all doing a similar thing and the Pharisees would say something like.... Then Jesus responds to the inquiry of the Pharisees: the framework verb is in the present tense. Mark then attaches the final two-member aphorism to the chreia with another imperfect.

The segment is evidently cast in the iterative mode. This suggests that the present tense in v. 25 is the equivalent of an iterative imperfect. I suspect that the present is used in such contexts because the narrators (a) are always tempted to make Jesus's speech more vivid, and (b) tend to confuse the iterative with the gnomic present, which occurs hundreds of times in aphorisms and other sayings of Jesus.

The segment is therefore to be understood as a typical event: disciples would shell grain on such occasions, and their critics would make complaints. And then Jesus might respond to such criticisms with a story like this one about David. Finally, Jesus would often quote his own aphorism on occasions like this.

Now observe what Luke and Matthew do with the same segment, with the text of Mark before them.

The sequence of verbs in Luke is:

6:1	ἔτιλλον (imperfect)	("would strip")
2	εἶπαν (aorist)	("said")
3	εἶπεν (aorist)	("answered")
5	ἔλεγεν (imperfect)	("used to say")

Luke seems to historicize the nucleus of the segment with the two aorists. But he is technically correct in utilizing the iterative imperfect for Mark's ἤρξαντο ("they began") with the infinitive: the subject is plural so we have a pseudo-iterative action. And he retains Mark's imperfect in introducing the aphorism as though it were a defocalizing conclusion: Jesus said this kind of thing on such occasions as the one just narrated.

The sequence of framework verbs in Matthew is:

12:1	ἤρξαντο τίλλειν	("began to strip")
2	εἶπαν (aorist)	("said")
3	εἶπεν (aorist)	("said")

Matthew retains Mark's initial construction in modified form, but then switches to the aorist. He does not introduce the climactic aphorism with a separate verb of saying, but attaches it to the nucleus of the segment as though it were part and parcel of the preceding remarks.

In sum, it appears that both Luke and Matthew move away from what Mark took to be a typical scene with typical elements clustered by the narrator, including a final, defocalizing aphorism of the sort Jesus might have said on such occasions. They are moving in the direction of a single event, but do not quite complete the transition. Luke is technically correct in his use of narrative markers, but Matthew takes the matter one step further in the direction of a singulative event than Luke. Again, Matthew historicizes.

Evidence from other Greek authors of the period will, I believe, substantiate the suggestions being advanced in this and earlier sections. Philostratus often employs the present in narration to indicate the opinion of the anonymous "they." I have noted numerous comparable examples of narrative markers and the use of tense in Josephus and the Shepherd of Hermas. We can be sure that the new edition of Blass-Debrunner-Funk, now in preparation, will have entirely new sections on narrative grammar and the use of the tenses.

17. Direct and Indirect Discourse

A few brief comments on direct and indirect discourse are pertinent to the concerns we are addressing.

In Mark 1:4 and the Lukan parallel in 3:3, the content of JB's proclamation is given in indirect discourse, which SV translates as: "calling for baptism and a change of heart that lead to forgiveness of sins." Matthew (3:2) has modified both the content and the form: "Change your [second plural] ways because Heaven's imperial rule is closing in." The form is now direct discourse; while the theme of repentance has been retained, an eschatological note has been added in the same words attributed to Jesus at 4:17. The question now arises: is this another instance of Matthew's historicizing proclivities? Specifically, is the change from indirect to direct discourse a mark of a maturing tradition?

It looks very much that way since Matthew replaces Mark's iterative participles in 1:14, 15 with an infinitive with ἄρχομαι: is this a change from a pure iterative to a simple inceptive, or is ἄρχομαι with infinitive another possible substitute for the iterative? In other words, is the inceptive imperfect with ἄρχομαι a stylistic variation on the pure iterative? I have not yet completed an examination of the comparative evidence and so a hard conclusion is not warranted. In any case, Matthew's shift to direct from indirect to direct discourse is clearly a move in the singulative and thus historicizing direction.

Recent work on poetics has resulted in numerous fine distinctions in the ways in which speech is presented in narrative. I am drawing here on

the sketch of Shlomith Rimmon-Kenan.[13] We may distinguish four ways
of presenting speech:

    (1) the bare act of speaking:
        JB preached (in the wilderness).

    (2) diegetic summary:
        JB preached about a change of heart and baptism.

(We cannot reconstruct the direct form from this summary.)

    (3) indirect discourse:
        JB called for people to change their hearts and be baptized.
        JB kept calling for baptism and a change of heart.

(We can imagine a direct form using the indirect as the basis.)

    (4) direct quotation or direct discourse
        JB said, "Change your ways because heaven's imperial rule is clos-
        ing in."

In the gospels direct and indirect discourse are sometimes alternated,
suggesting that some segments are a mixture of enactment and recounting. John 5:14–19ff. is a good example of this mixed mode. The words of
Jesus are quoted directly, no doubt because the narrator values the statements of Jesus more highly, and so they are more vividly presented, while
the words of the lame man and Jesus's critics are given in diegetic summary or indirect discourse. SV translates:

[14] Later, Jesus finds him in the temple and said to him, "Look, you are
well now. Don't sin any more, or something worse could happen to you."

[15] The man went and told the Judeans it was Jesus who had cured
him.

[16] And this is the reason the Judeans continued to hound Jesus: he
would do things like this on the sabbath day.

[17] (Jesus) would respond to them: "My Father never stops laboring,
and I labor as well."

[18] So this is the reason the Judeans then tried even harder to kill
him: Not only did he violate the sabbath; worse still, he would call God
his Father and make himself out to be God's equal.

[19] This is how Jesus would respond: "As God is my witness…"

Jesus's words in vv. 14 and 17 are quoted directly. The lame man is
quoted indirectly in v. 15. Nevertheless, v. 16 makes it clear that the scene

---

13. Shlomith Rimmon-Kenan, *Narrative Fiction: Contemporary Poetics* (London:
Methuen, 1983), 106–16.

is iterative: things like this happened more than once; they were typical. V. 18 is again iterative: the Judeans tried repeatedly to kill him. The words ascribed to Jesus in this verse are of course being reported by Jesus's opponents and so are given indirectly. Then the author of the Fourth Gospel opens the long discourse in 5:19 with another iterative verb of speaking, but the statements that follow are given in direct discourse. The words presented as direct quotations are, of course, pseudo-iteratives: they are the narrator's idea of what Jesus said on such occasions.

This is a blatant example of the alternation of direct and indirect discourse in a narrative segment essentially in the iterative mode.

18. Conclusions

In view of what was sketched in §§9–12 on showing and telling, memory and literacy, and the social construction of reality, our current views of enacted scenes and recounted segments may require revision. The revision in its broadest form can be stated this way: modern scholars are inclined by dint of habit to value direct quotation and enacted narration more highly for historical reference than they do indirect or free quotation and recounted narration, but in fact recounting and paraphrase are more likely to reflect proximity to actual events. This conclusion seems inevitable in view of what we now know about how the memory functions and how social reality is created by means of typifications.

In the first phase of the Jesus Seminar, we were right on target with rule of evidence 01: *In the oral transmission of Jesus's words, his disciples remembered only the core or gist of his sayings and parables, not his precise words.* But we may have goofed in formulating N1: *Only words reported as directly quoted speech are eligible to be considered words of Jesus.* Aside from memorable aphorisms and clichés, only indirectly quoted words are likely to reflect the first stage of the oral tradition. In our practice we have probably been wiser than our theory allowed.

In the assessment of narrative data, the seminar will need to be on guard against the illusion created by enacted or mimetic narrative: the narrator is using sleight-of-hand to create a "motion" picture. It is in the typification, especially if that typification does not square with the social reality of the first Christian enclaves, that there is likely to be the source of original information. The seminar should look to recounting rather than enactment for the historical core of the tradition (P14).

Four additional rules of procedure will assist the seminar in steering away from fathomless waters.

(P18) Assess for fact or fiction only those events open to neutral observers.

(Pl 9) Assess for fact or fiction only those events open to two or more observers.

(P20) Assess for fact or fiction only those events whose agency is open to public verification.

(P21) Assess for fact or fiction only those reports that do not require privileged knowledge.

We cannot assign the label historical to any event that is not subject in principle to verification by a neutral observer. Neutral in this case means an observer who is neutral with respect to the truth or falsehood of narrative statements.

We cannot assign the word historical to events not open to verification by at least two observers. In other words, events that are in principle private experiences cannot be verified.

We cannot assign the label historical to claims made by various reporters that God did this or that since such claims are not in principle verifiable.

We cannot assign the label historical to reports that require knowledge of mental states, intent, or the like, unless those reports are based on observable evidence.

In all these cases, however, the claim, explicit or implied, that such and such an event was historical opens that event to investigation. We cannot confirm or deny the claim that Mary was pregnant by the holy spirit or that God raised Jesus from the dead. But we can and should investigate the claims that Mary gave birth without sexual intercourse and that Jesus rose from the dead.

Bibliography

Berger, Peter L., and Thomas Luckmann. *The Social Construction of Reality: A Treatise in the Sociology of Knowledge.* New York: Doubleday, 1966.

Chatman, Seymour. *Story and Discourse: Narrative Structure in Fiction and Film.* Ithaca: Cornell University Press, 1978.

Funk, Robert W. *The Poetics of Biblical Narrative.* Sonoma: Polebridge, 1988.

Funk. Robert W., with Mahlon H. Smith. *The Gospel of Mark: Red Letter Edition*. Sonoma: Polebridge, 1991.

Genette, Gerard. *Narrative Discourse: An Essay in Method*. Translated by Jane E. Lewin. Ithaca: Cornell University Press, 1980.

Hirsch, E. P., Jr. *Cultural Literacy: What Every American Needs to Know*. New York: Vintage Books, 1988.

Ong, Walter J. *Orality and Literacy: The Technologizing of the Word*. London: Methuen, 1982.

Rimmon-Kenan, Shlomith. *Narrative Fiction: Contemporary Poetics*. London: Methuen, 1983.

Sanders, E. P., and Margaret Davies. *Studying the Synoptic Gospels*. Philadelphia: Trinity Press International, 1989.

Appendix 1: John the Baptist

Mark 1:4–8 // Matt 3:1–12 // Luke 3:2–20
Narrative Statements
(s = status; a = action)
(K = Mark; M = Matthew; L = Luke; J = John)

(s1)	JB appeared in the wilderness (of Judea).	K1:4; M3:1
(s2)	JB was son of Zechariah.	L3:2
(a3)	JB went into the whole region around the Jordan.	L3:3
(a4)	JB proclaimed	K1:4
(4.1)	baptism and a change of heart	K1:4
(4.2)	a change of heart	M3:2
(4.3)	God's imperial rule is closing in.	M3:2
(a5)	Everyone from the Judean countryside	K1:5; M3:5
	and all the residents of Jerusalem	K1:5; M3:5
	and all the region around the Jordan	M3:5
	streamed out to him.	K1:5; M3:5
(a6)	They were baptized by him in the Jordan river.	K1:5; M3:6
(a7)	They acknowledged their sins.	K1:5; M3:6
(s8)	JB dressed in camel hair.	K1:6; M3:4
(s9)	JB wore a leather belt around his waist.	K1:6; M3:4
(s10)	JB lived on locusts and wild honey.	K1:6; M3:4
(a11)	JB proclaimed	Cf. (5)
(11.1)	Someone more powerful than I will succeed me.	K1:7; M3:11
(11.2)	I am not fit to bend down and untie his sandal straps.	K1:7; M3:11; L3:16
(11.3)	I have been baptizing you with water.	K1:8; M3:11; L3:16
(11.4)	He will baptize you with holy spirit.	K1:8; M3:11; L3:16
(a12)	JB observes many Pharisees and Sadducees coming for baptism.	M3:7a
(a13)	Crowds come out to be baptized by him (before him).	L3:7b, 10a
(a14)	Toll collectors come to be baptized.	L3:12a
(a15)	Soldiers (come).	L3:14a
(a16)	John says	M3:7b, L3:7a
(16.1)	You spawn of Satan!	M3:7c, L3:7c
(16.2)	Who warned you to flee from the impending Doom?	M3:7d, L3:7d
(16.3)	Well then, start producing fruit suitable for a change of heart	M3:8, L3:8a
(16.4)	and don't even think of (start) saying to yourselves	M3:9a, L3:8b
(16.5)	We have Abraham as our father.	M3:9b, L3:8c
(16.6)	Let me tell you	M3:9c, L3:8d
(16.7)	God can raise up children for Abraham right out of these rocks.	M3:9d, L3:8e
(16.8)	Even now the axe is aimed at the root of the trees.	M3:10a, L3:9a

(16.9) So every tree not producing choice fruit gets cut down	M3:10b, L3:9b
(16.10) and tossed into the fire.	M3.10c, L3:9c
(a17) Crowds asked	L3:10a
(17.1) So what should we do?	L3:10b
(a18) JB answered	L3:11a
(18.1) Whoever has two tunics should share with someone who has none.	L3:11b
(18.2) Whoever has good should do the same.	L3:11c
(a19) Toll collectors asked	L3:12b
(19.1) Teacher, what should we do?	L3:12c
(a20) JB said to them	L3:13a
(20.1) Charge nothing above the official rates.	L3:13b
(a21) Soldiers asked him	L3:14a
(21.1) And we, what should we do?	L3:14b
(a22) JB said to them	L3:14c
(22.1) No more shakedowns!	L3:14d
(22.2) No more frame-ups either!	L3:14e
(22.3) And be satisfied with your pay.	L3:14f
(s22) People were filled with expectation.	L3:15a
(s23) People were trying to figure out whether JB might be the Anointed.	L3:15b
(a24) JB's answer was the same to everyone.	L3:16a
(a25) JB proclaimed	K1:7a–b
(25.1) I baptize you with water (for a change of heart).	L3:16c, M3:11d–e, K1:8a
(25.2) Someone more powerful than I is coming	L3:16c, M3:11d–e, K1:7c–d
(25.3) Whose sandal straps I am not fit (K: to bend down) and untie (M: to carry).	L3:16e, M3:11e, K1:7e
(25.4) He will baptize you with (holy] spirit (M, L: and fire).	L3:16f–g, M3:11f–g, K1:8b
(25.5) His pitchfork is in his hand.	L3:17a, M3:12a
(25.6) He'll thoroughly clear off his threshing floor.	L3:17b, M3:12b
(25.7) He'll gather his wheat into the granary.	L3:17c, M3:12c
(25.8) But the chaff he'll bum with a fire that can't be put out.	L3:17d, M3:12d
(a26) JB preached to the people with many other Exhortations	L3:18a
(a27) JB denounced Herod the tetrarch because of Herodias, his brother's wife.	L3:19
(a28) Herod shut John up in prison.	L3:20
(a29) Herod committed other crimes.	L3:20

Appendix 2: Rules of Procedure

(P1)   Reduce each narrative segment to narrative statements.

(P2)   Determine the action or complex of actions that constitutes the event—the change in status—narrated in that segment.

(P3)   Assess for fact or fiction the action or complex of actions that constitutes the event.

(P4)   Arrange action statements in the order of their generality.

(P5)   Assess for fact or fiction action statements at the highest level of generality.

(P6)   Arrange status statements in the order of their generality.

(P7)   Assess status statements for fact or fiction at the highest level of generalization.

(P8)   Assess status statements for fact or fiction at the highest level of generality specific to particular segments.

(P9)   Distinguish introductions and conclusions from nuclei in narrative segments and sequences of segments.

(P10) Isolate data derived from the order of segments and sequences.

(P11) Isolate data derived from the order of segments and sequences in the gospel narratives and evaluate such data very circumspectly: the connectives provided by the evangelists between and among segments are largely fictive and vary frequently from performance to performance, from source to source.

(P12) Identify the role of the narrator by determining voice and perspective and by noting marks of the narrator's presence. In assessing the historical basis of particular segments, the seminar should calculate the effect of limiting factors—factors based on voice, perspective, and presence—on what is narrated.

(P13) Distinguish showing from telling in each narrative segment.

(P14) In assessing the narrative reports of what Jesus did and said, isolate the gist of the reports and compare the gist with the typifications regnant in the community transmitting the materials out of which the gospels were created.

(P15) Identify the "debris" in the Jesus tradition-elements that have not been assimilated to the typifications characteristic of the transmitting communities.

(P16) Assess the "debris" in the tradition for fact or fiction.

(P17) Be especially cautious in the use of traditions that are often repeated in the gospels: their repetition may owe to domestication in emerging Christian communities, and they may thus not reflect earlier traditions.

(P18) Assess for fact or fiction only those events open to neutral observers.

(P19) Assess for fact or fiction only those events open to two or more observers.

(P20) Assess for fact or fiction only those events whose agency is open to public verification.

(P21) Assess for fact or fiction only those reports that do not require privileged knowledge [cf. (P12)].

The Jesus Seminar and the Quest

Robert Funk

In the Jesus Seminar and the Westar Institute, we have attempted to identify issues in the sphere of Bible and religion that matter. Then we endeavored to enlist serious scholars who would devote the time and effort to address these issues. Finally, we agreed at the outset to do our work in full public view and to report in terms that any reasonably literate reader could understand.

As our first topic we elected to investigate the historical Jesus. Americans have a perennial interest in Jesus, but as the century drew to a close that interest intensified. The result was the organization of the Jesus Seminar in 1985.

The Jesus Seminar is made up of fellows and associates. Fellows are scholars with an advanced degree in biblical or religious studies. Associates are interested nonspecialists. Westar has about thirty-five hundred members and another thirty-five hundred observers. About two hundred of these are scholars of the Bible or theologians. More than seventy-five fellows have signed each of the two major reports published thus far.

Protocols

The first steps we took in organizing the Jesus Seminar back in 1985 turned out to be crucial. We agreed from the outset to form an agenda of issues on which we would come to decision, no matter how provisional or tentative. That in itself is uncharacteristic of humanists who prefer to hold all questions in perpetual abeyance pending further review. We adopted collaboration as our group process in order to expand the basis of decision making. We agreed to make our work cumulative, which meant that we built on consensus judgments as we pursued our agenda; we identified what we had in common rather than concentrate on our differences. Academic critics of scholarly essays tend to make the worst case they can for the publications of their colleagues, whereas the friendly critics of great literary works attempt to make the best case they can for their authors. We have behaved against academic type in striving to make the best case for our texts and each other, without blunting or critical acumen. This, I judge, has been our sharpest departure from academic protocol that has resulted in our most significant achievement: the production of knowledge that makes a difference.

It may have been fortuitous that we assembled outside the university. We gathered beyond the confines but still within earshot of the churches, even beyond the demands of the seminaries training clergy. By dint of historical circumstance, we formed the seminar outside the boundaries of the professional guilds. That made it possible for us to establish different protocols. We did all of this at some risk to ourselves.

We insisted on holding our sessions in public and making reports in nontechnical language that any literate person could understand. Voting with colored beads and reporting with color-coded texts were ingredient to those aims. We took some additional risk in talking to reporters and appearing on talk shows. This aspect of our work has generated the most controversy.

We recognized at the outset that we are all facing an information glut in the electronic age. We are being bombarded with unsorted and undigested information from every quarter. On the subject of religion, the common view is that one opinion is as good as another. This conviction is a recipe for chaos, and that is just about what we have. By banding together and keeping our eye on a common goal, we had hoped to reduce confusion by a small fraction in *The Five Gospels* and *The Acts of Jesus*.

The Premises of the Quest

We have identified four premises of the quest.

(1) The quest of the historical Jesus is the pursuit of the discrepancy between the historical figure and the portraits of him in the gospels.

The naïve view is that Jesus did and said everything that is reported of him in the four New Testament gospels. After more than two centuries of critical work we know that is not true. The New Testament gospels are a mixture of folk memories and creative storytelling; there is very little hard history. In addition, almost all critical scholars doubt that the New Testament gospels were composed by eyewitnesses. Furthermore, we now have the text, in whole or in fragment, of eighteen additional gospels to consider. Like the New Testament gospels, they, too, must be evaluated critically.

We know there is a discrepancy between the historical figure and the portraits of him in the gospels because the Jesus of the Gospel of John differs markedly from the Jesus of the Synoptics—Mark, Matthew, Luke. And the Jesus of Mark differs from the Jesus portrayed in Matthew and Luke. Further, the Jesus of the Gospel of Thomas is not always the same Jesus as we find in the Synoptics. And the Jesus of the Sayings Gospel Q, used by Matthew and Luke in creating their gospels, presents a picture of Jesus that differs markedly from all the others.

In addition, the Jesus of the apostle Paul has features unknown to the gospel writers. The Jesus of the Apostles' Creed is known by his miraculous birth, death under Pontius Pilate, bodily resurrection, and anticipated return, but absolutely nothing is said about how he lived or what he taught. And the Jesus of the Nicene Creed of 325 CE is the second person of the trinity who existed as part of the godhead from the beginning.

All but the most conservative scholars of the Bible agree that the historical figure who lived in Galilee during the first quarter of the first century differs in at least some important respects from the way he is remembered and pictured in early Christian texts. There is a quest for the historical Jesus because most scholars believe the Galilean sage has been obscured at least in part by the authors of ancient Christian documents. We would not be looking for something that has not been lost.

(2) The problem, accordingly, is to distinguish fact from fiction in the twenty-two ancient gospels that contain reports about what he said and did. Many scholars hold the view that the ancient gospels contain virtually no reliable information about the historical figure. For them a quest of the historical Jesus is futile. But for those of us who think the gospels preserve some scattered information about him, even if only incidentally or accidentally, the quest is essentially a search for reliable data. Our job is to sort through all the information contained in the ancient gospels and other related texts and attempt to distinguish fictive elements from the facts. The first task of the quest is to establish a firm database from which to reconstruct features of the historical figure of Jesus.

(3) Those who undertake the quest do so because they believe they can isolate at least a small fund of reliable historical data. The fellows of the Jesus Seminar are questers because we hold the view that we can identify traces of the figure that has been obscured to one extent or

another by Christian hope and piety. The question is whether we can develop criteria that will enable us to discriminate fact from fiction in all the ancient gospels.

(4) If we succeed in assembling a significant database of reliable information, of what value are those data? Does knowledge of the historical Jesus carry any significance for Christian faith? That is the final question we put on our agenda.

The picture of Jesus found in the New Testament gospels and transmitted by the church through the centuries is a varied one. There are almost as many pictures of Jesus as there are churches and sects in Christendom. Nevertheless, the church has insisted, by and large, that not just any picture of Jesus will do as the basis of faith: the Jesus who is confessed as Lord must be Jesus of Nazareth. Because of this conviction, the churches have countenanced the investigation of their traditions in an effort to disclose the historical figure at the base of those traditions, the Jesus that undergirds faith insofar as that faith identifies its Lord with Jesus of Nazareth. For that reason, the seminar assumes that the quest has real, perhaps even critical, significance for faith.

The basic propositions underlying the quest, then, are these:

- The quest of the historical Jesus is the pursuit of the discrepancy between the historical figure and the representations of him in the gospels.
- The quest of the historical Jesus is the search for reliable data.
- The quest of the historical Jesus assumes that some reliable historical data are recoverable.
- Knowledge of the historical Jesus matters for faith.

The Jesus Seminar adopted these four propositions as the basis of its work. In so doing, it has acted in concert with the vast majority of critical scholars the world over.

The Agenda of the Jesus Seminar

The initial task of the seminar was to inventory the data—all the data. We did not limit ourselves to the four New Testament gospels; we avoided canonical bias by including all twenty-two gospels.[1]

---

1. Collected with fresh translations in M. Robert Miller, ed. *The Complete Gospels: Annotated Scholars Version*, rev. and expanded (Santa Rosa, CA: Polebridge, 1994).

We then sorted the data in to the actions reported of Jesus and the words attributed to Jesus. We further classified the materials by organizing the data into types of sayings and types of stories in accordance with the canons of form criticism.

The big job, which took us the first ten years, was to evaluate each item in the inventory. Papers were prepared and circulated in advance of each of our meetings (now amounting to twenty-eight sessions). Each item on the agenda was debated and discussed until the fellows were ready to indicate their judgments by voting. The object of voting was to determine whether there was a consensus among us and, if so, to discover its extent. The simple test was this: would you include this item—word or deed—in the data base to determine who Jesus was and what he said?

In the first two phases of the seminar we sorted through approximately 1,500 versions of 500 sayings attributed to Jesus and identified those words that, in the judgment of the fellows, most probably originated with him or were spoken by him in some proximate form. We wound up after six years of deliberations with a compendium of ninety aphorisms and parables that we think echo the voice of the historical Jesus.

When we had completed that task, we turned to 387 reports of 176 events and deeds and carried out a similar evaluative process. Twenty-nine of the 176 events were deemed to contain some historical information. In addition, we formulated and adopted 42 narrative statements based on information derived from stray data scattered across the gospels.

The result was the creation of a twin database: The first, on the words of Jesus, was published as *The Five Gospels* (1993), the second, covering the deeds of Jesus, as *The Acts of Jesus* (1998).[2]

Pursuing the Puzzle

It is common academic wisdom to beware of the scholar who can account for all the data. One can be sure he or she is manipulating the evidence. Research ought to begin with what your predecessors have left unexplained. The beginning is the puzzle others have not been able to solve. The puzzle the Jesus Seminar began with was why the parables and aphorisms, and the

---

2. Funk Robert W. and Roy W. Hoover, *The Five Gospels: The Search for the Authentic Words of Jesus* (San Francisco: HarperSanFrancisco, 1993); Robert W. Funk and the Jesus Seminar, *The Acts of Jesus: The Search for the Authentic Deeds of Jesus* (San Francisco: HarperSanFrancisco, 1998).

metaphorical language of Jesus, which play such a large role in the gospels, found so little place in earlier quests.

In pursuing this puzzle, we adopted the broad scholarly consensus on the history and relationships of the gospels. We affirmed with most scholars that Matthew and Luke were essentially revisions of Mark. We did not permit ourselves to make use of their revisions of Mark without powerful corroborating evidence. We assumed that Matthew and Luke also made use of the sayings gospel Q in supplementing Mark. We struggled with the difficulties in reconstructing the original text of Q. We acknowledged that some stray oral traditions may have been captured by Matthew and Luke. And we even conceded that the Fourth Gospel may have preserved some incidental historical data, in spite of the fact that many scholars dismiss John as of no real historical value. For example, we took seriously the observation that the first followers of Jesus were probably recruited from disciples of John in the Jordan Valley, reported only by John. We agreed that the Gospel of Thomas was useful in reconstructing the history of some individual traditions, as were other fragments of gospels. But nothing in our profiles of Jesus depends solely on data taken from Thomas or other extracanonical sources.

In our deliberations we held ourselves to the strict observance of this consensus. We did not permit each other to fudge. Out of dozens of individual decisions about particular sayings and parables, in retrospect we formulated "rules of evidence." Those rules reflect actual practice rather the theory of how the tradition grew and developed. It was on the basis of this complex method that we arrived at a shared database, which in turn functioned as the basis for individual profiles of the historical Jesus that bear some remarkable affinities. Those profiles are not monolithic, to be sure. But they do converge at many points.

Reporting

Our intention in creating a color-coded report was to make its contents immediately evident to the general reader without the necessity of reading hundreds of pages of commentary. We took as our model the red-letter editions of the New Testament widely known to students of the Bible. The original proposal was to print everything either in red or black: Jesus did or did not say or do it. We finally settled for four options:

Red meant that Jesus very probably said or did this.

Pink meant that Jesus probably said or did this.

Gray meant that Jesus probably did not say or do this (although in practice gray often meant that the data were ambiguous and no firm judgment was possible).

Black of course meant that Jesus very probably did not say or do this.

A final gray or pink designation in our reports will often reflect a mixed bag of colored beads, since we employed the weighted method of determining the final result.

Response

To our great surprise, *The Five Gospels* made it on to the religion best-seller list for nine months. Our associate members, many of whom attend our sessions, have been enthusiastic in their support of our work. We are now producing two-day seminar programs in churches across North America, New Zealand, Australia, and the United Kingdom at the rate of about two a month. Media interest has grown and matured. Some of our fellows are regular contributors to television documentaries. We celebrated the consummation of the first phase of our work with a four-day celebration in October of 1999. The Once and Future Jesus conference took a look at the future of Jesus and Christianity for the third millennium. A conference on The Once and Future Faith is scheduled for March of 2001.

In spite of this encouraging public reception, the response we have elicited from some colleagues who did not participate has been nothing short of uncivil. We have been the butt of rancor, vituperation, name calling, and scathing satire. Rather than enter into critical dialogue about the emerging database, some scholars have felt it appropriate to attack members of the seminar personally. In many cases, these responses have violated the canons of professional behavior.

There are three reasons, in my estimation, that we have gotten the kind of response we have.

First, we caught our colleagues by surprise in exposing widely held academic views to public scrutiny, perhaps for the first time in this century. The fact that the parish minister and priest have withheld this common information from their parishioners contributed to the surprise.

The revelation of a closely guarded secret deepened the chagrin felt by many colleagues. An angry rebuttal is often the defense needed to buy time for thought.

In the second place, *The Five Gospels* intervened directly in the way Scripture is read and interpreted. The quest began to destabilize the canon—the authority of the New Testament gospels—and to introduce strange new documents into the discussion. Scholars and lay persons alike are not inclined to welcome change, especially change that demands utter candor and complete honesty. Suddenly, scholars who had been dissembling for years were forced out into the open on questions they preferred to leave unanswered.

Thirdly, the reports of the seminar represented an attack on the previous consensus dating back to the popular book of Albert Schweitzer, *The Quest of the Historical Jesus* (see bibliography).[3] Schweitzer adopted the view of Johannes Weiss that Jesus was an apocalyptic prophet who believed the final days were at hand in his own time. The seminar, in contrast, came to the view that Jesus was not an apocalyptic prophet, but a sage in the tradition of Israelite wisdom. His parables and aphorisms had been overlaid with apocalyptic views at the behest of his first followers, who had come from the circle of John the Baptist. They brought John's views with them into the Jesus movement, and when Jesus was gone, those older views simply displaced Jesus's own views of the kingdom of God. The loss of a vulnerable Jesus, who was thought to be a failed prophet, meant that scholars and theologians had to rethink everything. Above all, it meant that the creation of the creeds as representations of Jesus might have to be reconsidered. That prospect provoked heated response.

Our critics continued to insist that Jesus was an average Jew who, according to them, believed and advocated what every average Jew believed and advocated that the end of the age was at hand. If he did not share that view, and if he did not express that view in Aramaic, then we had robbed him of his Jewishness. Few of our critics have recognized what a monolithic and denigrating view of Second Temple Judaism that is. And, of course, that view ignores the dozens of Jews who spoke and wrote in Greek during the period.

---

3. Albert Schweitzer, *The Quest of the Historical Jesus: A Critical Study of Its Progress from Reimarus to Wrede* (New York: Macmillan, 1961); trans. of *Geschichte der Leben-Jesu-Forschung* (Tübingen: Mohr Siebeck, 1906).

By looking for a single voice in a Galilean crowd the seminar launched its quest as a discovery venture. Our critics responded by turning their socalled third quest into an apologetic for the orthodox view based, for the most part, on the three synoptic gospels.

In the seminar we took as our primary problem how the Jesus tradition got from around 30 CE to the first narrative gospel, Mark, in the 70s. Our critics adopt the Synoptic Gospels as their starting point and roam around in those gospels indiscriminately as though the authors were eyewitnesses of the original events. They see little need to reckon with the forms of anecdotes that served as vehicles for the memories of Jesus, and they take even less notice of the formal structure of sayings that were likely to have survived twenty to fifty years or more of oral transmission. With the exception of the extremely conservative scholars, most do agree, however, that the Gospel of John is virtually without value as a source of information about Jesus.

It is worth taking note of the steady canonical bias in the protests of our critics. They use the Synoptics as though they were virtually reliable history but reject all extracanonical sources as secondary and devoid of any historical merit. They deride our use of Q and Thomas and the other fragmentary gospels.

In spite of the fact that the parables appear in their canonical sources, our critics refuse to make use of them as distinctive traces of Jesus's voice because, they argue, who can say what the parables mean? The aphorisms, too, come in for short shrift because they blend in with the wisdom tradition of Israel. These deft moves permit them to ignore the primary database we have identified, using both form and content as clues, as essential to the rediscovery of the historical figure.

The alternative view our critics propose is to begin with the deeds of Jesus. Yet they have trouble isolating any particular deed as the bedrock of the tradition, beyond Jesus's baptism at the hands of John and the crucifixion events no one contests who thinks Jesus was a historical person. They do not recognize the fundamental methodological problem put so pointedly by Julian Hills: the deeds of Jesus are reported, while the sayings of Jesus are repeated.[4] In other words, deeds are narrated from a third person perspective, while the authentic words of Jesus betray his own perspective.

---

4. Julian Hills's couplet "Sayings are repeated, deeds are reported" is quoted by Lane C. McGaughy, "The Search for the Historical Jesus: Why Start with the Sayings?," *The Fourth R* 9.5–6 (1996): 17–26.

In any case, the deeds of Jesus are literary artifacts apart from some interpretive assessment, and it is only Jesus who can really tell us what his acts were all about. For this his sayings are essential.

In clinging to the apocalyptic hypothesis, our critics are disposed to be literal-minded: the apocalyptic tradition is relentlessly literal and humorless. It is difficult to crack a joke if you think the world is about to end. And, of course, having a celebration just before Armageddon seems inappropriate. The seminar, on the other hand, by paying close attention to the parables and witticisms of Jesus, finds them filled with metaphor, hyperbole, parody, paradox, and ambiguity. The contrast between Jesus's authentic words and the apocalyptic tradition could not be stronger.

It is striking that none of our critics, so far as I can see, ever takes note of the collapse of the mythic universe or the information revolution through which we are passing. They seem to think the old symbols are still in place and functional. But then I can see why they do so: the credibility of the apocalyptic worldview requires it.

The Quest and Faith

Why did we undertake this particular task? The legacy of the scientific age is scientism, which falls out as literalism in the general population: truth in the popular mind refers only to what is literally true, which nearly always means empirically verifiable. That same mind in naïve believers assumes that everything reported in the Bible is literally true or the Bible is not true in any respect. Yet historians and theologians know that faith cannot guarantee a single fact—believing does not make anything so. In this atmosphere, we decided to submit everything to a rigorous historical test in order to frustrate the believer's fantasy while satisfying the appetite for the factual.

Yet a second, more profound effect was our ultimate goal: we wanted to clear away the literalistic obstructions that burden the Christian and other religious traditions and allow myths and rituals to emerge for what they truly are: expressions of the needs and aspirations of the human spirit.

Nevertheless, learning who Jesus was historically apart from any faith claims may also have direct salutary effects. The question for us is whether Jesus himself has any input into the conception and practice of the thing we call Christian faith. For the orthodox Christian community, faith was faith in the faith of the first disciples. They believed because the first disciples believed. And they allegedly believed what those disciples believed.

That set of relationships has tended to dominate the entire course of Christian history.

At the beginning, on the other hand, during the time Jesus went in and out among them, whatever faith Peter and others in the circle around Jesus had was inspired by Jesus himself. Their faith was not mediated by someone else. The question then arises: can we know enough of the historical Jesus for him to be the inspiration of our faith, an unmediated faith, so to speak?

The issue is even more complicated than that. For some in that first circle, Jesus himself may have become the object of faith. Some of his followers may have concluded, after Easter, that Jesus was the Messiah, or the son of man, by adoption. On this view, Jesus had become the object of faith.

For others, faith in Jesus meant to trust what he trusted. On that view, it was not Jesus who was the object of faith; on the contrary, his Father, God, was the true object of faith. Better yet, the kingdom of God was the real object of faith. And faith was not belief; it was trust. Jesus did not call on people to believe in God; he called on them to trust in God's presence among them, to trust the creation, including other human beings. As he viewed it, the world is God's kingdom or God's domain. God's domain was his perception of how the world is meant to thrive under the direct aegis of the Father.

In terms of the parties involved in the quest, the Jesus Party suggests that Jesus points to the kingdom of God. The Apostolic Party thinks that Peter points to Jesus as the object of faith. The Bible Party believes that the New Testament points to the apostles as the foundation of the faith.

It would appear that faith in the New Testament is a derivative faith, twice removed from the kingdom of God. Faith in Jesus is not the same thing as faith in God's imperial rule. Even faith in the faith of Peter and the apostles is secondhand faith. The question then becomes: Did Jesus call on his followers to believe that he was the Messiah, the apocalyptic son of Adam, or a miraculously begotten son of God? If he did not, were his followers justified in calling on subsequent believers to do so?

Jesus seems to have called on his followers to trust what he trusted, to believe that the world was God's domain, and to act accordingly. That dramatic shift in understanding could trail a radical reformation in its wake.

As the Jesus movement aged, an institution and an ideological orthodoxy began to emerge. As they did, the role of the words and deeds of Jesus began to diminish. What he did and said was gradually eclipsed by what was done to him-birth, crucifixion, resurrection-interpreted in the mythical framework of a dying/rising lord. By the time we come to the Apostles' Creed (possibly the mid-second century), the acts and words of Jesus are no longer central. Indeed, the creed itself has an empty center—it lacks any reference to what Jesus said and did, but includes only what was done to him.

The historical figure has been so overlaid with the Christian myth that the historical figure is overshadowed by the adoration of him as the Christ. In the course of this development, the iconoclast became an icon.

If the Christian movement readmits Jesus into its counsels, he will be a powerful critic of sedimented institutions and orthodoxies. That is what happened in the waves of reformation that swept through Europe in the sixteenth and following centuries. The rediscovery of the historical Jesus could again provoke a revision of Christian practice and belief.

Even a partial recovery of Jesus of Nazareth will serve to purge the clogged arteries of the institutional churches, arteries blocked with self-perpetuating bureaucracies and theological litmus tests designed to maintain the status quo. His voice will redefine the nature and parameters of the Christian life.

The recovery of the historical figure of Jesus may well serve as the catalyst of a new beginning for the Christian movement as it enters the third millennium. The words and deeds of Jesus were the catalyst of the original movement. There was an organized cluster of activities before there was an institution-a religion without dogma. The rediscovery of the historical Jesus may prompt the creation of a twenty-first century version of that early stage.

Bibliography

Funk, Robert W., and the Jesus Seminar. *The Acts of Jesus: The Search for the Authentic Deeds of Jesus.* San Francisco: HarperSanFrancisco, 1998.

———. *Gospel of Jesus.* Santa Rosa, CA: Polebridge, 1999.

Funk, Robert W., and Roy W. Hoover. *The Five Gospels: The Search for the Authentic Words of Jesus.* San Francisco: HarperSanFrancisco, 1993.

McGaughy, Lane C. "The Search for the Historical Jesus: Why Start with the Sayings?" *The Fourth R* 9.5–6 (1996): 17–26.

Miller, Robert J., ed. *The Complete Gospels: Annotated Scholars Version.* Rev. and exp. ed. Santa Rosa, CA: Polebridge, 1994.

Schweitzer, Albert. *The Quest of the Historical Jesus: A Critical Study of Its Progress from Reimarus to Wrede*. New York: Macmillan, 1961. Translation of *Geschichte der Leben-Jesu-Forschung*. Tübingen: Mohr Siebeck, 1906.

Part 7
The Academy and Publications

Transformation of the Academy and Publications

James B. Wiggins†

It is more than a little ironic to be considering the transformation of the academy as part of this presentation, because after his resignation from the Department of Religious Studies at the University of Montana in 1986, Bob Funk spent the last nineteen years of his life developing vehicles of direct communication and interaction with the public. As I view his accomplishments through the Westar Institute and its various ventures and the publications from his Polebridge Press, those expressed his near total disenchantment with institutions of higher education (assuming that is what is referred to as the "academy" in my assignment) and no less with traditional scholarly and professional societies. To be sure, he enlisted the participation of scholars who remained in the academy in his continuing ventures—notably, the Jesus Seminar, members of the board of the Westar Institute, and authors publishing through Polebridge Press—but only if they shared his conviction that a radical reformation of scholarship and publication is needed today.

In a recent issue of *The Fourth R* newsletter from the Westar Institute, Funk issued this clarion call:

> We are looking for professional scholars who have decided not to sit out the cultural transition through which we are now passing in the comfort of their library carrels…. We are looking for men and women who will join us in the fight to reduce ignorance and promote literacy. We seek those who are willing to put honesty and integrity above all other concerns…. The time for dissembling is past.[1]

---

1. Robert W. Funk, "Editorial: A Few Good People," *The Fourth R* 15.3 (2002): https://tinyurl.com/SBL1128b.

In that same piece, Funk continued: "We seek affiliation with persons and organizations that have achieved some sense of self-transcendence and yet who are sufficiently self assured to weather the critical storms ahead."[2] I do not believe that by that time in his life Funk regarded the Society of Biblical Literature or the American Academy of Religion to be among the organizations with which he sought to be affiliated in his projects. If any think otherwise, I would be interested in knowing the basis for that.

The irony, however, is that Funk left indelible marks upon both the study of the Bible and the study of religion, especially upon the Society of Biblical Literature and, only slightly less so, the American Academy of Religion! That was not widely recognized and appreciated in 1980, when the Executive Committee of the Board of Scholars Press terminated Scholars Press' contract with Funk as its director. That occurred within three months after the press was relocated to Chico, California, from Missoula, Montana. The ripple effects from those events in Chico spread over many years, as resentments and repercussions continued to be expressed by many people.

When the Annual Meeting met in Dallas in 1980 only a few weeks after that dramatic, traumatic event that resulted in Funk's departure from Scholars Press, the waters were deeply troubled, at least as I was aware of some of them in the form of difficulties confronting the American Academy of Religion. Others would be able, I am sure, to recall the situation then within the Society of Biblical Literature. The Society of Biblical Literature was celebrating its one hundredth anniversary at that meeting in Dallas as it learned of Funk's departure from Scholars Press and, effectively, his departure from the Society of Biblical Literature and the American Academy of Religion. Ernest Saunders opined in 1982 that "both Scholars Press and the Society in this first century had been led by this scholar-administrator into a new understanding of their natures and tasks and had been challenged to move in new directions."[3] It is to that new understanding of their natures and tasks that I want to attend.

---

2. Funk, "Editorial: A Few Good People."

3. Ernest W. Saunders, *Searching the Scriptures: A History of the Society of Biblical Literature, 1980–1980* (Scholars Press: Chico, CA, 1982), 67. I am grateful to Andrew Scrimgeour, who sent me this text.

Bob Funk's Academic Odyssey

Funk dreamed great dreams and generated encompassing visions. As a boy evangelist in his native Indiana, by all accounts he was a compelling and persuasive preacher. Then he went off to college, seminary, and graduate school and became ever more sophisticated as he honed his rhetorical skills and his remarkable insights and as he established his academic bona fides. He embarked upon a career as a university professor in 1953 that lasted through 1986 as he successively taught at Texas Christian University, Harvard, the American School of Oriental Research, Emory, Drew, Vanderbilt, and Montana. He established impressive scholarly credentials through several publications that appeared while he worked in the academy in those diverse sites. During that thirty-three year interval he was also from time to time an administrator of several academic departments and programs, a matter of importance later in this story.

The transition from primary appointments in theological and graduate studies while at Harvard, Emory, Drew, and Vanderbilt to an undergraduate department in a secular, tax-supported university in Montana was a significant move. That new academic setting provided a context and in some respects motivation for engaging so energetically in imagining new possibilities and generating new paradigms for studying religion and the Bible. It seems to me that Funk's working in that context during the years of his great involvement in and influence upon the Society of Biblical Literature and the American Academy of Religion contributed significantly to his seeking opportunities and means to transform learned societies into entities that could support new and different paradigms.

Journey into the Wilderness of Learned Societies

Funk's many enterprises in which he engaged from 1968, the year in which he finished serving on the faculty of Vanderbilt and joined the faculty at the University of Montana, until 1980 were ones that so directly and deeply impacted both the Society of Biblical Literature and the American Academy of Religion. The chronicle of the various positions he held during those years provides a skeletal outline of what will be fleshed out in the remarks that follow:

1968–1973 Executive Secretary of the Society of Biblical Literature
1968–1973 Board of Directors of the American Academy of Religion

1968–1973 Conference of Secretaries of the American Council of
           Learned Societies
1970–1972 Executive Committee of the Conference of Secretar-
           ies of the ACLS
1974–1975 President of the Society of Biblical Literature
1974–1980 Founder and Director Scholars Press

While carrying all those responsibilities, except for some leaves of absence from the Department of Religious Studies at Montana, Funk actively taught and also served as associate dean of the College of Arts and Sciences in 1971–1972 and as chair of the Department of Religious Studies from 1974 until 1976. I note those activities to underscore that he had considerable experience as an administrator in several different settings and in creating the new enterprise of Scholars Press. Those skills and capabilities continued to be called upon until his death in 2005 in running his Westar Institute and Polebridge Press. Funk wrote of that time in an unpublished draft of his memoirs these words: "I discovered during the next five years [1968–1973] that I had a head for numbers, strategy, and business that had not occurred to me earlier."[4] Those skills and growing acumen were to have far-reaching consequences. He expressed the issues he faced in these words: "to rescue the two organizations from bankruptcy and put them on a firm financial footing."[5] Solving those issues generated the master plan that he pursued until his departure from the societies in 1980.

In 1967 Jacob Neusner was the vice-president elect of the American Academy of Religion. The American Academy of Religion was in financial stress—too few sources of revenue and increasing expenses, especially incurred in publishing its journal. Neusner requested Funk to accept appointment as chair of the American Academy of Religion Publications Committee, and with it a seat on the American Academy of Religion Board of Directors. His concurrent involvement in and influence upon both the American Academy of Religion and the Society of Biblical Literature was then and to now remains unprecedented. Funk became the executive secretary of the Society of Biblical Literature in 1968 succeeding Walter Harrelson who had been acting executive secretary. I know of no other instance in which the executive secretary of the Society of Biblical

---

4. Robert W. Funk, "Bridge over Troubled Waters: From Seminary to the Jesus Seminar" (unpublished memoir), Part Five, 13.

5. Funk, "Bridge over Troubled Waters," Part Five, 13.

Literature concurrently served on the Board of Directors of the American Academy of Religion as Funk did from 1968 to 1973.

I believe that no assessment of the work of Funk in transforming the societies committed to fostering the study of the Bible and of religion in these organizations can honestly be recounted without emphasizing the connection and symbiotic relationship between him and Ray L. Hart during those critical years. Their remarkable collaboration developed through their serving together on the faculties of Drew, Vanderbilt, and Montana Universities.

It was in the rarified and pristine air of Missoula in the period from 1969 to 1980 that their creative energies really coalesced in ways that continue to be felt in both organizations. Hart was appointed as chair of the newly created Department of Religious Studies at the University of Montana in 1969 and accepted on the condition that the university also appoint another senior professor, Funk, and two assistant professors of their choice. Reflecting Hart's masterly political skills, the university acceded. By all accounts their relationship over the subsequent eighteen years was often stormy—Titans hurling their thunderbolts in many directions, sometimes at each other. Hart became deeply involved in the governance and direction of the American Academy of Religion and the effects of his influence continue therein until now. A major first step in that process was Hart's being appointed by Neusner to be the editor of the *Journal of the American Academy of Religion* in 1968—remember Funk was chair of the Publications Committee of the American Academy of Religion at that time. That position provided Hart with an *ex officio* seat on the American Academy of Religion Board of Directors. It does sound a little incestuous, doesn't it?

The synergy between Funk and Hart was creative, effective and long-lasting. They also enjoyed the benefit of an extraordinary group of colleagues on the faculty at Montana during those years—Lane McGaughy, our copanelist today, among them. Although I have no authenticated account of the ways and degrees in which those colleagues contributed to the ideas and projects of Funk and Hart as they worked together and separately within the American Academy of Religion and Society of Biblical Literature, I personally know or knew a number of them and can only surmise that they would have provided significant stimulation and support to their senior leaders.

The American Academy of Religion had only adopted its new name (formerly it was the National Association of Biblical Instructors—NABI) and declared its independence from the Society of Biblical Literature at its annual meeting in December 1963. One manifestation of this new-found autonomy of the American Academy of Religion was its holding its annual meetings in 1966, 1967, and 1968 separately from the Society of Biblical Literature.

I doubt it to have been coincidental that, after Funk's being only one year on the board of the American Academy of Religion and serving one year as executive secretary of the Society of Biblical Literature, the pattern of holding joint meetings of the two organizations was reestablished in 1969 when they met in Canada at the Royal York in Toronto. That arrangement will have continued for forty years before the decision of the American Academy of Religion to go its separate way from joint meetings with the Society of Biblical Literature happened, beginning in 2009, coincidentally again in Canada but in Montreal. (I predict that, though it may take a little more than three years, some arrangement will be made for the two societies to resume meeting at least *concurrently*, if not *jointly*—and, yes, there is a significant difference between those two kinds of arrangements—once again.[6])

Revamping the Structure of the Annual Meeting Programs of the Society of Biblical Literature and the American Academy of Religion

One of the early societal collaborations between Funk and Hart was to develop a new template for the structure of the annual meeting programs of the two societies. Programs arranged under the rubrics of sections, groups, seminars, and consultations provide the framework within which to assign program proposals from members who make presentations at annual meetings. Each of those categories, at least originally, was characterized in a distinctive way.

Sections were allocated more program slots than the other kinds of units in recognition of the consensus estimate of the continuing importance of the subject to be addressed by voluntary presenters within the sessions of sections. In comparison with sections, *groups* were designed to address new methodologies or areas of scholarly interest and generally were to have a more limited half-life than sections, but their importance in ongoing scholarly conversations is clearly recognized. Participants in

---

6. Editorial note: Wiggins's suspicion turned out correct, as the SBL and AAR began meeting jointly again in 2011.

groups were to be a continuing constituency for the life of the group. *Consultations* were to provide opportunities for scholarly engagement about new topics, issues and subjects with a very limited duration—as little as one or two years—within which to discover whether the participants would seek a more enduring structural designation in subsequent years. The other kind of program unit, the *seminar*, was conceived to provide a slot in the program when the work of a group of scholars who commit to be in dialogue with each other throughout the year, usually for a period of at least five years, will physically continue their conversation face to face. Attendees at the Annual Meeting may attend seminar sessions, but typically only as auditors. Plenary lectures and occasional gatherings jointly sponsored by the Society of Biblical Literature and American Academy of Religion have been the other typical components of annual meetings. This basic architecture of the programs of the societies continues with very few changes. This structure is one of the enduring legacies of Funk and Hart on the two organizations.

Both the Society of Biblical Literature and the American Academy of Religion also extend the opportunity to carefully vetted *affiliated societies* to meet in conjunction with the annual meeting, ordinarily before or after, but such groups plan their own programs and handle the logistics for their meetings. In more recent years the two societies have offered increased services to such groups by way of making arrangements for their meetings, and in some cases their meetings have even been scheduled concurrently with official programs of the Society of Biblical Literature and the American Academy of Religion.

Stimulating Publishing

The other major emphasis of Funk's concurrent tenure as executive secretary of the Society of Biblical Literature and as a member of the Board of Directors of the American Academy of Religion was upon the crucial importance of scholarly publication. I cannot ascertain whether he thought that focusing the restructuring of the program of the Annual Meeting on the elevation of serious scholarship would result in enhancing the quality and quantity of publications or that it would work the other way around.

A degree of influence on his emphasizing publications so heavily might have come from his formal involvement in the American Council of Learned Societies, which was one of the opportunities afforded him *ex officio* by his position as executive secretary of the Society of Biblical Literature. (Although the Society of Biblical Literature had been a member of the American Council of Learned Societies from its beginning, the American Academy of Religion was not accepted as a member of the American Council of Learned Societies until 1979.) The conviction that has always been at work in the American Council of Learned Societies is epitomized by this quotation: "The quality and value of a scholarly society must be measured finally by the character of its research work and the dissemination of it through publishing as the principal form of scholarly communication."[7] As I read the evidence, that thought confirmed Funk's convictions.

Funk envisioned a dramatic and even radical new direction for continuing and expanding the publication work of the Society of Biblical Literature and for stimulating a more extensive and higher quality publication program for the American Academy of Religion. High quality publications in the form of its journals, translations, commentaries, and monographs have been marks of the Society of Biblical Literature for well over a century and continue very impressively today. The American Academy of Religion has work to do to reach anything remotely approaching parity with the Society of Biblical Literature either in quantity and perhaps in quality, but it has made significant progress since the early 1970s. That is another effect of Funk's influence on the American Academy of Religion. It could not have happened, of course, without a widespread readiness with the American Academy of Religion to move in that direction. Beginning in 1974 he would be the founding director of Scholars Press, but there were several earlier developments that led to that. And some of them were indices of the master plan upon which Funk was embarked.

Funk quickly learned anything to which he turned his intelligence and imagination. He rapidly acquired a great deal of knowledge about the world of publication.[8] Among the aspects of that was familiarizing himself with different ways to print materials. In working with the university press at Montana to switch to offset rather than handset printing, Funk and Hart reduced the costs of printing the journals of the two societies by half or more in one fell swoop.

---

7. From the American Council of Learned Societies publication *Scholarly Communication* (Baltimore: Johns Hopkins University Press, 1979).

8. There is insufficient time to rehearse that education, but it is recounted in his unpublished memoirs.

Funk also became well acquainted with potential funding sources for a variety of undertakings that would emerge in subsequent years. Funk, with the assistance of many colleagues, persuaded major foundations, governmental agencies, and individual philanthropists to provide support for various projects in the years to come. Funk was accomplished at networking in ways that predated the widespread popular use of that notion. This kind of support from external sources was another step in securing the long-term financial sustainability of the two societies.

One other of his many accomplishments during his years as executive secretary that has matured and is extremely important in both the Society of Biblical Literature and the American Academy of Religion was his recognition of and elevation of the roles that regional groups of members would play in both. The regions of the two societies are not perfectly overlaid geographically, so it is not the case that all regional meetings combine the regional programs of both societies. Much more might be explored regarding the regional organizations, but time does not permit. Suffice it to say that Funk clearly saw that the national organizations would have to interconnect creatively and supportively with the regions to ensure the interests and futures of both.

An Interlude: The Council on the Study of Religion

If the Society of Biblical Literature was to become itself the publisher of scholarly work in many forms and if the American Academy of Religion were to be prodded to undertake its own publication program, Funk believed that stimuli from outside both societies might be very valuable. To that end Funk supported the creation of the Council on the Study of Religion in 1969. The Council on the Study of Religion initially had six scholarly society members, among them both the Society of Biblical Literature and the American Academy of Religion. It was housed in Waterloo, Ontario, and directed by Norman Wagner. The driving intention for that new organization was to develop "greater coordination of the field as a whole."[9] By 1970 the first issue of the *CSR Bulletin* was published.

It is my sense that Funk and the other founders of Council on the Study of Religion, particularly Claude Welch, envisioned the strong possi-

---

9. Cited by Saunders, *Searching the Scriptures*, 61. I have confirmed my own memory of several dates from this work.

bility, even likelihood, that the Council on the Study of Religion would not just *coordinate* but in many respects *consolidate* the field. The Council on the Study of Religion rapidly began providing a number of services to its member societies that chose to purchase them (and the Society of Biblical Literature and the American Academy of Religion did so):

- collection of membership dues and tracking of membership status;
- meeting planning and arrangements (such as negotiating rates at host hotel sites) including the coordination and allocations of meeting room for the programs of the two societies;
- its own publication program (the *CSR Bulletin*; *Religious Studies Review*; *Directory of Departments of Religion*).

The first International Congress of Learned Societies in the Field of Religion was held in Los Angeles in 1972, having been planned by a committee chaired by James M. Robinson.[10] Lane McGaughy was the on-site manager who was dispatched from Missoula by Funk to the then new Century City Hotel in Los Angeles for much of the preceding year to attend to the myriad of logistical arrangements and details. That meeting replaced the 1972 joint annual meeting of the Society of Biblical Literature and American Academy of Religion. Eighteen societies, mostly from North America, were convened. The magnitude of the 1972 Congress was significant in itself, but it was also the place in which attendees were first provided a book exhibit hall. That was another step in working for solvency for the two societies since the fees collected from publishers for display space has become a significant source of revenue. And for some members surveying all the materials on display in the exhibit hall has become a major reason for attending the Annual Meeting.

Increasing the registration fees for attending the Annual Meeting and linking the value of having a current membership in one or the other society (or a joint membership) were additional steps in the plan. For many years the dues in each society were linked to and equal to those in the other. Obviously, as membership has grown in both the Society of Biblical Literature and American Academy of Religion over the decades, the revenues from that source have also significantly increased.

---

10. I should note that during the decade of the 1960s Funk had collaborated with Robinson and Helmut Koestler on a number of projects and that the three, as I understand it, remained close colleagues.

Creating a New Thing: Scholars Press 1974–1980

Funk quickly realized that when the Council on the Study of Religion provided many of those services for a fee, the Society of Biblical Literature and the American Academy of Religion were expending resources that under some different arrangement they might have retained. That realization and the search for a vehicle to stimulate publication by both societies led Funk to the next major step. He took leave from Montana in 1972–1973 and spent months in Waterloo observing the operations of the Council on the Study of Religion staff. He returned to Missoula and launched Scholars Press in 1974. It was a manifestation of a recommendation that Funk had made in 1970 that publications by scholars in religion must intentionally and extensively engage other scholars in the other humanistic fields and disciplines. He recruited sponsors of this new undertaking from contiguous disciplines and the numbers grew to the point that by the early 1980's almost twenty societies from wide ranging fields had become collaborators in Scholars Press. That in itself was an unusual and important dimension of Scholars Press from the beginning. Incidentally, the Society of Biblical Literature and the American Academy of Religion remained members of the Council on the Study of Religion until the mid 1980s. Their withdrawals generated a significant amount of resentment and anger on the part of its officers and other member societies. It was subsequently renamed as the Council of Societies for the Study of Religion, and it continues to have its own publication program.

I am unable to establish the exact sequence and dates of the steps that ensued, but I know that Scholars Press grew dramatically from 1974 until 1979. One particular comment serves to capture Funk's contributions to and roles in the new venture:

> There was no time for a slow start…. It was an achievement that would cause even a veteran entrepreneur to marvel…. And behind it all were the energies and the daring of Bob Funk, functioning in the kaleidoscopic roles of editor, advertiser, administrator, scholar, purchasing agent, stock boy, technician, troubleshooter, and prophet. Koheleth and Gutenberg would have been dumbfounded.[11]

---

11. Saunders, *Searching the Scriptures*, 90.

Scholars Press became a publisher committed to expanding the publication programs of the two societies as well as those of its other sponsors. In 1975 a new entity called the Center for Scholarly Publishing and Services incorporated Scholars Press and "undertook to handle all bookkeeping and membership services of the Society as well as for other sponsoring institutions."[12] It was, however, a new entity in name only, and it continued almost universally to be referred to as Scholars Press until its dissolution in 2003.

The agreement in 1975 by most of its sponsors that Scholars Press would assume responsibility for providing membership services, financial record keeping, and meeting planning, along with publishing services entailed the necessity for growing the staff to include personnel with those capabilities and sufficient space within which to provide those services. The publishing services alone were extremely challenging. Scholars Press undertook to manage societal publications such as their journals and the dissertation series, monographs, translations, commentaries, and so forth that were accepted by their respective editorial boards and publication committees. Scholars Press also marketed and distributed the publications and collected the money for the sales of the publications. Significant amounts of cash had to be accounted for and accredited to its proper recipient sponsors' accounts. In short it became a significant business operation with a number of departments and numerous personnel. Having generated a new institution, Scholars Press, with all the business operations it provided, was an enormously important step in Funk's efforts to rescue the two organizations from bankruptcy and put them on a firm financial footing.

A decision was made by the board of Scholars Press, with the concurrence of the two societies, to find a new location for it. Eventually, it was decided to move to Chico, California where it would be connected with and subsidized by the State University of California in Chico. At least one of the reasons for that decision was that Charles Winquist, a professor at Chico, had been appointed to the position of executive director of the American Academy of Religion in 1978, and he was instrumental in securing an offer to house Scholars Press from the administration of Chico. Neither Missoula nor Chico were exactly on beaten travel paths, but both universities were very supportive of the press during the durations of its

---

12. Saunders, *Searching the Scriptures*, 65.

presence under their auspices and gratitude will ever be due to them for that support. Emory University became the permanent home of Scholars Press in 1985.

Funk's departure from Scholars Press on a September day in 1980 was painful to all concerned. The board of the press relieved him of his position and had the locks to the facilities changed. I have heard several accounts of what led the board to its decision. Some who participated in it have died. Others remain among us, but they, appropriately in my opinion, speak little about it, even when pressed. Funk's words regarding the matter include the remark that he was "anonymously accused of pilfering funds from the Press." A melancholy comment follows: "In my naiveté I had not imagined that my 'friends' no longer trusted me."[13] Elsewhere he referred to it as the "catastrophe in Chico." As observed earlier, rumors continued long into the future, and it was a bitter disappointment to Funk that his reputation was damaged by those events.

Funk's impact upon the Society of Biblical Literature and the American Academy of Religion was profound and far-reaching. The aspirations of both organizations were elevated, and many of those aspirations fulfilled through his challenging both to undertake ventures neither had previously dared. It is likely to remain the case, as Walter Harrelson remarked in 1973, "He has set an example for all future Executive Secretaries which is unfair even to mention to his successor."[14]

Funk returned to teach at the University of Montana from 1981 to 1986, after which he resigned and moved to California, where he established the Westar Institute and made Polebridge Press its publication vehicle. Others here have told us some of those stories.

Bibliography

American Council of Learned Societies. *Scholarly Communication*. Baltimore: Johns Hopkins University Press, 1979.

Funk, Robert W. "Bridge over Troubled Waters: From Seminary to the Jesus Seminar." Unpublished memoir.

———. "Editorial: A Few Good People." *The Fourth R* 15.3 (2002): https://tinyurl.com/SBL1128b.

---

13. Funk, "Bridge over Troubled Waters," Part Four, 4.
14. Cited by Saunders, *Searching the Scriptures*, 64.

Saunders, Ernest W. *Searching the Scriptures: A History of the Society of Biblical Literature, 1980–1980*. Chico, CA: Scholars Press, 1982.

Society of Biblical Literature—
Report of the Executive Secretary, 1968–1973

Robert W. Funk

1. The chief aims of this retrospective report are modest. I propose, first, to chart the course the officers, Council, and Society chose to run during the period 1968–1973. Charting after the fact permits the navigator to omit mention of storms, drift, and faulty compass readings. These omissions may suggest that our course has been less of an adventure than it has been. Secondly, it may prove illuminating to betray the impulses, instincts, working principles, vague concepts, determinations feats of the will, by which we have endeavored to tack the ship of the Society into the winds of economic and academic adversity or promise, as the case may be. And finally, a peek into the future may be permitted a retiring secretary.

This report is accordingly divided into three parts:

1. 1968–1973
2. Incantations against 1984
3. 1980 and Beyond

The secretary has reported to the Council and the Society on the state of the organization and its programs each year. In those reports, now to be placed in the Society's archives, I have endeavored to qualify as well as quantify the data. In this review, I may perhaps be excused from quantification, except by the way and as an afterthought. Quantified afterthoughts are appended to this report as appendices, which may, or may not, speak for themselves.

1. 1968–1973

2. It never occurred to me, when Walter Harrelson passed on the secretary's mantle late in 1967, that the revision of the constitution, then on the

Council agenda, would unleash a movement to alter the contours of the Society. A draft of the revision prepared by Robert A. Kraft and others was laid on the table in San Francisco in 1968. By then it was evident that we were doing more than adjusting a formal instrument. At the prolonged business meeting in Toronto in 1969, votes in striking numbers were cast, perhaps also a die of the future shape of things. At all events, a new mood, already in rudimentary evidence the preceding year, had taken firm root. It remained for the secretary to read the signs of the times and set out.

3. The revision of the constitution represents the formal climax of a set of forces set in motion, I believe, by Kendrick Grobel. Kendrick remarked to me on more than one occasion before his untimely death that he believed the Society ought to do more to expand the base of active participation, particularly in the case of younger scholars. He believed that too many able younger scholars were condemned to the Siberia of their first teaching assignments without hope of reprieve. He wanted to prevent the waste represented by that unnecessary exile.

It first came over me, as I think back on it, in Toronto in 1969, as Harry Orlinsky quipped his way through several tense moments, that the time had come to deliver the Society of Biblical Literature into the hands of its members; to expand the base of active participation and contract the base of passive relationship. In the air was a new conviction that scholarly communication was the primary function of the Society, and that meant communication between and among *all* members, and on *all* matters deemed by those members to be of significance. Kendrick Grobel's dream of drawing more younger scholars into active research, of relieving the tedium of service in outlying posts, had to become a reality, if the forces at work in that conviction were to be allowed to spend themselves fruitfully.

Once the fundamental direction became clear, the steps to be taken were more or less self-evident.

4. The first step to be taken was to broaden the real geographical base of the Society. This could be achieved in part, by new emphasis on the sections, and by the judicious rotation of Annual Meeting sites.

The annual pilgrimage to Union Theological Seminary during the Christmas holidays answered the scholarly devotion of too few to suit Kendrick Grobel's dream. Nevertheless, the 1968 meeting in San Francisco owed more or less to the accident of circumstance and the vigor of Victor R. Gold. But it was an omen.

President James Muilenburg had been able to host the 1968 meeting close to home. President Frank Beare was extended the same courtesy in Toronto the following year. The Royal York was a considerable improvement on the dormitories of Berkeley and Union, and the Society discovered other comforts of the convention hotel. Relief from laryngitis was not among them for Frank Beare. Registrations climbed to 650 in Toronto over approximately 400 in Berkeley the year before. Three hundred fifty registrations in New York no longer seemed significant.

The return to New York 1970 was not to Union but to the faltering New Yorker. President Orlinsky welcomed colleagues to his own backyard, the "fun city." Attendance at the meeting approached an all-time high. The return was not a reversion; it was part of the geographical sweep. The exclusive orientation of the Society to New York and New England died where it had been conceived. Henceforth the Society belonged to all of North America.

Meetings in Atlanta (1971) and Los Angeles (1972) proved that the Society could quit New York two years in a row and survive. Indeed, the tour had perhaps been too successful: smog, traffic jams, and high prices made New York too quickly a dim memory.

The secretary set out in 1968 to find out whether there really were sections and, if so, what they were about. The visits surprised the sections and alarmed the budget committee. Along the way, however, I came to know a battery of devoted sectional secretaries, who were subsequently to play a leading role in the Council. I also discovered that the sections were leading an active life of their own, for the most part, and at some remove from the life of the parent Society. As odd as it may sound, it struck me that the parent Society was really the section for New York and New England, and the other sections were more or less independent kingdoms. Naturally, I was intrigued to discover whether a reunion were possible.

Several of the sectional meetings had grown to proportions equal to those of the old national meetings at Union. Interest and activity in the sections picked up noticeably during 1968–1971. Secretaries importuned the Council for new support and got it. New sections were formed: Eastern Great Lakes; Pacific Northwest; Upper Midwest; and the old Middle Atlantic section became two, Hudson-Delaware and Chesapeake Bay. New allegiances were formed as the parent Society made its geographical rounds. Reunion was possible!

The secretaries of the sections met as a Conference of Secretaries for the first time, informally, in Berkeley. The conference has since become an important pre-Council meeting each year, sharing ideas, reviewing the Council agenda, coordinating sectional and national programs. Political intrigue has, of course, played no role in these meetings.

It was on my first visit to the Canadian section in 1968 that I encountered Norman Wagner, then secretary. He now doubtless regards that as an ill-fated visit he could well have done without.

The renewal of the sections has meant that few scholars, however removed from the major university centers, are without the stimulus of scholarly contact at least once during the year. And these contacts have become more productive with each passing year.

5. The second step was to broaden the leadership base of the society. When I was elected an associate in Council as a "younger scholar," it was respectfully suggested that I need not take an active role. I did not. It was clear that the leadership of the Society was intentionally restricted. It was a tautly if not tightly run ship.

The revision of the constitution, effected later, improved access to the Council and the committee structure of the Society. Indefinite terms came to an end. New offices and committees were created. Nominating Committees deliberately sought geographical, institutional, and ideological balance. Protestant domination receded even more. Canadians became Americans. Sectional secretaries canvassed their constituencies for suggestions of nominations and committee appointments. Aggressive executive secretaries are appropriately required to retire after a specified term.

The millennium has not dawned, but the leadership circle of the Society more nearly encompasses 10 percent of the active membership now than it did in 1967.

6. Expansion of active participation in the Annual Meeting seemed the next logical step. With this we come to the first material advance: more participation means that more research is being reported and hence presumably done.

The gain can be put tellingly in a compound sentence: in 1967 *thirty-nine* papers were read at the Annual Meeting in New York; for the meeting in Chicago in 1973, *forty* section, group, seminar, and consultation chairmen are at work. These forty chairmen will select and schedule about *two hundred* papers and reports out of many more submitted.

It is sometimes said that the quality of papers is not what it once was. I am unable to contest the assertion: I used to hear virtually everything read at one of the two sections of the Annual Meeting; now I hear only a fraction of the total and so cannot speak generally. I do know that W. F. Albright used to read only one paper; Frank Cross reportedly read more than one in Los Angeles in 1972. Henry Cadbury rarely appeared more than once in the old days; it has now become necessary to schedule the entire meeting around the program commitments of Robert Kraft. The increase in activity is not, however, all of this order: a great many younger, unknown, not well-known scholars are submitting their work to the judgment of peers at the Annual Meeting. Depreciation of quality, if any, results from an appreciation of scholarly production. The risk, it seems to me, is worth taking.

7. The expansion of the geographical and leadership bases of the Society and the increase of active participation in the Annual Meeting are not, in themselves, significant. If the Society is to fulfill its fundamental role, it must stimulate the production and dissemination of research in biblical and related fields. The fulfillment of this role meant moving in those new unspecifiable directions dimly forecast in 1968. As those directions took discernible shape, they appeared to be:

1. The reorganization of the Annual Meeting into sections and seminars (now also groups and consultations), under competent leadership;
2. The organization of the Committee on Research and Publications as the chief instigator of cooperative scholarly endeavor;
3. The launching of new publications programs as an outlet for research in progress and as a stimulus to new research.

Even the naming of them is more after than before the fact: at the beginning scarcely anyone could have predicted what would emerge.

8. The Gospels Seminar, with Krister Stendahl in the chair, took its first tentative step in Berkeley in 1968, and the International Organization for Septuagint and Cognate Studies was launched under the tutelage of Harry Orlinsky. Emergent patterns were in evidence.

M. Jack Suggs was appointed permanent chairman of the Gospels Seminar for the Toronto meeting; the seminar promptly spawned four task groups, which were to work under and report to the parent body. The Old Testament Form Criticism group and the Pseudepigrapha group, both subsequently to become seminars, were organized in 1969, with Gene Tucker and Walter Harrelson as chairmen. Consultations on the use of computers in biblical studies and on scholarly publishing were convened

(William Murdock and William Doty); Nag Hammadi specialists brought their manuscripts to the meeting and sat down for a serious session; linguistics, Greco-Roman religions, and the application of literary criticism to biblical studies were recognized for the first time as program units.

Toronto blossomed into New York: thirteen section chairmen produced a greatly expanded program of 160 items. Sections on Early Rabbinic Studies (Lou Silberman), Art and the Bible (Joseph Gutmann), and the Fourth Gospel (Moody Smith) began activity; the Seminar on Paul was organized with Nils Dahl as chairman, and the American Textual Criticism Seminar was reorganized in the course of an international consultation. Consultations on computers and publishing continued.

Twenty-one program unit chairmen became thirty-one in Atlanta (1971), became thirty-nine in Los Angeles (1972), will become forty in Chicago (1973). But numbers do not tell the story. The story to be told consists of chairmen and participants coming to the Annual Meeting in increasing numbers for high scholarly purpose of a more intimate and extended sort. It is still vogue to attend the stellar performance, but is now also possible to carry forward research and argument in smaller working groups. And the full diversity of interests and competencies represented in the Society are permitted expression in one form or another.

The reconception of the Annual Meeting has pulled more members into an active role in the life of the Society and reduced the purely passive relationship of members to what passes on the stage.

9. The account of the Annual Meeting in number 8 anticipates the function of the Committee on Research and Publications, in large measure.

James M. Robinson was elected the first chairman of the Research and Publications Committee in Toronto in 1969. With the skill for which he is famous, the new chairman began assisting with cooperative scholarly enterprises of a national, even international, nature.

The Nag Hammadi project was already well underway, but the team met regularly at the Annual Meeting and used the occasion to further its work on the gnostic texts. An International Consultation on Textual Criticism was held in New York in 1970, with support from the American Council of Learned Societies; the aim of the meeting was to further international cooperation and breathe fresh life into text-critical projects of long standing. The new committee spearheaded conversations on the use of computers in biblical studies, with the help of William Murdock, Malcolm Peel, and Norman Wagner.

The primary attention of the committee has been given to the seminars of the Society. In addition to organizing and reviewing seminars connected with the Annual Meeting, Chairman Robinson and James Hester created a Regional Seminar on Paul. The University of Redlands has supported the work of the seminar with a grant.

When the American Council of Learned Societies called for a list of research instruments needed in the field of religious studies, naturally the Research and Publications Committee was called upon to supply the data. A flurry of activity in the spring of 1972 resulted in a highly tentative compendium of needed tools, with descriptions and costs. The document was of some help in making the case for the funding of such instruments across the whole spectrum of the humanities to the National Endowment for the Humanities. The Council on the Study of Religion will now undertake to revise and expand the list, in consultation, of course, with the Society of Biblical Literature committee. Hopefully, some of the projects will eventually receive support.

10. In recent months, the work of the Committee on Research and Publications has been devoted largely to publications.

The first Seminar Papers were distributed, willy-nilly, at the registration desk in New York in 1970. Seminar Papers were bound in two volumes in 1971 and 1972. These publications have been the backbone of new publishing ventures on the part of the Society.

The Welch report, *Graduate Education in Religion*, and the Perrin Festschrift, sponsored by the New Testament Colloquium, were displayed and sold at the Atlanta meeting, along with a selection of Society of Biblical Literature Monographs. There we learned a very important fact of life: scholars will buy Society publications if they are inexpensive and readily available at annual and regional meetings.

The Research and Publications Committee determined to move ahead with innovative publishing in time for the International Congress, held in Los Angeles, 1–5 September 1972. The first two volumes of the new dissertation series appeared in time, along with the first two numbers of Texts and Translations, the Cartlidge-Dungan, *Sourcebook for the Study of the Gospels*, and Funk's *Beginning-Intermediate Greek Grammar*. The first volume of the new Septuagint and Cognate Studies series, two further volumes of Seminar Papers, along with previously published items, were added to the items for sale at the Society of Biblical Literature booth during the meeting.

More volumes of the Society of Biblical Literature Monograph series were sold at the congress than Abingdon Press had sold by mail during the preceding year. Altogether Society of Biblical Literature publications grossed more than $3,000—an impressive beginning!

The publications programs of the Society have continued to grow at a rapid rate. New volumes and new series are in process or contemplated. The Society took in an additional $3,000 by 31 December 1972 from sales, and regional meetings have now proved to be significant outlets for publications.

When I recall that the Council very nearly discharged the old Research Committee for want of purpose less than ten years ago, I am even more startled by the course events have taken since the organization of the new committee in 1970.

11. As officers and Council endeavored to deliver the Society into the hands of members, the Society was, from another point of view, being delivered to new challenges and opportunities. I have in mind the deeper currents of the academic times—currents that occasionally rise to the surface and trouble the waters.

Permit two generalizations: there has been a perceptible shift in the academic base of the profession (theological studies as a whole) from the seminary to the university-based department of religion; the academic base for biblical scholarship and teaching has visibly contracted. The first observation constitutes an interesting opportunity; the second threatens and challenges.

The emergence of a section on the Bible and the Humanities, under the chairmanship of David Dungan, reflects the growing opportunity of biblical scholars to address themselves to biblical questions in a purely humanistic—as opposed to ecclesiastical—context. It is not a new opportunity, but it has presented itself with new force, especially when connected with the second observation indicated above. And it is an opportunity which more and more members of Society of Biblical Literature have been inclined to explore, if I read the mood correctly. Perhaps I am extrapolating from my own experience: I could not have guessed ten years ago that the University of Montana would house a Department of Religious Studies, to which I would find myself joined.

As biblical chairs in seminaries have contracted, the need to expand the base for biblical studies in other contexts has grown more acute. Biblical scholars have responded by reshaping their work to those other contexts, principally the secular university. And the reshaping of biblical work has meant that the contours of research, of the Annual Meeting, of publications have altered.

These shifts have surfaced, in my judgment, in the reunion of the Society with the American Academy of Religion, formerly the National Association of Biblical Instructors, in New York in 1970. The last time the National Association of Biblical Instructors met with the Society of Biblical Literature was in Nashville in 1965. During the intervening years, the National Association of Biblical Instructors lost the character of a satellite group and became the most representative learned society in the field of religious studies. The transformation of the National Association of Biblical Instructors into the American Academy of Religion reflects the dramatic changes taking place in colleges and seminaries across the continent: biblical departments were rapidly becoming departments of religion with the most diverse components. The American Academy of Religion has endeavored to encompass all the major disciplines and subdisciplines, including biblical studies in a humanistic context. The reaffiliation of the American Academy of Religion and the Society of Biblical Literature, on new terms, has given tacit recognition to the changed academic situation, and, hopefully, presages a new era in biblical studies, now with twin allegiances.

12. The weak position of religious studies generally among the humanistic disciplines has given rise, in turn, to the Council on the Study of Religion, if I may speak boldly. It is the time for high resolve and unprecedented cooperation in the field; the Council on the Study of Religion is the result of that sense of the time of the times.

The Council on the Study of Religion is not, however, the child of alarm. Rather, it represents the end of an epoch and the beginning of a new one. It manifests the end of isolated specialization, of confessional differences, of the pretense that the study of religion, to be respectable, must be hidden under the bushel of a neutral discipline, such as philology, psychology, or sociology. And the Council on the Study of Religion reflects the new willingness to identify the study of religion as a legitimate humanistic enterprise, with its own intrinsic merits and claim upon public support, It embodies the self-identity of the field in a new and vigorous form. It asserts the human, rather than partisan, role of religion in the life of man.

It may be remarked, purely parenthetically, that biblical scholars have been called upon to lead this and the preceding enterprises. Norman

Wagner, the first executive director of the Council on the Study of Religion, was executive secretary-elect of Society of Biblical Literature before he was tapped for his new post; the Society of Biblical Literature gave him up to a higher cause. Harry M. Buck the former executive director of American Academy of Religion, and Robert A Spivey, his successor, are both New Testament scholars.

13. The narrative of the past six years would not be complete without some mention of fiscal matters.

Former Treasurer Virgil M. Rogers rightly sensed that the Society would be in trouble were it not to raise member dues from $9 to $15. The decision to raise dues was taken in 1969, along with other momentous decisions. While matters were not as bad as they seemed at that time, the resolution on the part of members has proved to be salutary. As a result, the fiscal position of the Society is today as sound as—a Yen or a Mark.

Annual surpluses in recent years have been made possible, in part, by the decision to change printers for the journal. Printing bills were cut in half by the move to the University of Montana Printing Department in 1971. The savings have been invested in other publications, also being produced at bargain basement rates.

The net worth of the Society has increased modestly in the past few years. The growth is represented in appendix 2.[1]

14. It is too recent in memory to rehearse the International Congress of Learned Societies in the Field of Religion, held in Los Angeles. Yet much effort of the preceding two years and more went into that congress; the chairman of the Committee on Research and Publications (also chairman of the Congress Committee), the executive secretary, Alan Sparks, George MacRae, Robert Wright, and many others devoted countless hours to preparation and planning. The burden of management fell on Lane C. McGaughy, who served as floor manager of the meeting. Such success as the congress enjoyed owes to the persons named and to our foreign guests, and the program chairmen of participating societies, the Institute for Antiquity and Christianity, the Claremont Graduate School, the School of Theology at Claremont, and the American Council of Learned Societies.

---

1. Editor's Note: Not included in this reprint.

Is it possible that we will undertake something like this again in 1980?

15. I set out to chart the course the Society has run during the period, 1968–1973. As predicted, that course has been represented schematically. I have not told the real story. I do not know the real story. If I did, I could not, or would not, tell it. You have no choice but to pause at your desk and imagine the real narrative to yourself.

2. Incantations against 1984

16. In the beginning, it was not apparent that the job of executive secretary would ever demand more than a lunch hour, or that it would last more than a year or two. Helmut Koester, then chairman of the Nominating Committee, assured me that it was so. A succession of capable secretaries: Lola LaRue, Bettye Ford, Carol Durant, Patricia Nolley, Joann Armour, Jayne Mitchell have endeavored to help me keep up the illusion, but in vain.

As unanswered correspondence deepened, travel mounted, books and journals lay unopened, I decided that a scholar or would-be scholar is justified in accepting administrative responsibilities only if other scholars are thereby enabled to achieve what would otherwise be beyond reach. The proper compensation for the loss in one's own output is a hundredfold gain in the output of colleagues. At that exchange rate I could sell with an easy conscience.

Even so, the bureaucracy remains. What wiles are there to protect against the sorcery of 1984? What stratagems enable one to defeat the bureaucracy and come to the heart of things? I did not know then, and I do not know now, but I have collected a desk drawer full of incantations for the purpose.

Perhaps the collection of incantations is the final deceptive stratagem of the bureaucracy.

17. At the threshold.
17.1. The secretary has assumed that the function of the Society is to help members do what they are already doing, only do it better.

In that case, one should open the door when someone knocks. Standard bureaucrat confuses the habitual "no" with the power to discriminate. "Yes" is the appropriate response whenever proposals do not merely equal or fall below past performance.

17.2. The generalization, "we can't do anything about that," is inadmissible. We can do something, however trivial, about every problem, however gross. The insurmountable obstacle is mostly a fictitious form in the stilted stance of the *status quo*.

17.3. In a bureaucracy credit must be multiplied to satisfy the claims upon it; mistakes and complaints, conversely, have no place to lodge. The secretary who fears 1984 should begin by making himself a repository of blame. Besides, critics are struck dumb by the admission of guilt.

18. At the hearth.

18.1. The secretary has assumed that the bureaucracy is necessary but an evil. Accordingly, it is to be cultivated and pruned, simultaneously, like vines. The bureaucracy is poison: there should be as little as possible, but what there is should be potent.

18.2. The size and shape of the organizational machinery should be commensurate with the active participation of at least 10 percent of the membership in the decision making process, and 100 percent in the review process.

18.3. The bureaucracy should not be permitted a life of its own. Dispense with officers, committees, institutions that are not oriented to the real work of the Society.

18.4. The bureaucracy should not be permitted the illusion of making substantive decisions, indeed any decisions. Material decisions are made by particular persons for particular reasons. The editor and editorial board make decisions regarding the content of the journal; the Council, secretary, and treasurer do not. Section and seminar chairmen are responsible for the content of their programs at the Annual Meeting; the Program Committee and the Committee on Research and Publications are not. The individual scholar determines the judgment he wishes to champion in his paper; the section chairman and editor of the journal do not.

18.5. Capable members should be kept rotating in and out of the power elite. Do not permit a leadership clique to develop; expel tenacious secretaries.

18.6. Nonfunctioning persons should not be permitted to occupy leadership posts. Officers and Council should be as demanding of themselves as they are of their printer.

18.7. For Secretaries: Never permit the substantive issues to be decided by experts who control the technologies. Acquire the knowledge to make an independent judgment yourself. Control the means, if necessary.

Unless you do, you will be a trailer hitched to other notions of where the Society should go.

18.8. Wherever possible in the work of the Society (Annual Meeting, publishing, business operations). The scholar is a craftsman who takes pride in his work; the craftsman is a scholar who understands what he is doing.

18.9. The fodder of the organization consists of deliberately taken initiatives. Officers must not sustain a passive relation to the bureaucracy.

18.10. The secretary should take more initiatives than can be accommodated. The Council should be prodded into saying "no" part of the time. It should be encouraged to say "yes." But it should not be allowed to say "yes" all of the time.

18.11. Reports are necessary to keep the membership informed, but they should be as succinct and revealing as possible. It would not hurt if they were well written.

18.12. The secretary must assume that members are always right in problems having to do with the bureaucracy. That is because academics are chronically incompetent in practical matters and must be nursed through fits of depression brought on by the mail service, computer, and convention hotel, so they can stay with, or get to, their work. Furthermore, it will save time in the long run.

18.13. And for laughs: The secretary should never let a letter lie on the desk more than two days without some reply. Answer it or throw it away.

19. Into the fire.

19.1. At the hearth one must be keenly alert to the danger of falling statuary: there one is prompted to inspect the household gods. To do so is to pass into the fire.

Every practice and tradition, every injunction and taboo, is to be examined with an eye to the question: Is this ceremony any longer telling? Has this prescription retained its cogency? The wise secretary will discard, revamp, and preserve.

The proportion will vary greatly among secretaries and the times. Now one, now the other, will be to the fore. The critical point is to keep the tradition in motion, vibrant.

19.2. As a corollary, the discerning secretary will harbor suspicions of every effort to suppress, limit, make to conform, subject to arbitrary control. In every effort to circumscribe arbitrarily, there is latent a tyrannical current. Conformity sucks oxygen away from the breath of imagination.

In order to encourage wholesome diversity, and guard against his own aspirations, the executive officer should write out a letter of resignation the day after election and entertain the thought of early retirement. If he does so, he will be most pleased when there are as many material judgments as there are responsible and informed parties to the debate.

19.3. A plethora of flames leaps from the hearth. The richest among them is the hue of the subject matter itself. The reluctant bureaucrat will attend those deep hues. There is to be spied the true drift of the subject matter, in concert with the trajectory of the discipline. The secretary who aspires to authentic leadership of the discipline he serves—in addition to nourishing the reserve fund—will spend long hours staring into the fire.

In my own defense, I may report that I did get around to installing a fireplace for the purpose.

19.4. The secretary of a learned society should be a practicing scholar. When he is not staring into the fire, his feet will be held there by the double demand upon his energy. And six years is the equivalent of a mild marathon.

3. 1980 and Beyond

20. Officers entering upon their tenure are required to plan and project. Retiring officials are permitted to prophesy. The difference is that the first may be held accountable for promises; the latter are merely indulged. Fortunately, the latter may also be ignored.

The following predictions and proposals are in part unfinished business. While I do not offer them lightheartedly, I will not go so far as to claim attention for them.

21. The centennial celebration of the Society looms before us in 1980. It would be appropriate on that occasion to review the state of the discipline and probe its foundations.

By that I do not mean simply a recapitulation of the state of knowledge and research. I mean rather a penetrating assessment of the aims and methodologies of biblical scholarship and the relation of that scholarship to institutions of higher learning, to church and synagogue, to the American tradition, and to the culture at large. It is time, in my judgment, for latter day Jeromes to look up, if only momentarily, from their foolscap and take stock of what is going on about them and in them.

Looking up and around involves at least a history and analysis of American biblical scholarship. That is one task to which the Society should address itself, unrelentingly, if for no other reason than that biblical scholarship on these shores will not fully mature until it comes to terms with its own past. Biblical scholars in North America have too long regarded themselves as poor cousins of richer uncles in Europe. There are signs that those legendary uncles are being robbed of their own patrimony, and there are other indications that the commitments of European biblical scholarship will no longer serve the demands to which American scholars must answer.

22. As a token of advancing maturity and as a means of celebrating its first century, the Society should undertake to sponsor a major cooperative scholarly project or projects, one or more to be completed by 1980. Among the possibilities may be mentioned a critical edition of a compendium of primary texts; new translations of ancient texts in economical editions; a new dictionary of the Bible, perhaps a subject rather than a word dictionary; lexica and grammars of relevant languages; compendia of archaeological data; bibliographic and abstracting tools. Whatever the specific projects, they should be undertaken with direct Society sponsorship, prepared and published by the Society alone or in concert with a university or commercial press, and the income earmarked for subsequent research and publishing programs.

23. Also in recognition of its one hundredth anniversary, the Society should reprint the earlier issues of the *Journal of Biblical Literature*. Inexpensive methods of reproduction would put a full run of the journal within reach of most members of the Society and all libraries, especially on a subscription plan, say, for $5 a volume, at the rate of two or three volumes a year. For those who do not want the full run, a series of volumes representing the best articles on given topics could be produced at equally modest prices. A microfiche edition of one or the other is a further, highly desirable item.

24. It is perhaps crucial to the health of the discipline that the Society establish one or more advanced research institutes and/or archives, in conjunction with one or the other of the major graduate centers in North America. Such institutes/archives would serve to nurture advanced research. In particular, the shape and direction of the field would be under constant surveillance. The publications of the Society and its members would be deposited in the archives. Younger and older scholars would be brought to the institutes, and scholars would similarly be loaned to more

remote institutions for stipulated periods. These institutes/archives would be funded by the host institution, the Society, and external sources.

It is my intention to elaborate this suggestion in a subsequent issue of the *CSR Bulletin*.

25. The innovative publishing programs of the Society constitute the single most important new means for the exchange of scholarly information. The future of these programs extends far beyond 1980. It is safe to predict that the Society will expand its publishing activities indefinitely. Among the many challenges and opportunities that lay before us, I may be permitted to mention a few that invite prompt attention.

25.1. Of top priority, as it seems to me, is the reconception of the Monograph series. This already prestigious series should seek increasingly to attract the ranking scholars in the Society to its lists. Inexpensive technical and nontechnical monographs can do as well in relatively inexpensive formats under the sponsorship of the Society as in the hands of commercial houses. Indeed, the Society may soon offer the primary outlet for such monographs.

25.2. As indicated above, the Society should undertake the creation and publication of a major research instrument as part of its centennial celebration. It is but a short and logical step to suggest that the Society should assume the primary responsibility for the development and maintenance of most research tools in the biblical field, whether on its own or in conjunction with a university or commercial press.

25.3. The Society publishing programs merits investment in still other forms. I would suggest that the series of Sources for Biblical Study should be considerably enlarged, particularly so as to include modules of material for use by students and teachers in conventional university courses. The Society has too long shunned its immediate responsibility to the undergraduate and graduate student.

25.4. A series of studies of important biblical scholars in the American tradition should be launched at the earliest possible date. A history of the Society would be an important monument to the one hundredth anniversary. Analyses of recent trends and innovations in American biblical scholarship is a must, if not for the journal, then for a series of occasional papers.

25.5. The Society should recognize the incipient happy wedding of literary criticism and biblical criticism by inaugurating a series devoted to this exchange. Seminars in both the Old Testament and New Testament fields have generated sufficient productive power to warrant such a series.

25.6. Finally, the Society has wisely commissioned the first volumes in a joint series with the American Academy of Religion devoted to religion and the arts. The first volume contains studies of the Dura synagogue. Subsequent volumes will range over the whole field of the arts. Works related to the biblical field should appear regularly in this series.

26. Some mention should be made of micropublications. The day is not far away when scholars and libraries will trade primarily in microforms. The Society should seize the initiatives and begin its micropublishing program by nurturing demand: a good quality reader could be marketed at a substantial discount to members, at the same time as the first texts and tools are being produced on microfiche. Micropublication should follow actual scholarly need closely: those texts and tools should be published for which there is real demand. To be sure, inaccessibility and high cost will make many texts and tools in microfiche highly desirable: why not have the work on one's desk for pennies, when physical copies are available only in the library because of the price?

27. The horizons that open before the imagination in contemplating the future of Society sponsored publishing suggest that we will soon have to abandon our rough-and-ready methods. It will soon not be possible to operate out of a professor's office, with a part-time secretary and a friendly but unpaid designer. The best suggestion that has occurred to me is one I elaborated in the June 1973 issue of the *CSR Bulletin*: a scholar's press organized by a consortium of learned societies, perhaps amalgamated with a university press. The Society's volume alone now requires more attention than a professor with a full teaching load can give it.

When all is said and done, I believe the key to a successful publications program sponsored directly by the Society, in collaboration with other learned associations, is management. It is possible to enlist authors of quality among our own members; superb editors are working with minimal support; but it is very difficult to keep costs to a minimum, and market journals and books at prices that most members will find attractive, indeed irresistible. Success means, of course, the free exchange of information and judgment between and among scholars. Unless this is achieved, all other successes, for example, financial success, spell failure. I repeat: the key to success in a fundamental sense is close and imaginative management.

As something of an untutored pioneer in this regard, I have one or two suggestions to offer. It is crucial, I judge, to have as managers of a scholarly publishing program or press only those who are scholars by instinct and practice and stringent managers by nature and necessity. A suitable manager is one who has published on tables of stone and wrung water from a rock. It is still important, in my estimation, to retain university connections, in spite of widespread budgetary retrenchments. The university has much to offer by way of hospitality even in its poverty, much that the scholar cannot do without. Manuscript preparation and editing will have to be carried out by the author, for the most part, and funded largely by the host institution in order to keep costs down. In other words, other publishing programs will have to be run as the journal and monograph series have been run. Further, many manuscripts will be reproduced from camera-ready typescript; others will be set on in-house equipment, such as the society now has operational at the Council on the Study of Religion office; commercial composition will be the exception.

It has now become clear to me that the Society will want to run its own minimal printing facility, doubtless in partnership with others societies. It will not install a letterpress, but it may depend on its connections with a university press with such facilities and the ties it maintains with other university and commercial shops.

Distribution will become much more efficient as we gain experience in marketing through the Council on the Study of Religion. It is necessary to bear in mind that scholars, as their own publishers, are publishing preeminently for themselves; they cannot afford the vanity of those authors who demand that technical biblical works be bestsellers. Royalties will be paid as we grow older and more confident; the societies will make money and plow it back into research; and publishing opportunities will expand. Of these things, there is no doubt. To reach that happy plateau will require the patience and trust of all parties to the experiment.

28. The heartening publishing experiment in which we are currently involved owes to a happy congruence of circumstance. Al Madison and the University of Montana Printing Department enables us to learn the trade firsthand and presented us with the first opportunities to adventure. Small initial successes prompted us to be bolder. Successive expansions of our experiments could not have been undertaken without the assistance of our associate secretary, Lane McGaughy, and the pleasant efficiency of Betty Christiansen of the University Clerical Services, not to mention my secretary. Even so, it astounds me in retrospect what we were able to achieve with so few in so short a time.

It is some reconstruction of this favorable circumstance that is ingredient to further successes, I have no doubt, albeit in some new and perhaps unanticipated configuration.

29. The centennial and publications have thus far dominated these remarks. I should now like to turn to a budget of miscellaneous items, which represent, in part, those things I left undone, and, in part, objectives I recognized too late in my tenure to pursue.

29.1. In order to enlarge the proportion of the membership engaged in the decision-making process in the Society, I propose that the principal elections of the Society be conducted by mail ballot. For example, the principal national officers should be so elected. Mail ballot would enable a larger proportion of the membership to participate than can attend the Annual Meeting (cf. no. 18.2).

29.2. The bulk of the membership of Society of Biblical Literature is concentrated in an area dissected by a line that runs from New York to Chicago. As I thought about the rotation of the sites of the Annual Meeting, it occurred to me that a reasonable distribution would be: in two years out of three the Annual Meeting should be located in that area of concentrated membership bounded by New York-Washington-Saint Louis-Chicago-Toronto-Boston-New York, and in the third the Annual Meeting should be circulated to the other sections of the nation (Southeast, Southwest, West, Upper Midwest).

29.3. The official name for the regional organizations of Society of Biblical Literature, currently *sections*, should be changed to *region*, in order to conform to the American Academy of Religion usage and eliminate the confusion with program units called sections.

29.4. In view of the cost of holding a national meeting, it should perhaps be considered whether a series of regional meetings should be substituted, at least once in a decade or so; I am not sure that regional meetings would adequately replace the national meeting, even on rare occasions, but I believe the idea worthy of reflection.

29.5. It has always been a source of consternation to me that there is such poor exchange of used scholarly books in North America. I think it must owe to poor marketing facilities. In any case, I wonder whether a book exchange would work. I have in mind a cheap publication advertising used books and libraries; sales would be consummated by parties directly with each other after they had learned of opportunities for buying and selling through the book exchange. A small percentage of the sale price, on an honor basis, would be remitted to the Society to support the publication.

29.6. Some serious attempt needs to be made to expand the secular academic base for biblical studies, especially in view of the contracting seminary base (cf. no. 11). At the same time, the adaptation of biblical studies to the secular university context has become a new challenge to the Society. A special presidential commission might serve to open the question up, collect the facts, and make recommendations to the Council regarding ways of meeting these challenges.

30. A not-so-miscellaneous item concerns the name of the Society. I visited with the chairman of the National Endowment for the Humanities on one occasion when he remarked the political impossibility of using the name of the Society in connection with Congressional appeals. I have since pondered the problem: What could we call the Society of Biblical Literature (1) that would comport with its subject matter and aim, and (2) be less problematic for public funding agencies? I do not have the answer to the question. But I am persuaded that "biblical literature" is misleading nomenclature in contemporary society, perhaps even in the university. What we study is the history of religious movements in Western antiquity, not just their canonical literatures (recall biblical archaeology, Ugarit, Qumran, Nag Hammadi). Society of Biblical Literature should perhaps expand its horizons formally in the direction it has steadily moved for its hundred years, strike a new comity arrangement with the American Academy of Religion, and make its aim the study of religion in Western antiquity. Society for the Study of Religion and Religions in Western Antiquity is a bit cumbersome. A set of reprinted journals could be offered as a prize for the best suggestion of a new name for the Society—one that is finally adopted by the Council and the membership at large.

31. As in the case of the Apostle, if it were permissible to boast, there are many things about which I might boast. That is only to say that I have derived much satisfaction from my tenure as secretary of the Society; I have endeavored to veil my pride in this report, doubtless unsuccessfully. But I am dropping even the pretense in this final remark.

A secretary should be measured, not by the specific achievements of his tenure but by the stature of the men required to replace him. The fact that Norman Wagner, now the executive director of the Council on the Study of Religion and business manager of Society of Biblical Literature as a part of that responsibility, and George MacRae, the secretary-elect of Society of Biblical Literature, were required to take up my duties is a form of flattery not to be gainsaid. If they are not in fact both needed, I am proud that they were persuaded that they were needed. That they think so is as important as the fact.

32. The preceding outburst of pride leads me to a prediction by way of postscript: I predict that the Society of Biblical Literature, or the Society of Biblical Literature/the American Academy of Religion, will shortly have a full-time executive secretary.

The Learned Society as
Publisher and the University Press

Robert W. Funk

1. The Learned Society as Publisher

The learned society has as its fundamental aim the production and dissemination of scholarly information in that discipline or subject matter area to which it is devoted. Typically, the society stimulates production by making it possible to exchange information easily in published form and in public forum. The annual meeting has served as the principal public forum, the journal (and related publications) as the print medium. Until recently, the learned association was able to fulfill its function by these effective though limited means.

The professional association is currently under heavy pressure to expand its publishing activities. Professional memberships have climbed steadily since 1950, but the size of the association journal has tended to remain constant under the weight of spiraling production costs. Similarly, the monograph series has been beset by importunate scholars and failing association funds. The conflict between the need for more pages and insufficient funds has brought more than one society to the brink of fiscal disaster. Under amateur management, most associations have assumed that the only option was to compromise their purpose. A few have conducted a more radical review of the possibilities.

The plight of the learned society has been aggravated by the near failure of the commercial bookmaker and the university press. Book prices have skyrocketed. Retrenchment has been the order of the day. Many lists have been pruned of scholarly books, and scholarly manuscripts find less frequent consideration. The commercial house has been forced—or perhaps has chosen—to become more commercial still: the annual sales chart, like the Nielsen ratings, is the arbiter to which all-wise editors and programmers must submit. The university press has suffered both from shrinkage in the general book market and from cuts in university budgets. In any case, the university press has been able to serve the exchange of scholarly information only in a limited way and with indifferent success, with some notable exceptions.

Contraction in publishing outlets has made it more difficult for scholars to exchange information and to submit their work to the critical assessment of peers. Prices have all but choked the life out of the private research library. The inability to buy has contributed, will-nilly, to the inability to publish: the circle is vicious. The scholar has been unable, or unwilling, or insufficiently informed, to break out of the circle, and the professional association, until quite recently, did not conceive it as its responsibility to address problems so mundane and of such magnitude.

The curtailment of the private research library has made the scholar theoretically more dependent on the institutional library. But that library is no better placed than the individual scholar with respect to purchasing power, relatively speaking. Library budgets have scarcely kept pace with inflation, and the library bureaucracy has responded even less nimbly than the learned association to the deterioration of its primary function.

As a consequence of these mounting pressures, scholarship has been forced to ask itself, through the medium of the learned association, whether the responsibility for the dissemination of scholarship was not passing into new hands. A further, immediate question was whether conventional modes of publication could not be executed more efficiently and less expensively. Beyond this matter lay speculation regarding promising new forms of scholarly communication. In short, the learned association suddenly found itself facing tasks previously assumed to be the primary responsibility of the commercial press, the university press, and the institutional library.

2. Scholars Learn about Scholarly Publishing

A number of learned societies in the field of religious studies set out, half a decade ago, to rescue themselves from bankruptcy and to put their journals and monographs on a firm financial basis. They began by raising member dues. But this move did not stem the inflationary tide. It became necessary to cut back the number of pages being printed or pare production costs significantly. It was in exploring the second option that these societies discovered rudiment number 1:

2.1. *The learned society can contract for its own composition and print-ing, by diligent shopping, at rates substantially below those charged by pro-fessional management firms.* The three principal societies in the field of religion cut their printing and distribution bills in half by adopting this procedure.

The discovery of further economic first principles followed rapidly upon the first:

2.2. *The distribution overhead for the journal and monograph published for a specialized audience (and only for them) adds very little to the overhead costs of running a national office.*

2.3. *The bulletin of the learned societies or conglomerate of learned societies is a reasonably effective means of marketing the scholarly journal and mono-graph printed in short runs.*

2.4. *Scholars are more apt to buy their own books if physical copies are made available to them at the annual and regional meetings.*

2.5. *Members of the society are proving to be effective book agents for and among themselves.*

The professional associations in the field of religious studies have now joined in a Council on the Study of Religion, which serves most business functions of constituent groups. Journals, monographs, and other publi-cations are being promoted and distributed through that office. The *CSR Bulletin* is the principal but not the only instrument. The annual meeting, which is also a joint venture, has become a major means of distributing publications. Members are volunteering to serve as book agents at regional meetings and for university bookstores.

The Society of Biblical Literature organized its first national seminar in 1968. The seminar was defined as a closed-membership group at work on a common problem; members were required to prosecute their work throughout the year as well as at the annual meeting. For this purpose, a publications exchange was the necessary instrument: papers and memo-randa were rapidly duplicated and circulated to the other members of the group; replies were treated similarly. The seminars then began publishing the principal papers each year as "proceedings." It was in connection with the publications exchange and the proceedings, that a further fact came to attention.

2.6. *Memoranda and papers being prepared by scholars could be typed up as camera-ready copy with no additional expense, and the cost of composition could be eliminated.* The application of this principle made it possible to publish inexpensively, not only memoranda and proceedings, but also collections of papers, collections of primary texts, even monographs. Two dissertation series have been launched with minimal capital, by working directly from typescripts.

Since composition costs figure heavily in the production of any journal or book, learned societies have been exploring the possibilities of doing their own composition. The Modern Language Association and the American Anthropological Association, after rocky beginnings, have now established that:

2.7. *Learned societies can do much of their own composition in-house, at rates well below commercial rates.* The advent of the IBM cold type system and new photo-composers have put in-house composition within the reach of most societies. Nevertheless, some composition will continue to be done at the source, and some will be purchased from commercial houses. Cheaper composition has made it possible to expand the number of pages being published while holding the line on costs.

Scholars are slow learners in practical matters. It has taken some time to unlearn the commercial axiom that only the large edition is financially viable. Correlatively, it has taken a while to establish that:

2.8. *The learned society has a relatively small but highly specialized market which it can exploit in significant ways in the interests of scholarship: the society is justified in producing a book in an edition of two hundred copies if there are two hundred scholars who want just that book.* The society thus need not concern itself that the book not "sell" in the commercial sense. It need not because the technology is now available to publish books in short editions at prices significantly below customary market prices.

In the case of publications that have a potential sale of considerable size, storage is a bothersome problem. In the process of reprinting back issues of bulletins and journals, several societies learned that:

2.9. *It is virtually as cheap to run second printings (by cheap reproduction methods) as it is to run a long first printing (i.e., the unit cost is not significantly greater): this eliminates or greatly reduces the need for storage.* The printings of most publications of the Council on the Society of Religion societies are being determined on the basis of sales projections for eighteen–twenty-four months.

The learning that has gone on by officers and publications committees has been salutary for those scholars who did not know or did not realize how dependent they were on the printer and publisher for the continued vitality of their work. Scholars have learned that they can do some things better for themselves. They have also learned that there are limits to which they are advised to subscribe. The chief limit is this:

2.10. *The learned society is a publisher chiefly of and for itself, including those libraries that collect in its discipline(s) or subject matter area(s).* The learned society cannot market efficiently beyond the circumference of its own membership and subscribers, nor should it try. When it publishes a work that is likely to command a wide sale, the learned society is advised to publish jointly with a university press or commercial house. This may be formulated as a further axiom:

2.11. *Works with a market potential extending beyond the confines of the learned society should be published jointly with a house possessing adequate marketing facilities.* The jointly published work holds great promise for the future. The learned society has learned that the most important commodity it has is knowledge: it must seek some return from the production and dissemination of knowledge, in order to be able to repeat the cycle. However, it cannot perpetuate the mentality that is sinking the university press, namely, that the commercial house has the right to publish winners, while the university press and the learned society are confined to economic losers.

2.12. *The learned society should join in the publication of salable works, the returns from which would be used to further research and the production of still further works.* This admonition applies especially to collaborative works (dictionaries, encyclopedias, editions of primary texts, etc.), text and sourcebooks for student use, the publication of primary texts and data.

In seeking to develop its own publishing program, the learned society has no desire to impair the commercial house and university press further. On the contrary, some success on the part of the association may awaken the industry to new possibilities. Meanwhile, the society can undertake positive measures to assist the conventional house with its publications. Among those measures:

2.13. *The association should undertake to market, through the "bookclub" or comparable device, carefully selected works published elsewhere.*

2.14. *The association should enlist publishers (and librarians) to serve on its publications committee, in the interests of closer liaison and the resolution of common problems.*

3. Scholars Learn about Scholars Publishing

Scholars have been able to learn something about themselves as publishers in the course of learning something about publishing. One of the most surprising things we learned about ourselves is this:

3.1. *Scholars will accept the unconventional, cheaply produced book, provided it is serious scholarship (i.e., provided cheap reproduction does not mean careless content).* The first observation is contained in a second, larger one:

3.2. *Scholars will enthusiastically support their learned association's publishing program, provided that program really serves their needs, and provided the profits go to support further scholarship.* The enthusiasm of members requires testing over a long period of time, of course. Sales are one form of tangible support, and sales in several societies have been remarkable. Another, perhaps more telling, sign of support is the willingness of leading scholars to serve as editors and on editorial boards. Here, again, the associations generally have a long tradition of positive response. The question of royalties and stipends can scarcely be avoided in these new publishing programs, and it is interesting that scholars have devised the means to circumvent or reduce the drain on the association treasury in this regard. These actions and reactions have indicated that:

3.3. *Scholars are willing to contribute editorial services freely and gratis, they are willing to forego or wait upon royalties, provided they are publishing for themselves.* It follows that author and editing costs are generally much lower than in commercial publishing.

Most scholars are nostalgic about the private library once the hallmark of the serious scholar. They have not given up book buying of their own volition; they have been driven from it by outrageous prices designed to recover costs from the first wave of institutional sales. They therefore recognize:

3.4. *The learned society's publishing effort aims to retrieve the scholar's private library from oblivion by disseminating basic information rapidly and cheaply.* Connected with this is the further recognition that:

3.5. *The learned society's publishing program is designed to aid the institutional library in a time of severe economic pinch.*

4. Scholars Learn about Publishing

Just as scholars have learned a great deal about themselves as they ventured into publishing, they have also learned some basic things about publishers. Perhaps "learned" is not the right word; "brought to consciousness" may be more accurate.

It has become clear to many scholars serving on publications committees:

4.1. *Commercial publishers have allowed themselves to be boxed in by conventional publishing methods and by the lure of the mass market.* Unfortunately, everything commercial houses do is geared to the two underlying assumptions. It is no wonder that they have classed themselves out of the scholarly publishing business, but it is a wonder that scholars did not awake to this fact sooner.

It is equally clear that university presses have followed commercial houses in the one assumption but not the other:

4.2. *University presses have assumed that conventional publishing methods alone were open to them, but they have further assumed that "university presses are non-profit institutions that exist largely to publish specialized scholarly works that are not publishable commercially."*[1] It scarcely needs to be said that the two things are not commensurate, except on the further assumption that the university press is highly subsidized. The current economic squeeze reveals how precarious that further assumption is.

It has often been claimed that the editorial processes of the commercial and university press justify their existence. Another thing scholars have become acutely aware of, however, is:

---

1. William C. Becker and John B. Putnam, "The Impending Crisis in University Publishing," *Scholarly Publishing* 3 (1972): 196.

4.3. *Commercial houses and university presses do not necessarily eliminate "bad" books and publish only the "good" books: they have biases of their own, oriented to and bossed by the mass market and the eccentricities of a few editors.* Moreover, they are often dependent on the material judgments of those same scholars, in camera, who would otherwise give their opinions, in public, in the learned society. That is simply to say, the editorial judgments of the learned society are probably better grounded than the comparable process in the conventional house. Where professional editors are required, the learned society can hire freelance editors as readily as the commercial house.

Scholars have not been reticent, in the past, in giving publishers their advice. Much of that advice went unheeded, particularly when it concerned scholarly needs and spiraling prices. Without claiming that scholars earlier were prepared to give sound advice, it can be claimed that scholars have learned a new lesson in this regard.

4.4. *Commercial publishers sit up and listen when they are confronted, not with advice, but with performance.* The limited successes already enjoyed by learned societies as publishers have won them a measure of fresh attention. A new basis for cooperation has been laid.

5. Scholarly Habits and The Means Of Publication

The plight of publishers and publishing in recent years has been the result, in part, of a basic shift in the working habits of scholars. The modification of the scholar's habits has been prompted by new technologies. However, the impact of new technologies on the working habits of scholars has only begun to be felt further and more radical shifts are likely to follow. Fact and speculation are here intertwined in the barest sketch.

The copying machine has freed the scholar from immediate dependence on the physical copy of the book and journal and relieved him of long hours of arduous note-taking. It has made out-of-print materials more accessible and diminished the advantage of living across the yard from Widener Library. It has made possible the immediate exchange of information and opinion, at the very threshold of experiment and hypothesis. It has also thrown the copyright law into confusion.

The copying machine and the copy center have made demand publishing a reality: single copies of books or journals can be produced virtually on demand.

These developments mean that the scholar is less dependent on the local library: he can borrow and copy remotely.

The scholar has trimmed his book and journal budget because he is inundated with print and swamped by price. His professional journals cover much more than his immediate interests, so he depends more and more on indexing and abstracting services (soon to be computerized), while his journals accumulate as files to be consulted or are discontinued. He waits for the review to tell him which books to read thoroughly and hence to buy. The articles of other specialists come to him originally as preprints and later as offprints. He therefore works primarily with indices, abstracts, the review journal, and the preprint. He will buy the cheap publication to scan and throw away or read and add to his library, but the average scholarly book is beyond his financial reach, unless he has some prior indication that it is indispensable to his work.

The advent of micropublishing promises to revolutionize the scholar's life all over again. Although his librarian will have discouraged him, the scholar will be persuaded of the benefits of micropublishing and the microfiche reader through his learned association. Journals in the future will probably be published only in microform; orders for particular articles will be based upon previously published abstracts. Primary sources and collections of data will be made available for pennies on microfiche. Specialized publications of all types will be reduced to microform before mailing (postal rates will see to that). The microfiche reader will come to be as commonplace in the scholar's office as the typewriter now is.

Learned societies are now taking the lead in introducing the microfiche reader to the scholar. The association will market reader and fiche conjointly until scholarly habits have been turned permanently into new channels. Institutional libraries will then be able to follow suit and halt the relentless expansion of library buildings.

Scholars have also modified or are modifying their habits as regards the textbook. (In this connection, please note appendix 1). Fewer texts are being adopted. Teachers are recommending more books, requiring fewer. The paperback has the distinct advantage. The publication roughly the length of the week's assignment has an ever greater advantage. The scholar-teacher yearns for the text and sourcebook that is published as a series of fifty–one hundred page separates, that is, as segments from which he can assemble his own compendium. What he can't get in this form he is increasingly tempted to copy, even for his students.

The active scholar is accustomed to attending the annual meeting of his professional association and "publishing" a scholarly treatise in oral form. For this his university pays travel and often hotel bills. Assuming an annual meeting of 2,500 scholars, and assuming an average travel bill of $100 and an average hotel bill of $100, the cost comes to a staggering half million dollars for the oral publication of three or four hundred papers. Oral publication and the association meeting are doubtless necessary for other reasons. Nevertheless, the learned society should perhaps think of a biennial meeting and the university consider supporting scholarly communication in a variety of forms out of old travel and phone budgets: the saving on the one would permit significant expansion in other, perhaps more efficient means of scholarly communication.

Technologies potentially significant for scholarly communication have not been adequately explored. The learned society and the university must join in seeking more efficient and less costly means of disseminating scholarly information, and these in turn must be correlated with developing scholarly habits.

6. The University Press and The Learned Society

Directors of university presses are speaking frequently of the impending crisis in university publishing. The university press is under threat, if not under siege. The learned society has much to lose by the demise of the university press; a retrenchment in scholarly publishing anywhere is a loss to the profession. At the time the university press is contracting its programs, the learned society is in the process of expanding its publishing services. Considerations advanced above endeavor to account for this paradoxical phenomenon. The further question needs to be asked: is it advisable to join the needs of the learned society to the facilities of the university press?

From the viewpoint of the learned society, it seems fair to say at once that the university press would not serve the learned society well without undergoing considerable modification. Nevertheless, the needs of scholarship and the university prompt us to explore every possibility in times of financial duress.

Assuming that the university press were willing to modify its aims and practices, what would the university press stand to gain from affiliation with a cluster of learned societies, say as little as three or as many as ten? Possible gains may be stated succinctly:

6.1. *The university press would gain one or more self-edited, fully subsidized publishing programs of considerable prestige. Such programs might involve publishing budgets of $100,000 to $250,000 a year.*

6.2. *The publishing programs of the learned societies would serve as a floor under the operations of the university press.*

6.3. *Identifiable, highly specialized markets come with the constituencies of affiliated learned associations, to be cultivated by the university press for all its publishing programs.*

6.4. *A consortium of learned societies in related disciplines or subject matter areas would provide the university press with the basis for specialization, if it chose.*

6.5. *The university press would gain a pool of experienced consultants, editors, authors, who would be willing to work on the same terms as for the learned society.*

6.6. *The university press would have direct access to certain promotional channels: bulletins, journals, annual meetings.*

6.7. *The university press might gain the determination and boldness to rescue scholarly publishing from the doldrums and experiment with new forms of scholarly communication.*

6.8. *The university press would benefit, presumably, from affiliation with a group of prestigious learned societies.*

7. The Learned Society and the University Press

Officers of learned societies are rightly alarmed at burgeoning publication lists and programs. Scholars do not want to be distracted from research any longer than necessary. Consolidation under experienced management appears advisable (the AAA and sister groups have provided a model). Too much success could lead to premature failure. There are thus reasons the learned society should seek affiliation with sister associations and with an organization that could manage part or all of its publishing efforts.

Affiliation with a university press could bring the following benefits to a consortium of learned societies:

7.1. *The learned societies would gain a stable institutional base for publishing programs.* This is especially significant in those cases where the national office of the society "floats."

7.2. *Affiliation with a university press would afford associations the possibility of avoiding the high rent district in New York or Washington.*

7.3. *The learned societies would benefit from technical assistance and experience, assuming that the university press has some professional staff.*

7.4. *The learned society might have access, through the university, to some funds or grants that would not otherwise be available.* The recent grant of the Mellon Foundation to support publishing in the humanities is a case in point (limited to university presses).

7.5. *The learned societies would have access, through the university, to a pool of scholarly consultants and editors on the faculty of the sponsoring institution.* This would not be the case were a group of learned societies to establish a press apart from a university context.

7.6. *The learned societies would have access, indirectly, to the American Association of University Presses.*

7.7. *The learned societies would benefit, presumably, from affiliation with a prestigious university press imprint.*

8. Proposals for Articles of Affiliation

Joining the publishing programs of several professional associations with that of a university press will involve considerable adjustment. Effective merger will require a period of years. Some consolidation, however, could take place at once. Negotiations leading to first steps would involve the following points (no effort has been made to draw up an exhaustive list):

8.1. *The university press would agree to accept established association publication programs intact, with editorial autonomy for editors and editorial boards. This applies to journals, monograph series, and the like.*

8.2. *New publishing programs sponsored by an association would be negotiable, but the presumption would be for acceptance, provided the sponsoring society supplied the risk capital.*

8.3. *The learned societies affiliated with the university press would have a voice in the election of the director of the university press.*

8.4. *The learned societies would have seats on the governing board of the university press.*

8.5. *The use of imprints, whether of the university press or the association, on specific publications would be subject to advance negotiation and agreement.*

8.6. *The publishing program of the university press, aside from association programs, would be subject to the control of the governing board. Insofar as possible, university press publications would be coordinated with those of affiliated associations or adjusted to the needs of the host faculty.*

8.7. *It would be the primary responsibility of the university press to contract for composition and printing.*

8.8. *The university press would be charged with developing an effective marketing program.*

8.9. *The distribution of excess income on particular publishing ventures would vary, in accordance with prior agreements. The income from journals, for example, is the primary support of the learned association. In other cases, the university press might share any surplus with the sponsoring society, after deducting overhead.*

8.10. *The university press would not be expected to risk capital on behalf of the association(s). Conversely, the associations would not be expected to support university press ventures out of society money.*

8.11. *The university would be required to furnish the university press and the associations with a guaranteed overhead rate (with provision for inflation) for those services provided by the university.*

8.12. *Affiliation would be subject to dissolution upon twelve-months notice by either party.*

9. Signs of the Times

A group of learned societies in related humanistic fields are currently undergoing reorganization. There has been some preliminary talk of joining in the creation of a consolidated national office and a joint press. Whether these talks will mature remains to be seen.

The American Council of Learned Societies has expressed interest in the establishment of a scholar's press. The National Endowment for the Humanities has indicated interest in supporting the creation and publication of research instruments and tools in the humanistic field. The Mellon Foundation has taken recognition of the plight of scholarly publishing in the humanities in its recent grant.

The possibility of bringing these movements together and affiliating with a university press seems remote, but it may be the time for high resolve and unprecedented cooperation.

Appendix 1

William C. Becker advances the following reasons for the decline in university press sales:[2]

1. Levelling off or cutback in college and university library acquisition budgets.
2. Cutback in US federal funds to higher education for book acquisition.
3. Changes in the teaching approaches at the college and university level.
4. Scholars are buying fewer copies of clothbound books because they can't afford them; they buy a book for their personal libraries only when it is a "must."

---

2. Becker and Putnam, "Impending Crisis in University Publishing," 202–3.

Bibliography

Becker, William C., and John B. Putnam. "The Impending Crisis in University Publishing." *Scholarly Publishing* 3 (1972): 195–207.

Religious Studies as Witches Brew

Robert W. Funk

1. The question that seems to persist wherever religious studies is promoted or practiced as an academic discipline is this: is religion a proper subject matter for a university department? A correlative question concerns the discipline or congeries of disciplines that is or are apposite to the study of religion. Put differently, does religious studies have a definable professional profile—a cogent methodology or methodologies joined to a circumscribed sphere of investigation?

To many of our colleagues in the university, religious studies has the semblance of a witches' brew: something we have concocted from a little of this and a little of that, an agglomerate rather than a conglomerate, whose bulk consists of lizards and toads, hair and nail pairings, bat wings and warts. The vapors given off by this concoction when heated are thought— by the witches whose products they are—to be laced with potencies and portents. That is, advocates tend to lay claim to virility and the powers of prognostication, where the evidence seems to indicate—to the microbiologist or nuclear engineer—no more than the ignorant fancies of a prescientific mentality.

I do not wish to argue the case in this form or even to restate it more precisely. That is to say, I do not regard extended conversations with physicists whose religious development was arrested at age six, or with chemists who think the university in the Western tradition was organized around 1920, or with anthropologists who think religious studies and Sabbath school to be synonyms, to be particularly enlightening. Charming, perhaps, but not enlightening. I want, rather, to take up with the symptoms as I have encountered them over a long period of time and in a variety of institutions, in an effort to assess whether what religious studies has become, in its posttheological development, has not, in fact, tended to support the impression of a witches' brew rather than the profile of a rigorous discipline. In other words, these reflections are for insiders only, for those who came to this gathering on a broom.

Let me be more literal and hence specific in the symptoms to which I refer.

2. Symptoms of Witches' Brew

2.1. In religious studies our past continues to haunt us. Our departments have developed out of theological schools, out of Bible departments in colleges and universities without seminaries, out of traditional theological curricula. Of course, we need not hide our ancient and distinguished academic tradition. Until quite recently, the theological faculty was the center or the university and the one place at which advanced studies were possible. Theologically trained ministers, priests, and teachers were the cultural and intellectual leaders of most communities. Nevertheless, these reasons for respect no longer obtain. Religious studies is differently placed, and rather more poorly placed, because of its inevitable connection with theological schools and curricula.

This relationship may be less debilitating in Canada, because of its British connections, than it is in the United States. But even where the relationship is not detrimental to the institutional status of departments of religious studies, it continues to influence that curriculum, if for no other reason than that most faculty were trained in theological faculties.

It is unnecessary to describe the theological curriculum which tends to be imitated, weakly, in departments of religious studies. It need only be pointed out that (1) our secular colleagues continue to suspect us, our neutrality, our commitment to scientific investigation, because of our origins and our continued subdued service to professional theological curricula; and (2) those lingering connections and influences have hindered our ability to face our own problem squarely and with a clear vision.

I am less concerned about what our colleagues think of us than I am about what we think of ourselves, although the former certainly presents us with needless handicaps. I can express those best merely by referring to my experience in the American Council of Learned Societies as a representative of the Society of Biblical Literature. I became weary, after a few years, of explaining that, no, we were not an organized group of Bible teachers, but a full-fledged discipline that had contributed much to the study of Semitic languages and culture, to Near Eastern archaeology, to a mastery of the Hellenistic period, which most classicists snub, to the creation of grammars, dictionaries, reference works for the study of western antiquity, and the like. No other representative of any discipline, no matter how new or arcane, was asked so frequently about his or her credentials. I never failed to point out that our founding fathers were Ezra, who lived several centuries before Christ, and Jerome, who hailed from the fourth century after Christ. Our new world branch, I suggested, was more recent, but still much older than most of the associations represented in the ACLS. And I delighted to claim W. F. Albright as an average member.

The drag of the past has been more fateful with respect to our self-conception. We seem not to be able to give up traditional curricular divisions and traditional ways of approaching our subject matter. While our aims have shifted markedly since World War II, we nevertheless are riddled with ambiguities, with ghosts we are unable to exorcise.

2.2. Problems of parentage are connected with problems of subject matter. Aside from the influence of theological curricula, we have tended to proliferate our subject matter until our colleagues think it must cover heaven and earth, which it does. We have set out our wares like a great cafeteria, with unlimited entrees, side dishes, and desserts. We have dabbled in all the religious traditions of the world, and we have followed out the cultural tentacles of religion wherever they lead. Since they lead virtually everywhere, we have touched most of the bases of the other arts and humanities and many of the social sciences. We are not afraid to tackle music, the visual arts, architecture, literature, history, philosophy, and the rest. In brief, we have spread out all over the academic map.

It is understandable that these maneuvers make our colleagues in other disciplines (1) feel threatened, (2) nervous, (3) hostile.

2.3. The proliferation of subject matter is correlative with the difficulty of defining the phenomenon we are investigating and presumably teaching. There are as many definitions of religion as there are teachers of religion. When asked by colleagues to circumscribe our work, we stumble. I shall have suggestions about this problem anon.

2.4. The diffuseness of subject matter corresponds to the profusion of methodologies brought to its study. Scholarship in the biblical field is still primarily philological, although we have archaeology in its several branches, theories and practice of interpretation or hermeneutics, literary criticism, now structuralism, poststructuralism, sociology, anthropology, phenomenology, and countless other -ologies which I do not even comprehend. And this list is limited to biblical studies. Were we to extend it to the other domains of religious studies, we would encompass just about every procedure known to humanists and social scientists.

Colleagues in related disciplines are rightly apprehensive about our ability to master and utilize all the methodologies we pretend to own.

2.5. The symptoms just described contribute to a problem of collegial comity, or the encroachment of one domain on another. Members of the English department believe they study English literary texts with the help of their method, literary criticism. Anthropologists and sociologists believe that they have definable subject matters joined to distinctive methodologies (whether they do or not we need not contest in this context). Historians pretend to be clear about their areas of investigation and the methodology or methodologies appropriate to the production of historical knowledge. Something roughly comparable may be said of professional philosophy and philosophers. Now, in view of this panorama of certainties, religious studies appears to hold an unclear object in view, which it studies with no methodology of its own, but rather with methodologies borrowed, as our colleagues think, from them and their disciplines.

There is much ignorance behind criticisms of this order. But there is also this truth: we in religious studies have not deliberately, or at least not with evident success, come to a working consensus of what we do and how we do it. This tends to leave us vulnerable.

2.6. The preeminent symptom of religious studies as witches' brew concerns our aims. We teach religious studies to our students to what end?

Many of our critics claim that we lack a bread-and-butter aim, like composition, or accounting, or math, or even French. I believe we have a proper response to this criticism, but I do agree that we have not articulated it very well or very consistently.

Allied with this alleged lack is the suspicion that we are, in fact, not neutral with respect to our subject matter, that we do, in practice, advocate Christianity, or Judaism, in hidden and pervasive ways. This suspicion is raised on the part of those who believe we should rob students of any respect for these religious traditions, who think we should proselytize in the name of secularism or scientism or something akin.

The suspicions of secular colleagues are inflamed by other, equally well meaning academics, who think we in religious studies should inculcate religion, at least in some form, and instill values in our students. They urge us to take responsibility for teaching the values they themselves do not want to espouse or advocate. They regard us as surrogate chaplains, all the more effective because of our disguise.

Academic cross currents of this order create a haze under which we are more or less free to introduce a little bit of the witches' potency, trade a smidgen in the portent syndrome, in other words, play the secret role of guru.

It is at this point that we have been less than honest with ourselves, our students, our colleagues, and our larger constituency. I believe we have trafficked in the warm heart of religion too frequently, that we have not come clean about our aims, that we have, as a consequence, failed to demand of ourselves a firm answer to queries about our specific instructional goals.

3. Qualifications

It may be disarming at this point to insert a notice of my qualifications for addressing this topic.

The author is a chronic failure in every attempt to remedy the deficiencies just sketched. I have tried often and failed steadily to reform theological curricula, both in my own institution and in schools under the jurisdiction of others. I have tried with only very limited success to form a religious studies curriculum at a secular institution of my own choosing. I cannot honestly say that I have been able to meet any of these criticisms, or symptoms, to my satisfaction.

On the other hand, I am fundamentally dissatisfied with our current lot. I am brash enough to think we can and should do something about it. I am willing to cheer others on where I myself have dropped the baton.

4. Proposals

4.1. Our lot as an academic department might improve in the world if we were to assume an ostensive definition of our subject matter and let it go at that. We could claim that we study and teach religious traditions. Everyone knows or pretends to know what the Christian tradition is, or what the Jewish tradition is, and by extension, what other religious tradition might conceivably be.

This strategy has the advantage of keeping the definition simple. It has the further advantage of being acceptable to those who object to the word religion, for example, Native Americans: it is apparently unclear to them that their traditions should in any sense be called religious. In any case, Christian tradition, Jewish tradition, et cetera would be acceptable and relatively clear.

It has the further advantage of direct analogies. The English department treats the tradition of English and American letters; the French department studies and transmits the French language and culture. Religious studies would simply study and transmit the religious traditions of the world.

This way of defining our subject matter also permits us to be as complex as we wish and the subject matter dictates. Religious traditions may in fact be the cultural phenomenon par excellence, as many scholars think, embracing as it often does most other manifestations of culture. It is therefore easily possible to pursue the study of religious traditions into cultural artifacts broadly, without dissembling: after all, religion does touch music, the visual and plastic arts, including architecture, letters, and other cultural expressions, particularly those that abut ceremony and liturgy.

4.2. Using an ostensive definition of religion as religious tradition may not solve our problems. It can, and no doubt will, be argued that such a loose definition only intensifies the problem. Be that as it may, I believe we can move beyond the problem of definition by adopting a pragmatic view, like the one suggested.

How is a department to define its own contours?

In response to this question, I would suggest several basic guidelines: 4.2.1. Religious studies ought to provide students with the means to become basically literate in their own religious tradition (presumably Christianity or Judaism; Islam in coming years, perhaps). Other literacies, local in nature, require special resolution. We expect students in this continent to read and write English (or French; or Spanish, or Black!, etc.) tolerably well. We expect other literacies of them, such as math and the physical sciences. Yet we seem not to want to make much of a case for basic literacy in the language of one's own religious tradition. I believe we should be up front and firm on this point (vis-a-vis colleagues who fear literacy).

4.2.2. Literacy in one's own religious tradition seems to me to require at least two points of reference, one of which is the contemporary, current, living manifestation(s) of that tradition, the other is some remote and presumably signal point in the origin or development of that tradition. For

Christianity that might be its formative years in late antiquity, the Middle Ages, the Reformation, or the nineteenth century. With a firm grasp on a remote form of the tradition and an insightful view of one's own position in history, there is an outside chance that the student will be able to function reasonably intelligently in relation to that tradition, either negatively or positively. After all, I want to help the physicist of my acquaintance whose religious maturation was arrested at age six, who speaks Christianity only in the form of nursery talk.

4.2.3. Literacy stools require three legs for functional balance, or, to use a surveying metaphor, locating ourselves wants a triangulation point. Literacy in one's own tradition is likely to be precariously balanced without a steadying leg in an alien tradition. The third guideline, consequently, is a relatively mature grasp of a non-native religious tradition (i.e., for Christians and Jews, an oriental tradition, Native American traditions, or perhaps Islam).

4.2.4. I would further suggest that the orientation of the department be to religious tradition as a language. By that I mean: religious traditions may best be understood in their reach as symbol or value systems dependent upon a common, supporting language that carries those traditions. In other words, what is transmitted is transmitted in words and symbols.

The term tradition may be understood as the process by which opinions, beliefs, customs, are handed down, or it may be understood as the content of what is handed down. The content of tradition, broadly conceived, is any cultural continuity consisting of experience that has passed the test, which in turn provides orientation and norms for present and future common activities. More specifically, a tradition consists of habituated and inherited ways of perceiving, feeling, thinking, doing which characterize a particular people in particular periods or epochs, and these ways are transmitted from generation to generation by a system of signs.

In orienting itself to tradition as language, religious studies should assign itself responsibility for studying and transmitting both the process and the content. A medieval cathedral or a piece of liturgy or altar art may be as significant to the process as the Council of Nicea or the canon of the New Testament.

4.3. More requires to be said about the shape of religious studies than that it is a three-legged stool of one proximate and two remote pillars of tradition. Whether or not the department takes this precise shape, there are further practical considerations that ought to play a fundamental role in curricular and staffing decisions. Permit me to suggest a few, with brief comment.

4.3.1. Canonical Literacy List

Chaos follows in a tradition that loses its canon. One of the problems facing scholars of English letters is that there is no working consensus of what constitutes a minimal canon of high English letters. Without exemplary norms from which to work, it is extremely difficult to convey to students a sense of the tradition. Inability to agree on items that ought to be in every list means that the English curriculum is made up of the whimsies of current members. The message that confusion conveys is not lost on students. We have entered what appears to be the period of the privatization of all norms, which signals, in turn, the tyranny of mass norms: educated judgments, because divided against themselves, give way to untutored tastes.

We in religious studies (and elsewhere in the university) ought to take resolve in this matter. We need to discipline ourselves to forming a canon of primary and secondary works, the mastery of which would constitute basic literacy in a religious tradition. That list should be made up of works that represent the three legs of our stool; and the works in it should be those that can be and are taught by all members of the staff. The list should be put in the hands of students, particularly majors, who would then know what we expect of them by way of minimum achievement.

The criterion of a canon of essential works for a study of Christianity or Judaism would be agonizing to form. It would be difficult even if it were confined to two points of reference: a proximate point in one's own tradition and a selected remote point along the rise and development of that tradition. Nevertheless, it should be attempted.

Compromise would be in order from the outset. Special interests would have to be recognized, of course, but they should not be allowed to obscure the fundamental issue: functional literacy in Christianity or Judaism.

Permit two further parochial and personal comments.

Were one of the legs of the stool of my department the biblical foundations of Christianity and/or Judaism, I would argue immediately that the biblical canon itself is far too large and indiscriminate to be included as a whole on the list. The glossaries and commentaries have become too extended for the elementary comprehension of biblical texts for us to think of covering the bible in its entirety. Careful selection is essential.

Recently I was invited to help select twelve moments in the biblical tradition to serve as the foci of twelve public television shows of one hour duration. Each moment was also to illustrate the usefulness, cogency of the historical-critical method of bible study. There is a challenge to test one's metal, and a helpful one. We should submit ourselves to the test.

I have asked myself, as you no doubt have, what texts, primary and secondary, proved most significant, in retrospect, to my own education. I am drawn, of course, to the Jesus tradition, segments of the Pauline corpus, Second Isaiah, along with portions of the Pentateuch, as you expect of a student of the bible. However, many of the secondary texts that proved decisive to me did not come to my attention until after I had left graduate school. Why was that? I can only reply that my teachers were so centered on their specialties that they failed to inquire whether their trees collectively constituted a forest.

4.3.2. Norms for Literacy Test

Assuming we can agree on a canonical literacy list, the next question is whether we can agree on the norms or instrument for measuring literacy. I do not propose to develop this suggestion, except to say that, if we know what students should read to be literate, we should be able to specify what that literacy entails.

4.3.3. Local Competencies and the Moulding of the Stool

It has been suggested that religious studies should develop a more definitive profile consisting of two three-legged stools (one each for Christianity and Judaism) and a common canon. Are we then to ignore technical competencies so painfully acquired? As Paul would put it, God forbid!

The design of the stool should be guided, in the first instance, by competencies already present in departmental staff. While we cannot slight the student's received religious sensibility, we may certainly allow for considerable diversity in putting down more remote points of reference. These should of course be directly related to the training and skills faculty bring to their work.

4.3.4. The Religious Studies Curriculum and Contiguous Departments

Conceiving the three-legged religious studies stool must take into account not only the present and anticipated resources of the department, it should also relate to and build on the strengths of related departments in the university. I may be permitted one or two examples by way of illustration.

At the University of Montana, we have an outstanding medievalist in the history department and a competent philosopher who specializes in medieval philosophy and letters. These two, together with our own philosopher-theologian of Thomist familiarity, permits us to offer a small but cogent medieval Christian leg to our stool. Needless to say, deans, chairs, curriculum committees have fought us tooth and nail over this shameless breach of departmental curricular decorum.

At Vanderbilt University the classics department kindly furnishes the university with a Hellenist who was, and is, indispensable to New Testament students there.

In general, I am a strong advocate of developing legs, particularly the third, alien leg, only in relation to correlative competencies. For example, we have a Native American specialist in religious studies at Montana, but he is supported by two colleagues in anthropology, one linguist who specializes in Colville (local) languages, and a small program of Native American studies. We *have* not developed Buddhist studies at Montana because Japanese is not taught, and we have only the barest offerings in Japanese history and culture.

Religious studies is naturally interdisciplinary by virtue of its several methodologies. It ought also to be intercompetency. And it could achieve the latter readily by conceiving aspects of its curriculum as the study of periods or movements. If you will permit this further personal reference, one of the most exciting seminars I have ever organized was one on the Bible in the American Tradition: The Chicago School, in which a historian of American institutions and a historian of American letters joined me in investigating the city of Chicago, the formation of the University of Chicago, the Chautauqua movement, and various other aspects of middle America from 1875 to World War I, as they impinged upon and were informed by the Chicago way of interpreting the Bible. Rarely have students and faculty benefited so much from a wholistic approach to a topic.

4.3.5. Religious Studies in Relation to Setting

It goes virtually without saying that religious studies ought to be developed in relation to its setting beyond but proximate to the university community. It makes sense at Montana to give attention to Native American traditions, located as the university is in a state with six Indian reservations and a significant Native American population. On the other hand, it does not make much sense to have a department of black studies: we have one, but we import both faculty and students to populate it, since there is little established black population in Montana. Decisions in this regard call for circumspection and careful, long-range planning.

4.3.6. Religious Studies: Methods of Approach

I cannot quit this topic finally without some comment on our methods of approach to the subject matter, particularly to our own native traditions, Christianity and Judaism.

All too often, it seems to me, we confine ourselves to the more traditional analyses of religious texts and institutions: Bible, church, and synagogue. We tend to slight the insights that would alert students to the proclivities and presentments of their own religious tradition, as they are formed and protected by regnant sensibilities. We do not, for example, often study the current reality sense and ask what that sense admits or excludes on its own authority. During the 70's I found it helpful to include analysis of some of the centerpieces of the drug culture, such as the works of Carlos Castaneda, as a means of interrogating the religious sensibilities seated in front of me. In interpreting the parables, Kafka and Borges are better instructors than I. Robert Jewett and John Lawrence have shown that an American monomyth competes successfully with classical mythologies, partly because the living American mythology is transmitted through films, television, and the cult of so-called comic books.

We need not hesitate to present Hansel and Gretel as a myth of maturation, which stands opposed to Superman and his community, in which people never grow up. The Lone Ranger should be exposed to the Lord of the Rings, and Star Wars makes an interesting foil for Revelation.

Whatever the technique, our way of addressing the subject matter should include an expose of prevalent myths, symbol systems, paradigms of reality. Otherwise, what religion is all about, ln whatever tradition, will remain a chimera, a fancy without bearing on the real.

5. Professional Hostages and Their Ransom

5.0. In suggesting that religious studies bring its own ship about and head her into the wind, I am implying that the profession itself will require some modest amount of redirection. The modification of habits of long standing will require persuasive sanctions.

5.1. We are taught to respond to the tinkling bell initially by being hired for specific tasks and paid for executing them. We are reviewed, retained, promoted, and tenured for the same reason, or ostensibly the same reason. Why can we not turn these powerful sanctions to account for the cause?

What about a job ad that runs like this:

> Wanted: a young scholar willing to learn and teach a basic library of religious texts jointly identified; skilled in the analysis of the current practice of religion on the American scene; proficient in a period or movement of the western tradition; eager to join in a team-taught sequence on that movement or period; ready to correlate research and publishing with pedagogical aims; open to change and growth over the years in the company of others similarly disposed.

I have been vague in the job description at points at which given departments could be more specific. One could, for example, indicate the period or movement desired, or give a list of options, in relation to other facets of the program already in place. And one could be more definite about features of the American religious scene with which the department needed help.

5.2. If one is skeptical of this approach, one has every right to be, since it flies in the face of habits of mind long since entrenched in members of the profession. Moreover, those habits have been institutionalized, for the most part. These obstacles feed one's natural skepticism.

Where is the graduate program in religion that will train young scholars for a program of this order?

What foundation or agency will fund research of the kind probably entailed, without forcing the applicant to camouflage it as something else?

What university review committee, dean, and vice president will honor departmental recommendations for promotion and tenure based on such high cooperation, such sacrifice for the sake of learning?

What of senior colleagues—those of us who came into the department with high hopes but who have been pressed into the ruts dug by predecessors enterprise?

What of our retooling and remaking? Will someone fund that enterprise?

Who will decide on a suitable leave policy supportive of this program?

Assuming that research can be pursued and consummated in this atmosphere, where will it be published? Will scholarly journals open their pages to new questions and issues? Will publishers recognize a market for the product?

And, finally, to what professional association will the new breed belong?

These are the principal questions that arise when we begin to speak of reordering the game. And they represent the forces that tend to keep us all in place. And yet it does not seem to me that any one of them, or several of them, or all of them taken together, is or are insurmountable. It is just that we have not drawn the plan and developed the strategy to get through them, or around them, to our goal.

7 March 1981
corrected, 8 April 1981

Legends of the School of Scribes
or
The Seventy Pens of Power

Robert W. Funk

Book 1

Once upon a time, during the First Age of the world, in a land far away to the east, there dwelt a proud and stiff-necked people, who were short and stocky of build, wore sandals on their hairy feet, and took as many meals a day as they could get. They were especially fond of bagels and lox but didn't care for pork. Their evenings were spent listening to minstrel-comedians who played the violin and smoked expensive cigars.

Their minstrels sang frequently of the great prophets who were believed to have talked with God. One of the old prophets, with whom this story begins, is reported to have taken a dry bath in the sea, stumbled around in the desert, and climbed a high mountain in a thunderstorm. He wrote down ten words in a stone notebook, which wasn't a very bright thing to do, since it later took a large cart and a brace of oxen to haul his records around.

One of the new prophets, who ran a cabinet shop on the side, is said to have taken a wet bath in the river, stumbled around in the desert, and climbed a low mountain on a sunny afternoon. He wrote his ten words in the sand. This practice, too, led to problems for librarians since they now had to maintain sandboxes. And readers became indignant: one could not

A presentation given at the Centennial Banquet of the Society of Biblical Literature, Dallas, Texas, November 8, 1980.

check out a sandbox for close study and it is very difficult to curl up with a sandbox on a rainy afternoon.

The ten words of each of the great prophets were handed around hither and yon, now in this form, now in that, until the twenty words became twenty thousand, and the words were embellished with many vignettes and stories, as minstrels are wont to do. In order to care for this growing collection of tales, a guild of scribes was created, whose responsibility it was to polish the stone notebooks and rake the boxes of sand. The shear strain of this labor led to the discovery of papyrus and wet soot, which came just in time to save what remained of the seashore.

About this time or on the third day, whichever came first, the king of Egypt sent a gift of seventy pens of power to the sacred scribes. These precocious pens were thought to have fallen from the seventh heaven at the beginning of the Age. In any case, seventy scribes wielding the seventy pens of power copied the words of the prophets onto loose sheets of papyrus tied clumsily together at the corner with discarded shoelaces. This was the beginning of the Book.

One covey of scribes copied the words of the old prophet onto sheets, a considerable stack of which was knocked onto the floor of the Scrollery by a passing shepherd. In the confusion that followed, the sheets were jumbled and the thread of the story lost. The foreman of guild came to be known as P, for reasons that emerged only in the Third Age.

The leader of the second bevy of scribes was called Q, which stands for Quadruple. The name refers to the quaint practice of creating four versions of every text.

There were also leaders named R and S. The latter made a beautiful copy of the Book, now referred to simply as S; no one knows what happened to R and the rest of the alphabet.

Book 2

At the hands of P and Q and other members of the guild, the twenty words were further augmented with insertions, additions, comments, glosses, marginal and otherwise, together with an elaborate system of dots. And the First Age drew to a close.

During the Second Age, the sacred scribes devoted themselves to copying the words from one book into another using the pens of power. They took oaths not to alter the text by so much as one dot; of the meaning of the words they knew very little, but of devotion to the letter of the text they were enthralled. In addition to their vineyards, which the scribes attended assiduously, they made cheap copies of the Book and placed them, willy-nilly, in wayside inns as a cure for insomnia in the weary traveler.

Book 3

The Third Age dawned with the invention of movable wooden type and the printing press, developed out of the wine press, and this made the life of the scribes more tolerable: they could now devote themselves with greater resolve to their vineyards and to debates over the dots in the text. The printing press made obsolete the pens of power, or so it was thought. Broken point went unrepaired; ink wells went dry. The pens were put away in storage at Catherine's mountain motel, along with a master copy of the Book made by S and the two denarii of the Good Samaritan. The end of the Third Age drew near.

Book 4

The guild of scribes was invaded, toward the close of the Age, by evil and pernicious influences. These deleterious spirits initially took one of two forms: in one, certain of the scribes began to talk of amending the text; in another, leading scribes undertook to offer their opinions on the meaning of the text. The one movement came to be known as dot criticism; the other paraded under the rubric, Herman tactics, because the tactics were invented by a scribe called Herman.

Dot criticism and Herman tactics were overshadowed for a time by the pretensions of Sir Frank of the Cross. Sir Frank announced the discovery of old, lost sandboxes along the shore of the Sea of death, which contained, in an archaic tongue, copies of the ten words of the old prophet. But Sir Frank refused to exhibit his sandboxes, and man began to doubt that the sandboxes existed, or that they had writing on them. They were even more skeptical of his claim that the best boxes contained writing in a new and profane tongue. According to the best informed opinion, the boxes had long since been raked and such writing as there was lost forever.

The deceptions of Sir Frank paled into insignificance alongside the treachery of J. Merry Robinhood and his band of quiltrthoats. According to Merry, there existed another whole version of the Book written in characters unknown to the fathers and the old scribes. He averred, further, that these scriptures provided a new and different picture of both the new and the old prophets, the authenticity of which the guild of scribes could scarcely question.

J. Merry was supported in this idle boast by Maid Karen of Kingsley, who pretended to find women lurking in every obscure passage, and by Knight Ron of Camerot, whose brother Thomas conspired with him to forge a new thesaurus of the second prophet in a vile southern tongue.

Meanwhile, a new aberration appeared in the far West in the latter days. A band of rebel scribes organized by Robert of Sonoma established a lair among the vineyards and ignited the bead controversy. When these twisted minds were not munching grapes, they were promoting the fabrication that the original ten words of new prophet were lost during the First Age and buried under a mountain of oral debris. What was preserved in the Book, according to them, was mostly invented by Peter, Paul, and Mary, who were also the creators of Q, M, and L. The chorus was provided by Smith of Morton Major, who alleged to have discovered a secret version of the whole sordid affair while searching for his glasses in the Vatican library over a lunch hour. During their conclaves, the outlaws would throw their colored beads on a round table to see whether there were more black or red. The preponderance of black gave the scribe the privilege of tearing one page out of the Book. When the Book dwindled to a few pages, a rump party began to claim the beads were loaded.

Book 5

One day J. Merry Robinhood was crossing a narrow bridge and was accosted there by Friar Dom of the Cross That Spoke. Friar Dom knocked J. Merry off the log with his staff and became preeminent among the vineyard waywards. His story forms the last chapter of this fateful and sad tale.

Friar Dom came from a land filled with snakes and rocks. He learned stealth from the snakes before his patron saint came and drove them into the sea. The rocks taught him to be cunning, since he had to transport them across the water to a broad plain where they formed the cross that spoke. Later the stones became the first hospice for exiled Irish poets. Among his early exploits, Friar Dom climbed high in a castle in Cork and kissed the blarney stone, which left him at a loss for words. The Friar was short of stature and so he also came to be known as Little Dom, although some called him Dom Little.

Little Dom fanned the bead controversy by proposing that the tale of the death of the latter prophet was created, like his vestment, out of whole cloth. Two early scribes, he claimed, copied the work of each other, so that both accounts were equally secondary. And on these stories there developed two kinds of variations. One was occasioned by the performances of the camp jesters, who sang and recited the words but never kept to the text. These were called financial variations, because the sale of tickets to the performances paid the travel expenses of the band.

The other variation was inspired by Herman tactics. In this form, the scribes quoted the received words but meant something entirely different by them. Such was the perversity of these performers.

Little Dom published this nefarious tale using one of the pens of power, lost for many centuries, which he claimed to have found in a Paris gutter.

Friar Dom was known for his quips. "An oral mind," he once said, "is not the same thing as a tin ear," the clever meaning of which is that a mental cavity cannot be filled by listening to a brass band. But the most famous of his aphorisms—he was given to the short, pithy, meaningless phrase—fired the bead controversy even more. "The original words of the second prophet are preserved for us only in financial variations or in summaries of variations. There is not a red bead in the lot."

Later, when it was asked who had said coined that marvelous phrase and whether it had any real significance, a wise but anonymous sage replied, "The answer to both questions in Dom Little."

Part 8
A Letter and Interviews

Letter to Graduate Seminar Students, Graduate Department of Religion, Vanderbilt University

Robert W. Funk

From the long cluttered desk in the far comer, overlooking the dirty ramp of steps. A rainbird chatters away, struggling to bring the pavement to green life. A girl hurries across the lawn, homebound. Three students sprawl on the ground.

Time: weeks past insistent deadlines; too soon for leisure of mind. Esteemed Colleagues!

The approach of summer signals the cessation of semantic scrutiny, the return of cerebral lethargy. The rhythm of the year retrieves the beat of cascading waters. The door of solitude and solicitude for things long covered by winter's white stands open. It is just as well. The drone of didactic dandies easily frays the fragile sprout of spirit.

Your letters came to my jaded hearing with surprising melody. Somewhere there, underneath the jumble of ideographs, often badly ordered, frequently misspelled, I detected an emergent voice. I cannot say that I was overwhelmed with your detailed knowledge of Acts or the letters of Paul of Tarsus, nor was I singularly impressed with care for words. Yet, in a babel of voices still seeking a tongue, I thought I could hear speech struggling to be born. I thought I should communicate my intuition to you, since letters, by nature, elicit response, and it seemed out of the question to write to each of you in turn. Random comments scrawled on margins scarcely substitute for direct address. Then, too, I wondered whether some notice, some intimation, might not prompt you to nurse that voice into greater life during the coming weeks of distraction.

The letter was written in spring 1969.

The sense of speech aborning, mind you, was not universally evoked: some letters and some parts of letters were as lifeless as the moon. Nevertheless, what encountered me ask the predominant contest to win something to say, to win the words in which something could be said.

Let me speak of the ways in which your language was deceptive, to you and to me. Only by so doing can I come to the reason I was able, for the most part, to read signs of life between the lines.

It is clear, I judge, that the fictive letter was a hurdle, for most of you, too high to clear. What I mean can be put simply: there was too often no one listening at the other end. The lack of a presence drove you to converse with yourself, to hold a mock dialogue. Conversation of this order tends to be incestuous: only those supremely disciplined can talk with themselves without falling prey to their own voices. On the other hand, those who wrote letters to real persons were similarly unable to credit the recipient as an auditor. Mothers, cousins, and friends would have been appalled at the opaque jargon! Nonunderstanding and misunderstanding would have reigned!

I asked myself: Does the woodenness of these letters mean that we have forgotten how to hold a conversation! That we have yet to learn to rap?

The bogus letter form was doubtless precipitated by the phony language. Some of you wrote in the language of Paul or the language of Bultmann and so were taken captive by a language not your own. I don't remember a single instance where the word "faith" struck me as authentic. You simply traded in vacuous hieroglyphics. But some of you refused the language of the texts and poke your own tongue. Was I encouraged by that bravado? I am sorry to disappoint you. Most of you who wrote living idiom refused the subject matter! For opposite reasons, consequently, very little of significance erupted into speech.

You may well be wondering, in view of what I have said, what there was in your letters to give me heart.

I was intrigued by the contest itself. The contest which pitted writer against words, writer against subject matter. The vast majority of you knew the language you were using—whether your own or that of the texts—was phony. You also knew—though you were not disposed to say so—that you had not gotten the subject matter into view. What is to be said and the saying, you assumed, had to emerge together. That they did not is something to which your letters gave mute but powerful testimony. Lurking there in the language itself was the struggle!

And there was something even more decisive. Many of you sensed that what Paul was talking about in his letters had something to do with speech itself. Shall we say that Paul's talk of faith, and flesh, and spirit, and sin, impinges upon the authenticity of speech, and thereby upon how we are placed in the world? Can we say that sin, for Paul, is the loss of powerful, liberating discourse? To put it that way may sound odd. Yet consider how Paul strives to effect speech sufficiently powerful to liberate his hearers from the "principalities and powers" and for a life of faith. To confess Jesus as the Christ meant nothing for Paul unless the confession liberates!

One of you wrote: "Why does the watered down bullshit always get the upperhand?" That's an illuminating question. It gets the upperhand because man is prone to forsake his humanity, to sacrifice the impending future for a comforting but prone past, as a means of abrogating his responsibility for the world and himself. Sin is giving oneself to "watered down bullshit." Faith is the freedom to live into the future, to sing and dance new songs.

Many of you, I believe, apprehended as much. For this reason you were also able to see that you had to read between the lines of Paul's speech, to attend to what he was saying rather than merely to the words. If you failed to bring what he was saying to speech afresh, it may only be because that is not an easy task. It may not be ours to accomplish. In any case, you can now also understand why I read, not just your words, but there between the lines the essential contest in which you were and are dimly engaged. To judge speech "according to the flesh" is to take words at face value; to judge speech "according to the spirit" is to attend to what is being said, in and through language, that takes up the past, the tradition, our habituated way of putting things, into a powerful new idiom for the present, into which man may live as a creature free for the future.

Because you were fighting the letter and fighting the words, you gave evidence of knowing all this by way of not knowing it. Lack is the threshold of discovery. We look only for what we miss. May your destitution increase and your quest intensify!

A Conversation with Robert W. Funk
about the Society of Biblical Literature

Selections

Ernest W. Saunders

ES: Well let me get you started by asking about, well really a pivotal year was 1969, right? Is that the year that the new constitution went into effect.

RF: It's the year we adopted it.

ES: You came into office the year before, or two years before.

RF: I was elected at the meeting in 1967, so the first year I was in office was 1968.

ES: Now I know Bob Kraft was on that committee on the revision of the constitution.

RF: Yeah, Bob was the key person.

ES: But I wondered if you could reflect a little bit about what were some of the precursors, to use a favorite term of yours, of this event. In other words, there was a lot that was going on before the committee was appointed for the revision of the constitution. I don't know whether you were a part of that but you certainly inherited the results of them very quickly and that really just precipitated all manner of change beyond that point. But do you remember or can you recall some of the things that were involved there? What do you think led up to so drastic a revision of the constitution? That's been revised many, many times over the years, but this was a major change.

RF: I think probably, Ernie, the original impetus for modifying that constitution was fairly innocent.

The interview took place on March 25, 1979; edited by Andrew D. Scrimgeour.

ES: Ah, so! They didn't even dream of all of this?

RF: No, I think not. I think there was an inclination at first and this antedates me. Just to tinker with the document because some things in it needed adjustment, and I don't even know what those things were anymore. But if I remember correctly, that committee was already formed when I became secretary.

ES: I think that's true. I think I picked up the concern for revising the constitution as early as 1967, as I recall.

RF: That sounds plausible. But I believe there were some other things at work that many of us were not conscious of or not aware of at the time that soon became evident. The external factor was the enormous growth in the membership in the Society and its distribution over the country in a way that had never really been operative before. No, my memories of the SBL when I first joined it in the fifties were that it was essentially an up-East, Ivy League club to which the more aggressive and aspiring of the rest of us in other parts of the country made an annual pilgrimage to hear the greats. And we sort of all took a back seat to that annual show. With that growth and membership and the rise of additional institutions, up-start institutions in other parts of the country, meant that a number of the sections had grown as large as the national society.

ES: When you visited the Southern section, you discovered that it had membership almost as large and attendance almost as large as we had in the parent organization.

RF: Now the Midwest section was always very large too, of course. It was joined there with the American Oriental Society, but even so, as you know, that group had its own life too, and still does, to a certain extent. It's one of the few sections that's not really integrated.

ES: I guess what I am really after is—it seemed to me, you know, in retrospect as I look at that constitution, that involved in it, whether they knew it or not, was almost a reconceptualization of what the Society [could be].

RF: Now while you're asking about that—When we were talking a little bit about the winds that were blowing that made this possible, I had spent some time with Kendrick Grobel, who was my teacher, during the period when he was secretary. And Kendrick was a man with some vision and when he became secretary, he began to function (I remember talking to him about this) as the program chairman for the first time. You know, Charlie Kraft had that job, and I don't think he had anything to do with the program, because it was a separate thing.

ES: Grobel followed Kraft, did he?

RF: Yeah, that's right.

RF: Well we talked about program because I had been involved, along with a number of others, in the formation of some rump groups. You know we organized that New Testament Colloquium which met every year.

ES: I wanted to ask about that.

RF: And Kendrick was anxious to get more leadership into the Council, including [some of] his students. He managed, at one point, to get me elected into the Council, and I remember when I first went there, I was advised by Morton Enslin and others, that junior members of the Council did not take an active role.

It was at one of those early meetings, when I was a junior member of the Council, Bruce Metzger proposed that we dismantle the Research Committee, because it really didn't have anything to do. He had been chairman for a number of years, and they had never done anything. And I remember that I just couldn't resist. And I took to my soapbox and listed about fifteen things I thought the Society ought to be doing and asked why it was that we had not gone after some of the basic projects that we were always complaining about the Germans dominating and suggested that the Society might well take the lead in things like … a lexicon and collections of texts and other research instruments and so on. And that didn't go over very well.

But that was still in the period. That was pretty close to the period I was elected, because I think my last year on the Council, or maybe next to the last year on the Council, was when I was in Germany and that was in '66–'67 (or was it '65–'66; it was '65–'66 I think). Well, and then, I don't know whether I mentioned in that '73 report you read today, but what for me was supposedly the single most important event was Kendrick's last year, and I don't recall what year that was—was it the year of the one hundredth meeting, or was it the following year? He had resigned at Vanderbilt and was going back to Oberlin to get back to music and the place of his first love to teach there until his retirement, and he asked me to stay over after the last meeting and join him for dinner because he wanted to talk to me about Vanderbilt.

As it turned out, he urged his colleagues to consider me to be his successor, which they did. But we talked awhile that evening, and we went up to one of those Chinese restaurants at 125th Street and spent the evening up there. Then after we had talked about Vanderbilt, we talked about the Society, and I guess I was curious enough to want to learn as much as I could, so I really questioned him on a number of things. And a number of the policies which I tried to enunciate later, he really had put into my head. He said one of the things he regretted the most was that the Society was really not open to young scholars. They went out to these institutions in the hinterlands and got lost. Nobody really encouraged them to develop [as] scholars. The attrition rate was really very high, and he thought that the waste was so enormous. He had a funny relationship to his own teaching career. He had been rather badly treated at Vanderbilt, probably for more than one reason. He certainly was a learned man and had a wide range of skills and knowledge; he was a fine musician, for example, he knew a great deal about the history of music and, of course, one of the things that made it difficult for him was that he was so close to the [Neo-Orthodox] theology. But at any rate, his career at Vanderbilt had not been admirable, and he told me that night that he had decided to go back to Oberlin because he had invested so much of his life in graduate students and really had very little to show for it. And he sort-of laid it on me to think about going to Vanderbilt, and he was hopeful they would offer me that chair.

And I felt that charge very strongly; I didn't know at the time that this SBL thing was going to come my way, too. But anyway, we talked a great deal about airing out the Society a little bit, and he gave me some insights into the Program Committee which not many of my colleagues know. At that time the Program Committee received abstracts for whole, entire papers in the event members had not read before, you may remember, and just as the journal is refereed, the papers at the annual meetings were refereed.

ES: Well, all that ———

RF: Oh yeah, when I became secretary, that was still true. But, of course, they didn't get many submissions, and in 1967, there were [only about] thirty-nine items on the [program].

ES: Yes, I remember; it was a very low number.

RF: But he said what was wrong. It was that the senior members, their papers were accepted without review. It was only people on the outside whose papers were scrutinized. And he felt that was not fair because, he said, to be frank with you, there are a number of senior scholars who read every year and who have no right to be on the program. Well, we talked a little bit about domination of the Society by the New England schools. [By contrast] what was happening in the regions is that they were going up to their own inclination.... I guess he worried a little bit about biblical scholarship losing its way, and by that time (let's see by this date, 1965, it must have been 1965). I don't remember when he died, well he may have lived awhile after, come to think of it. He didn't die immediately.

It was already becoming evident that the departments of religion were no longer biblical departments. And the professional base of biblical scholarship was retracting rapidly, and I remember we talked about that issue. So when I came, two or three years later, to this constitution revision business …, I was filled with a lot of those ideas…. So conceptually a lot of that material had been churning in my head….

ES: Was Kendrick Grobel, had he been in conversation with some of your own peers? I think of people like Walter Harrelson, who else would I bring to mind? Oh, Jim Robinson, who were increasingly disturbed also by the monopolistic role of the Society, or was that group which I am referring quite separated from and not in conversation with Grobel.

RF: No, Kendrick was one of the senior advisors to that New Testament Colloquium from the beginning—he and Amos [Wilder], Hans Jonas, I can only think of those three. No, he was active in that and some of these same concerns he was expressing in that group, and he felt it important to be involved in what he took to be a growing restlessness of younger scholars who nevertheless had pretty good credentials and were beginning to stir.

No, I have to tell you the sequel to this. Robinson and [Walter] Harrelson and Walter to be sure—because Walter was my predecessor. I think Walter really intended to step into this, and no sooner had he taken the job than he was elected dean [at Vanderbilt]. It was really by accident that I landed into the job. No, not quite by accident, but it's conceivable had Walter not been elected dean, he would have done the next stint. What happened was that by happenstance, Helmut Koester was made chairman of the Nominating Committee, the year Walter quit or resigned and he and [Kendrick] and Harrelson had talked a bit…. I think Larry Toombs just had it only one year.

ES: Yes, he had only one year, I know. And then his health apparently broke, and he couldn't sustain it.

RF: So, Walter had something of a bad conscience about that and said well if you decide you want to do it, nominate one of my colleagues, and we'll make the transition easier and we'll support it here at Vanderbilt, and I'll be at hand to help you with the transition. But I guess I will remember always as if it were yesterday.

I was at home one evening. I remember standing in the upstairs hallway talking on the phone, when Helen [Grobel] called me. And [Kendrick] and Jim were on the line. Jim was in California. Jim had already moved to California then, and they wanted to have a conference call because we had already started a thing then and that work was beginning to press in on us some. We were having difficulty, and we were all trying to do translations and various things. We had started *Journal for Theology and the Church*, and I had assumed the editorship of that.... What they had agreed was we probably should divide up responsibilities and not all of us try to be engaged in everything. See there was a time when I was going to work with Jim Robinson and really invest a lot of time in learning the [German] language and helping with that project, and they were both committed in spending time on *Journal for Theology and the Church*. What we agreed on on the phone that night was that Jim would assume the primary responsibility for the Nag Hammadi project.... And Helmut volunteered to become the chairman of the New Testament editorial board and assume the primary responsibility for running that, in exchange for which I would have to agree to be the secretary of the Society. So that's how I got into it.

ES: Doesn't sound like a bad arrangement. But I think both you and Ken Clark had certain advisory roles in the development of this constitution even if you didn't work on the committee, itself, at least I got that impression as I read the records so that you had some influence on the shape of it.

RF: I was deeply involved in that but was I not on the committee?

ES: Well maybe you were. I was under the impression that you weren't listed formally on that committee, but I have a distinct recollection that Clark, somewhat to my surprise, had some input on this, and your name certainly was in among that record.

RF: I drafted a part of that, I know, I remember that. Kraft and I divided up responsibilities in drafting sections and worked back and forth. It's conceivable I was not, or I might have been ex officio or something like that.

ES: Yeah, you may have been, of course.

RF: There had been a lot of discussion, I think they had been working on that; my memory or impression is that the committee had already worked on that for a couple of years.

ES: Yes, and apparently, I can understand what you mean by saying they may not have been as conscious of the outset of what they were doing. Because it went through quite a process actually—a presentation to the Society and then referral back or tabled, and a revised form of this was offered and so it was at the Toronto meeting when it was finally adopted but even then within a year there were a couple of articles that were altered to some measure, but what I was after was the constitution certainly represented a new understanding of what the Society was about and how it was to serve its publics.

RF: Yeah, on that there is no doubt.

ES: Now the records don't indicate and you are only left to imagine how much resistance there was from the old guard, especially I think perhaps from Morton Enslin, but were there others who were very unhappy about what they saw to be substantive changes in the structure of the organization?

RF: Yes, there was resistance. We had some very tense moments in Berkeley in '68, and that was on the table, and some of the important articles were being voted on. I can't remember now the names of the people. I'm not sure I can remember them [even] if I had the list of the Council in front of me. There was resistance for many reasons. Virgil Robbins, for example, was very resistant to any modification that took the power of the purse away from the treasurer. Morton Enslin regarded himself above the ebb and flow of this because he felt, as he kept reminding us, that he had been appointed editor for life. He didn't care what the constitution said.

Yeah, but I think what pleased me most about it and what gave me the most courage was the fact that people like Frank Beare and Harry Orlinsky [supported it]. I have always been very close to Morton Enslin, who kept saying these are things that we have to do; for the most part, they are just self-evident things, and they have got to be done and let's move forward. And there were other senior scholars, Herb May. Now, Herb May, he was a pillar of strength in all of this, and poor Herb was given that awful job of having to deal with Morton at the Toronto meeting—gee, I felt sorry for him, and he had also been close to Morton over the years. So in the end I think I have to say, Ernie, that people like Bob and myself, and of course, Bob was regarded as part of the establishment even though he was young. He had been very close to people like Morton; he had was the right hand of Mort. I don't think we'd ever had brought it off if the people I have named or other people like them had not been right in the center of it. Had people like Frank and Harry not been in the chair [as president] in those two succeeding years, we would have never made it....

ES: Now out of that shift in the structure of governance of the Society emerged a new section of programming. I don't at the moment recall whether that was implicit in the constitution or whether it was a development from, an outgrowth of, the constitution, where no longer did you have an assembly of people who had been brought together to listen to a chosen few to give more formal papers, but that there were groups, there were sections, there were seminars. Can you tell me about how that notion of what a program ought to look like and how research and corporate research activities could be built into the study? How did that come about?

RF: Well I think the answer to that is relatively simple. Walter could not really function as the secretary and one of the things I did for him that year was to go to the ACLS meetings and became immediately an active member of the Council of Secretaries, and being as nosey as I am, I just tried to find out as much as I could about other organizations, and then the first year I was secretary, I was really sort of embroiled in ACLS activities, and it isn't hard to pick out societies that are really on the march and the executive officers knew what they were doing. And I just made it my business to find out how they ran their groups, and what succeeded and what didn't. In addition to which we had really developed a rather different kind of program for the New Testament Colloquium, because we felt need for the opportunity to work in seminar style on given topic, on a common topic. So already by 1968, we had the first meeting of the Gospel Seminar in 1968, which was the first meeting I ran. We hadn't finished the revision of the constitution, and when I went to Stendahl and Jack Suggs about this idea of organizing a national seminar to take on a major topic, why, they said, they didn't know why that hadn't been thought up before. It's just so natural.

ES: Just think of a Gospel Seminar, but behind that was the New Testament Colloquium wasn't it?

RF: Well, just the idea of it was, in other words, I had already been experimenting a little bit with this, and what I found was that the old style meeting had become passe in all the better societies. There were doing a whole range of different things,

ES: That's a very helpful insight.... And it's important because it's another demonstration of the need for any professional society to be in interaction with other learned societies.

A Conversation with Robert W. Funk
during his visit to Melbourne

Richard Treloar

RT: Don Cupitt once used the image of the long-legged fly skating across the pond surface to describe the space, the flatter dimensions in which religious thought needs to be conducted in our age. He said: "The pond skater is light, resourceful, fast-moving and well able to survive.... Like the pond skater's world our theology must be perfectly horizontal."[1] I suspect you have some sympathy with that image, and yet you do continue to use language in your writing that is suggestive of the transcendent. You speak of "God's domain" and "that which lies beyond the rim of present sight." In what sense do you think it is still meaningful or credible in the twenty-first century to speak about God and divinity?

RF: I think it's really problematic to be able to speak about God, simply because the term conjures up for most people categories that are no longer really conscionable for serious philosophers and theologians. The God "up there" or the God "out there" is so problematic on the basis of what we now know about the history of the universe. We've had to really rethink all the metaphors we use for transcendence, for mystery, for notions of the world and life, and we can't take literally things that lie beyond what we can see with our eyes and hear with ears and touch with our fingers. Those are the metaphors that I think require considerable subtlety as we try to develop rapprochement with the sciences. What has happened to us is the sciences have nearly put theology out of business through the last four hundred years, and we allowed ourselves to be painted into a corner as theologians which is really unfortunate. But I think in the second half of

---

The interview took place on July 6, 2000.

1. Author's note to Don Cupitt, *The Long-Legged Fly: A Theology of Language and Desire* (London: SCM, 1987).

the twentieth century we began to break out of that box. People like Don Cupitt who you mentioned is, in my judgment, one of the really pioneering spirits that has helped us see the theological problems we have based on the kind of orthodox dogmas that are no longer really friends of ours—friends because they can't be sustained in anything like their traditional form in relation to what we now know of the physical world.

RT: On that question of science and religion, you have said that "the truths of religion are more like the truths of poetry than the truths of empirical science, and yet the truths of religion and the truths of science [and history] are divorced only at great risk."[2] How do you see those kinds of truths holding together in the case of biblical narratives such as the Adam and Eve story which, as you say, have been largely deliteralized by the rise of new cosmologies? How can those different sorts of truths hang together?

RF: I think one of the things we have lost is the myth of Adam and Eve, the myth of origins in that primitive form. Since we can no longer conceive of human life beginning as it is depicted in Gen 1 and 2, we have had to rethink those issues. Darwin has forced us to do that. The age of the earth that we now know about has forced us to do that. From my perspective the one thing that remains that I think is very profound about that story is the doctrine of original sin. Although I don't think human beings are sinful by birth or by disposition, I think the one thing that is clear to us in the modern West is that human beings have this propensity to be able to deceive themselves. There is nothing we cannot sublimate, there is nothing we cannot rationalize, and we do so all the time to our peril. So what has leapt to the top of the scale of virtues in my agenda is absolutely honesty—integrity—if we lose that, I don't think we have anything going for us as a species.

RT: So there is still, in a sense, a scientifically true statement there about the human condition in that narrative?

RF: Yes. We may have to learn to tell other stories to express it, but it's still there.

RT: I really liked the description of "God's domain according to Jesus's" in your theses setting out "The Coming Radical Reformation,"[3] things like

---

2. Robert W. Funk, *Honest to Jesus: Jesus for a New Millennium* (New York: HarperSanFrancisco, 1996), 2.

3. Published by Polebridge Press in the Westar Institute's journal *The Fourth R* 11.4 (July/August 1998): https://tinyurl.com/SBL1128a; see especially theses 12–18.

trust in the order of creation, the essential goodness of neighbor; the celebration of life—there's a real optimism there which sounds to me very much like Good News. I'm wondering if this is what has maintained your love of and interest in Scripture and what does it allow you to hope for personally?

RF: That's the heart of it. I think there is a lot of optimism there, although I don't think Jesus was just naive, although he may well have been a peasant, although that is still in dispute. He certainly had a kind of wisdom that goes together with the great sages of Israel, and I think in that wisdom there was a lot of optimism.

I'm afraid I have never been able to achieve the kind of trust that he had in his fellow human beings. I still have a great deal of difficulty with that, but I have a great deal of difficulty with many of the things that he advocated and apparently practiced. But there's where the hope is: in the challenge to be better human beings, to learn to live together, and to learn to care for the planet that is our home. That, I think, is in the consciousness of all of us who are aware of what is going on in the modern world. If we don't learn to care for the planet then we may put ourselves out of business.

RT: I don't know if you are aware that the Anglican Church in Australia was embroiled in controversy last Easter over the meaning of Jesus's resurrection? In your tenth of those twenty-one theses you say that "Jesus did not rise from the dead, except perhaps in some metaphorical sense. The meaning of the resurrection is that a few of his followers ... finally came to understand what he was all about." Does that mean that early Christianity was a form of Gnosticism after all? Is this a case of "salvation-by-understanding" for those early disciples of Jesus?

RF: Gnostic in that sense, yes, I think that's accurate, although there are other senses in which I think this movement was not gnostic. One of the things we know about Gnosticism, at least about its predominant forms, is that it depreciated the physical world. I don't think that is present in Jesus of Nazareth, and I think in any tradition that I want to be affiliated with the depreciation of the physical universe is not a part of that.

RT: —the dualism that goes with that?

RF: Yes, I think that's right; I don't think we want to fall back into that. Although I realize in saying that, that there are other religious traditions in which dualism is a fundamental proposition, and I have to respect the rights of other people who look at the world differently than I do. But I think the future lies with those of us who affirm the world, even with its chaos and its evil and its disasters. I like to be optimistic at least. I think it's hard to laugh if you are an apocalypticist: that the world has got so bad that it needs to be destroyed. I think laughter is the thing we have to cultivate and nurture so that we don't lose our sense of proportion.

RT: Are there other forms of apocalypticism, do you think, such as outlined by your colleague John Dominic Crossan, which might be more consistent with the historical Jesus? Apocalypticism as justice, as an over-turning of the status quo—is that a different sort of apocalypticism that the churches can still subscribe to, in your view?

RF: Yes, I think so. But again, you know, the problem I have is the same problem I have with the word *God*. When I say the word God imme-diately people who hear me say that associate a certain set of things with that term. I think that's also true with the use of the word *apocalyptic* or *eschatological*. What comes to mind for most people is not exactly what we mean by that, and what Dom Crossan has tried to do is to redefine the term. I don't know whether we can salvage it or not, but I believe that Jesus did have a kind of eschatology, but it wasn't a literal eschatology. And I would agree, if we don't learn to behave as human beings we will destroy ourselves. So there is an apocalyptic element in that.

RT: Ethics is clearly on important theological index for you, as you've just suggested, indeed you reject some traditional atonement theories on the basis that they are "subethical." And yet the Bible, you say, including presumably authentic admonitions of Jesus, won't provide us with a blue-print for living as such.[4] Where should we, as Christians and as human beings, look for ethical guidance and formation, if not to the mind and character of the historical Jesus, insofar as we can know it?

RF: It's really to look at the historical Jesus for hints. I now like to think of the body of the Christian lore as a compendium of wisdom, of crucial insights. They are discrete insights but they are related to each other, and they have to be transposed and translated from one culture into another because they are culture-bound. That's the reason I think we just can't take over-literally everything that Jesus said and did, because the world he inhabited and the self he was would be different if he were alive today, living let's say in the culture here in Melbourne, or in some other part of the world. He would have been a different person and probably would have been a different sage. He might have been more like Gandhi or like Martin Luther King or like somebody else—maybe Nelson Mandela—to think of people who have been, in my judgment, sort of Christ-like in their

---

4. See Funk, "Coming Radical Reformation," thesis 20.

being in the modern world. But certainly very different than I imagine Jesus of Nazareth to have been in his time and place.

RT: You mentioned the problem of evil before. Some theologies, most notably perhaps "process theology," have attempted to qualify the power of God in order to affirm the goodness of God and of the created order.[5] You seem to do something similar in rejecting the idea of God as a being who exists and acts outside of nature meting out special providence. The implications of this for prayer are clearly enormous. Is there still a place, do you think, in such a theological vision for intercessory prayer? And what are we to make of Jesus's own prayer and worship?

RF: Let's begin with the Jesus part of that question. The worldview that he had, that he adopted, was clearly a different one than we have, and so his prayer life was undoubtedly different from what we know of any prayer life for ourselves. Although I suspect there are certain points at which the two really do touch.

I like the way Bishop Spong talks about his prayer life as something that happens to him when he's in contact with other people in the world, that the way of relating to other people is a form of prayer. I like that idea, and I think that is probably also true of Jesus.

One of our colleagues in the seminar, a Methodist pastor by the name of Hal Tosick, has developed this notion that Jesus always prayed in fragments and he always prayed in relation to concrete situations, although he is represented as going off by himself and meditating. Nevertheless, Rev'd Tosick has argued that the substantial prayer-life of Jesus was probably an open and public one where he blessed people or he allowed them to minister to him, and to do so in a kind of prayerful relationship.

For my part I think I've learned a little bit from the Eastern traditions and now prefer to think of prayer more as listening, more as meditation. I think the notion that prayer is talking perhaps goes together with anthropocentric notion we have of the world: that God ought to listen to us because we are important. I would prefer really to reverse that and say that what we need to learn to do is listen—listen to others, listen to the world about us, listen to the unseen.

And what I'm going to say in these lectures here[6] basically is that we need to cultivate what I call the "glimpse." I think those little snatches of

---

5. See Funk, "Coming Radical Reformation," theses 4 and 5.

6. July 7–9, 2000, at St Michael's Church, Collins Street, Melbourne: "The End of the Christian Era?," "The Challenge of Jesus," and "A Faith for the Future."

transcendence that we occasionally are given as gifts are the only things we really have to build on—those occasional insights provided us by others and by our relation to the physical world, to learn to cultivate those and to put them together in the whole story seems to me to be where the future lies. And that, I think, is what prayer is all about.

RT: You have been described in publicity material for that series of lectures as bringing "a critical and pragmatic approach to Christianity." Your founding membership of the Jesus Seminar as a body of scholars who meet regularly to discuss and vote on issues related to the authenticity of Jesus's words and deeds seems to bear out the "pragmatic" tag and the corporate dialogical method of the seminar has been seen as one of its greatest achievements. How does that sort of "truth-by-democratic-consensus" approach to scholarship (if I might call it that) avoid generating its own constraining orthodoxy—the very sort of "political correctness" that you say so often seduces scholars away from their true task of candor and honesty?[7]

RF: It's no different in principle, I suppose, than the councils of the church over the centuries have been. The difference is that we don't have any authority. We are not an institution. We don't own an institution. We have no interest in declaring anybody a heretic who doesn't agree. Indeed the seminar is made up of people who disagree with each other.

What is unique about the group is that we have agreed to emphasize what we have in common rather than what distinguishes us from each other—to major in ecumenism in a broad sense, not just an ecumenism that crosses the denominations but one that embraces other religious traditions as well. And to keep a steady focus on the consensus seems to me to be absolutely essential if our religious traditions are to survive in the increasingly secular world.

I think scholars are doing themselves a great disservice by continuing this kind of mindless criticism of each other in public. Scholarly debate is one thing; but the sort of ad hominem to which we have been subjected often in the seminar I think is unbecoming of academics, to say nothing of Christianity. I'm a little bit embarrassed, by the way, for the kind of acrimony that's now abroad in the land here about the election of Peter Carnley. It seems to me to be—well, to put it kindly—not really appropriate!

RT: The world loses some patience, doesn't it?

---

7. See Funk, *Honest to Jesus*, 10.

RF: It really does, and it makes people inside the church look as though they don't really know what they are doing, and don't understand their own tradition. I just think that's unfortunate. I believe we can do better if we put our minds to it; if everybody recognizes that we are going through, or passing over, this critical cultural watershed—probably the greatest one now that has taken place in the history of the West.

I think we are in a new age that is going to be unlike anything that has happened in the West, at least, in the last four or five thousand years. I don't know what globalism is going to bring, but we can already begin to see that instant communication and mobility, and the advance of the sciences and all that sort of thing is going to transform our lives.

If we insist on hanging on to those social and psychological securities that were in place in the old tradition I think we are going to lose out in the long run. In that case I think Christianity is going to become increasingly isolated in its various denominational forms and will become ghettoized eventually—pretty much like Orthodox Judaism has, and the same thing is happening to the Muslim tradition, which is going to have to come out of its shell if it wants to be part of the modern world. We are all pretty much in the same boat in that regard. So I'm urging a certain maturity in the way we look at things rather than to be so protective of our fiefdoms.

RT: You've spoken a little bit about Jesus as a sage, and I think that very few in the churches would take issue with your claim in *Honest to Jesus* that "Jesus is one of the great sages of history whose insights should be taken seriously" along with those of other seers, both ancient and modern.[8] I'm wondering if that's all that we can say about him at the end of the day, what difference do you think the "Five Gospels" project of the seminar makes?

By way of example, why is it any more important to know with a degree of accuracy what the human being Jesus said than the human being Socrates? Why not simply allow the tradition that has built up around him to bear his wisdom to us—the wisdom you have spoken of—as we do the works of Plato in Socrates's case? Do you think that the work of the seminar would be more urgent if its claims about Jesus were greater, somehow, than that?

RF: I think what's dying in our tradition in the modern world are the traditional orthodox claims about Jesus. I guess my own apprehen-

---

8. Funk, *Honest to Jesus*, 302–3.

sion about this is that those orthodox claims expressed, for example, in the creeds—the Nicene Creed and the Apostles' Creed—will take Christianity with it. I think there is a richness in this tradition that's worth salvaging, that's worth recovering.

I think Jesus of Nazareth was a visionary for his times. I think that he was trying to produce a movement that was transethnic, certainly transtribal. I think a mission to the gentiles was implicit in what he was doing from the very beginning, even though he himself may not have gone to the gentiles. Paul of Tarsus saw that right away.

I think insights of that sort, his regard for human beings, his way of using things out of nature as his paradigms—of trust for example: the birds and the flowers of the field and that sort of thing—is a very worthwhile tradition. It reunites us with other primitive forms of religion that reconnect us with the natural world in a way in which modern, sophisticated, philosophical traditions do not. Orthodox Christianity really does not have much to say about our relation even to each other; certainly nothing to say about our relations with the natural world, the world of nature.

RT: Do you think the resurgence of Trinitarian theology will help Christianity to recover some of that sense of the essential relatedness of existence?

RF: I'm not sure I know what that means—the resurgence of Trinitarian Christianity. Perhaps that's its aim? If so, I'd be all in favor of it. But again, that doctrine carries such metaphysical overtones that I think it's very difficult to use it now in a meaningful way. I'm afraid if we just throw the baby out with the bathwater as we proceed in the third millennium, if Christianity remains tied to those outmoded ways of thinking we may lose the insights of Jesus of Nazareth. And, I think, ultimately the great prophets of Israel.

RT: So the concern for accuracy, then, is driven by that concern to recover the richness?

RF: That's right; to recover the richness, to preserve the heart of the tradition, to go back and rediscover the roots, to try to reinvent the tradition in a new form. And by a new form I mean a new mythology, a new set of metaphors that will be suitable to carry it forward into the next millennium. That's a big task. I'm certainly not going to contribute much to it! I think it's too soon in the process to know what direction it will take. But it's a worthy enterprise.

RT: You mentioned the creed a moment ago, and in a more recent work, *Honest to Jesus*, you say that "The creed left a blank where Jesus should have come."[9] What other sorts of statements about Jesus's life would you like to see in the creed, or is the credal form itself just too problematic anyway?

RF: Well the creed is really a story, so I don't think the story form is problematic, but this is the way I would put it: what we should have done in Christianity is to retell the story with differences—if we had kept it plastic, fluid, across the centuries it would have been a much better instrument, and we wouldn't be being forced to abandon it.

You see the Greeks learned this in a very interesting way. They had a contest every year in Athens to tell the old stories but to tell them in new ways, so a story without a fixed canon is what we need—a functional story without a fixed text. Now we have some living myths that function in that way. The one that fascinates me is the Arthur myth, which is not unlike the Christ myth. There are a couple of things about the Arthur cycle that I think are worthwhile. One is we can tell the story over and over again so long as we don't just repeat it in the same form. It's adapted to new and different circumstances or conditions that makes it appeal in the same way.

RT: Like midrash?

RF: Yes, like midrash. And the second thing is that the hero is flawed; that always makes for a great story, to have a hero who has to go out into the desert, by the way, and be subject to all the temptations—it's right there in the gospels, but we choose to ignore that. I mean, here is a Jesus who turns down the options that Mark then turns around and has him adopt as a miracle worker and so on. You see the body of the gospel really contradicts the temptation story at the head of the gospel. But we've tended to ignore that.

What we need are stories about Jesus that have something of a flawed figure in the sense that he has his problems too—there in the garden by the way is another nice part, you see, which does represent him rather differently, but we lose all that in the creed. We lose it because he has been so exalted. And then in the Byzantine churches he is no longer represented in the wall panels; we only paint him on the ceiling. He becomes the cosmic Christ. In other words, he has become so remote, so irrelevant, we keep him entirely out of the way. We don't want for him to get in the way of what functions in the world down here below. I think what we did in the end was killed him by "kicking him upstairs," so to speak.

RT: Does that make the gospel stories into "tragedy," in the literary sense?

---

9. Funk, *Honest to Jesus*, 303.

RF: If we took the accounts that we have that are self-contradictory, and took them as stories, you see, they would function much better. What we did was subtract way from them and took only the frame: the miraculous birth and the crucifixion and the resurrection and the ascension, and embodied those in the creed. And then in the Nicene Creed we even got away from that and made it even more abstract yet. So we kept abstracting away from the concrete narrative which was okay in the metaphysical context; it worked alright. But then we took it too seriously, and now we are stuck with it.

RT: What Derrida would call "white mythology," where you actually forget what genre it is in which you're speaking.

RF: Yes.

RT: According to British scholar N. T. Wright, we're currently in the "Third Quest" for the historical Jesus—one which seeks to understand Jesus within his Jewish environment. Do you see that as one of the greatest contributions to the study of Christian origins that the Jesus Seminar makes, especially in our post-Holocaust context, and, if so, what might be some of the implications or learning from this insight for the churches?

RF: You have touched on a very difficult theme. Tom Wright has a set notion of what the Jewishness of Jesus means. Tom Wright seems to know a lot more about Judaism in that period than I think most of us do. He thinks everybody in that period was an apocalypticist in some form or another, and I just don't agree.

Judaism is a very diverse set of convictions and ways of living, both in Palestine in the south and in Galilee as well as in the diaspora. You can look at the list of Jewish writings that have been preserved from let's say three hundred years either side of Jesus of Nazareth—it's an incredibly rich and diverse tradition. Where Jesus fits in that pattern is very difficult to say. I think in some respects he is something of a misfit I think he doesn't really belong to any of the major traditions, but the ones he is closest to are traditions like the Second Isaiah, for example, or the wisdom tradition that was living in his day and time. Tradition of Ben Sirach would be an example of somebody I think he was relatively close to. That's one side of the issue.

The other side, of course, is that the rediscovery of the Jewishness of Jesus—if one can speak in that odd way, I mean, how we ever lost that notion is beyond me—is an essential thing in our post-Holocaust period. I mean, we have to put an end to the acrimony between these two traditions. It is just unbelievable that Christians have kept it alive. Reconciliation with our Jewish brothers, I think, is an essential. If we are not able to do that, we don't deserve to belong to this tradition at all.

I really, for the most part, find very little difference between my own religious convictions and those of Reformed Jews. Jewish scholars that I know, those involved in the quest, and I wish we had more of them, by the way (we do have two or three Jewish scholars in the seminar)—that's been a really wholesome experience for most of us to engage jointly in trying to recover something of this figure. I think that's been one of the most satisfying aspects of my connection with the seminar over the years.

To go back to Tom Wright, I think the Third Quest and the way in which he has become an advocate of it, I think is really a new form of apologetics. He really wants to salvage orthodoxy but to do so in a kind of reformed platform where he understands a number of these things metaphorically—for example, he thinks the eschatology of Jesus can be deliteralized and he thinks that's what Jesus intended it to be. I find that strange, to argue, on the one hand, that he was an apocalypticist, and, on the other hand, that he could understand it only symbolically.

So I really think that the divide between those who are involved in the Third Quest and what I call the "Renewed Quest" is the difference between apologetics and the genuine historical inquiry that is a "no holds barred" proposition. But I am sure he would disagree with that!

RT: Your final thesis of those twenty-one theses concerns the language of faith, and, to me, this goes to the very heart of your critique of Christian orthodoxy. It seems to me there is a proper caution, a sort of theological modesty to which I believe our postmodern context recalls the churches in their God-talk.

Being an Anglican for whom worship is the primary language of theology (*lex orandi, lex credendi,* and so on) how do those sorts of insights impact upon what I might be able to "say" to and about God in worship? Is it reasonable to expect that worship might be anything more than "strong poetry" (that phrase you use used to indicate that which gives us "a glimpse of what lies beyond the rim of the present sight")?[10]

RF: The liturgy originally was nothing more than strong poetry. We've turned it into metaphysics, we've given it ontological status, which is the reason it has died. Those philosophical canons are just no longer viable if we understand those terms literally. And what people like Marcus Borg

---

10. Funk, "Coming Radical Reformation," thesis 19.

have done, and when I talk with Mark about this he says "Well, I can't recite the creed anymore and take it seriously, but I can sing it." I think that's his way of saying "I want you to understand I am not making any philosophical affirmations when I sing the Creed."

But then the question arises not just for Mark but for a person like Don Cupitt. You see he can continue to participate in the liturgy as an Anglican priest, but he says "I just understand it altogether differently." I don't think that's going to work very much longer.

What I see happening is that more and more people are abandoning the church because they can't swallow the language, even metaphorically, in the liturgy. If the church wants to continue to function as a worshipping community I think it's got to invent new language. That's going to be very difficult to do but I think it's absolutely essential. I have no idea what that language should be, or has to be, but I don't think it can be the traditional language.

RT: Does that instinct come from the conviction in your earlier work that language, in a sense, creates the world—that language partly creates reality for us and therefore It needs to be apposite to the reality we inhabit?

RF: Yes, if you will permit me to recall that it is a cycle. It not only creates the world; it maintains the world and then it destroys the world as it becomes crystallized and dies. So language is a cycle, and if it is a living language tradition, that's one thing, and the language of the liturgy was a living tradition until four hundred years ago, but no longer. And we've gone on repeating it which means that more and more it's losing its vibrancy, its vitality. It's comforting for people.

One of the things that amazed me during the six-week tour that (my partner) Char and I had in England just a couple of months ago was how many atheists love to go to church! Just to be in one of those medieval cathedrals and participate in the traditional liturgy, it's somehow comforting, even though they don't believe a word of it. Those things will hang around for a long time, but they will eventually die, and they are dying.

RT: Can the buildings themselves, can the arts and architecture give us that "glimpse" as well, of what lies beyond?

RF: They can. Unfortunately, as Winston Churchill once said, we mold our buildings and then our buildings mold us forever after (or something like that).

RT: There's a series "In the Mind of the Architect" on the public broadcasting network here at the moment which has used that very phrase.

RF: That's a wonderful insight, and I think, although those cathedrals are going to stand for another thousand years in all probability, what I see happening in England is they are being turned into museums and art centers because they aren't being used anymore for the function for which they were originally intended. And if the church in England does become disestablished, more and more of those cathedrals will be used for other purposes.

I was in Edinburgh recently where one of the cathedrals has become really a center for the arts. Well, that's a good function for it, but all of that is to say that those buildings work together with the theology they reflected and as beautiful and impressive as they are, they can no longer function for most of us the way they once did. I say that with a good deal of regret. I'm not happy that we are all having to suffer through these enormous changes, but there is something exhilarating about it at the same time, and that's the reason I'm not willing to become a pessimist.

RT: On that slightly more personal level, in a foreword to your early work *Language, Hermeneutic, and the Word of God*,[11] you make a couple of very interesting comments. In fact you begin that foreword with a warning: "He who lays a violent hand on his tradition must beware of failing statuary."[12] Looking back over some forty years of public scholarship, would you see yourself as having laid such a hand on your tradition, and has there been any falling statuary?

RF: Do you want me to show you the scars?! Sure. It's a perilous business, and it takes I think a considerable amount of courage, but it has to be linked with foolhardiness. I think those of us who have engaged in this, people like Cupitt, for example, Rudolf Bultmann who was my mentor (I learned to distrust some things in the tradition from him, although he died an absolutely orthodox Lutheran), going back to David Friedrich Strauss in the nineteenth century, and then to my friend down in New Zealand, Lloyd Geering, who suffered a good deal of this in recent days.

All of these people are very courageous. Jack Spong is another example, and, by the way, I gave the Easter sermon at Christ Church in Edinburgh after Evensong—they didn't make it a part of the service; I think they were a little bit hesitant! They offered to, and I suggested maybe I would do it

---

11. Robert W. Funk, *Language, Hermeneutic, and the Word of God: The Problem of Language in the New Testament and Contemporary Theology* (New York: Harper & Row, 1966).

12. Funk, *Language, Hermeneutic, and the Word of God*, xi.

after Evensong. But Bishop Holloway was there and we had a wonderful conversation following that. He's another one, you see, who has risked an awful lot to face the issues.

So I'm heartened by all this, although I recognize that those of us who have engaged in it can't be regarded as heroes. In a certain sense we are high risk-takers, we are a little foolhardy, we think there's too much at stake—

RT: —fools for Christ perhaps?

RF: Yes, something like that. I like that expression of Paul, actually; yes, I think that's a pretty good one. But I think that's true of any great tradition that's undergoing monumental changes—there always have to be people who are willing to take the risk. That was true of the great Greek tradition. I think of Socrates pretty much in the same category as I do Jesus of Nazareth, as somebody who challenged the old traditions, somebody who was willing to die for it—

RT: —who'd pursue a question, and wouldn't let the question go?

RF: And then when the time came and he was convicted of corrupting the youth of Athens and was given the opportunity to escape on the part of his friends, he said, "No. I'm not willing to break the laws of the state. If I've been condemned to death, I am ready to die." Now that's integrity!

RT: On that issue, you decry the "brokerage system" by which the church has dispensed rites of passage from outsider to insider, sinner to righteous as being inherently self-interested.[13] I wonder (1) where the Eucharist fits into that brokerage system, and (2) notwithstanding the objective of the Westar Institute and the Jesus Seminar to engage in public theology, is there still a danger that academic theologians today similarly act as brokers of "right understanding" which, in much the same way, becomes a sort of rite of passage into spiritual maturity?

RF: Well of course, brokerage is necessary. And that's because human societies, like colonies of ants and bees, organize themselves. So there will be brokers always in any social system. The only question is whether in a society like ours that is more egalitarian than it has ever been in human history—and that really came with the rise of the middle class, as we all know, sociologically speaking—we need to reduce the brokerage element to a considerable extent by depriving it of its temptation to be self-perpet-uating, and depriving it of the power to impose social control. You see, in effect, that's what it was in the Middle Ages—a form of social control.

---

13. Funk, "Coming Radical Reformation," theses 15 and 16.

I was listening the other night on television to a biography of Thomas Jefferson and was reminded, almost to my amazement, that when Jefferson was growing up in the age of the Enlightenment in the middle seventeen-hundreds heresy was still a state crime and you could be punished or even executed for being a heretic. It has been that recent that that sort of thing was possible. In most Western societies that's no longer possible, to be executed for just being a heretic, or punished. It's still possible, I suppose, in Muslim societies—at least in those that are closed—but that's really now, isn't it, a thing of the past.

But the brokerage systems, you see, are still in place. I am just appalled that the Southern Baptists think they can continue to suppress women in the name of the patriarchal system that's there in the Bible, that women shouldn't be entitled to serve as pastors or shouldn't have any function in the churches. That will ghettoize the Southern Baptist Convention sooner than anything—in fact it is already splitting that denomination; it's going to be two or three denominations before very long.

So those of us that mediate this kind of knowledge to the public must take care always to represent our opinions as being tentative, in the process of revision. We do Jesus Seminar "on the road" programs; now we are doing them all over the world. One of the rules we have is that we never send only one scholar at a time. We always send at least two so they can disagree with each other and do so publicly. We do that not just because we like to be contentious, but because we want to make it clear that all of our conclusions are provisional.

RT: So that's part of the limitation of the work of reconstruction, that it's never absolute, never finished?

RF: That's right. Somebody is going to come along and do it better than we have done it, we know that. History has taught us that, if it hasn't taught us anything else, and we should just reckon with that possibility. I know we've made mistakes, I just don't happen to know where we made them. If I did we'd go back and correct them now. But somebody else will see where we've made them down the road a ways and will fix them, I hope. If we can get that kind of tradition going it will I think reduce the brokerage aspect of the tradition.

RT: As an inherently self-perpetuating ritual, I wonder if the Eucharist is somehow caught up at the center of that?

RF: That really I think is the heart of what I would like to see happen, and here I am absolutely one with my colleague Dom Crossan. I would perhaps go even further—I think all we need to do is take the altar out of the chancel, remodel it as a round table and move it into the center of the sanctuary and have people sit around it so it is a place where we come together and bond as a community of faith, rather than a place where we are absolved from our guilt by the blood of Christ. Sharing the bread and the wine is a very basic symbol, a ritual that all societies and cultures know. I think it is very much worth preserving in that form.

RT: A sort of covenant of salt?

RF: Exactly. We have to think up new rituals for that. But I was in Brisbane a couple of years ago and I went to, I think, the only Catholic church I have been invited to speak in. And, lo and behold, they had taken the altar out of the chancel and moved it into the center of the sanctuary and put the chairs around it—in a Catholic church! I asked them how they got away with it. He said, "Well, the bishop has written this parish off! He doesn't care what they do over there."

RT: Part of being prepared to be an outsider, I guess?

RF: I guess. The priest who had cooked this all up and who was in charge was away when I was there. I don't know whether he was away by design, but it was a very interesting experience. Anyway, I'm all in favor of remodeling the Eucharist, and the idea of the round table is borrowed from the Arthur legend and the notion that it is an egalitarian table—and that again reduces the brokerage element.

I am also an advocate of taking the cross down off of the steeple and off of the altar and painting it on the floor or inscribing it on the floor where the priest or the preacher stands and understanding it as a symbol of absolute integrity. When you stand on the cross you cannot tell a lie, you cannot dissemble, or you should not dissemble.

RT: Is that the primary symbol the cross is for you—a symbol of integrity?

RF: Yes—well, again, I don't want to claim that as the exclusive meaning of the cross but it is one way. My Jewish friends and colleagues tell me that they wonder whether it is ever going to be possible for Jews to be comfortable with that symbol. I'm quite prepared to give it up if that's the case. I don't think we can afford to keep a symbol that divides us. If it is salvageable, I think it is salvageable only if we put it in a new form: we create it with a new form and a new function so that it doesn't carry any of the old connotations of Christ-killers and so on.

We have one member of the seminar who has been with us from the beginning who is a Jewish rabbi who tells stories about his youth in Brooklyn and what the cross came to mean to him: that he was stoned on his way home from school. He said, "I just doesn't know whether I can manage to be comfortable in a church that has a cross as the basic symbol."

RT: You have to respect that sort of experience.

RF: In my lifetime that sort of thing still happens, apparently. I have Jewish friends too who are secular as all get-out. We had a Jewish colleague on our staff for a while who I guess you would have to say was pretty secular. He was really not connected with the synagogue in any important way until his son came along and got old enough, and then he had to decide whether he wanted to be a Jew or not. But it was a problem for him. He was a very sophisticated guy, a lawyer by trade, and believed in what we were doing and was a great supporter. But that's the reason symbols are powerful: they function even when we don't want them to function.

RT: And in ways we can't control?

RF: Yes.

RT: In *Honest to Jesus*, again in a prologue, you describe authentic Christian life in its seeking of the kingdom of God in terms of exile and exodus—a sort of journeying without arriving—and in that prologue you speak very candidly about your own intellectual and spiritual trek that has brought you to this point. At one stage you write there "I began ... with a string of beliefs and very little faith."[14] I wonder if you could just say a little bit about what you see as the essential difference, and what has been most significant in moving you from one to the other?

RF: I wish I knew what moves me to do that. What I came to see is that it's the quest itself, the journey itself, that is the saving feature of this tradition or of any great religious tradition. And that's what I think we have in common with the sciences, if I may just digress: it's the willingness to give up our old propositions and try out new ones and that I think is the faith that's involved in the exodus or in the exile. It's interesting to me that people like Jack Spong have picked that up. He describes himself as a Christian in exile, even though he's a bishop in the church. And that's the appropriate metaphor, to regard yourself as an outsider or an outcast.

RT: It's a different metaphor from a pilgrimage, isn't it?

RF: It is, because I suppose what you mean by pilgrimage is one is going to a holy site?

RT: It's goal-oriented.

---

14. Funk, *Honest to Jesus*, 3.

RF: It's goal-oriented, yes, it is different to a pilgrimage. It's the willingness to be left out, to leave home; and that's the reason I think the parable of the Prodigal [Son] is one of the most powerful stories Jesus told. The way I would sum that up is that in order to come home you have to leave home.

RT: Because you do also use the language of odyssey, which suggests that sort of desire somehow to return, but to return as someone different.

RF: By the way, that's what makes the *Iliad* and the *Odyssey* such a great poem [sic]. The Odysseus who left was not the Odysseus who came back.

Bibliography

Cupitt, Don. *The Long-Legged Fly: A Theology of Language and Desire.* London: SCM, 1987.

Funk, Robert W. "The Coming Radical Reformation: Twenty-One Theses." *The Fourth R* 11.4 (July/August 1998): https://tinyurl.com/SBL1128a.

———. *Honest to Jesus: Jesus for a New Millennium.* New York: HarperSanFrancisco, 1996.

———. *Language, Hermeneutic, and the Word of God.* New York: Harper & Row, 1966.

Robert W. Funk Chronology, 1926–2005

Edited and updated by Andrew D. Scrimgeour

A listing of dates for Funk's education, academic appointments, offices, ventures, and major publications.

1926	Born, July 18, Evansville, Indiana
1947	AB, Classics, Butler University, Indianapolis, Indiana
1950	BD, Philosophy of Religion, Christian Theological Seminary, Butler University
1951	MA, Semitics, Butler University
1953	PhD, New Testament and Philosophy, Vanderbilt University, Nashville, Tennessee
1953–1956	Teaching at Texas Christian University, Fort Worth
1956–1957	Teaching at Harvard Divinity School, Cambridge, Massachusetts
1957–1958	Annual Professor, W. F. Albright Institute of Archaeological Research, Jerusalem
1958–1959	Teaching at Emory University, Atlanta, Georgia
1959–1966	Teaching at Drew University, Madison, New Jersey
1961	Editor and translator, *A Greek Grammar of New Testament and Other Early Christian Literature*, by F. Blass and A. Debrunner
1965–1966	Guggenheim Fellow and Fulbright Senior Scholar, University of Tubingen, Germany
1966	*Language, Hermeneutic, and Word of God*
1966–1969	Teaching at Vanderbilt Divinity School, Nashville, Tennessee
1968–1973	Executive Secretary, Society of Biblical Literature
1968–1973	Board of Directors, American Academy of Religion
1969–1986	Teaching at University of Montana, Missoula

1970–1972	Executive Committee, American Council of Learned Societies
1973	*A Beginning-Intermediate Grammar of Hellenistic Greek*
1973–1974	American Council of Learned Societies Fellow, University of Toronto
1974–1975	President, Society of Biblical Literature
1974–1980	Founder and Director, Scholars Press
1975	*Jesus as Precursor*
1980	William Rainey Harper Award for Statecraft in Support of Biblical Scholarship
1981–2005	Founder and President, Polebridge Press
1982	*Parables and Presence: Forms of the New Testament Tradition*
1985–2005	Founding Chair, the Jesus Seminar
1986–2005	Founder and Director, Westar Institute
1986–1998	Cochair, with John Dominic Crossan, the Jesus Seminar
1988	*The Poetics of Biblical Narrative*
1993	*The Five Gospels: The Search for the Authentic Words of Jesus* (with Roy W. Hoover and the Jesus Seminar)
1996	*Honest to Jesus: Jesus for a New Millennium*
1998	*The Acts of Jesus: The Search for the Authentic Deeds of Jesus* (with the Jesus Seminar)
2002	*A Credible Jesus: Fragments of a Vision*
2005	Doctor of Humane Letters, Butler University
Died, September 3, Santa Rosa, California

Robert W. Funk Publications

Edited and updated by Andrew D. Scrimgeour

1947

- ◆ "Dollar Gets Warm Reception in Europe, Minister Discovers." *The Indianapolis Star*. 29 June 1947.

1955

- ◆ "The Christian College and the Cultural Crisis." *The Christian Evangelist* 95:5–6, 13.
- ◆ "Let's Review the Restoration Plea." *The Christian Evangelist* 95:802–3.
- ◆ *New Testament Life and Literature*. Fort Worth: Texas Christian University Press.

1956

- ◆ "The Enigma of the Famine Visit." *JBL* 75:130–36.

1958

- ◆ "The 1958 Sounding at Pella" (coauthor with H. N. Richardson). *BA* 21:82–96.
- ◆ "The Citadel of Beth-zur." *BASOR* 150:8–20.
- ◆ "Papyrus Bodmer II (P66) and John 8:25." *HTR* 51:95–100.

1959

- ◆ "The Wilderness." *JBL* 78:205–14.

1960

♦ "Humiliation-Exaltation: The Structure of the New Testament Proclamation." *DrewG* 30:143–50.

1961

♦ Blass, Friedrich, and Albert Debrunner. *A Grammar of the Greek
New Testament and Other Early Christian Literature.* Translated from
German and revised by Robert W. Funk. Chicago: University of Chi-
cago Press; Cambridge: Cambridge Press.

1962

♦ "[First] Consultation on Hermeneutics" (with John B. Cobb). *ChrCent*
79:783–84; repr. in *DrewG* 33 (1963):123–26.
♦ "Conzelmann on Luke." Review of *The Theology of St. Luke,* by Hans
Conzelmann; *Die Mitte der Zeit: Studien zur Theologie des Lukas,* by
Hans Conzelmann. *JBR* 30: 299–30.
♦ *Interpreter's Dictionary of the Bible.* 4 vols. New York: Abingdon.
Articles on the following subjects: Awl, Ax, Bar, Bellows, Brick Kiln,
Chalkstones, Distaff, Dyeing, Furnace, Hammer, Hatchet, Herodium,
Jewels and Precious Stones (New Testament), Lamp (New Testament
period), Masada, Mortar, Pestle, Razor (total words: 10,265).
♦ "New Testament Literature 1960–62: A Potpourri." *DrewG* 33:34–44.

1963

♦ "The Hermeneutical Problem and Historical Criticism." *DrewG*
33:142–53.

1964

♦ "Creating an Opening: Biblical Criticism and the Theological Curriculum." *Int* 18:387–406.
♦ "Colloquium on Hermeneutics." *ThTo* 21:287–306.
♦ "The Hermeneutical Problem and Historical Criticism." Pages 164–97
in *The New Hermeneutic.* Vol. 2 of *New Frontiers in Theology.* Edited
by James M. Robinson and John B. Cobb. New York: Harper & Row.

- "'How Do You Read?' (Luke 10:25–37)." *Int* 18:56–61.
- "The Interpreter's Dictionary of the Bible: A Review Article." *DrewG* 34:99–105.
- "Logic and the Logos" [The Second Consultation on Hermeneutics]. *ChrCent* 81:1175–77.

1965

- "Das hermeneutische Problem und die historische Kritik." Pages 209–51 in *Die Neue Hermeneutik*. Vol. 2 of *Neuland in der Theologie*. Edited by James M. Robinson and John B. Cobb. Zurich: Zwingli Verlag.
- Editor: *The Bultmann School of Biblical Interpretation: New Directions?* *JThC* 1. "Foreword," ix–xi.
- "The Old Testament in Parable: A Study of Luke 10:25–37." *Encounter* 26:251–67.
- "Parable." *Children's Religion* 26:14–16.
- Editor: *Translating Theology into the Modern Age*. *JThC* 2. New York: Harper & Row.

1966

- *Language, Hermeneutic, and Word of God: The Problem of Language in the New Testament and in Contemporary Theology*. New York: Harper & Row.
- "Saying and Seeing: Phenomenology of Language and the New Testament." *JBR* 34:197–213.

1967

- "The Apostolic *Parousia*: Form and Significance. Pages 249–68 in *Christian History and Interpretation: Studies Presented to John Knox*. Edited by William Reuben Farmer, C. F. D. Moule, and Richard R. Niebuhr. Cambridge University Press.
- Editor: *Distinctive Protestant and Catholic Themes Reconsidered*. *JThC* 3. New York: Harper & Row.
- "The Form and Structure of II and III John." *JBL* 86:424–30.
- Editor: *History and Hermeneutic*. *JThC* 4. New York: Harper & Row.

1968

- Editor: *God and Christ: Existence and Provenance. JThC* 5. New York: Harper & Row.
- "Myth and the Literal Non-literal." Pages 57–65 in *Parable, Myth, and Language*. Edited by Tony Stoneburner. Cambridge, MA: The Church Society for College Work.

1969

- "Apocalyptic as a Historical and Theological Problem in Current New Testament Scholarship." *JThC* 6:175–91.
- Editor: *Apocalypticism. JThC* 6. New York: Herder & Herder.
- "A History of Beth-zur"; "The Bronze and Iron Age Pottery." Pages 4–17 and 35–53 in *The 1957 Excavation at Beth-zur*. AASOR 38. Cambridge, MA: American Schools of Oriental Research.
- *Rudolf Bultmann, Faith and Understanding*. Vol. 1. Edited with an introduction (pp. 9–27) by Robert W. Funk. London: SCM.

1970

- "Bet-Tsur." Pages 60–63 in *Encyclopedia of Archaeological Excavations in the Holy Land*. Hebrew ed. Jerusalem: Israel Exploration Society; Ramat-Gan: Massada Press.
- Editor: *Schleiermacher as Contemporary. JThC* 7. New York: Herder & Herder.

1971

- "Beyond Criticism in Quest of Literacy: The Parable of the Leaven." *Int* 25:149–70.
- "Book Catalogues and Other Hyperboles." *CSR Bulletin* 2:10–22.
- "The Parables: A Fragmentary Agenda." Pages 287–303 in *Jesus and Man's Hope*. Vol. 2. Pittsburgh Theological Seminary: A Perspective Book.

1972

- "Axioms and Arenas of the Academic Association, An Executive Secretary's View." Pages 23–35 in *Report of the Task Force on Scholarly*

Communication and Publication. Edited by George MacRae. Waterloo, Ontario: Council on the Study of Religion.

◆ *A Beginning-Intermediate Grammar of Hellenistic Greek*. Incomplete ed. Missoula, MT: Society of Biblical Literature.

◆ "Jesus and Kafka." *CAS Faculty Journal* 1:25–32.

◆ "Parsing Code for Hellenistic Greek: Preliminary Proposals." Pages 315–30 in vol. 2 of *Society of Biblical Literature 1972 Proceedings*. Missoula, MT: Society of Biblical Literature.

1973

◆ *A Beginning-Intermediate Grammar of Hellenistic Greek*. 2nd corr. ed. 3 vols. SBLSBS 2. Missoula, MT: Scholars Press. 3rd ed. Polebridge, 2013.

◆ "The Looking-Glass Tree Is for the Birds." *Int* 27:3–9.

◆ "The Learned Society as Publisher and the University Press." *CSR Bulletin* 4.3:3–13.

◆ "Society of Biblical Literature—Report of the Executive Secretary, 1968–73." *CSR Bulletin* 4.4:8–28.

◆ Translator (with R. Philip O'Hara and Lane C. McGaughy) and editor: Rudolf Bultmann, *The Johannine Epistles*. Hermeneia. Philadelphia: Fortress.

1974

◆ "Critical Note." *Semeia* 1:191–94.

◆ "The Good Samaritan as Metaphor." *Semeia* 2:74–81.

◆ "The Journal of the Future: A Trinitarian View." *CAS Faculty Journal* 2:56–60.

◆ "The Narrative Parables." *St. Andrews Review*:299–323.

◆ "*Semeia* and the Stuff and Style of Scholarship." *Semeia* 1:275–78.

◆ Editor: *A Structuralist Approach to the Parables. Semeia* 1.

◆ "Structure in the Narrative Parables of Jesus." *Semeia* 2:51–73.

1975

◆ "Beth-Zur." Pages 263–67 in *Encyclopedia of Archaeological Excavations in the Holy Land*. English ed. Jerusalem: Israel Exploration Society; Ramat-Gan: Massada Press.

- *Jesus as Precursor.* SemeiaSt 2. Philadelphia: Fortress; Missoula MT: Scholars Press.
- "Mission, Milieu, Management: The Mood of the University Under Fiscal Crisis." *CAS Faculty Journal* 4.1:6–34.
- "Scholars Press as Vector: What Difference Does It Make?" *Scholia* 1:10–15.
- "The Significance of Discourse Structure for the Study of the New Testament." Pages 209–21 in *No Famine in the Land: Studies in Honor of John L. McKenzie.* Edited by James Flanagan and Anita Weisbrod Robinson. Missoula, MT: Scholars Press.

1976

- "The Watershed of the American Biblical Tradition: The Chicago School, First Phase, 1892–1920." *JBL* 95:4–22. Repr. pages 169–88 in *Presidential Voices: The Society of Biblical Literature in the Twentieth Century.* Edited by Harold W. Attridge and James C. VanderKam. Society of Biblical Literature, 2006.

1977

- "Issues in Scholarly Publishing: Part 1." *Scholarly Publishing* 9:3–17.
- Editor: *Literary Critical Studies of Biblical Texts. Semeia* 8.
- "The Narrative Parables: The Birth of a Language Tradition." Pages 43–58 in *God's Christ and His People: Studies in Honour of Nils A. Dahl.* Edited by Nils Alstrup Dahl, Jacob Jervell, and Wayne A. Meeks. Oslo: Universitetsforlaget.
- "Scholars Press as Vector." *Scholia* 1:10–15.
- "Scholars Press Simplified." *Scholia* 2:9–17.
- "Symposium on Biblical Criticism." *ThTo* 33:362.

1978

- Editor: *Early Christian Miracle Stories. Semeia* 11.
- "The Form of the New Testament Healing Miracle Story." *Semeia* 12:57–96.
- "Issues in Scholarly Publishing: Part 2." *Scholarly Publishing* 9:115–30.

1979

+ "Scholars Press Applies for an NEH Challenge Grant: Whence and Whither the Press." *Scholia* 9:17–22.

1981

+ "On Dandelions: The Problem of Language." *JAAR* 48.2:79–87.
+ "Parable, Paradox, Power: The Prodigal Samaritan." *JAAR* 48.1:83–97.

1982

+ *Parables and Presence: Forms of the New Testament Tradition.* Philadelphia: Fortress.

1984

+ Translator and editor (with Ulrich Busse): Ernst Haenchen. *John: A Commentary on the Gospel.* 2 vols. Hermeneia. Philadelphia: Fortress.

1985

+ *New Gospel Parallels.* Vol. 1: *The Synoptic Gospels.* Vol. 2: *John and the Other Gospels.* Philadelphia: Fortress.
+ "Form and Function." *Forum* 1.1:51–58.
+ "A Forum for Focused Discussion." *Forum* 1.1:3–5.
+ "From Parable to Gospel: Domesticating the Tradition." *Forum* 1.3:3–24.
+ "The Issue of Jesus." *Forum* 1.1:7–12.
+ "Pen Fellows." *Forum* 1.3:31–32.
+ "Polling the Pundits." *Forum* 1.1:31–50.

1986

+ "The Beatitudes and Turn the Other Cheek: Recommendations and Polling." *Forum* 2.3:103–28.
+ "Matters of Moment: Inaugural Editorial of the *WestWord* Magazine." Forum 2.2:65–68.
+ "Poll on the Parables." *Forum* 2.1:54–80.

1987

- "The Hitching Post." *Westar Magazine* 1.3:2–3, 9.

1988

- "Gospel of Mark: Parables and Aphorisms." *Forum* 4.3:124–43.
- *The Parables of Jesus: Red Letter Edition.* A Report of the Jesus Seminar (with Bernard B. Scott and James R. Butts). Santa Rosa, CA: Polebridge.
- *The Poetics of Biblical Narrative.* Santa Rosa, CA: Polebridge.

1989

- "An Advocate for Religious Literacy." *The Fourth R* 2.5:1, 9.
- "Don't Look for Jesus on Clouds of Glory." *The Fourth R* 2.3:1, 6–7.
- "The Emerging Jesus." *The Fourth R* 2.6:1, 11–15.
- "The Lord's Prayer: Does It Go back to Jesus?" *The Fourth R* 2.1:1, 4–6.
- "A New Blass-Debrunner-Funk." *The Fourth R* 2.5:9.
- "Scholars Version: Translator's Guidelines." *The Fourth R* 2.5:4.
- "Time Marches On, Part 1." *The Fourth R* 2.2:1–2, 6, 8.
- "Time Marches On, Part 2." *The Fourth R* 2.3:4–5.
- "Unraveling the Jesus Tradition: Criteria and Criticism." *Forum* 5.2:31–62.
- "What Books Belong to the Bible." *The Fourth R* 2.5:2.
- "What Jesus Is Emerging?" *The Fourth R* 2.4:1, 6–7.

1990

- *Mark.* Vol. 1.2 of *New Gospel Parallels.* Rev. ed. Santa Rosa, CA: Polebridge.
- "Criteria for Determining the Authentic Sayings of Jesus." *The Fourth R* 3.6:8–10.
- "In the Heart of America: Redeemer Figures and Mythic Spaces." *The Fourth R* 3.4:1–4.
- "Mark and Street Lingo" (with Arthur J. Dewey). *The Fourth R* 3.5:10–11.
- "Scholars Version: Calling a Spade a Spade." *The Fourth R* 3.5:12, 14.
- "Report from the Jesus Seminar." *The Fourth R* 3.6:13–14.
- "Where Have All the Students Gone?" *The Fourth R* 3.2:8–10.

1991

- *The Gospel of Mark: Red Letter Edition* (with Mahlon H. Smith). Santa Rosa, CA: Polebridge.
- "How Jesus Became God." *The Fourth R* 4.6:10–13.
- "Press Release: Westar 1991 Spring Meeting." *The Fourth R* 4.2:1–3.
- "Press Release: Westar Fall 1991 Meeting." *The Fourth R* 4.6:1–3.
- "Rules of Oral Evidence Determining the Authentic Sayings of Jesus." *The Fourth R* 4.2:8–10.
- "Translation Notes." *The Fourth R* 4.3:16.

1992

- "Demons: Identity and Worldview." *The Fourth R* 5.3:15.
- "The Four-Year Political Circus: Can You Fool All the People All the Time?" *The Fourth R* 5.4:10–12.
- "Hansel and Gretel, The Lone Ranger, and the Lord of the Rings." *The Fourth R* 5.5:4–9.
- "Jesus and the Apocalypse." *The Fourth R* 5.2:1–7.
- "The Jesus That Was." *The Fourth R* 5.6:1–4.
- "Oxyrhynchus Gospel 840" (draft translation) and general editor of The Scholars Version project. *The Complete Gospels.* Edited by Robert J. Miller. Santa Rosa, CA: Polebridge.
- "Press Release: Jesus Seminar Spring Meeting." *The Fourth R* 5.2:8–11.

1993

- "Call for a Canon Council." *The Fourth R* 6.3:7, 13.
- *The Five Gospels: The Search for the Authentic Words of Jesus* (with Roy W. Hoover and the Jesus Seminar). New York: Macmillan.
- "God and the Emperor in Waco." *The Fourth R* 6.3:14–16.
- "The Gospel of Jesus and the Jesus of the Gospels." *The Fourth R* 6.6:3–10.
- "The Jesus Seminar: Phoenix in the Fall." *The Fourth R* 6.2: inside back cover.
- "On Distinguishing Historical from Fictive Narrative." *Forum* 9.3–4:179–216.
- "Report: The Jesus Seminar." *The Fourth R* 6.2:12–16.

- "Tongues of the Wise: How to Answer Critics of *The Five Gospels*." *The Fourth R* 6.6:2, 15.

1994

- Foreword to *The Complete Gospels*. Revised and expanded edition. Edited by Robert J. Miller. Sonoma, CA: Polebridge.
- *Jesus as Precursor*. Edited by Edward F. Beutner. Rev. ed. Santa Rosa, CA: Polebridge.
- "The Resurrection of Jesus: Reports and Stories." *The Fourth R* 7.4:3–15.

1995

- "Bookshelf: The Resurrection of Jesus." *The Fourth R* 8.1:3–16.
- "Profiles of Jesus: Protocol." *The Fourth R* 8.5/6:21–22.

1996

- *Honest to Jesus: Jesus for a New Millennium*. San Francisco: HarperSanFrancisco, 1996.
- "Jesus befreien: Die US-Debatte urn den Mann aus Nazareth." *EvK*:512–15.
- "Jesus of Nazareth: A Glimpse." *The Fourth R* 9.1/2:17–20.

1997

- "The Incredible Creed." *The Fourth R* 10.3/4:7–22.

1998

- *The Acts of Jesus: The Search for the Authentic Deeds of Jesus* (with the Jesus Seminar). San Francisco: HarperSanFrancisco.
- "The Coming Radical Revolution." *The Fourth R* 11.4:3.
- "The Jesus Seminar on the Road in New Zealand." *The Fourth R* 11.5:15–16.
- "The Quest of the Historical Jesus: Problem and Promise." *Intersections* 5 (Summer): 14–22.
- "Twenty-One Theses and Notes." *The Fourth R* 11.4:8–10.

1999

- *The Gospel of Jesus according to the Jesus Seminar* (with the Jesus Seminar). Santa Rosa, CA: Polebridge.
- "The Once and Future Jesus." Pages 5–25 in *The Once and Future Jesus*. With Thomas Sheehan, Marcus Borg, John Shelby Spong, Karen King, John Dominic Crossan, Lloyd Geering, Gerd Luedemann, and Walter Wink. Santa Rosa, CA: Polebridge.

2000

- "Editorial." *The Fourth R* 13.3:2.
- "Editorial." *The Fourth R* 13.6:2.
- "The Incredible Canon." Pages 24–46 in *Christianity in the Twenty-First Century*. Edited by Deborah A. Brown. New York: Crossroad.
- Richard Treloar, interviewer. "Transcript of a Conversation with Robert Funk." *Colloq* 32:151–67.

2001

- "Editorial." *The Fourth R* 14.4:2.
- "A Faith for the Future." Pages 1–17 in *The Once and Future Faith*. Santa Rosa, CA: Polebridge.
- "Jesus as Itinerant Sage: True or False?" *The Fourth R* 14.2:19–20.
- "The Jesus Seminar and the Quest." Pages 130–39 in *Jesus Then and Now: Images of Jesus in History and Christology*. Edited by Marvin Meyer and Charles Hughes. Harrisburg, PA: Trinity Press International.
- "Milestones in the Quest for the Historical Jesus." *The Fourth R* 14.4:9–11, 14–18.
- "A War of Worlds." *The Fourth R* 14.5:6–8.
- "The Westar Recipe." *Forum* 2/4.2:297–301.

2002

- *A Credible Jesus: Fragments of a Vision*. Santa Rosa, CA: Polebridge.
- "Editorial." *The Fourth R* 15.1:2.
- "Editorial." *The Fourth R* 15.3:2.
- "Editorial." *The Fourth R* 15.5:2.

- "Editorial." *The Fourth R* 15.6:2.
- "The End of a Great Tradition." Pages 25–27 in *Faith, Truth, and Freedom: The Expulsion of Professor Gerd Lüdemann from the Theology Faculty at Göttingen University, Symposium and Documents*. Binghamton, NY: Academic Studies in Religion and the Social Order, Global Publications, Binghamton University.
- "Jesus: A Voice Print." Pages 9–13 in *Profiles of Jesus*. Edited by Roy W. Hoover. Santa Rosa, CA: Polebridge.
- "Letters of Concern for Prof. Gerd Lüdemann." Pages 111–16 in *Faith, Truth, and Freedom: The Expulsion of Professor Gerd Lüdemann from the Theology Faculty at Göttingen University, Symposium and Documents*. Binghamton, NY: Academic Studies in Religion and the Social Order, Global Publications, Binghamton University.
- "The Once and Future New Testament." Pages 541–57 in *The Canon Debate*. Edited by Lee Martin McDonald and James A. Sanders. Peabody, MA: Hendrickson.
- "Rewards Are Intrinsic." *The Fourth R* 15.2:15–16,18.

2003

- "Editorial." *The Fourth R* 16.1:2, 20.
- "Editorial." *The Fourth R* 16.2:2, 18.
- "Editorial." *The Fourth R* 16.4:2.
- "The Mythical Matrix and God as Metaphor." *Forum* 2/3.2:381–99.
- "The Sunday Morning Experience: A Codicil to Robert Price." *The Fourth R* 16.6:15–18.

2004

- "Do the Gospels Contain Eyewitness Reports?" *The Fourth R* 17.2:15–18.
- "Editorial." *The Fourth R* 17:6:2, 20.

2005

- "Editorial." *The Fourth R* 18.1:2, 20.
- "Metaphor and Reality, Editorial." *The Fourth R* 18.4:2, 18.

2006

- "Commencement Address." *The Fourth R* 19.2:18–19.
- *Funk on Parables: Collected Essays.* Edited with an introduction by Bernard Brandon Scott. Santa Rosa, CA: Polebridge.

2007

- *Just Call Me Bob: The Wit and Wisdom of Robert W. Funk.* Edited with an introduction by Andrew D. Scrimgeour. Santa Rosa, CA: Polebridge.